Pamela; or, virtue rewarded. In a series of familiar letters from a beautiful young damsel to her parents. ... By Mr. Samuel Richardson. In four volumes. Volume 3 of 4

Samuel Richardson

Pamela; or, virtue rewarded. In a series of familiar letters from a beautiful young damsel to her parents. ... By Mr. Samuel Richardson. In four volumes. Volume 3 of 4

Richardson, Samuel
ESTCID: T091178
Reproduction from British Library
Also issued as part of: 'The novelist's magazine' vol.20, London, 1780-88. P.634 misnumbered 364.
London : printed for Harrison and Co., 1785.
364[i.e.634]p.,plates ; 8°

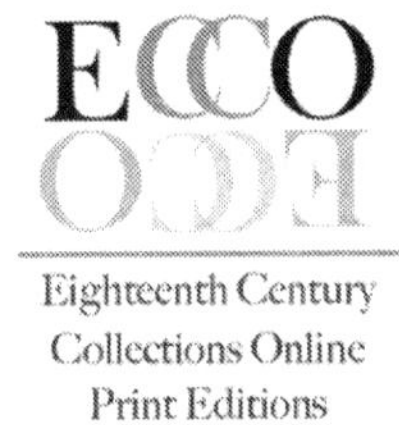

Gale ECCO Print Editions

Relive history with *Eighteenth Century Collections Online*, now available in print for the independent historian and collector. This series includes the most significant English-language and foreign-language works printed in Great Britain during the eighteenth century, and is organized in seven different subject areas including literature and language; medicine, science, and technology; and religion and philosophy. The collection also includes thousands of important works from the Americas.

The eighteenth century has been called "The Age of Enlightenment." It was a period of rapid advance in print culture and publishing, in world exploration, and in the rapid growth of science and technology – all of which had a profound impact on the political and cultural landscape. At the end of the century the American Revolution, French Revolution and Industrial Revolution, perhaps three of the most significant events in modern history, set in motion developments that eventually dominated world political, economic, and social life.

In a groundbreaking effort, Gale initiated a revolution of its own: digitization of epic proportions to preserve these invaluable works in the largest online archive of its kind. Contributions from major world libraries constitute over 175,000 original printed works. Scanned images of the actual pages, rather than transcriptions, recreate the works ***as they first appeared.***

Now for the first time, these high-quality digital scans of original works are available via print-on-demand, making them readily accessible to libraries, students, independent scholars, and readers of all ages.

For our initial release we have created seven robust collections to form one the world's most comprehensive catalogs of 18th century works.

Initial Gale ECCO Print Editions collections include:

History and Geography
Rich in titles on English life and social history, this collection spans the world as it was known to eighteenth-century historians and explorers. Titles include a wealth of travel accounts and diaries, histories of nations from throughout the world, and maps and charts of a world that was still being discovered. Students of the War of American Independence will find fascinating accounts from the British side of conflict.

Social Science

Delve into what it was like to live during the eighteenth century by reading the first-hand accounts of everyday people, including city dwellers and farmers, businessmen and bankers, artisans and merchants, artists and their patrons, politicians and their constituents. Original texts make the American, French, and Industrial revolutions vividly contemporary.

Medicine, Science and Technology

Medical theory and practice of the 1700s developed rapidly, as is evidenced by the extensive collection, which includes descriptions of diseases, their conditions, and treatments. Books on science and technology, agriculture, military technology, natural philosophy, even cookbooks, are all contained here.

Literature and Language

Western literary study flows out of eighteenth-century works by Alexander Pope, Daniel Defoe, Henry Fielding, Frances Burney, Denis Diderot, Johann Gottfried Herder, Johann Wolfgang von Goethe, and others. Experience the birth of the modern novel, or compare the development of language using dictionaries and grammar discourses.

Religion and Philosophy

The Age of Enlightenment profoundly enriched religious and philosophical understanding and continues to influence present-day thinking. Works collected here include masterpieces by David Hume, Immanuel Kant, and Jean-Jacques Rousseau, as well as religious sermons and moral debates on the issues of the day, such as the slave trade. The Age of Reason saw conflict between Protestantism and Catholicism transformed into one between faith and logic -- a debate that continues in the twenty-first century.

Law and Reference

This collection reveals the history of English common law and Empire law in a vastly changing world of British expansion. Dominating the legal field is the *Commentaries of the Law of England* by Sir William Blackstone, which first appeared in 1765. Reference works such as almanacs and catalogues continue to educate us by revealing the day-to-day workings of society.

Fine Arts

The eighteenth-century fascination with Greek and Roman antiquity followed the systematic excavation of the ruins at Pompeii and Herculaneum in southern Italy; and after 1750 a neoclassical style dominated all artistic fields. The titles here trace developments in mostly English-language works on painting, sculpture, architecture, music, theater, and other disciplines. Instructional works on musical instruments, catalogs of art objects, comic operas, and more are also included.

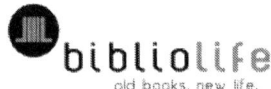

Preface to the Third and Fourth Volumes.

THE Two former Volumes of PAMELA met with a success greatly exceeding the most sanguine expectations and the Editor hopes, that the Letters which compose these, will be found equally written to NATURE, avoiding all romantick flights, improbable surprises, and irrational machinery, and that the passions are touched, where requisite, and rules, equally *new* and *practicable*, inculcated, throughout the whole, for the *general conduct of life* and, therefore, he flatters himself, that they may expect the good fortune, which *few continuations* have met with, to be judged not unworthy the *first* part, nor disproportioned to the more exalted condition in which PAMELA was destined to shine, as an affectionate *wife*, a faithful *friend*, a polite and kind *neighbour*, an indulgent *mother*, and a beneficent *mistress*, after having in the two former volumes supported the character of a dutiful *child*, a spotless *virgin*, and a modest and amiable *bride*.

The reader will easily see, that in so great a choice of materials, as *must arise from a multitude of important subjects, in a married life, to* such geniuses and friendships as those of Mr and Mrs B the Editor's greatest difficulty was, how to bring them within the compass which he was determined not to exceed And it having been left to his own choice, in what manner to digest and publish the letters, and where to close the work, he had intended, at first, in regard to his other avocations, to have carried the piece no farther than the two former volumes.

It may be expected, therefore, that he should enter into an explanation of the reasons whereby he was provoked into a necessity of altering his intention. But he is willing to decline saying any-thing upon so well-known a subject.

The Editor has been much pressed with importunities and conjectures, in relation to the person and family of the gentlemen, who are the principal persons in the work all he thinks himself at liberty to say, or is necessary to be said, is only to repeat what has been already hinted, that the story has it's foundation in truth and that there was a necessity, for obvious reasons, to vary and disguise some facts and circumstances, as also the names of persons, places, &c

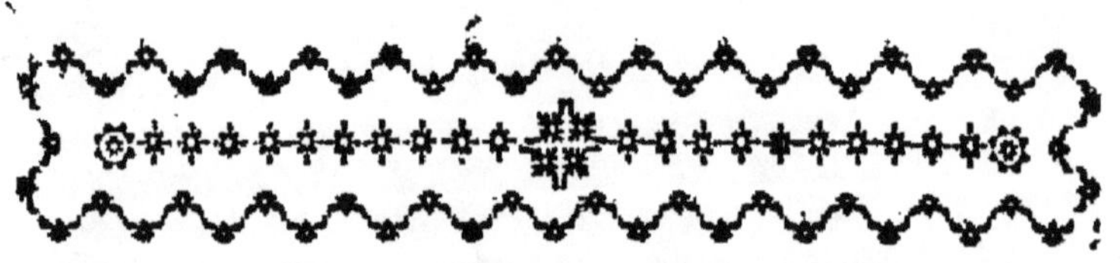

PAMELA;

OR,

VIRTUE REWARDED.

VOLUME THE THIRD

LETTER I

MY DEAR FATHER AND MOTHER,

WE arrived here last night, highly pleased with our journey, and the occasion of it May God bless you both with long life and health, to enjoy your sweet farm, and pretty dwelling, which is just what I wished it to be And don t make your grateful hearts too uneasy in the possession of it, by your modest diffidence of your own worthiness for, at the same time, that it is what will do honour to the best of men, it is not so *very* extraordinary, considering his condition, as that it will give any one cause to censure it as the effect of a too partial and injudicious kindness for the parents of one whom he *delighteth to honour*

My dear master (why should I not still call him so, bound to reverence him as I am, in every light that he can shine in to the most obliged and sensible heart?) holds his kind purpose of fitting up the large parlour, and three apartments in the commodious dwelling he calls yours, for his entertainment and mine, when he shall permit me to pay my duty to you both, for a few happy days together; and he has actually given orders for that purpose, and that the three apartments be *so* fitted up, as to be rather suitable to *your* condition, than his *own*, for, he says, the plain simple elegance which he will have to be observed in the rooms, as well as the furniture, will be a variety in his retirement to this place, that will make him return to his own with the greater pleasure, and, at the same time, when we are not there, will be of use for the reception of any of your friends, and so he shall not, as he kindly says, rob the good couple of any of their accommodations

The old bow windows he will have preserved, but will not have them sashed, nor the woodbines, jessamines, and vines, that run up against them destroyed, only he will have larger panes of glass, and convenienter casements, to let in more of the sweet air and light, to make amends for that obstructed by the shades of those fragrant climbers For he has mentioned three or four times, how gratefully they dispensed their intermingled odours to us, when, the last evening we stood at the window in our bed-chamber, to hear the responsive songs of two warbling nightingales, one at a distance, the other near, which took up our delighted attention for above two hours, and charmed us the more, as we thought their season had been over And when they had done, he made *me* sing him one, for which he rewarded me with a kiss, saying—
'How greatly do the innocent pleasures
'I now hourly taste, exceed the guilty

'tumults that used formerly to agitate 'my unequal mind!—Never talk, my 'Pamela, as you frequently do, of obligation to me: one such hour as I now 'enjoy is an ample reward for all the benefits I can confer on you and your's 'in my whole life!'

The parlour indeed will be more elegant, though that is to be rather plain than rich, as well in it's wainscot as furniture, and to be new floored. The dear gentleman has already given orders about it, and you will soon have workmen with you to put them in execution. The parlour-doors are to have brass hinges and locks, and to shut as close, he tells them, as a watch-case. 'For who knows, said he, 'my dear, but we shall have full 'added blessings, in two or three charming boys and girls, to place there in 'their infancy, before they can be of 'age to be benefited by your lessons 'and example? And besides, I make no 'doubt, but I shall entertain there some 'of my chosen friends, in their excursions, for a day or so.'

How am I, every hour of my life, overwhelmed with instances of God Almighty's goodness and his!—O spare, blessed Father of Mercies, the precious life of this excellent man, and increase my thankfulness, and my worthiness, and then—But what shall I say?—Only, that then I may *continue* to be what I am, for more blessed, and more happy, in my own mind, surely I cannot be.

The beds he will have of cloth, because he thinks the situation a little cold, especially when the wind is easterly, and because he purposes to be down in the early spring season, now-and then, as well as in the latter autumn, and the window-curtains of the same, in one room red, in the other green, but plain, lest you should be afraid to use them occasionally. The carpets for them will be sent with the other furniture, for he will not alter the old oaken floors of the bedchamber, nor yet of the little room he intends for my use, to withdraw to, when I choose not to join in such company as may happen to fall in. 'Which, my dear,' says he, 'shall be as little as is possible, only particular friends, who may be disposed 'once in a year or two to see, when I am 'there, how I live with my Pamela, and 'her parents, and how I pass my time 'in my retirement, as I shall call this: 'for otherwise, perhaps, they will be 'apt to think I am ashamed of company 'I shall always be pleased with.—Nor 'are you, my dear,' continued he, 'to 'take this as a compliment to yourself, 'but a piece of requisite policy in me, 'for who will offer to reproach me for 'marrying, as the world thinks, below me, when they shall see, that such 'a reproach, as they intend it, is so far 'from being so to me, that I not only 'pride myself in my Pamela, but take 'pleasure in owning her relations as 'mine, and visiting them, and receiving 'visits from them, and yet offer not to 'set them up in such a glaring light, as 'if I would have the world forget (who 'in that case would always take the more 'pleasure in remembering) what they 'were? And how will it anticipate low 'reflection, when they shall see, I can 'bend my mind to partake with them 'the pleasures of their humble but decent life?—Ay,' continued he, 'and 'be rewarded for it too, with better 'health, better spirits, and a better mind; 'so that, my dear,' added he, 'I shall 'reap more benefit by what I propose to 'do, than I shall confer.'

In this generous manner does this best of men endeavour to disclaim, (though I must be very ungrateful, if, with me, it did not inhance) the proper merit of a beneficence which is natural to him, and which, indeed, as I tell him, may be in one respect depreciated, inasmuch as (so excellent is his nature) he cannot help it if he would.—O that it was in my power to recompense him for it! But I am poor, as I have often said, in every thing but will—and that is *wholly* his: and what a happiness is it to me, a happiness I could not so early have hoped for, that I can say so without *reserve*; since the dear object of my happiness requires nothing of me but what is consistent with my duty to the Supreme Benefactor, the first mover and cause of all his own happiness, of my happiness, and of that of my dear, my ever-dear parents!

But whither does the inchanting subject lead me! I am running on to my usual length, though I have not the same excuse for it, for heretofore I had nothing to do but to write. Yet, I am sure, if I do exceed a little, *you* will be pleased with it, and you have moreover a right to rejoice with me in the days of my felicity, after your indulgent hearts had been so much pained by a long succession

of

of my fears and my dangers, which only ought to be remembered now, as subjects of thankful exultation, by *your dutiful and happy daughter*.

LETTER II.

MY DEAREST DAUGHTER,

I Need not repeat to you the sense your good mother and I have of our happiness, and of our obligations to your honoured spouse you both were pleased witnesses of it every hour of the happy fortnight you passed with us But still, my dear, we hardly know to address ourselves even *to you*, much less to the *'Squire*, with the freedom he so often invited us to take for, I don't know how it is, but though you are our daughter, and are so far from being lifted up by your high condition, that we see no difference in your behaviour to us, your poor parents, yet when we look upon you as the lady of so fine a gentleman, we cannot forbear having a kind of respect, and—I don't know what to call it—that lays a little restraint upon us And, yet we would not, methinks, let our minds be run away with the admiration of worldly grandeur, so as to set too much by it.

But your merit, and your prudence, my dear daughter, is so much above all we could ever have any notion of and to have gentry come only to behold you, and admire you, not so much for your genteelness, and amiableness neither, as for your behaviour, and your affability to poor as well as rich, and to hear every one calling you an angel, and saying, you *deserve* to be what you are, makes us hardly know how to look upon you, but as an angel indeed! I am sure you have been a good angel to us, since, for your sake, God Almighty has put it into your honoured husband s heart to make us the happiest couple in the world. But little less, indeed, we should have been, had we only, in some far distant land, heard of our dear child s happiness, and never partaken of the benefits of it ourselves But thus to be provided for! Thus kindly to be owned, and called Father and Mother by such a brave gentleman! and thus to be placed, that we have nothing to do but to bless God, and bless him, and bless you, and hourly pray for you *both*, is such a providence, my dear child, as is too mighty to be borne by us, with equalness of temper, and we kneel together every morning, noon, and night, and weep and rejoice, and rejoice and weep, to think how our unworthiness is distinguished, and how God has provided for us in our latter days, when all that we had to fear was, that, as we grew older and more infirm, and worn out by hard labour, we should be troublesome where, not our pride, but our industrious wills, would have made us wish not to be so, —but to be intitled to a happier lot for this would have grieved us the more, for the sake of you, my dear child, and your unhappy brother's children for it is well known, that, though we pretend not to boast of our family, and indeed have no reason, yet none of us were ever sunk so low as I was to be sure, partly by my own fault, for, had it been for your poor aged mother s sake only, I ought not to have done what I did for John and William, for, so unhappy were they, poor lads! that what I could do, was but as a drop of water to a bucket

But yet the issue has shewn, that, (if I may presume to say so) what I did was not displeasing to God, inasmuch as I have the comfort to see that my reliance on him, while I was doing what though some thought *imprudent* things, yet not *wrong* things, is so abundantly rewarded, beyond expectation and desert Blessed be his holy name for it!

You command me—Let me, as writing to Mr B s lady, say *command*, though as to my dear *daughter*, I will only say *desire* and, indeed, I will not, as you wish me not to do, let the one condition, which was accidental, put the other, which was natural, out of my thought. you spoke it in better words, but this was the sense.—But you have the gift of utterance, and education is a fine thing, where it meets with such talents to improve upon as God has given you.—But let me not forget what I was going to say—You *command*—or, if you please—you *desire* me to write long letters, and often—And how can I help it, if I would? For when here, in this happy dwelling, and this well-stocked farm, in these rich meadows, and well-cropt acres, we look around us, and which way soever we turn our heads, see blessings upon blessings, and plenty upon plenty, see barns well-stored, poultry increasing, the kine low-

 ing

ing and crouding about us, and all fruitful, and are bid to call all these our own. And then think, that all is the reward of our child's virtue!—O my dear daughter, who can bear these things!—Excuse me!—I must break off a little! For my eyes are as full as my heart, and I will retire to bless God, and your honoured husband.

So, my dear child, I now again take up my pen; but reading what I had written, in order to carry on the thread, I can hardly forbear again being in one sort affected. But do you think I will call all these things my own?—Do you think I will live rent-free?—Do you think I would? Can the honoured 'squire believe, that having such a generous example before me, if I had no gratitude in my temper before, I could help being touched by such an one as he sets me? If his goodness makes him know no mean in giving, shall I be so greedy as to know none in receiving?—Come, come, my dear child, your poor father is not so sordid a wretch neither. He will shew the world, that all these benefits are not thrown away upon one, who will disgrace you as much by his temper, as by his condition: what though I cannot be as worthy of all these favours as I wish, I will be as worthy as I can. And let me tell you, my dear child, if the king and his royal family (God bless 'em!) be not ashamed to receive taxes and duties from his subjects, if dukes and earls, and all the top gentry, cannot support their bravery, without having their rents paid, I hope I shall not affront the 'squire, to pay to his steward, what any other person would pay for this noble stock, and improving farm: and I will do it, if it please God to bless me with life and health. I should not be worthy to crawl upon the earth, if I did not. And what did I say to Mr Longman, the faithful Mr Longman? Sure no gentleman had ever a more worthy steward than he: it was as we were walking over the grounds together—and observing in what good order every thing was, he was praising some little contrivances of my own, for the improvement of the farm, and saying, how comfortably he hoped we might live upon it. 'Ay, Mr Longman, said I, 'comfortably indeed: but do you think I could be properly said to *live*, if I was not to pay as much rent for it as another?'—'I can tell you,' said he, 'the 'squire will not receive any thing from you, Goodman Andrews.—Why, man, he has no occasion for it: he's worth a power of money, besides a noble and clear estate in land.—Ad's heartlikins, you must not affront him, I can tell you that: for he's as generous as a prince, where he takes, but he is hasty, and will have his own way.'—'Why, for that reason, Mr Longman, said I, 'I was thinking to make *you* my friend!'—'Make *me* your friend! You have not a better in the world, to my power, I can tell you that, nor your dame neither, for I love such honest hearts: I wish my own brother would let me love him as well, but let that pass.—What I can do for you, I will, and here's my hand upon it.'

'Well then,' said I, 'it is this: let me account to you at the rent Farmer Dickens offered, and let me know what the stock cost, and what the crops are valued at, and pay the one as I can, and the other quarterly, and not let the 'squire know it till you can't choose, and I shall be as happy as a prince; for I doubt not, by God's blessing, to make a comfortable livelihood of it besides.'—'Why, dost believe, Goodman Andrews, said he, 'that I would do such a thing?—Would not his honour think if I hid one thing from him, I might hide another!—Go to, go to, honest heart, I love thee dearly: but can Mr B. do too much for his lady, think'st thou? Come, come,' (and he jeer'd me so, I could not tell what to say to him) 'I wish at bottom there is not some pride in this.—What, I warrant, you would not be too much beholden to his honour, would you?'—'No, good Mr Longman, said I, 'it is not that, I'm sure. If I have any pride, it is only in my dear child—to whom, under God, all this is owing.—But some how or other it shall be so.'

And so, my dear daughter, I resolve it shall, and it will be, over and above, one of the greatest pleasures to me, to do the good 'squire service, as well as to be so much benefited and obliged by him.

Our eldest grandson Thomas is very desirous to come and live with us: the boy is honest, and, they tell me, industrious. And cousin Burroughs wants me to employ his son Roger, who understands the business of a farm very well.

It

It is no wonder, that all one's relations should wish to partake of our happy lot, and if they *can* and *will* do their business as well as others, I see not why relationship should be an objection but yet, I think, one would not *beleaguer*, as one may say, your honoured husband with one's relations. You, my best child, will give me always your advice, as to my carriage in this my new lot, for I would not for the world be thought an incroacher And I am sure you have so much prudence, that there is nobody's advice fitter to be followed than your's

Our blessing (I am sure you have blessed us!) attend you, my dearest child, and may you be as happy as you have made us, (I cannot wish you to be happier, because I have no notion how it can be, in this life) conclude us, *your ever-loving father and mother*,

JOHN *and* ELIZ ANDREWS

May we hope to be favoured now-and-then with a letter from you, my dear child, like some of your former, to let us know how you go on? It would be a great joy to us indeed it would — But we know you'll have enough to do without obliging us in this way So must acquiesce,

LETTER III

MY DEAR FATHER AND MOTHER,

I Have shewed your letter to my beloved.—Don't be uneasy that I have, for you need not be ashamed of it, since it is my pride to have such honest and grateful parents and I'll tell you what he said to it, as the best argument I can use, why you should not be uneasy, but enjoy without pain or anxiety all the benefits of your happy lot

'Dear, good souls! said he, 'how does every thing they say, and every thing they write, manifest the worthiness of their hearts! No wonder, Pamela, you love and revere such honest minds, for that you would do, were they not your parents and tell them, that I am so far from having them believe, that what I have done for them is only the effect of my affection for their daughter, that let 'em find out another couple as worthy as themselves, and I will do as much for them Indeed I would not place them,' continued the dear obliger, 'in the *same* county, because I would wish *two* counties to be bless'd for their sakes Tell them, my dear, that they have a right to what they enjoy on the foot of their own *proper* merit, and *bid* them enjoy it as their patrimony and if there can any thing arise, that is more than they themselves can wish for, in the way of life they choose to live, let them look round among their own relations, where it may be acceptable, and communicate to them the like solid reasons for rejoicing in the situation they are pleased with and do you, my dear,' continued he, 'still farther enable them, as you shall judge proper, to gratify their inlarged hearts, for fear they should deny any comfort to themselves in order to do good to others.'

I could only fly to his generous bosom, (for this is a subject which most affects me) and, with my eyes swimming in tears of grateful joy, and which overflowed as soon as my bold lips touched his dear face, bless God, and bless him, with my whole heart, for speak I could not! But, almost choak'd with my joy, sobb'd to him my grateful acknowledgments.—He clasped me in his arms, and said—'How, my dearest, do you overpay me for the little I have done for your parents! If it be thus to be bless'd for conferring benefits so insignificant to a man of my fortune, what joys is it not in the power of rich men to give themselves, whenever they please!—Foretastes, indeed, of those we are bid to hope for, which can surely only exceed these, as *then* we shall be all intellect, and better fitted to receive them'—'Tis too much!—too much,' said I, in broken accents:—'How am I oppressed with the pleasure you gave me!—O, Sir, bless me more gradually, and more cautiously—for I cannot bear it!' And, indeed, my heart went flutter, flutter, flutter, at his dear breast, as if it wanted to break it's too narrow prison, to mingle still more intimately with his own

Surely, surely, my dear, my beloved parents, nobody's happiness is so great as mine!—If it proceeds thus from degree to degree, and is to be augmented by the hope, the charming hope, that the dear second author of your blessings and mine, be the uniformly good as well as the partially kind man to us, what a felicity will this be! and if our prayers shall be heard, and

and we shall have the pleasure to think, that his advances in piety are owing not a little to them, and to the example God shall give us grace to set, then, indeed, may we take the pride to think, we have repaid his goodness to us, and that we have satisfied the debt, which nothing less can discharge.

Thus, then, do I set before you imperfectly, as I am forced to do, the delight your grateful, your honest hearts give us, I say, imperfectly, and well I may, for I might as easily paint sound, as describe the noble, the sublime pleasures, that wind up my affections to even a painful height of rapture on such occasions as this: and I desire, as he often bids *me*, that *you* will take to yourselves the merit of thus delighting us both, and then think with less uneasiness, of the obligation you are under to the best of friends.—And indeed it is but doing justice to his beneficent temper, to think, that we have given him an opportunity of exercising it, in a way so agreeable to it, and I can tell by the ardour of his speech, by the additional lustre that it lights up in his eyes, naturally so lively, and by the virtuous endearments, refined on these occasions above what sense can know, that he has a pleasure, a joy, a transport, in doing what he does of this sort, that is it's own reward, as every virtuous and noble action must be to a mind that can be delighted with virtue for it's own sake, and can find itself enlarged by the power of doing good to worthy objects Even I, my dear parents, know this by experience, when I can be an humble means to make an honest creature happy, though not related to myself, and yet I am but a third-hand dispenser, as I have* elsewhere said, of these comforts; and all the light I communicate, as, I once before observed †, like that of the moon, is but borrowed from his sunny radiance

Forgive me, my dear, my worthy parents, if my stile on this subject be raised above that natural simplicity, which is more suited to my humble talents But how can I help it? For when the mind is elevated, ought not the sense we have of our happiness to make our expressions soar equally? Can the affections be so highly raised as mine are on these occasions, and the thoughts creep groveling, like one's ordinary self? No, indeed!—Call not this, therefore, the gift of utterance, if it should appear to you in a better light than it deserves It is the gift of gratitude, a gift which makes you, and me too, *speak* and *write*, as I hope it will make us *act*, above ourselves — And thus will our gratitude be the inspirer of joy to our common benefactor; and his joy will heighten our gratitude, and so we shall proceed, as cause and effect to each other's happiness, to bless the dear man who blesses us.—And will it be right then to say, you are uneasy under such (at least as to your wills) returned and discharged obligations? God Almighty requires only a thankful heart for all the mercies he heaps upon the children of men my dear Mr. B. who, in these particulars, imitates Divinity, desires no more —You *have* this thankful heart,—yes, you have, and that to such a high degree of gratitude, that nobody can exceed you

But yet, my dear parents, when your worthy minds would be too much affected with your gratitude, so as to lay you under the restraints you mention, to the dear gentleman, and for his sake, to your dependent daughter, then let me humbly advise you, that you will at such times, with more particular, more abstracted aspirations, than at others, raise your thoughts upwards, and consider who it is that gives *him* the opportunity, and pray for him and for me, for *him*, that all his future actions may be of a piece with this noble disposition of mind, for *me*, that I may continue humble, and consider myself blest for your sakes, and in order that I may be, in some sort, a rewarder in the hands of Providence, of this it's dear excellent agent; and then we shall look forward, all of us, with pleasure *indeed* to that state, where there is no distinction of degree, and where the humble cottager shall be upon a par with the proudest monarch

O my dear, dear parents, how can you, as in your *postscript*, say—'May we 'not be *favoured* now and then with a 'letter?' Call *me* your daughter, your Pamela—I am no lady to you —I have more pleasure to be called your comfort, and to be thought to act worthy of the sentiments with which your examples, cautions, and instructions, have inspired me, than in any other thing in this life, my determined duty to our common benefactor,

* See Vol II p 238 † See Vol II p. 236.

nefactor, the best of gentlemen and husbands, excepted And I am sure, God has blessed me for your sakes, and has thus answered for me all your prayers; nay, *more* than answered all you or I could have wished or hoped for We only prayed, only hoped, that God would preserve *you* honest, and *me* virtuous: and see, O see, my excellent parents, how we are crown'd with blessings upon blessings, till we are the talk of all that know us —You for your honesty, I for my humility and virtue!—that virtue which God's grace inspired, and your examples and lessons, with those of my dear good lady, cultivated, and which now have left me nothing to do but to reap all the rewards which this life can afford; and if I walk humbly, and improve my blessed opportunities, will heighten and perfect all in a still more joyful futurity

Hence, my dear parents, (I mean, from the delight I have in writing to you, a delight which transports me so far above my own sphere) you'll see, that I *must* write to you, and cannot help it, if I would, And *will* it be a great joy to you!—And is there any thing that can add to your joy, think you, that is in the power of your Pamela, that she would not *do?*—O that the lives and healths of my dearest Mr B and my dearest parents, may be continued to me! And who then can be so blest as your Pamela?

I *will* write, *depend* upon it, I will—on every occasion:—and you augment my joys, to think it is in my power to add to your comforts Nor can you conceive the pleasure I have in hoping that this your new happy lot may, by relieving you from corroding care, and the too wearing effects of hard labour, add, in these your advanced years, to both your days.—For, so happy am I, I can have no grief, no pain, in looking forward, but from such thoughts as remind me, that one day either you from me, or I from you, must be separated

But it is fit, that we so comport ourselves, as that we should not imbitter our present happiness with prospects too gloomy—but bring our minds to be cheerfully thankful for the present, wisely to enjoy that *present* as we go along—and at last, when all is to be wound up, lie down, and say—'*Not mine*, but *Thy* '*will be done*!'

I have written a great deal, yet have much still to say relating to other parts of your kind, your acceptable letter, and so will soon write again: for I must think every opportunity happy, whereby I can assure you, how much I am, and will ever be, without any addition to my name, if that will make you easier, *your dutiful*

PAMELA.

LETTER IV.

MY DEAREST FATHER AND MOTHER,

I Now write again, as I told you I should in my last—but I am half afraid to look back on the copy of it, for your worthy hearts, so visible in your letter and my beloved's kind deportment upon shewing it to him, raised me into the frame of mind that was bordering on extacy yet am I sure, I wrote my heart. But you must not, my dear father, write to your poor Pamela so affectingly. Your *steadier* mind could hardly bear your own moving strain, and you were forced to lay down your pen, and retire: how then could I, who love you so dearly, if you had not, if I may so say, *increased* that love by fresh and stronger instances of your worthiness, forbear being affected, and raised above myself!—But I will not again touch upon this subject.

You must know then, that my dearest spouse commands me, with his kind respects, to tell you, that he has thought of a method to make your *worthy hearts* easy, those were his words 'And this 'is, said he, 'by putting that whole 'estate, with the new purchase, under 'your father's care, as I at first intend'ed*, and he shall receive and pay, and 'order every thing as he pleases, and 'Longman, who grows in years, shall be 'eased of that burden Your father,' said he, 'writes a very legible hand, and 'he shall take what assistants he pleases: 'and do you, Pamela, see to that, that 'this new task may be made as easy and 'pleasant to him as possible He shall 'make up his accounts only to you, my 'dear And there will be several pleasures arise to me upon it,' continued

* See Vol II, page 269.

he 'first, that it will be a relief to honest Longman, who has business enough on his hands besides. Next, it will make the good couple easy, that they have an opportunity of enjoying that as their due, which now their too grateful hearts give them so many causeless scruples about. Thirdly, it will employ your father's time, more suitably to *your* liking and *mine*, because with more ease to himself, for you see his industrious will cannot be satisfied without doing something In the fourth place, the management of this estate will gain him more respect and reverence among the tenants and his neighbours, and yet be all in his own way For, my dear, added he, 'you ll see, that it is always one point in view with me, to endeavour to convince every one, that I esteem and value them for their own intrinsick merit, and want not any body to distinguish them in any other light, than that in which they have been accustomed to appear'

So, my dear father, the instrument will be drawn, and brought you by honest Mr Longman, who will be with you in a few days, to put the last hand to the new purchase, and to give you possession of your new commission, if you please to accept of it; as I hope you will, and the rather, for my dear Mr. B's third reason, and because I know that this trust will be discharged as worthily and as sufficiently, after you are used to it, as if Mr Longman himself was in it —And better it cannot be Mr Longman is very fond of this relief, and longs to be down to settle every thing with you, as to the proper powers, the method, &c.—And he says, in his usual way of phrasing, that he ll make it as easy to you as a glove.

If you do accept it, my dear Mr. B will leave every thing to you, as to rent, where not already fixed, and likewise, as to acts of kindness and favour to be done where you think proper; and he is pleased to say, that with his bad qualities, he was ever deemed a kind landlord, and this I can confirm in fifty instances to his honour 'So that the old gentleman,' said he, 'need not be afraid of being put upon severe or harsh methods of proceeding, where things will do without, and he will always have it in his power to befriend an honest man, by which means the province will be intirely such a one as suits with his inclination. If any thing difficult or perplexing arises,' continued he, 'or where a little knowledge in law-matters is necessary, Longman shall do all that and your father will see, that he will not have in those points a coadjutor that will be too hard hearted for his wish: for it was a rule my father set me, and I have strictly followed, that although I have a lawyer for my steward, it was rather to know how to do *right* things, than oppressive ones, and Longman has so well answered this intention, that he was always more noted for composing differences, than promoting law-suits'

I dare say, my dear father, this will be an acceptable employment to you, on the several accounts my dearest Mr. B was pleased to mention and what a charming contrivance is here! God forever bless his considerate heart for it!—To make you useful to him, and easy to yourself as well as respected by, and even a benefactor to all around you! What can one say to all these things!—But what signifies exulting in one's gratitude for *one* benefit;—every hour the dear man heaps new ones upon us, and we have hardly time to thank him for one, but a second, and a third, and so on to countless degrees, confound one, and throw back one's words upon one's heart before they are well formed, and oblige one to sit down under all with profound silence and admiration

As to what you mentioned of the desire of cousin Thomas, and Roger, to live with you, I endeavoured to sound what our dear benefactor's opinion was. He was pleased to say—'I have nothing to choose in this case, my dear Your father is his own master he may employ whom he pleases, and, if they are not wanting in respect to him and your mother, I think, as he rightly observes, relationship should rather have the preference, and as he can remedy inconveniencies, if he finds any, by all means let every branch of your family have reason to rejoice with him'

But I have thought of this matter a good deal, since I had the favour of your letter, and I hope, since you condescend to ask my advice, you will excuse me, if I give it freely, yet entirely submitting all to your liking.

In the first place, then, I think it would be better to have *any body* than relations; and that for these reasons.

One

One is apt to expect more regard from relations, and they more indulgence, than strangers can have reason for

That where there is such a difference in the expectations of both, it is hardly possible but uneasiness must arise

That this will subject you to bear it, or to resent it, and to part with them If you bear it, you will know no end of impositions if you dismiss them, it will occasion ill-will They will call you unkind, and you them ungrateful, and as, it may be, your prosperous lot will raise your enviers, such will be apt to believe *them* rather than *you*

Then the world will be inclined to think that we are crouding upon a generous gentleman a numerous family of indigent people, and though they may be ever so deserving, yet it will be said—' The girl ' is filling every place with her relations, ' and *beleaguering*, as you significantly express it, ' a worthy gentleman And this will be said, perhaps, should one s kindred behave ever so worthily And so,

In the next place, one would not, for *their* sakes, that this should be done, who may live with *less* reproach, and *equal* benefit, any-where else for I would not wish any one of them to be lifted out of his station, and made independent, at Mr B s expence, if their industry will not do it, although I would never scruple to do any thing reasonable to promote or assist that industry, in the way of their callings

Then it will possibly put others of our relations upon the same expectations of living with you, and this may occasion ill-will among them, if some be preferred to others in your favour

Then, my dear father, I apprehend, that our beloved and honoured benefactor would be under some difficulty, from his natural politeness, and regard for you and me —You see how kindly, on all occasions, he treats you both, not only as the father and mother of his Pamela, but as if you were his own father and mother and if you had any-body as your servants there, who called you cousin, or grandfather, or uncle, he would not care, when he came down, to treat them on the foot of common servants, though they might nevertheless think themselves honoured (as they would be, and as I am sure I shall always think *myself*) with his commands And would it not, if they are modest and worthy, be as great a difficulty upon *them*, to be thus distinguished, as it would be to *him* and to *me*, for *his* sake? For otherwise, (believe me, I hope you will, my dear father and mother) I could sit down and rejoice with the meanest and remotest relation I have But in the world s eye, to every body but my best of parents, I must, if I have ever so much reluctance to it, appear in a light that may not give discredit to his choice

Then again, as I hinted, you will have it in your power, without the least injury to our common benefactor, to do kinder things by any of our relations, when *not* with you, than you can do, if they *live* with you

You may lend them a little money to put them in a way, if any thing offers that you think will be to their advantage You can fit out my she-cousins to good reputable places.—The younger you can put to school, or, when fit, to trades, according to their talents, and so they will be of course in a way to get an honest and creditable livelihood

But, above all things, one would as much discourage, as one could, such a proud and ambitious spirit in any of them, as should want to raise itself by favour instead of merit, and this the rather, for that, undoubtedly, there are many more happy persons in low than in high life, take number for number all the world over

I am sure, although four or five years of different life had passed with me, I had so much pride and pleasure in the thought of working for my living with you, my dear parents, if I could but get honest to you, that it made my confinement the more grievous to me, and even, if possible, aggravated the apprehensions attending it

But I must beg of you, not to harbour a thought, that these my reasons proceed from the bad motives of a heart tainted with pride on it's high condition. Indeed there can be no reason for it, to one who thinks after this manner:—the greatest families on earth have some among them who are unhappy and low in life, and shall such a one reproach me with having twenty low relations, because they have, peradventure, not above five? or with ten, because they have but one, or two, or three?—Or should I, on the other hand, be ashamed of relations who had done nothing blame-worthy, and whose poverty (a very necessary state in the scale of of beings) was all their crime, when there is hardly any great family, but has produced instances of persons guilty of bad actions, *really* bad, which have reduced them to a distress we never knew? Let the person who would reproach me with *low birth*, which is no disgrace, and what I *cannot help*, give me no cause to retort upon him *low actions*, which *are* a disgrace to any station, the more so the higher it is, and which he *can help*, or else I shall smile with contempt at his empty reproach; and could I be half so proud *with cause*, as he is *without*, glory in my advantage over him.

Let us then, my dear father and mother, endeavour to judge of one another, as God, at the last day, will judge of us all; and then the honest peasant will stand fairer in our esteem than the guilty peer.

In short, this shall be my own rule—Every one who acts justly and honestly, I will look upon as my relation, whether he be so or not; and the more he wants my assistance, the more intitled to it he shall be, as well as to my esteem; while those who deserve it not, must expect nothing but compassion from me, and my prayers, were they my brothers or sisters. 'Tis true, had I not been poor and lowly, I might not have thought thus; but if it be a right way of thinking, it is a blessing that I was so, and that shall never be matter of reproach to me, which one day will be matter of justification.

Upon the whole then, I should think it adviseable, my dear father and mother, to make such kind excuses to the offered services of my cousins, as your better reason shall suggest to you, and to do any thing else for them of *more* value, as their circumstances may require, or occasions offer to serve them.

But if the employing them, and having them about you, will add any one comfort to your lives, I give up intirely my own opinion, and doubt not every thing will be thought well of, that you shall think fit to do.

And so I conclude with assuring you, that I am, my ever-dear parents, *your dutiful and happy daughter.*

The copy of this letter I will keep to myself, till I have your answer to it, that you may be under no difficulty how to act in either of the cases mentioned in it.

LETTER V.

MY DEAREST DAUGHTER,

HOW shall I do to answer, as they deserve, your two last letters? Surely no happy couple ever had such a child as we have! But it is in vain to aim at words like your words, and equally in vain for us to offer to set forth the thankfulness of our hearts, on the kind office your honoured husband has given us, for no reason but to favour us still more, and to quiet our minds in the notion of being useful to him. God grant I may be able to be so!—Happy shall I be, if I can! But I see the generous drift of his proposal; it is only to make me more easy from the nature of my employment, and in my mind too, overloaden, as I may say, with benefits; and at the same time to make me more respected in my new neighbourhood.

I can only say, I most gratefully accept of the kind offer; and since it will ease the worthy Mr Longman, shall with still greater pleasure do all I can in it. But I doubt I shall be wanting in ability, I doubt I shall: but I will be just and honest however. That, by God's grace, will be within my own capacity; and that, I hope, I may answer for.

It is kind, indeed, to put it in my power to do good to those who shall deserve it: and I will take *double* pains to find out the true merit of such as I shall recommend to favour, and that their circumstances be really such as I shall represent them.

But one thing, my dear daughter, let me desire, that I may make up my accounts to Mr Longman, or to his honour himself, when he shall make us so happy as to be here with us. I don't know how—but it will make me uneasy, if I am to make up my accounts to you; for so well known is your love to us, that though you would no more do an unjust thing, than, by God's grace, we should desire you, yet this same ill-willing world might think it was like making up accounts to one's self.

Do, my dearest child, get me off of this difficulty, and I can have no other; for already I am in hopes I have hit upon a contrivance to improve the estate, and to better the condition of the tenants at the same time, at least not to worst them, and which, I hope, will please every body.

but

but I will acquaint Mr Longman with this, and take his advice, for I will not be too troublesome either to you, my dear child, or to your spouse.—If I could act so for his interest, as not to be a burden, what happy creatures should we both be in our own minds!—We find ourselves more and more respected by every one, and so far as shall be consistent with our new trust, we will endeavour to deserve it, that we may interest as many as know us in our own good wishes and prayers for the happiness of you both.

But let me say, how much convinced I am by the reasons you give for not taking to us any of our relations. Every one of those reasons has it's force with us. How happy are we to have so prudent a daughter to advise with! And I think myself obliged to promise this, that whatever I do for any of them above the amount of forty shillings at one time, I will take your direction in it, that your wise hints, of making every one continue their industry, and not to rely upon favour instead of merit, may be followed. I am sure this is the way to make them *happier*, as well as *better* men and women, for, as I have often thought, if one were to have a hundred pounds a year in good comings-in, it would not do without industry; and with it, one may do with a quarter of it, and less.

In short, my dear child, your reasons are so good, that I wonder they came not into my head before, and then I needed not to have troubled you about the matter: but yet it ran in my own thought, that I could not like to be an incroacher.—for I hate a dirty thing, and in the midst of my distresses, never could be guilty of one. Thank God for it.

You rejoice our hearts beyond expression at the hope you give us of receiving letters from you now-and-then: to be sure it will be the chief comfort of our lives, next to seeing you, as we are put in hope we sometimes shall. But, yet, my dear child, don't let us put you to inconvenience neither. Pray don't: you'll have enough upon your hands without —to be sure you will.

The workmen have made a good progress, and wish for Mr Longman to come down, as we also do.

You need not be afraid we should think you proud, or lifted up with your condition. You have weathered the first dangers, and but for your fine clothes and jewels, we should not see any difference, indeed we should not, between our dear Pamela, and the much respected Mrs B——. But God has given you too much sense to be proud or lifted up. I remember in your former writings, a saying of the squire's, speaking of you, my dear child, that it was for persons who were not used to praise, and did not deserve it, to be proud of it*. In like sort one may say, it is for persons of little sense to be proud, but you, my dear child, every one sees, are *above* it: and that, methinks, is a proud word, is it not? If one was not—I don't know how,—half stupid, I believe—one would be raised by your high stile of writing. But I should be more than half stupid, I'm sure, to aim at it.

Every day brings us instances of the good name his honour and you, my dear child, have left behind you in this country. Here comes one, and here comes another, and a third, and a fourth, and—'Goodman Andrews, cries one, and, 'Goody Andrews,' cries another—(and some call us Mr and Mrs but we like the other full as well) 'when heard you 'from his honour? How does his lady 'do?—What a charming couple are 'they?—How lovingly they live!—'What an example do they give to all 'about them!' Then one cries—'God 'bless 'em both, and another cries—'Amen,' and so says a third and a fourth, and all say—'But when do you 'expect them down again?—Such a-'one longs to see 'em—and 'such a one 'will ride a day's journey, to have but 'a sight of 'em at church.' And then they say—'How this gentleman praises 'them, and that lady admires them.'—O my dear child, what a happiness is this! How do your poor mother and I stand fixed to the earth to hear both your praises, our tears trickling down our cheeks, and our hearts heaving as if they would burst with joy, till we are forced to take leave in half words, and hand-in-hand go in together to bless God, and bless you both! O my daughter, what a happy couple have God and you made us!

Your poor mother is very anxious about her dear child. I will not touch upon a matter so very irksome to you to hear of. But, though the time may be some months off, she every hour prays

* See Vol. II. p. 129.

for your ſafety and happineſs, and for all the increaſe of felicity that his honour's generous heart can wiſh for. That is all we will ſay at preſent: only, that we are, with continued prayers and bleſſings, my deareſt child, *your loving father and mother,*

J. *and* E. ANDREWS.

Yet one word more!—and that is—our *duty* to your honoured huſband. We muſt ſay ſo now, though he forbad us ſo often before. You cannot, my dear child, imagine how aſhamed I was to have my poor letter ſhewn to him. I hardly remember what I wrote, but it was from my heart, I'm ſure, ſo I needed not to keep a copy: for an honeſt mind muſt always be the ſame, in caſes that cannot admit of change, ſuch as thoſe of my thankfulneſs to God and to him. But don't ſhew him all I write; for I ſhall be afraid of what I ſay, if I think any body but our daughter ſees it, who knows how to allow for her poor parents defects.

LETTER VI.

FROM LADY DAVERS TO MRS. B.

MY DEAR PAMELA,

I Had intended to have been with you before this, but my lord has been a little indiſpoſed with the gout, and Jackey has had an intermitting fever; but they are pretty well recovered, and it ſhall not be long before I ſee you, now I underſtand you are returned from your Kentiſh expedition.

We have been exceedingly diverted with your papers. You have given us, by their means, many a delightful hour, that otherwiſe would have hung heavy upon us, and we are all charmed with you. Lady Betty, as well as her noble mamma, has always been of our party, whenever we have read your accounts. She is a dear generous lady, and has ſhed many a tear over them, as indeed we all have; and my lord has not been unmoved, nor Jackey neither, at ſome of your diſtreſſes and reflections. Indeed, Pamela, you are a charming creature, and an ornament to your ſex. We wanted to have had you among us a hundred times, as we read, that we might have loved, and kiſſed, and thanked you.

But after all, my brother, generous and noble as he was, when your trials were over, was a ſtrange wicked young fellow; and happy it was for you both, that he was ſo cleverly caught in the trap he had laid for your virtue.

I can aſſure you, my lord longs to ſee you, and will accompany me; for, he ſays, he has but a faint idea of your perſon. I tell him, and tell them all, that you are the fineſt girl, and the moſt improved in perſon and mind, I ever beheld; and I am not afraid, although they ſhould imagine all they can in your favour, from my account of you, that they will be diſappointed when they ſee you, and converſe with you. But one thing more you muſt do for us, and then we will love you ſtill more; and that is, you muſt ſend us the reſt of your papers, down to your marriage at leaſt; and farther, if you have written farther; for we all long to ſee the reſt, as you relate it, though we know in general what has paſſed.

You leave off* with an account of an angry letter I wrote to my brother, to perſuade him to give you your liberty, and a ſum of money; not doubting but his deſigns would end in your ruin, and, I own it, not wiſhing he would marry you; for little did I know of your merit and excellence, nor could I, but for your letters ſo lately ſent me, have had any notion of either. I don't queſtion but, if you have recited my paſſionate behaviour to you, and when I was at the hall, I ſhall make a ridiculous figure enough; but I will forgive all that, for the ſake of the pleaſure you *have* given me, and will ſtill farther give me, if you comply with my requeſt.

Lady Betty ſays, it is the beſt ſtory ſhe has heard, and the moſt inſtructive; and ſhe longs to have the concluſion of it in your own words. She ſays now-and-then—'What a hopeful brother you have, 'Lady Davers! O theſe intriguing gentlemen!—What rogueries do they not 'commit! I ſhould have had a fine huſband of him, had I received your propoſal! The *dear* Pamela would have run in 'his head, and had I been the firſt lady 'in the kingdom, I ſhould have ſtood 'but a poor chance in his eſteem; for, 'you ſee, his deſigns upon her began† 'early.'

* See Vol. II. p. 155, & 274. † Vol. I. p. 51.

She

She says, you had a good heart to go back again to him, when the violent wretch had driven you from him on such a slight occasion but yet, she thinks the reasons you give * in your relation, and your love for him, (which then you began to discover was your case) as well as the event, shewed you did right

But we ll tell you all our judgments, when we have read the rest of your accounts. So pray send them as soon as you can, to (I won't write myself sister till then) *your affectionate*, &c

B. DAVERS

LETTER VII.

MY DEAR GOOD LADY,

YOU have done me great honour in the letter your ladyship has been pleased to send me, and it is a high pleasure to me, now all is so happily over, that my poor papers were in the least diverting to you, and to such honourable and worthy persons as your ladyship is pleased to mention. I could wish, my dear lady, I might be favoured with such remarks on my conduct, so nakedly set forth, (without any imagination that they would ever appear in such an assembly) as may be of use to me in my future life, and make me, by that means, more worthy than it is otherwise possible I can be, of the honour to which I am raised Do, dearest lady, favour me so far I am prepared to receive blame, and to benefit by it, and cannot expect praise so much from my *actions* as from my *intentions*, for, indeed, these were always just and honourable but why, even for these, do I talk of praise, since, being prompted by impulses I could not resist, it can be no merit in me to have been governed by them?

As to the papers following those in your ladyship s hands, when I say, that they must needs appear impertinent to such judges, after what you know, I dare say your ladyship will not insist upon them yet I will not scruple briefly to mention what they contain

All my dangers and trials were happily at an end to that they only contain the conversations that passed between your ladyship s generous brother and me, his kind assurances of honourable love to me, my acknowledgments of unworthiness to him, Mrs Jewkes s respectful change of behaviour towards me, Mr. B 's reconciliation to Mr Williams, his introducing me to the good families in the neighbourhood, and avowing before them his honourable intentions A visit from my honest father, who (not knowing what to conclude from the letter I wrote to him before I returned to your honoured brother, desiring my papers from him) came in great anxiety of heart to know the worst, doubting I had at last been caught by a stratagem, that had ended in my ruin His joyful surprize to find how happy I was likely to be All the hopes given me, answered, by the private celebration of our nuptials—an honour so much above all that my utmost ambition could make me aspire to, and which I never can deserve! Your ladyship s arrival, and anger, not knowing I was actually married, but supposing me a vile wicked creature, in which case I should have deserved the worst of usage. Mr B 's angry lessons to me, for daring to interfere, though I thought in the tenderest and most dutiful manner, between your ladyship and himself The most acceptable goodness and favour of your ladyship afterwards to me, of which, as becomes me, I shall ever retain the most grateful sense My return to this sweet mansion in a manner so different from my quitting it, where I had been so happy for four years, in paying my duty to the best of mistresses, your ladyship's excellent mother, to whose goodness, in taking me from my poor honest parents, and giving me what education I have, I owe, under God, my happiness The joy of good Mrs Jervis, Mr Longman, and all the servants, on this occasion. Mr B 's acquainting me with Miss Godfrey's affair, and presenting to me the pretty Miss Goodwin, at the dairy-house. Our appearance at church, the favour of the gentry in the neighbourhood, who, knowing your ladyship had not disdained to look upon me, and to be favourable to me, came the more readily into a neighbourly intimacy with me, and still so much the more readily, as the continued kindness of my dear benefactor, and his condescending deportment to me before them, (as if I had been worthy of the honour done me) did credit to his own generous act

These, my lady, down to my good parents setting out to this place, in order to

* See Vol. II p 153.

be settled by my honoured benefactor's bounty, in the Kentish farm, are the most material contents of my remaining papers: and though they might be the most agreeable to those for whom only they were written, yet, *as* they were principally matters of course, after what your ladyship has with you, *as* the joy of my fond heart can be better judged of by your ladyship, than describ'd by me, and as your ladyship is acquainted with all the particulars that can be worthy of any other's person's notice but my dear parents, I am sure your ladyship will dispense with your commands, and I make it my humble request, that you will.

For, Madam, you must needs think, that *when* my doubts were dispelled, *when* I was confident all my trials were over, *when* I had a prospect before me of being so abundantly rewarded for what I had suffered, *when every* hour rose upon me with new delight, and fraught with fresh instances of generous kindness from such a dear gentleman, my master, my benefactor, the son of my honoured lady, your ladyship must needs think, I say, that I must be *too* much affected, my heart must be *too* much opened, and especially as it then (relieved from its past anxieties and fears, which had kept down and damped the latent flame) first discovered to me impressions of which before I hardly thought it susceptible.—So that it is scarce possible, that my *joy* and my *prudence*, if I were to be tried by such judges of delicacy and decorum as Lord and Lady Davers, the honoured countess, and Lady Betty, could be so *intimately*, so *laudably* coupled, as were to be wished: although, indeed, the continued sense of my unworthiness, and the disgrace the dear gentleman would bring upon himself by his generous goodness to me, always went hand in-hand with my *joy* and my *prudence*, and what these considerations took from the *former*, being added to the *latter*, kept me steadier and more equal to myself, than otherwise it was possible such a young creature as I could have been.

Wherefore, my dear good lady, I hope I stand excused, and shall not bring upon myself the censure of being disobedient to your commands.

Besides, Madam, since you inform me, that my good Lord Davers will attend your ladyship hither, I should never dare to look his lordship in the face, if all the emotions of my heart on such affecting occasions, stood confessed to his lordship; and indeed, if I am ashamed they should to your ladyship, and to the countess and Lady Betty, whose goodness must induce you all three to think favourably, in such circumstances, of one who is of your own sex, how would it concern me, that the same should appear before such gentlemen as my lord and his nephew?—Indeed I could not look up to either of them in the sense of this.—And give me leave to hope, that some of the scenes, in the letters your ladyship had, were not read to gentlemen: your ladyship must needs know which I mean, and will think of my two grand trials of all. For though I was the innocent subject of wicked attempts, and so cannot, I hope, suffer in any one's opinion for what I could not help, yet, for your dear brother's sake, as well as for the decency of the matter, one would not, when one shall have the honour to appear before my lord and his nephew, be looked upon, methinks, with that levity of eye and thought, which, perhaps, hard-hearted gentlemen may pass upon one, by reason of those very scenes, which would move pity and concern in a good lady's breast, for a poor creature so attempted.

So, my dear lady, be pleased to let me know, if the gentlemen *have* heard all.—I hope they have not.—And be pleased also to point out to me such parts of my conduct as deserve blame: indeed, I will try to make a good use of your censure, and am sure I shall be thankful for it,—for it will make me hope to be more and more worthy of the honour I have, of being exalted into such a distinguished family, and the right the best of gentlemen has given me to stile myself *your ladyship's most humble, and most obliged servant,*

P. B.

LETTER VIII

FROM LADY DAVERS, IN REPLY.

MY DEAR PAMELA,

YOU have given us all a great disappointment in declining to oblige me with the sequel of your papers. I was a little out of humour with you at first,—I must own I was.—for I cannot bear denial, when my heart is set upon any thing. But Lady Betty became your advocate, and said, she thought you very excusable, since, no doubt, there might

be

be many tender things, circumstanced as you were, which might be well enough for your parents to see, but for nobody else, and relations of our side least of all, whose future intimacy, and frequent visits, might give occasions for raillery and remarks, that might not be otherwise agreeable I regarded her apology for you the more, because I knew it was a great baulk to her, that you did not comply with my request But now, child, when you know me more, you ll find, that if I am obliged to give up one point, I always insist on another, as near it as I can, in order to see if it be only *one* thing I am to be refused, or *every* thing, in which last case, I know how to take my measures, and resent.

Now, therefore, this is what I insist upon, that you correspond with me in the same manner that you did with your parents, and acquaint me with every passage that is of concern to you, beginning with your accounts how you spent your time, both of you, when you were in Kent, for, you must know, we are all taken with your duty to your parents, and the discretion of the good couple, and think you have given a very edifying example of filial piety to all who shall hear your story, for if so much duty is owing to parents, where nothing can be done for one, how much more is it to be expected, where there is a power to add to the natural obligation, all the comforts and conveniences of life? We people in upper life, you must know, love to hear how gratitude and unexpected benefits operate upon honest minds, who have little more than plain artless nature for their guide, and we flatter ourselves with the hopes of many a delightful hour, by your means, in this our solitary situation, as it will be, if we are obliged to pass the next winter in it, as my lord and the earl threaten me, and the countess, and Lady Betty, that we shall Then let us hear of every thing that gives you joy or trouble and if my brother carries you to town, for the winter, while he attends parliament, the advices you will be able to give us of what passes in London, and of the publick entertainments and diversions he will take you to, as you will relate them in your own artless and natural observations, will be as diverting to us, as if we were at them ourselves For a young creature of your good understanding, to whom all these things will be quite new, will give us, perhaps, a better taste of them, their beauties, and defects, than we might have before For we people of quality go to those places, dressed out and adorned, in such manner, outvying one another, as if we considered ourselves as so many parts of the publick entertainment, and are too much pleased with ourselves to be able so to attend to what we see, as to form a right judgment of it and, indeed, we, some of us, behave with so much indifference to the entertainment, as if we thought ourselves above being diverted by what we come to see, and as if our view was rather to trifle away our time, than to improve ourselves by attending to the story or the action

See, Pamela I shall not make an unworthy correspondent altogether, for I can get into thy grave way, and moralize a little now-and-then and if you'll promise to oblige me by your constant correspondence in this way, and divest yourself of all restraint, as if you were writing to your parents, (and I can tell you, you ll write to one who will be as candid and as favourable to you as they can be) then I am sure we shall have truth and nature from you, and these are things which we are generally so much lifted above, by our conditions, that we hardly know what they are

But I have written enough for one letter, and yet, having more to say, I will, after this, send another, without waiting for your answer, which you may give to to both together, and am, mean time, *yours*, &c

B DAVERS.

LETTER IX.

DEAR PAMELA,

I Am very glad thy honest man has let thee into the affair of Sally Godfrey. But pr'ythee, Pamela, give us an account of the manner in which he did it, and of thy thoughts upon it, for that is a critical case, and according as he has represented it, so shall I know what to say of it before you and him for I would not make mischief between you for the world

This, let me tell you, will be a trying part of your conduct For he loves the child, and will judge of you by your conduct towards it He dearly loved her mother, and, notwithstanding her fault, she well deserved it for she was a sensible, ay, and a modest lady, and of an

ancient

ancient and genteel family But he was heir to a noble estate, was of a bold and enterprizing spirit, fond of intrigue— Don't let this concern you—You'll have the greater happiness and merit too, if you can hold him—And, 'tis my opinion, if any-body can, you will.—Then he did not like the young lady's mother, who sought artfully to intrap him So that the poor girl, divided between her inclination for him, and her duty to her designing mother, gave into the plot upon him, and he thought himself—vile wretch as he was for all that!—at liberty to set up plot against plot, and the poor lady's honour was the sacrifice.

I hope you spoke well of her to him I hope you received the child kindly.—I hope you had presence of mind to do this —For it was a nice part to act, and all his observations were up, I dare say, on the occasion —Do, let me hear how it was there's my good Pamela, do And write, I charge you, freely, and without restraint, for although I am not your mother, yet am I *his* eldest sister, you know—and as such—come I will say so, in hopes you'll oblige me—*your* sister, and so intitled to expect a compliance with my request- for is there not a duty in degree, to elder sisters from younger?

As to our remarks upon your behaviour, they have been much to your credit, I can tell you that but, nevertheless, I will, to encourage you to enter into this requested correspondence with me, consult Lady Betty, and will go over your papers again, and try to find fault with your conduct; and if we can see any thing censurable, will freely let you know our minds

But, before-hand, I can tell you, we shall be agreed in one opinion, and that is, that we know not who would have acted as you have done, upon the whole

So, Pamela, you see I put myself upon the same foot of correspondence with you —Not that I will promise to answer every letter- no, you must not expect that — Your part will be a kind of narrative, purposely designed to entertain us here, and I hope to receive six, seven, eight, or ten letters, as it may happen, before I return one but such a part I will bear in it, as shall let you know our opinion of your proceedings and relations of things —And as you wish to be found fault with, as you say, you shall freely have it, (though not in a splenetick or ill natured way) as often as you give occasion Now, you must know, Pamela, I have two views in this One is, to see how a man of my brother's spirit, who has not denied himself any genteel liberties, (for it must be owned he never was a common town rake, and had always dignity in his roguery) will behave himself to you, and in wedlock, which used to be freely sneered by him the next, that I may love you more and more, which it will be enough to make me do, I dare say, as by your letters I shall be more and more acquainted with you, as well as by conversation, so that you can't be off, if you would

I know, however, you will have no objection to this, and that is, that your family affairs will require your attention, and not give you the time you used to have for this employment But consider, child, the station you are raised to does not require you to be quite a domestick animal You are lifted up to the rank of a lady, and you must act up to it, and not think of setting such an example, as will derive upon you the ill-will and censure of other ladies —For will any of our sex visit one who is continually employing herself in such works as either must be a reproach to herself, or to them?—You'll have nothing to do but to give orders You will consider yourself as the task mistress, and the common herd of female servants, as so many negroes directing themselves by your nod, or yourself as the master-wheel, in some beautiful piece of mechanism, whose dignified grave motions is to set a-going all the under-wheels, with a velocity suitable to their respective parts —Let your servants, under your direction, do all that relates to household management they cannot write to entertain and instruct, as you can So what will you have to do?—I'll answer my own question in the first place, endeavour to please your sovereign lord and master, and let me tell you, any other woman in England, be her quality ever so high, would have found enough to do to succeed in that Secondly, to receive and pay visits, in order, for his credit as well as your own, to make your fashionable neighbours fond of you Then, thirdly, you will have time upon your hands (as your monarch himself rises early, and is tolerably regular for such a brazen face as he has been) to write to me in the manner I have mentioned, and expect, and I see plainly, by your stile, that

that nothing can be easier for you, than to do this

And thus, and with reading, may your time be filled up with reputation to yourself, and delight to others, till a fourth employment puts itself upon you, and that is (shall I tell you in one word, without mincing the matter?) a succession of brave boys, to perpetuate a family that has for many hundred years been esteemed worthy and eminent, and which, being now reduced, in the direct line, to him and me, *expects* it from you, or else, let me tell you, (nor will I baulk it) my brother, by descending to the wholesome cot—Excuse me, Pamela,—will want one apology for his conduct, be as excellent as you may.

I say this, child, not to reflect upon you, since the thing is done, for I love you dearly, and will love you more and more—but to let you know what is expected from you, and to encourage you in the prospect that is already opening to you both, and to me, who have the welfare of the family I sprung from so much at heart, although I know this will be attended with some anxieties to a mind so thoughtful and apprehensive as yours seems to be

O but this puts me in mind of your solicitude for fear the gentlemen should have seen every thing contained in your letters—But this I will particularly speak to in a third letter, having filled my paper on all sides and am, till then, *yours*, &c

B Davers

You see, and I hope will take it as a favour, that I break the ice, and begin first in the indispensibly expected correspondence between us

LETTER X

FROM THE SAME

AND so, Pamela, you are very solicitous to know, if the gentlemen have seen every part of your papers? I can't say but they have nor, except in regard to the reputation of your saucy man, do I see why the part you hint at might not by read by those to whom the rest might be shewn

I can tell you, Lady Betty, who is a very nice and delicate lady, had no objection to any part, though read before men only now-and-then, crying out—'O the vile man!—See, Lord Davers, 'what wretches you men are!' And, commiserating you—'Ah! the poor Pa'mela! And expressing her impatience to hear on, how you escaped at this time, and at that, and rejoicing in your escape. And now-and-then—'O Lady Davers, 'what a vile brother you have! I hate 'him perfectly —The poor girl cannot 'be made amends for all this, though he 'has married her Who, that knows 'these things of him, would wish him to 'be hers, with all his advantages of per'son, mind, and fortune? And such-like expressions in your praise, and condemning him, and his wicked attempts

But I can tell you this, that except one had heard every tittle of your danger, how near you were to ruin, and how little he stood upon taking any measures to effect his vile purposes, even daring to attempt you in the presence of a *good* woman, which was a wickedness that every *wicked* man could not be guilty of, I say, except one had known these things, one should not have been able to judge of the merit of your resistance, and how shocking those attempts were to your virtue, insomuch that life itself was endangered by them nor, let me tell you, could I in particular, have so well justified him for marrying you, (I mean with respect to his own proud and haughty temper of mind) if there had been room to think he could have had you upon easier terms

It was necessary, child, on twenty accounts, that we, your and his well wishers and his relations, should know that he had tried every stratagem, and made use of every contrivance, to subdue you to his purpose, before he married you and how would it have answered to his intrepid character, and pride of heart, had we not been particularly led into the nature of those attempts, which you so nobly resisted, as to convince us all, that you have deserved the good fortune you have met with, as well as all the kind and respectful treatment he can possibly shew you?

Nor ought you to be concerned who sees any the most tender parts of your story, except, as I said, for *his* sake, for it must be a very unvirtuous mind, that can form any other ideas from what you relate, than those of terror and pity for you Your expressions are too delicate to give the nicest ear offence, except at him.—

You paint no scenes but such as make his wickedness odious, and that gentleman, much more lady, must have a very corrupt heart, who could, from such circumstances of distress, make any reflections, but what should be to your honour, and in abhorrence of such actions. Indeed, child, I am so convinced of this, that by this rule I would judge of any man's heart in the world, better than by a thousand declarations and protestations. I do assure you, rakish as Jackey is, and freely as I doubt not that Lord Davers has formerly lived, (for he has been a man of pleasure) they gave me by their behaviour on these tenderer occasions, reason to think they had more virtue, than not to be very apprehensive for your safety; and my lord several times exclaimed, that he could not have thought his brother such a libertine neither.

Besides, child, were not these things written in confidence to your mother? And, bad as his actions were to you, if you had not recited all you could recite, would there not have been room for any one, who should have seen what you wrote, to imagine they had been still worse? — And how could the terror be supposed to have had such effects upon you, as to endanger your life, without imagining you had undergone the worst that a vile man *could* offer, unless you had told us, what that was which he *did* offer, and so put a bound, as it were, to one's apprehensive imaginations of what you suffered, which otherwise must have been injurious to your purity, though you could not help it?

Moreover, Pamela, it was but doing justice to the libertine himself to tell your mother the whole truth, that she might know he was not so very abandoned, but that he could stop short of the execution of his wicked purposes, which he apprehended, if pursued, would destroy the life, that, of all lives, he would choose to preserve; and you owed also thus much to your parents peace of mind, that after all their distracting fears for you, they might see they had reason to rejoice in an uncontaminated daughter. And one cannot but reflect, now all is over, and he has made you his wife, that it must be a satisfaction to the wicked man, as well as to yourself, that he was not more guilty than he *was*, and that he took no more liberties than he *did*.

For my own part, I must say, that I could not have accounted for your fits, by any descriptions short of those you give; and had you been less particular in the circumstances, I should have judged he had been still *worse*, and your person though not your mind less pure, than his pride would expect from the woman he should marry; for this is the case of all rakes, that though they indulge in all manner of libertinism themselves, there is no class of men who exact greater delicacy than they, from the persons they marry, though they care not how bad they make the wives, the sisters, and daughters of others.

I have run into length again, so will only add, (and send all my three letters together) that we all blame you in some degree for bearing the wicked Jewkes in your sight, after the most impudent assistance she gave to his lewd attempt; much less, we think, ought you to have left her in her place, and rewarded her for her vileness could hardly be equalled by the worst actions of the most abandoned procuress.

I know the difficulties you labour under, in his arbitrary will, and in his intercession for her: but Lady Betty rightly observes, that he knew what a vile woman she was, when he put you into her power, and no doubt employed her, because he was sure she would answer all his purposes, and that therefore she should have had very little opinion of the sincerity of his reformation, while he was so solicitous in keeping her there, and in having her put upon a foot, in the present on your nuptials, with honest Jervis.

She would, she says, had she been in your case, have had *one* struggle for her dismission, let it have been taken as it would; and he that was so well pleased with your virtue, must have thought this a natural consequence of it, if he was in earnest to reclaim.

I know not whether you shew him all I write, or not: but I have written this last part in the cover, as well for want of room, as that you may keep it from him, if you please. Though if you think it will serve any good end, I am not against shewing to him all I write. For I must ever speak my mind, though I were to smart for it; and that nobody can or has the heart to make me do, but my bold brother. So, Pamela, for this time, *Adieu*.

LETTER

LETTER XI.

MY GOOD LADY,

I Am honoured with your ladyship's three letters, the contents of which are highly obliging to me and I should be inexcusable if I did not comply with your injunctions, and be very proud and thankful for your ladyship's condescension in accepting of my poor scribble, and promising me such a rich and invaluable return, of which you have given me already such ample and such delightful instances I will not plead my defects, to excuse my obedience I only fear, that the awe which will be always upon me, when I write to your ladyship, will lay me under so great a restraint, that I shall fall short even of the merit my papers have already made for me, through your kind indulgence But nevertheless, sheltering myself under your goodness, I will chearfully comply with every thing your ladyship expects from me, that is in my power to do

You will give me leave, Madam, to put into some little method, the particulars of what you desire of me, that I may speak to them all for, since you are so good as to excuse me from sending the rest of my papers, (which indeed would not bear in many places) I will omit nothing that shall tend to convince you of my readiness to obey you in every thing else.

First then, your ladyship would have the particulars of the happy fortnight we passed in Kent, on one of the most agreeable occasions that could befal me.

Secondly, an account of the manner in which your dear brother acquainted me with the affecting story of Miss Godfrey, and my behaviour upon it

And, thirdly, I presume your ladyship, and Lady Betty, expect that I should say something upon your welcome remarks on my conduct towards Mrs Jewkes

The other particulars contained in your ladyship's kind letters will naturally fall under one or other of these three heads—But expect not, my lady, though I begin in method thus, that I shall keep up to it If your ladyship will not allow for me, and keep in view the poor Pamela Andrews in all I write, but will have Mrs B in your eye, what will become of me? —But, indeed, I promise myself so much improvement from this correspondence, that I enter upon it with a greater delight than I can express, notwithstanding the mingled awe and diffidence that will accompany me, in every part of the agreeable task.

To begin with the first article:

Your dear brother and my honest parents—(I know your ladyship will expect from me, that on all occasions I should speak of them with the duty that becomes a good child)—I say, then, your dear brother, and they, and myself, set out on the Monday morning for Kent, passing through St. Albans to London, at both which places we stopped a night, for our dear benefactor would make us take easy journies, and on Wednesday evening we arrived at the sweet place allotted for the good couple We were attended only by Abraham and John, on horseback, for Mr Colbrand, having sprained his foot, was in the travelling-coach with the cook, the house maid, and Polly Barlow, a genteel new servant, whom Mrs. Brooks recommended to wait on me

Mr Longman had been down there for a fortnight, employed in settling the terms of an additional purchase to this pretty well wooded and well watered estate, and the account he gave of his proceedings was very satisfactory to his honoured principal. He told us, he had much ado to dissuade the tenants from pursuing a formed resolution of meeting their landlord on horseback, at some miles distance, for he had informed them when he expected us but knowing how desirous Mr B was of being retired while he staid here this time, he had ventured to assure them, that when every thing was settled, and the new purchase actually entered upon, they would have his presence among them now-and then, and that he would introduce them all at different times to their worthy landlord, before we left the country

The house is large and very commodious, and we found every thing about it, and in it, exceeding neat and convenient, which was owing to the worthy Mr Longman's care and direction. The ground is well stocked, the barns and out-houses in excellent repair, and my poor father and mother have only to wish, that they and I may be deserving of half the goodness we experience from the bountiful mind of your good brother.

But indeed, Madam, I have the pleasure of discovering every day more and more, that there is not a better disposed, and more generous man in the world than himself, insomuch that I verily think he has not been so careful to conceal his *bad* actions as his *good* ones. His heart is naturally beneficent, and his beneficence is the gift of God to him for the most excellent purposes, as I have often been so free as to tell him.—Pardon me, my dear Lady. I wish I may not be impertinently grave: but I find a great many instances of his considerate charity, which hardly any body knew of, and which, since I have been his almoner, could not avoid coming to my knowledge.—But this possibly, is no news to your ladyship. Every body knows the generous goodness of your *own* heart: every one that wanted relief tasted the bounty of your excellent *mother*, my late honoured lady: so that 'tis a *family grace*, and I have no need to speak of it to *you*, Madam.

This cannot, my dear lady, I hope, be construed as if I would hereby suppose ourselves less obliged. Indeed I know nothing so God-like in human nature as this disposition to do good to our fellow-creatures; for is it not following immediately the example of that gracious Providence which every minute is conferring blessings upon us all, and by giving power to the rich, makes them but the dispensers of its benefits to those that want them? But yet as there are but too many objects of compassion, and as the most beneficent mind in the world cannot, like Omnipotence, do good to all, how much are they obliged who are distinguished from others? And this, kept in mind, will always contribute to make the benefited receive, as thankfully as they *ought*, the favours of the obliger.

I know not if I write to be understood in all I mean, but my grateful heart is so over-filled when it is employed on this subject, that methinks I want to say a great deal more at the same time that I am apprehensive I say too much.—Yet, perhaps, the copies of the letters I here inclose to your ladyship, (that marked [I.] written by me to my father and mother, on our return hither from Kent, that marked [II.] from my dear father in answer to it, and that marked [III.] mine in reply to his*) will, (at the same time that they may convince your ladyship, that I will conceal nothing from you in the course of this correspondence, that may in the least amuse and divert you, or that may better explain our grateful sentiments) in a great measure, answer what your ladyship expects from me, as to the happy fortnight we passed in Kent.

And here I will conclude this letter, choosing to suspend the correspondence, till I know from your ladyship, whether it will not be too low, too idle for your attention, whether you will not dispense with your own commands for my writing to you when you see I am so little likely to answer what you may possibly expect from me, or whether, if you insist upon my scribbling, you would have me write in any other way, be less tedious, less serious—in short, less or more any thing. For all that is in my power, your ladyship may command from, *Madam, your obliged and faithful servant,*

P. B.

Your dearest brother, from whose knowledge I would not keep any thing that shall take up any considerable portion of my time, gives me leave to proceed in this correspondence, if you command it: and is pleased to say, he will content himself to see such parts of it, and *only* such parts, as I shall shew him, or read to him.—Is not this very good, Madam?—O my lady, you don't know how happy I am!

LETTER XII.

FROM LADY DAVERS TO MRS. B.

MY DEAR PAMELA,

YOU very much oblige me by your chearful compliance with my request. I leave it intirely to you to write in what manner you please, and as you shall be in the humour to write, when you take up your pen; for then I shall have you write with less restraint: for, you must know, that what we admire in *you*, are truth and nature, and not studied or elaborate epistles. We can hear at church, or we can read in our closets, fifty good things that we expect not from you, but we cannot receive from any-body else the pleasure of sentiments flowing with that artless ease, which so much affects us when we read your letters. Then, my

* See Letters I. II. III. of this Volume.

sweet

ſweet girl, your gratitude, your prudence, your integrity of heart, your humility, ſhine ſo much in all your letters and thoughts, that no wonder my brother loves you as he does

But I ſhall make you proud, I doubt, and ſo by praiſe ruin thoſe graces which we admire, and, but for that, cannot praiſe you too much.—In my conſcience, if thou canſt hold as thou haſt begun, I believe thou *wilt have him all to thyſelf*, and that was once, more than I thought ever any woman on this ſide the ſeventieth year of his age would ever be able to ſay The letters to and from your parents we are charmed with, and the communicating of them to me, I take to be as great an inſtance of your confidence in me, as it is of your judgment and prudence, for you cannot but think, that we, his relations, are a little watchful over your conduct, and have our eyes upon you, to obſerve what uſe you are likely to make of the power you have over your man, with reſpect to your own relations

Hitherto all is unexampled prudence, and you take the right method to reconcile even the proudeſt of us to your marriage, and make us not only love you, but reſpect your parents, becauſe their honeſty will, I perceive, be their diſtinguiſhing character, and they will not forget themſelves, nor their former condition

I can tell you, you are exactly right, for if you were to be an *incroacher*, as the good old man calls it, my brother would be one of the firſt to ſee it, and he would gradually think leſs and leſs of you, till poſſibly he might come to deſpiſe you, and to repent of his choice for the leaſt ſhadow of an impoſition, or low cunning, or mean ſelfiſhneſs, he can not bear.

In ſhort, you're a charming girl, and Lady Betty ſays ſo too, and moreover adds, that if he makes you not the beſt and *faithfulleſt* of huſbands, he cannot deſerve you, for all his fortune and birth And in my heart, I begin to think ſo too

But won't you oblige me with the ſequel of your letter to your father? For, you promiſe, my dear charming ſcribbler, in that you ſent to me, to write again to his letter, and I long to ſee how you anſwer the latter part of it, about your relations deſiring already to come and live with him I know what I *expect* from you But let it be what it will, ſend it to me exactly as you wrote it, and I ſhall ſee whether I have reaſon to praiſe or reprove you For ſurely, Pamela, you muſt leave one room to blame you for ſomething. Indeed I can hardly bear the thought, that you ſhould ſo much excel as you do, and have more prudence, by nature, as it were, than the beſt of us get in a courſe of the genteeleſt education, and with fifty advantages, at leaſt, in converſation, that *you* could not have, by reaſon of my mother's retired life, while you were with her, and your cloſe attendance on her perſon

But I'll tell you what has been a great improvement to you it is your own writings This itch of ſcribbling has been a charming help to you For here, having a natural fund of good ſenſe, and a prudence above your years, you have, with the obſervations theſe have enabled you to make, been flint and ſteel too, as I may ſay, to yourſelf ſo that you have ſtruck *fire* when you pleaſed, wanting nothing but a few dry leaves, like the firſt pair in old Du Bartas, to ſerve as tinder to catch your animating ſparks. So that reading conſtantly, and thus uſing yourſelf to write, and enjoying beſides the benefit of a good memory, every thing you heard or read became your own, and not only ſo, but was improved by paſſing through more ſalubrious ducts and vehicles, like ſome fine fruit grafted upon a common free ſtock, whoſe more exuberant juices ſerve to bring to quicker and greater perfection the downy peach, or the ſmooth nectarine with it's crimſon bluſh

Really, Pamela, I believe, I, too, ſhall improve by writing to you—Why, you dear ſaucy-face, at this rate, you'll make every one that converſes with you, better, and wiſer, and *wittier* too, as far as I know, than they ever before thought there was *room* for 'em to be

As to my own part, I begin to like what I have written myſelf, I think and your correſpondence will poſſibly revive the poetical ideas that uſed to fire my mind, before I entered into the drowſy married life, for my good Lord Davers's turn happens not to be to books, and ſo by degrees, my imagination was in a manner quenched, and I, as a dutiful wife ſhould, endeavoured to form my taſte by that of the man I choſe But after all, Pamela, you are not to be a little proud (I can tell you that) of my correſpondence, and I could not have thought

thought it e er would have come to this but you'll have the penetration to observe, that I am the more free and unreserved, to encourage *you* to write without restraint for already you have made us a family of writers and readers, so that Lord Davers himself is become enamoured of your letters, and desires of all things he may hear read every one that passes between us Nay, Jackey, for that matter, who was the most thoughtless, whistling, sauntring, fellow you ever knew, and whose delight in a book ran no higher than a song or a catch, now comes in with an inquiring face, and vows he'll set pen to paper, and turn letter-writer himself, and intends (if my brother won't take it amiss, he says) to begin to *you*, provided he could be sure of an answer.

I have twenty things still to say, for you have unlocked all our bosoms And yet I intended not to write above ten or a dozen lines when I began;—only to tell you, that I would have you take your own way, in your subjects, and in your stile.—And if you will but give me hope, that you are in the way I so much wish to have you in, I will then call myself your affectionate sister, but till then, it shall only barely be *your correspondent*,

B Davers.

You'll proceed with the account of your Kentish affair, I doubt not.

LETTER XIII

MY DEAR GOOD LADY,

WHAT kind, what generous things are you pleased to say of your happy correspondent! And what reason have I to value myself on such an advantage as is now before me, if I am capable of improving it as I ought, from a correspondence with so noble and so admired a lady! I wish I be not now proud indeed!—To be praised by such a genius, and my honoured benefactor's worthy sister, whose favour, next to his, it was always my chief ambition to obtain, is what would be enough to fill with vanity a steadier and a more equal mind than mine

I have heard from my late honoured lady, what a fine pen her beloved daughter was mistress of, when she pleased to take it up But I never could have had the presumption, but from your ladyship's own motion, to hope to be in any manner the subject of it, much less to be called your correspondent

Indeed, Madam, I *am* proud, very proud of this honour, and consider it as such a heightening to my pleasures, as only *that* could give, and I will set about obeying your ladyship without reserve

But permit me, in the first place, to disclaim any merit, from my own poor writings, to that improvement which your goodness imputes to me What I have to boast, of that sort, is owing principally, if it deserves commendation, to my late excellent lady

It is hardly to be imagined what pains her ladyship took with her poor servant. Besides making me keep a book of her charities dispensed by my hands, she caused me always to set down, in my way, the cases of the distressed, their griefs from their misfortunes, and their joys in her bountiful relief, and so I was entered early into the various turns that affected worthy hearts, and was taught the better to regulate my own, especially by the help of the fine observations which my good lady used to make to me, when I read to her what I wrote. For many a time has her generous heart overflowed with pleasure at my remarks, and with praises, and I was her good girl, her dear Pamela, her hopeful maiden, and she would sometimes snatch my hand with transport, and draw me to her, and vouchsafe to kiss me, and always was saying, what she would do for me, if God spared her, and I continued to be deserving

O my dear lady! you cannot think what an encouragement this condescending behaviour and goodness was to me Indeed, Madam, you *cannot* think it

I used to throw myself at her feet, and embrace her knees, and, my eyes streaming with tears of joy, would often cry—'O continue to me, my dearest lady, the 'blessing of your favour, and kind in'structions, and it is all your happy, 'happy Pamela can wish for'

But I will proceed to obey your ladyship, and write with as much freedom as I possibly *can* for you must not expect, that I can entirely divest myself of that awe which will necessarily lay me under a greater restraint, than if I was writing to my father and mother, whose partiality for their daughter made me, in a manner, secure of their good opinions.

And

And now, that I may shorten the work before me, in the account I am to give of the sweet fortnight that we passed in Kent, I inclose not only the copy of the letter your ladyship desired me to send you, but my father's answer to it, which, with those you have already, will set before your ladyship all you want to see in relation to the desire some of my kindred had to live with my father, and my own opinion on the occasion And I am humbly confident you will join in sentiment with me for persons are less doubtful of approbation, when their minds are incapable of dark reserves, or such views as they would be afraid should be detected by any watchful observer of their conduct and your ladyship gives me double pleasure, that you are pleased to have an eye upon mine; first, because I hope it will be such as will generally bear the strictest scrutiny, and next, because, when my actions fall short of my intentions, I presume to hope your ladyship will be as kind a monitor to me, as you are a correspondent; and then I shall have an opportunity to correct myself, and be, as near as my slender talents will permit, what your ladyship would have me to be

As the letters I sent before, and those I now send, will let your ladyship into several particulars, such as a brief description of the house and farm, and your honoured brother's intentions of retiring thither now-and then, of the happiness and gratitude of my dear parents, and their wishes to be able to deserve the comforts his goodness has heaped upon them; and that in stronger lights than I am able to set them, I will only, in a summary manner, mention the rest and particularly,

That the behaviour of my dear benefactor to me, to my parents, to Mr Longman, and to the tenants, was one continued series of benignity and condescension He endeavoured, in every kind and generous way, to encourage the good couple to be free and chearful with him, and seeing them unable to get over that awe and respect, which they owe him above all mankind, and which they sought to pay him on all occasions, he would take their hands, and more than once called them by the nearest and dearest names of relationship, as if they were his own parents, and I believe would have distinguished them oftener in this manner, but that he saw them too much affected with his goodness to bear the honour (as my dear father says in his first letter) with *equalness of temper*, and he seemed always to delight in being particularly kind to them before strangers, and before the tenants, and before Mr Sorby, and Mr. Bennet, and Mr Shepherd, three of the principal gentlemen in the neighbourhood, who with their ladies came to visit us, and whose visits we *all* returned, for your dear brother would not permit my father and mother to decline the invitation of those worthy families

Judge you, my dear lady, with what a joy these kind distinctions, and his sweet behaviour, must fill their honest hearts. Judge of my grateful sentiments and acknowledgments, of these hourly instances of his goodness, and judge of the respect with which this must inspire every one for the good couple And when once Mrs Bennet had like to have said something of their former condition, which she would have recalled in some confusion, and when she could not, apologized for it, the dear gentleman said—'All is 'well, Mrs Bennet no apologies are 'necessary, and to assure you they are 'not, I ll tell you myself what you cannot have heard so particularly from 'others, and which were I to endeavour 'to conceal, would be a piece of pride 'as stupid as despicable.' So, in a concise manner, he gave them an account of my story, so much to my advantage, and so little to his own, in the ingenuous relation of his attempts upon me, that you can't imagine, Madam, how much the gentry were affected by it, and how much, in particular, they applauded him for the generosity of his actions to me, and to my dear parents And your ladyship will permit me to observe, that since the matter is circumstanced as it is, policy, as well as nobleness of mind, obliged him to this frankness and acknowledgment; for having said *worse* of himself, and as *mean* of my parents fortunes, as any one could think, what remained for the hearers but to *applaud*, when he had left them no room to *reproach*, not so much as in thought?

Every day we rode out, or walked a little about the grounds, and while we were there, he employed hands to cut a vista through a coppice as they call it, or rather a little wood, to a rising ground, which fronting an old-fashioned balcony in the middle of the house, he ordered it to be planted like a grove, and a pretty alcove to be erected on it's summit, of which

which he has sent them a draught, drawn by his own hand. And this, and a few other alterations, mentioned in my letter to my father, are to be finished against we go down next.

The dear gentleman was every hour pressing me, while there, to take one diversion or other, frequently upbraiding me, that I seemed not to *choose* any thing, urging me to propose sometimes what I could *wish* he should oblige me in, and not always to leave it to him to choose for me; saying, he was half-afraid, that my constant compliance with every thing he proposed, laid me sometimes under a restraint; and he would have me have a will of my own, since it was impossible, that it could be such as he should not take a delight in conforming to it.

But, when (as I told him) his goodness to me made him rather study what would oblige me than himself, even to the prevention of all my wishes, how was it possible for me not to receive with pleasure and gratitude every intimation from him, in such a manner as that, though it might seem to be the effect of an implicit obedience to his will, yet was it (nor could it be otherwise) intirely agreeable to my own?

I will not trouble your ladyship with any further particulars relating to this happy fortnight, which was made up all of white and unclouded days, to the very last; and your ladyship will judge better than I can describe, what a parting there was between my dear parents, and their honoured benefactor and me.

We set out, attended with the good wishes of crowds of persons of all degrees, for your dear brother left behind him noble instances of his bounty, it being the *first* time, as he bid Mr. Longman say, that he had been down among them since that estate had been in his hands.

But permit me, Madam, to observe, that I could not forbear often, very often, in this happy period, to thank God in private, for the blessed terms upon which I was there, to what I should have been, had I gracelessly accepted of those which formerly were tendered to me; for your ladyship will remember, that the Kentish estate was to be part of the purchase of my infamy.*

We returned through London again, by the like easy journies, but tarried not to see any thing of that vast metropolis, any more than we did in going through it before, your beloved brother only stopping at his banker's, and desiring him to look out for a handsome house, which he purposes to take for his winter residence. He chooses it to be about the new buildings called Hanover Square; and he left Mr. Longman there to see one, which his banker believed would be fit for him.

And thus, my dear good lady, I have answered your first commands, by the help of the letters which passed between my dear parents and me, and conclude this, with the assurance that I am, with high respect, *your ladyship's most obliged, and faithful servant,*

P. B.

LETTER XIV.

MY DEAREST LADY,

I Now set myself to obey your ladyship's second command, which is, to give an account in what manner your dear brother broke to me the affair of the unfortunate Miss Godfrey, with my behaviour upon it: and this I cannot do better, than by transcribing the relation I gave at the time, in letters to my dear parents, which your ladyship has not seen, in these very words.

[See Vol. II. p. 277, beginning 'My dear Mr. B.' down to p. 283.]

Thus far, my dear lady, the relation I gave to my parents, at the time of my being first acquainted with this melancholy affair.

It is a great pleasure to me, that I can already flatter myself, from the hints you kindly give me, that I behaved as you wished I should behave. Indeed, Madam, I could not help it, for I pitied most sincerely the unhappy lady; and though I could not but rejoice, that I had had the grace to escape the dangerous attempts of the dear intriguer, yet never did the story of any unfortunate lady make such an impression upon me as her's did: She loved *him*, and believed, no doubt, he loved *her* too well to take ungenerous advantages of her soft passion for him, and so, by degrees, put herself into his power; and too seldom, alas! have the noblest-minded of the seducing sex the mercy or the goodness to spare the poor creatures that do!—And then this love, to be sure, is a sad thing, when once it is suffered to

* See Vol. I. p. 116.

reign,—a perfect tyrant!—requiring an unconditional obedience to its arbitrary dictates, and deeming every instance of discretion and prudence, and virtue itself, too often, but as so many acts of rebellion to its usurped authority.

And then, how do even blemishes become perfections in those we love? Crimes themselves too often, to inconsiderate minds, appear but as human failings; and human failings are a *common cause*, and every frail person excuses them for his or her own sake.

Then 'tis another misfortune of people in love, they always think highly of the beloved object, and lowly of themselves; such a dismal mortifier is love!

I say not this, Madam, to excuse the poor lady's fall: nothing can do that; because virtue is, and ought to be, preferable to all considerations, and to life itself. But, methinks, I love this dear lady so well for the sake of her edifying penitence, that I would fain extenuate her crime, if I could; and the rather, as, in all probability, it was a *first love* on *both* sides, and so he could not appear to her as a *practised* deceiver.

Your ladyship will see by what I have transcribed, how I behaved myself to the dear Miss Goodwin; and I am so fond of the little charmer, as well for the sake of her unhappy mother, though personally unknown to me, as for the relation she bears to the dear gentleman whom I am bound to love and honour, that I must beg your ladyship's interest to procure her to be given up to my care, when it shall be thought proper. I am sure I shall act by her as tenderly as if I was her own mother. And glad I am, that the poor unfaulty baby is so justly beloved by Mr. B.

But I will here conclude this letter, with assuring your ladyship, that I am *your obliged and humble servant*,

P. B.

LETTER XV.

MY GOOD LADY,

I Now come to your ladyship's remarks on my conduct to Mrs. Jewkes, which you are pleased to think too kind and forgiving, considering the poor woman's baseness.

Your ladyship says, that I ought not to have borne her in my sight, after the impudent assistance she gave to his lewd attempts, much less to have left her in her place, and rewarded her. Alas! my dear lady, what could I do? a poor prisoner, as I was made, for weeks together, in breach of all the laws of civil society, without a soul who durst be my friend, and every day expecting to be ruined and undone, by one of the haughtiest and most determined spirits in the world!— And when it pleased God to turn his heart, and incline him to abandon his wicked attempts, and to profess honourable love to me, his poor servant, can it be thought I was to insist upon conditions with such a gentleman, who had me in his power, and who, if I had provoked him, might have resumed all his wicked purposes against me?

Indeed, I was too much overjoyed, after all my dangers past, (which were so great, that I could not go to rest, nor rise, but with such apprehensions, that I wished for death rather than life) to think of refusing any term that I could yield to, and keep my honour.

And though such noble ladies, as your ladyship and Lady Betty, who are born to independency, and are hereditarily, as I may say, on a foot with the highest-descended gentleman in the land, might have exerted a spirit, and would have had a right to have chosen your own servants, and to have distributed rewards and punishments to the deserving and undeserving, at your own good pleasure; yet what had I, a poor girl, who owed even my title to common notice to the bounty of my late good lady, and had only a kind of imputed significancy of person, though enough to make me the subject of vile attempts; who, from a situation of terror and apprehension, was lifted up to an hope, beyond my highest ambition, and was bid to pardon the bad woman, as an [illegible]ce, that I could forgive his own hard usage of me, who had experienced so often the violence and impetuosity of his temper, which even his beloved mother never ventured to oppose till it began to subside, and then, indeed, he was all goodness and acknowledgment, of which I could give your ladyship more than one instance.

What, I say, had I to do, to take upon me lady airs, and to resent?

But, my dear ladies, (let me, in this instance, bespeak the attention of you both) I should be inexcusable, if I did not tell you all the truth, and that is, that I not only forgave the poor wretch, in regard to *his commands*, but from *my own inclination* also

If I am wrong in saying this, I must submit it to your ladyships, and, as I pretend not to perfection, am ready to take the blame I shall be found to deserve in your ladyships judgments but indeed, were it to do again, I verily think, I could not help forgiving her And were I not able to say this, I should be thought to have made a mean court to my master's passions, and to have done a wrong thing with my eyes open which, I humbly conceive, no one should do

When full power was given me over this poor creature, (seemingly at least, though it might possibly have been resumed, and I might have been re-committed to her s, had I given him reason to think I made an arrogant use of it) you cannot imagine what a triumph I had in my mind over the mortified guilt, which (from the highest degree of insolence and imperiousness, that before had hardened her masculine features) appeared in her countenance, when she found the tables likely to be soon turned upon her

This change of behaviour, which at first discovered itself in a sullen awe, and afterwards in a kind of silent respect, shewed me, what an influence power had over her, and that when she could treat her late prisoner, when taken into favour, so obsequiously, it was the less wonder the bad woman could think it her duty to obey commands so unjust, when her obedience to them was required from her master

To be sure, if a look could have killed her, after some of her bad treatment, she had been slain over and over, as I may say but to me, who was always taught to distinguish between the person and the action, I could not hold my resentment against the poor passive machine of mischief one day together, though her actions were so odious to me.

I should indeed except that time of my grand trial, when she appeared so much a wretch to me, that I saw her not (even after * two days that she was kept from me) without great flutter and emotion of heart, and I had represented to your brother before, how hard a condition it was for me to forgive so much unwomanly wickedness †

But, my dear ladies, when I considered the matter in one particular light, I could the more easily forgive her, and *having* forgiven her, *bear her in my sight*, and act by her (as a consequence of that forgiveness) as if she had not so horridly offended —Else how would it have been forgiveness - especially as she was ashamed of her crime, and there was no fear of her repeating it

Thus then I thought on the occasion —' Poor wretched agent, for purposes ' little less than infernal ! I *will* forgive ' thee, since *thy* master and *my* master ' will have it so And indeed thou art ' beneath the resentment even of such a ' poor girl as I I will *pity* thee, base ' and abject as thou art And she who ' is the object of my *pity*, is surely beneath my *anger* My eye, that used ' to quiver and tremble at thy haughty ' eye, shall now, with conscious worthiness, take a superior steadiness, and ' look down thy scowling guilty one into ' self-condemnation, the state thou couldst ' never cast mine into, nor from it wilt ' be able to raise thine own ! Bear the ' reproach of thine own wicked heart, ' low, vile, woman, unworthy as thou ' art of the *name*, and chosen, as it should ' seem, for a foil to the innocent, and to ' make purity shine forth the brighter, ' the *only* good use such wretches as thou ' can be of to others (except for examples ' of penitence and mercy) This will ' be punishment enough for thee, without my exposing myself to the imputation of descending so near to a level ' with thee, as to resent thy baseness, ' when thou hast no power to hurt me '

Such were then my thoughts, my proud thoughts, so far was I from being guilty of *intentional* meanness in forgiving, at Mr B s interposition, the poor, low, creeping, abject, *self*-mortified and *master*-mortified Mrs Jewkes !

And do you think, ladies, when you revolve in your thoughts, *who* I was, and *what* I was, and what I had been *designed* for; when you revolve the amazing turn in my favour, and the prospects before me (prospects so much above my hopes, that I left them intirely to Providence to direct for me, as it pleased, without daring to look forward to what those prospects seemed naturally to tend,) when I could see my haughty persecutor become my repentant protector, the lofty spirit that used to make me tremble, and to which I never could look up without

* See Vol. I, p. 126 † Ibid p. 227.

awe,

lwe, except in those animating cases, where his guilty attempts, and the concern I had to preserve my innocence, gave a courage more than natural to my otherwise dastardly heart when this impetuous spirit could stoop to request one whom he had sunk beneath even her usual low character of his servant, who was his prisoner, under sentence of a ruin worse than death, as he had intended it, and had seized her for that very purpose, could stoop to acknowledge the vileness of that purpose, could say, at one time, that my forgiveness of Mrs Jewkes should stand me in greater stead than I was aware of Could tell her, before me, that she must for the future shew me all the respect that was due to one he must love* at another, acknowledged before her, that he had been stark naught, and that I was very forgiving† Again‡, to Mrs Jewkes, putting himself on a level with her, as to guilt—' We are both in generous hands and indeed, if Pamela did ' not pardon *you*, I should think she but ' half forgave *me*, because you acted by ' my instructions ' another time to the same §—' We have been both sinners, ' and must be both included in one act ' of grace '

When, I say, I was thus lifted up to the state of a sovereign forgiver, and my lordly master became a petitioner for himself, and for the guilty creature, whom he put under my feet, what a triumph was here for the poor Pamela! And could I have been guilty of so mean a pride, as to trample upon the poor abject creature, when I found her thus lowly, thus mortified, and wholly in my power? For so she seemed actually to be, while I really thought so and would it have been good manners with regard to my master, or policy with respect to myself, to doubt it, after he had so declared?

Then, my dear ladies, while I was enjoying the soul charming fruits of that innocence which the Divine Grace had enabled me to preserve, in spite of so many plots and contrivances on my master's side, and such wicked instigations and assistances on hers, and all my prospects were improving upon me beyond my wishes, when all was sunshine, unclouded sunshine, and I possessed my mind in peace, and had nothing to do but to be thankful to Providence, which had been so gracious to my unworthiness, when I saw, as I said above, my persecutor become my protector, my active enemy, no longer my enemy, but creeping with slow, doubtful feet, and speaking to me with awful hesitating doubt of my acceptance, a stamp of an insolent foot, now turned into curtseying half-bent knees, threatening hands into supplicating folds, and the eye unpitying to innocence, running over with the sense of her own guilt, a faultering accent on her late menacing tongue, and uplifted handkerchief—' I see she will be ' my lady and then I know how it will go ' with me‖, —Was not this, my ladies, a triumph of triumphs to the late miserable, now exalted Pamela?—Could I do less than pardon her? And having declared that I did so, was I not to shew the sincerity of my declaration?

Indeed, indeed, my dear good ladies, I found such a subject for exultation in this providential change of my condition, that I had much ado to subdue my rising pride, and thought there was more danger of being lifted up, (every moment, to see such improving contrition on the poor creature's part) than to be supposed guilty of a meanness of heart, in *stooping* (yes, Madam, that was then the proudly proper word, in the elevation wherein I found myself) to forgive her!—And, what!—should I not forgive a creature for that very baseness which, happily withstood, had so largely contributed to exalt me? Indeed, my dear good ladies, permit me to repeat, I could not choose but to forgive her!—How could I?—And would it not have been out of character in me, and against all expectation of my high-souled (though sometimes, as in my case, for a great while together, meanly-acting) master, if I had not?

Would it not have shewn him, that the low born Pamela was incapable of a generous action, had she refused the *only* request her humble condition had given her the opportunity of granting, at that time, with innocence? Would he not have thought the humble cottager as capable of insolence, and vengeance too, in her

* See Vol I page 127
† Vol II page 164.
‡ Vol II page 165
§ Vol II page 200.
‖ Vol. I page 130.

turn, as the better born? and that ſhe wanted but the power, to ſhew the like unrelenting temper, by which ſhe had ſo grievouſly ſuffered?—And might not this have given him room to think me (and to have juſtified and proſecuted his purpoſes accordingly) nearer to an arrogant kept miſtreſs, than an humble and obliged wife?

'I ſee, (might he not have ſaid) the 'girl has ſtrong paſſions and reſent'ments, and ſince ſhe has, will be *acted*, 'and ſometimes *governed* by them.—'I will improve upon this hint ſhe herſelf 'has now given me, by her inexorable 'temper—I will gratify her revenge, till 'I turn it upon herſelf. I will indulge 'her pride, till I make it turn bitter to her 'ſoul; for a wife I cannot think of in 'the low-born cottager, eſpecially when 'ſhe has lurking in her all the pride and 'arrogance, (you know, my lady, his haughty way of ſpeaking of our ſex) 'of 'the better deſcended.—And by a little 'perſeverance, and watching her un'guarded hours, and applying tempta'tions to her paſſions, I ſhall firſt diſco'ver them, and then make my advantage 'of them.'

Might not this have been the language, and this the reſolution, of ſuch a dear wicked intriguer?—For, my lady, you can hardly conceive the ſtruggles he apparently had to bring down his high heart to ſo humble a level. And though, I hope, all would have been, even in this *worſt* caſe, ineffectual, through Divine grace, yet how do I know what lurking vileneſs might have appeared by degrees in this frail heart, to have encouraged his deſigns, and to have augmented my trials and my dangers? And perhaps downright violence might have been uſed, if he could not, on one hand, have ſubdued his paſſions, nor, on the other, have overcome his pride. A pride, that every one, reflecting upon the diſparity of birth and condition between us, would have dignified with the name of *decency*, a pride that was become ſuch an eſſential part of the dear gentleman's character, in this inſtance of a wife, that although he knew he could not keep it up, if he made *me* happy, yet it was no ſmall motive in his chooſing me, in one reſpect, becauſe he expected from me more humility, more ſubmiſſion, than he thought he had reaſon to flatter himſelf would be paid him by a lady equally born and educated; and of this I will ſend your ladyſhip an inſtance, in a tranſcription from that part of* my journal you have not ſeen, of his leſſons to me, on the occaſion your ladyſhip ſo well remembers, of my incurring his diſpleaſure by interpoſing between yourſelf and him,† in your miſunderſtanding at the Hall; for, Madam, I intend to ſend, at times, any thing I think worthy of your ladyſhip's attention, out of thoſe papers you were ſo kind as to excuſe me from ſending you in the lump, and many of which muſt needs have appeared very impertinent to ſuch judges.

Thus, could your ladyſhip have thought it?—have I ventured upon a ſtrange paradox, that even this ſtrongeſt inſtance of his debaſing himſelf, is not the weakeſt of his pride; and he ventured once at Sir Simon Darnford's to ſay, in your ladyſhip's hearing, as you may remember, that, in his conſcience, he thought he ſhould hardly have made a tolerable huſband to any body but Pamela‡. And why? For the reaſons you will ſee in the incloſed papers, which give an account of the nobleſt and earlieſt curtain lecture that ever girl had: one of which is, that he expects to be *borne* with, (*complied* with, he means,) even when in the wrong: another, that a wife ſhould never ſo much as expoſtulate with him, though he *was* in the wrong, till by complying with all he inſiſted upon, ſhe ſhould have ſhewn him, ſhe deſigned rather to convince him for his *own* ſake, than for *contradiction's* ſake: and then another time, perhaps he might take better reſolutions§.

I hope, from what I have ſaid, it will appear to your ladyſhip, and to Lady Betty too, that I am juſtified, or at leaſt excuſed, in pardoning Mrs. Jewkes: and I have yet another reaſon behind, for doing ſo, had ſhe been as abſolutely in my power, as the wiſh of the moſt reſenting perſon in the world could have made her; and that is, the hope I had, that the poor creature, by being continued in a family, where the gentleman gave hopes of ſo deſirable a reformation, and where the example of the perſon he

* See Vol. II. page 258, & *ſeq.*
† Ibid. page 260.
‡ See Vol. II. page 257.
§ Ibid. page 260.

was

was about to honour in so eminent a degree, beyond all that could have been hoped for by her a few days before, might possibly contribute to make her change her manner of thinking, as well as acting

I looked upon the poor wretch, in all her deportment to me, in my days of trial, as one devoted to perdition, as one who had no regard to a future state, but while she could live in ease and plenty for a poor remainder of years, cared not what she did, and was ready to undertake any thing which persons of power and riches would put her upon, and who, were she to be turned off disgracefully, at my desire besides that I should thereby shew myself to be of an implacable spirit, might have been entertained by some profligate persons, to whose baseness such a woman might be useful, and that then her power to do mischief would have been augmented, and she would have gone on more successfully to do the devil's work, and several innocent creatures might have been entangled, like so many thoughtless flies, in the insnaring web of this venomous hearted spider, which I had so happily escaped 'Is it not better then, thought I, 'if I can imprint *conviction* 'upon the poor wretch, whom its hopeful forerunner *shame* had already taken hold of, 'and add the delightful 'hope of mischiefs prevented, to that of 'a soul reclaimed? And may not I, who have been so hardly used by her, for *that* very reason, have more influence upon her than any other person, even the best of divines, could have?

Nay, would not this behaviour of mine, very probably, operate on a much higher and nobler subject, her dear naughty master, and let *him* see the force and amiableness of conquering one's self? that there must be something in that duty which could make so young a creature regard it, in an instance so difficult to some minds, (and especially to the passionate and high born) that of forgiving injuries, where there is a power to revenge, and of returning good for evil?

And then, when no sullen behaviour to the poor wretch, on my side, took place, no distant airs were affected, no angry brow put on, nor sharpness of speech used, towards one who might expect all these from me, would it not shew him, that I was sincere in my forgiveness? that I was not able to bear malice? was a stranger to revenge? had truly that softness of nature, and placableness of disposition, which he holds to be the greatest merit in our sex, and which, I dare say, your ladyship will join with me in opinion, is indispensably necessary to the happy life of the person who is his wife?

Then I have no notion of that slight distinction I have so often heard between *forgive* and *forget*, when persons have a mind to split hairs, and to distinguish away their Christian duties by a word, and say—'*I must forgive such an action,* '*but I will never forget it* when I would rather say—'*I will remember such* '*an action, in order for my future guard*; 'but *I will forgive it as often as I re-* '*member it* or else *I will try to forget* '*it for ever, if it will occasion a breach* '*in my Christian charity*'

I will only add, that I thought it would not be wrong to keep her, as, besides what I have mentioned, it would induce the world to think, that Mr B had not gone such very wicked lengths, as might have been imagined, if she had not been supportable to me in the same house. And who knows, moreover, what she might have reported of both, had she been dismissed?

How, then, dearest ladies, if these considerations have any weight, could I act any otherwise than I did, either with respect to your honoured brother, myself, or the poor woman? And when I tell your ladyships, that I have all the reason in the world to be pleased with this manner of acting, when I consider the confidence it hath given me with Mr B and (what I was very desirous of) the good effects it hath had upon the woman herself, I dare say, both your ladyships opinions will be in my favour on this head

But your dear brother has just sent me word, that supper waits for me, and the post being ready to go off, I defer till the next opportunity what I have to say as to these good effects, and am, in the mean time, *your ladyship's most obliged and faithful servant,*

P B.

LETTER XVI

MY DEAR LADY,

I Will now acquaint you with the good effects my behaviour to Mrs Jewkes has had upon her, as a farther justification of my conduct towards the poor woman

That

That she began to be affected as I wished, appeared to me before I left the Hall, not only in the conversations I had with her after my happiness was completed, but in her general demeanour also to the servants, to the neighbours, and in her devout behaviour at church; and this still further appears by a letter I have received from Miss Darnford. I dare say your ladyship will be pleased with the perusal of the whole letter, although a part of it would answer my present design; and in confidence, that you will excuse, for the sake of its other beauties, the high and undeserved praises which she so lavishly bestows upon me, I will transcribe it all.

FROM MISS DARNFORD TO MRS B.

'MY DEAR NEIGHBOUR THAT WAS,

'I Must depend upon your known goodness to excuse me for not writing before now, in answer to your letter of compliment to us, for the civilities and favours, as you call them, which you received from us in Lincolnshire, where we were infinitely more obliged to you, than you to us.

'The truth is, my papa has been much disordered with a kind of rambling rheumatism, to which the physicians, learnedly speaking, give the name of *arthritica vaga*, or the flying gout; and when he has ever so little, (it signifies nothing concealing his infirmities, where they are so well known, and when he cares not who knows them) he is so peevish, and wants so much attendance, that my mamma, and her two girls (one of whom is as waspish as her papa, you may be sure I don't mean myself) have much ado to make his worship keep the peace; and I being his favourite, when he is indisposed, because I have most patience, if I may give myself a good word, he calls upon me continually, to read to him when he is grave, which is not often indeed, and to tell him stories and sing to him, when he is merry; and so I have been employed as a principal person about him, till I have frequently become sad to make him chearful, and happy when I could do it at any rate. For once in a pet, he flung a book at my head, because I had not attended him for two hours, and he could not bear to be slighted by little bastards, that was his word, that were fathered upon him for his vexation. O these men! Fathers or husbands, much alike! the one tyrannical, the other insolent; so that, between one and t'other, a poor girl has nothing for it, but a few weeks courtship, and perhaps a first month's bravery, if that; and then she is as much a slave to a husband, as she was a vassal to her father—I mean, if the father be a Sir Simon Darnford, and the spouse a Mr B.

'But I will be a little more grave, for a graver occasion calls for it, and yet an occasion that will give you real pleasure. It is the very great change that the example you have left behind you has had upon your housekeeper.

'You desired her to keep up as much regularity as she could among the servants there; and she is next to exemplary in it, so that she has every one's good word. She speaks of her lady not only with respect, but reverence, and calls it a blessed day for all the family, and particularly for herself, that you came into Lincolnshire. She reads prayers, or makes one of the servants read them, every Sunday night, and never misses being at church, morning and afternoon; and is preparing herself, by Mr Peters's advice and direction, for receiving the sacrament, which she earnestly longs to receive, and says it will be the seal of her reformation.

'Mr Peters gives us this account of her, and says she is full of contrition for her past mis-spent life, and is often asking him, if such and such sins can be forgiven? and among them, names her vile behaviour to her angel lady, as she calls you.

'It seems she has written a letter to you, which passed Mr Peters's revisal, before she had the courage to send it; and prides herself that you have favoured her with an answer to it, which, she says, when she is dead, will be found in a cover of black silk next her heart; for any thing from your hand, she is sure, will contribute to make her keep her good purposes; and for that reason she places it there; and when she has any bad thoughts, or is guilty of an faulty word, or passionate expression, she recollects her lady's letter, and that recovers her to a calm, and puts her again into a better frame.

'As she has written to you, 'tis possible I might have spared you the trou-

'ble

'ble of reading this account of her, but 've you will not be displeased, that so 'free a liver and speaker should have 'some testimonial besides her own assur'ances, to vouch for the sincerity of her 'reformation.

'What a happy lady are you, that 'persuasion dwells upon your tongue, 'and reformation follows your example! 'We all hear continually of your excel'lences. Every body is proud of speak'ing of you, and of having something to 'say of what they observe in you. This 'makes us long more and more to see 'you here again. My papa t'other day 'said, he wished you'd undertake him.

'This is not the least of what is ad'mirable in you, that professed rakes and 'libertines, who take upon themselves 'to ridicule seriousness in every body 'else, speak of you with reverence, and 'while they attribute pharisaical pride, 'or affectation, or hypocrisy, to other 'good persons, they say, you are a credit 'to religion, and that adorns you, and 'you that.

'Happy, thrice happy Mrs. B.! May 'you long live the ornament of your 'sex, and a credit to all your acquaint'ance! Such examples as you set, how 'are they wanted in an age so depraved? 'I fear not making you proud, since 'praise but puts the worthy upon enlarg'ing their deservings: for who, as I 'heard you once say, can sit down easy 'under imputed commendations they do 'not deserve? If they will not disclaim 'the praise they have not merited, when 'applied to their conduct, they give an 'earnest, by receiving it, that they will '*endeavour* to do it, and ought never to 'rest till they have made themselves a 'title to it.

'Happy Mr. B.!—But why say I so? 'since with more propriety, I may say, 'happy every one who sees, who knows, 'who converses with Mrs. B. not more 'the glory of the humble cot, than the 'ornament of the stately palace!

'If you knew how I love you, you 'would favour me with your presence 'and conversation, if it was in your own 'power to do so, and then I would 'rank myself among the *happiest*, and 'call myself, *The happy*

'POLLY DARNFORD.'

Your ladyship will, as I said, forgive me what may appear like vanity in this communication. Miss Darnford is a charming young lady. I always admired her, but her letters are the sweetest, kindest!—But I am too much the subject of her encomiums, and so will say no more, but add here a copy of the poor woman's letter to me, and your ladyship will see what an ample correspondence you have opened to yourself, if you go on to countenance it.

'HONOURED MADAM,

'I Have been long labouring under 'two difficulties, the desire I had 'to write to you, and the fear of being 'thought presumptuous, if I did. But 'I will depend on your goodness, so often 'tried, and put pen to paper, in that 'very closet, and on that very desk, which 'once were so much used by your dear 'self, when I was acting a part, that now 'cuts me to the heart, to think of. But 'you forgive me, Madam, and shewed 'me you had too much goodness to re'voke your forgiveness. And could I 'have silenced the reproaches of my own 'heart, I should have had no cause to 'think I had ever offended.

'But, Oh! Madam, how has your 'goodness to me, which once filled me 'with so much gladness, now, on reflec'tion, made me sorrowful, and at times 'miserable—To think I should act so 'barbarously as I did, by so much swee'ness, and so much forgiveness! Every 'place that I remember to have used you 'hardly in, how does it now fill me with 'sadness, and makes me often smite my 'breast, and sit down with tears and 'groans, bemoaning my vile actions, and 'my hard heart! How many places are 'there in this melancholy fine house, that 'call one thing or other to my remem'brance, that give me remorse! But 'the pond and the woodhouse, whence 'I dragged you so mercilessly, after I 'had driven you to despair almost, what 'thoughts do they bring to my remem'brance!—Then my wicked instigations '—What an odious wretch was I!

'Had his honour been as abandoned 'as myself, what virtue had been destroy'ed between *his* orders and *my* too rigo'rous execution of them, nay, stretch'ing them, to shew my wicked zeal, to 'serve a master, whom, though I ho'noured, I should not (as you more 'than once hinted to me, but with no 'effect at all, so resolutely wicked was 'my heart) have so well obeyed in his 'unlawful commands!

'His

'His honour has made you amends, has done justice to your merits, and so atoned for all his fault. But as for *me*, it is out of my power ever to make reparation. All that is left me, is, to let your ladyship see, that your pious example has made such an impression upon me, that I am miserable now in the reflection upon my past guilt.

'You have forgiven me, and GOD will, I hope; for the creature cannot be more merciful than the Creator, that is all my hope.—Yet sometimes, I dread that I am forgiven here, at least not punished, in order to be punished the more hereafter!—What then will become of the unhappy wretch, that has thus lived in a state of sin, and had so qualified herself by a course of wickedness, as to be thought a proper instrument for the worst purposes that any one could be employed in?

'Good your ladyship, let not my honoured master see this letter. He will think I have the boldness to reflect upon him, when, God knows my heart, I only write to condemn myself, and my *unwomanly* actions, as you were pleased often most justly to call them.

'But I might go on thus for ever accusing myself, not considering whom I am writing to, and whose precious time I am taking up. But what I chiefly write for, I am not come to yet, that is, to beg your ladyship's prayers for me. For oh, Madam, I fear I shall else be for ever miserable! We every week hear of the good you do, and the charity you extend to the bodies of the miserable. Extend, I beseech you, good Madam, to the unhappy Jewkes, the mercy of your prayers, and tell me if you think I have not sinned beyond hope of pardon; for there is a woe denounced against the presumptuous sinner.

'Your ladyship so assured me, at your departure, on the confession of my remorse for my misdoings, and my promise of amendment, that you would take it for a proof of my being in earnest, if I would endeavour to keep up a regularity among the servants here, if I would subdue them with kindness, as I had owned myself subdued, and if I would endeavour to make every one think, that the best security they could give of their doing their duty to their master in his *absence*, was by doing it to God Almighty, from whose all-seeing eye nothing can be hid. This, I remember, your ladyship told me, was the best test of fidelity and duty, that any servants could shew, since it was impossible without religion but that worldly conveniency, or self-interest, must be the main tie, and so the worst actions might succeed, if servants thought they should find their sordid advantage in sacrificing their duty.

'So well am I convinced of this truth, that I hope I have begun the example to good effect, and as no one in the family was so wicked as I, it was therefore less difficult to reform them, and you will have the pleasure to know, that you have now servants here, whom you need not be ashamed to call yours.

''Tis true, I found it a little difficult at first to keep them within sight of their duty, after your ladyship departed; but when they saw I was in earnest, and used them courteously, as you advised, and as your usage of me convinced me was the rightest usage, when they were told I had your commands to acquaint you how they conformed to your injunctions, the task became easy, and I hope we shall all be still more and more worthy of the favour of so good a lady, and so bountiful a master.

'I dare not presume upon the honour of a line to your unworthy servant. Yet it would pride me much, if I could have it. But I shall ever pray for your ladyship's and his honour's felicity, as becomes *your undeserving servant*,

'K. JEWKES.'

I have already, with these transcribed letters of Miss Darnford and Mrs Jewkes, written a great deal; but nevertheless, as there yet remains one passage in your ladyship's letter, relating to Mrs Jewkes, that seems to require an answer, I will take notice of it, if I shall not quite tire your patience.

That passage is this, Lady Betty rightly observes, says your ladyship, that he knew what a vile woman she [Mrs Jewkes] was, when he put you into her power, and, no doubt, employed her, because he was sure she would answer all his purposes; and that therefore she should have had very little opinion of the sincerity of his reformation, while he was so solicitous in keeping her there.

She

She would, ſhe ſays, had ſhe been in your caſe, have had one ſtruggle for her diſmiſſion, let it have been taken as it would; and he that was ſo well pleaſed with your virtue, muſt have thought this a natural conſequence of it, if he was in earneſt to become virtuous himſelf.

But alas! Madam, he was not ſo well pleaſed with my virtue for its own ſake, as Lady Betty thinks he was. He would have been glad at that very time, to have found me leſs reſolved on that ſcore. He did not ſo much as *pretend* to any diſpoſition to virtue. No, not he!

He had entertained, as it proved, a ſtrong paſſion for me. This paſſion had been heightened by *my reſiſting of it*. His pride, and the advantages he had both of perſon and fortune, would not let him brook controul; and when he could not have me upon his own terms, God turned his evil purpoſes to good ones; and he reſolved to ſubmit to mine, or rather to ſuch as he found I would not yield to him without. For all this time I had no terms to propoſe. Neither my low fortunes, my unjuſt captivity, nor my ſex, nor unexperienced youth, (not a ſoul near me whom I could call my friend, or whoſe advice I could aſk) permitted me to offer any terms to him, had I been diſpoſed to have diſputed his will, or his interceſſion for the woman; which, as I have ſaid, I was not. I had but one ſteady purpoſe to adhere to, and having grace given me to adhere to that, he reſolved, ſince he could not conquer his paſſion for me, to make me his with honour. But ſtill I doubt, as I ſaid, this was not for the love of virtue at that time. That came afterwards, and I hope will always be his governing motive, in his future actions; and then I ſhall be happy indeed!

But Lady Betty thinks, I was to blame to put Mrs. Jewkes upon a foot, in the preſent I made on my nuptials, with Mrs. Jervis. But the caſe was rather this, that I put Mrs. Jervis on a foot with Mrs. Jewkes; for the dear gentleman had *named* the ſum he would have me give Mrs. Jewkes*, and I would not give Mrs. Jervis *leſs*, becauſe I loved her better; nor *more* could I give her, on that occaſion, without making ſuch a difference between two perſons equal in ſtation, on a ſolemnity too where one was preſent and aſſiſting, the other not, as would have ſhewn ſuch a partiality, as might have induced their maſter to conclude, I was not ſo ſincere in my forgiveneſs, as he hoped from me, and as I really was.

But a ſtronger reaſon ſtill was behind, that I could, in a much more agreeable manner, both to Mrs. Jervis and myſelf, ſhew my love and my gratitude to the dear good woman: and this I have taken care to do, in the manner I will ſubmit to your ladyſhip, at the tribunal of whoſe judgment I am willing all my actions, reſpecting your dear brother, ſhall be tried. And I hope your ladyſhip will not think me a too profuſe or laviſh creature. I hope you won't have reaſon for it. Yet, if you think you have, pray, my dear lady, don't ſpare me; for if you ſhall judge me profuſe in one article, I will endeavour to ſave it in another.

But I will make what I have to ſay on this head the ſubject of a letter by itſelf; and am, mean time, *your ladyſhip's moſt obliged and obedient ſervant,*

P. B.

LETTER XVII.

MY DEAR LADY,

IT is needful, in order to let you more intelligibly into the ſubject where I left off in my laſt, that your ladyſhip ſhould know, that your generous brother has made me his almoner, as I was my late dear lady's, and has ordered Mr. Longman to pay me fifty pounds † quarterly, for purpoſes of which he requires no account, though I have one always ‡ ready to produce; and he has given me other ſums to enable me to do all the good I can to diſtreſſed objects, at my firſt ſetting out. Thus enabled, your ladyſhip knows not how many honeſt hearts I have made glad already, and how many more I hope to rejoice before a year is at an end, and yet keep within my limits.

Now, Madam, as I knew Mrs. Jervis was far from being eaſy in her circumſtances, thinking herſelf obliged to pay old || debts for two extravagant children, who are both dead, and maintaining in ſchooling and clothes three of their children, which always keeps her bare, I took upon me one day, as ſhe and I ſat together, at our needles, to ſay to her, (as we are always running over old ſtories,

* See Vol. II. p. 209. † Ibid. p. 270. ‡ Ibid. p. 274. || Vol. I. p. 54.

when we are alone) 'My good Mrs. Jervis, will you allow me to ask you after your own private affairs, and if you are tolerably easy in them?'

'You are very good, Madam,' said she, 'to concern yourself about my poor matters, so much as you have to employ your thoughts about, and so much as every moment of your time is taken up, from the hour you rise, to the time of your rest. But I can with great pleasure attribute it to your bounty, and that of my honoured master, that I am easier and easier every day.'

'But tell me, my dear Mrs. Jervis,' said I, 'how your matters *particularly* stand. I love to mingle concerns with my friends, and as I hide nothing from *you*, I hope you'll treat *me* with equal freedom; for I always loved you, and always will, and nothing but death shall divide our friendship.'

She had tears of gratitude in her eyes, and taking off her spectacles—'I cannot bear,' said she, 'so much goodness!—Oh! my lady!'

'Oh! my Pamela, say,' replied I. 'How often must I chide you for calling me any thing but your Pamela, when we are alone together!'

'My heart,' said she, 'will burst with your goodness! I cannot bear it!'

'But you *must* bear it, and bear still greater exercises to your grateful heart, I can tell you that. A pretty thing, truly! Here I, a poor helpless girl, raised from poverty and distress, by the generosity of the best of men, only because I was young and sightly, shall put on lady airs to a gentlewoman born, the wisdom of whose years, and her faithful services and good management, make her a much greater merit in this family, than I can pretend to have! And return, shall I? in the day of my power, insult and haughtiness for the kindness and benevolence I received from her in that of my indigence!—Indeed, I won't forgive you, my dear Mrs. Jervis, if I think you capable of looking upon me in any other light than as your daughter, for you have been a mother to me when the absence of my own could not afford me the comfort and good counsel I received every day from you.'

Then moving my chair nearer her, and taking her hand, and wiping, with my handkerchief in my other, her reverend eyes.... 'Come, come, my dear second mother,' said I, 'call me your daughter, your Pamela. I have passed many sweet hours with you under that name; and as I have but too seldom such an opportunity as this, open to me your worthy heart, and let me know, if I cannot make my *second* mother as easy and happy as our dear master has made my *first*.'

She hung her head on her shoulder, and I waited till the discharge of her tears gave time for utterance to her words, provoking only her speech, by saying—'You used to have three grandchildren to provide for in clothes and schooling. They are all living, I hope?'

'Yes, Madam, they are living: and your last bounty (twenty guineas was a great sum, and all at once!) made me very easy and very happy!'

'How easy, and how happy, Mrs. Jervis?'

'Why, my dear lady, I paid five to one old creditor of my unhappy son's, five to a second, and two and a half to two others, in proportion to their respective demands; and with the other five I paid off all arrears of the poor childrens schooling and maintenance; and every one is satisfied and easy, and all declare they will never do harsh things by me, if they are paid no more.'

'But tell me, Mrs. Jervis, what you owe in the world, put all together, and you and I will contrive, with justice to our best friend, to do all we can, to make you quite easy; for, at your time of life, I cannot bear that you shall have any thing to disturb you, which I can remove, and for my dear Mrs. Jervis, let me know all.'

'Come, I know your debts, (dear, just, good woman as you are!) like David's sins, are ever before you: so come,' putting my hand in her pocket, 'let me be a friendly pickpocket: let me take out your memorandum book, and we will see how all matters stand, and what can be done. Come, I see you are too much moved; your worthy heart is too much affected,' (pulling out her book, which she always had about her) 'I will go to my closet, and return presently.'

So I left her to recover her spirits, and retired with the good woman's book to my closet.

Your dear brother stepping into the parlour just after I had gone out, 'Where's your lady, Mrs. Jervis?' said he. And being

being told, came up to me —'What ails 'the good woman below, my dear?' said he 'I hope you and she have had 'no words?'

'No, indeed, Sir,' answered I 'If 'we had, I am sure it would have been 'my fault but I have picked her pocket 'of her memorandum-book, in order to 'look into her private affairs, to see if I 'cannot, with justice to our common 'benefactor, make her as easy as you, 'Sir, have made my other dear parents

'A blessing, said he,' upon my charm-'er's benevolent heart! — I will leave 'every thing to your discretion, my 'dear —Do all the good you prudently 'can to your Mrs Jervis

I clasped my bold arms about him, the starting tear testifying my gratitude 'Dearest, dear Sir,' said I, 'you affect 'me as much as I did Mrs. Jervis and 'if any one but you had a right to ask, 'what ails your Pamela? as you do, 'what ails Mrs Jervis? I must say, I 'am hourly so much oppressed by your 'goodness, that there is hardly any bear-'ing one's own joy

He saluted me, and said, I was a dear obliging creature 'But, said he, 'I 'came to tell you, that after we have 'dined, we'll take a turn, if you please, 'to Lady Arthur's she has a family of 'London friends for her guests, and begs 'I will prevail upon you to give her 'your company, and attend you myself, 'only to drink tea with her, for I have 'told her, we are to have friends to sup 'with us'

'I will attend you, Sir,' replied I, 'most willingly, although I doubt I am 'to be made a shew of

'Something like it, said he, 'for she 'has promised them this favour

'I need not dress otherwise than I am?'

'No, he was pleased to say, I was always what he wished me to be

So he left me to my *good works*, (those were his kind words) and I ran over Mrs Jervis's accounts, and found a balance drawn of all her matters, in one leaf, in a very clear manner, and a thankful acknowledgment to God, for her master's last bounty, which had enabled her to give satisfaction to others, and do herself great pleasure, as she had written underneath

The balance of all was thirty five pounds eleven shillings and odd pence, and I went to my escritoir, and took out forty pounds, and down I hasted to my good Mrs Jervis, and I said to her— 'Here, my dear good friend, is your 'pocket book, but are thirty-five or 'thirty-six pounds all you owe, or are 'bound for in the world?'

'It is, Madam, said she, 'and enough 'too It is a great sum, but 'tis in 'four hands, and they are all in pretty 'good circumstances, and so convinced 'of my honesty, that they will never 'trouble me for it, for I have reduced 'the debt every year something, since I 'have been in my master's service'

'Nor shall it ever be in any body's '*power*, said I, 'to trouble you I'll 'tell you how we'll order it

So I sat down, and made her sit down by me 'Here, my dear Mrs Jervis, is 'forty pounds It is not so much to 'me now, as the * two guineas were to 'you, that you would have given me, if 'I would have accepted of them, at my 'going away from this house to my fa-'ther's, as I thought But I will not '*give* it you neither, at least at *present*, 'as you shall hear indeed I won't make 'you so uneasy as that comes to But 'here, take this, and pay the thirty five 'pounds odd money to the utmost far-'thing, and the remaining four pounds 'odd will be a little fund in advance to-'wards the children's schooling And 'thus you shall repay it I always de-'signed, as our dear master added five 'guineas per annum to your salary, in 'acknowledgment of the pleasure he 'took in your services when I was Pa-'mela Andrews, to add five pounds per 'annum to it from the time I became 'Mrs B But from that time, for so 'many years to come, you shall receive 'no more than you did, till the whole 'forty pounds be repaid And so, my 'dear Mrs Jervis, you won't have any 'obligation to me, you know, but for 'the advance, and that is a poor mat-'ter, not to be spoken of and I will 'have leave for it, for fear I should die'

Had your ladyship seen the dear good woman's behaviour, on this occasion, you would never have forgotten it She could not speak tears ran down her cheeks in plentiful currents her modest hand put gently from her my offering hand, and her bosom heav'd, and she sobb'd with the painful tumult that seemed to struggle within her, and which, for some few moments, made her incapable of speaking

* See Vol I p 57.

[illegible] I [illegible] and putting my arm [illegible] her [illegible], and kissing her [illegible]—'My [illegible], 'never [illegible] too much [illegible] I [illegible]—and [illegible] my feet, for I was [illegible] enough to understand [illegible] —'My God A- '[illegible] and she—I [illegible] her, and [illegible] to [illegible] together—'My God [illegible], [illegible] her [illegible] my [illegible] [illegible] together, for many 'happy years! And [illegible] 'what [illegible] gentleman, [illegible] his 'and [illegible] 'any [illegible]!'

'Dear good woman, said I, rising and raising her, 'do you think you shall 'ou [illegible] praises and praises to the 'Fountain [illegible] mercies—Do you 'think you shall?—And while I am im- 'powered to do good to so many worthy 'objects abroad, shall I forget to make 'my dear Mrs Jervis happy at home?'

And thus, my lady, did I force upon the good woman's acceptance the forty pounds.

Permit me, Madam, to close this letter here, and to resume the subject in my next, till when I have the honour to be *your ladyship's most obliged and faithful servant,*

P. B.

LETTER XVIII

MY DEAR LADY,

I Now resume my last subject where I left off, that your ladyship may have the whole before you at one view.

I went after dinner, with my dear benefactor, to Lady Arthur's, and met with fresh calls upon me for humility, having the two natural effects of the praises and professed admiration of that lady's guests, as well as my dear Mr B—'s, and those of Mr and Mrs Arthur, to guard myself against; and your good brother was pleased to entertain me in the chariot going and coming, with an account of the orders he had given in relation to the London house, which is actually taken, and the furniture he should direct for it: so that I had no opportunity to tell him what I had done in relation to Mrs Jervis.

But after supper, retiring from company to my closet, when his friends were gone, he came up to me about our usual bed-time. He enquired kindly after my employment, which was trying to read in the French Telemachus: for, my lady, I am learning French, I'll assure you! And who, do you think, is my master?—Why, the best I *could* have in the world, your dear brother, who is pleased to say, I am no dunce. How inexcusable should I be, if I was, with such a master, who teaches me on his knee, and rewards me with a kiss whenever I do well, and says, I have already nearly mastered the accent and pronunciation, which he tells me is a great difficulty got over.

I requested him to render into English two or three places that were beyond my reach; and when he had done it, he asked me, in French, what I had done for Mrs Jervis?

I said—'Permit me, Sir, (for I am 'not proficient enough to answer you in 'my new tongue) in English, to say, I 'have made the good woman quite hap- 'py; and if I have your approbation, I 'shall be as much so myself in this in- 'stance, as I am in all others.'

'I dare answer for your prudence, my 'dear,' he was pleased to say; 'but this 'is your favourite. Let me know, when 'you have so bountiful a heart to stran- 'gers, what you do for your favourites?'

I then said—'Permit my bold eye, Sir, 'to watch yours, as I obey you; and 'you know you must not look full upon 'me then, for if you do, how shall I 'look at you again; now see, as I pro- 'ceed, whether you are displeased? for 'you will not chide me in words, so 'partial have you the goodness to be to all 'I do.'

He put his arm round me, and looked down [illegible] and then, as I desired; for, O! Madam, he is all condescension and goodness to his unworthy, yet grateful Pamela! And I told him all I have written to your ladyship about the forty pounds.—'And now, dear Sir, said I, half hiding my face on his shoulder, 'you have heard what I have done, chide 'or beat your Pamela, if you please: it 'shall be all kind from you, and matter 'of future direction and caution.'

He raised my head, and kissed me two or three times, saying—'Thus then I 'chide, I beat, my angel!—And yet I 'have one fault to find with you, and let 'Mrs Jervis, if not in bed, come up to 'us, and hear what it is; for I will *expose* 'you, as you deserve, before her.' My

Polly

Polly being in hearing, attending to it now as I wanted her assistance to undress, I bade her call Mrs Jervis. And though I thought from his kind looks, and kind words, as well as tender behaviour, that I had not much to fear, yet I was impatient to know what my fault was, for which I was to be exposed.

The good woman came, and as she entered with all that modesty which is so graceful in her, he moved his chair further from me, and, with a set aspect, but not unpleasant, said—' Step, Mrs ' Jervis, your lady, (for so, Madam, he will always call me to Mrs Jervis, and to the servants) ' has incurred my ' censure, and I would not tell her in ' what, till I had you face to face.'

She looked surprized—now on me, now on her dear master, and I, not knowing what he would say, looked a little attentive.—' I am sorry—I am very sorry ' for it, Sir, said she, curtseying low— ' but should be more sorry, if *I* were the ' unhappy occasion.'

' Why, Mrs Jervis, I can't say but it ' is on your account that I must blame ' her.'

This gave us both confusion, but especially the good woman, for still I hoped much from his kind behaviour to me just before.—And she said—' Indeed, ' Sir, I could never deserve—'

He interrupted her. ' My charge ' against you, Pamela, said he, ' is that ' of niggardliness, and no other; for I ' will put you both out of your pain. You ' ought not to have found out the me- ' thod of repayment.

' The dear creature, said he, to Mrs Jervis, ' seldom does any thing that can ' be mended; but, I think, when your ' good conduct deserved an annual ac- ' knowledgment from me, in addition ' to your salary, the lady should have ' shewed herself no less pleased with your ' service than the gentleman.—Had it ' been for old acquaintance-sake, for ' sex sake, she should not have given me ' cause to upbraid her on this head.— ' But I will tell you, that you must look ' upon the forty pounds you have, as the ' effect of a just distinction on many ac- ' counts; and your salary from last ' quarter-day shall be advanced, as the ' dear niggard intended it some years ' hence, and let me only add, that when ' my Pamela first begins to shew a cold- ' ness to her Mrs Jervis, I shall then su- ' spect she is beginning to decline in that ' humble virtue, which is now peculiar ' to herself, and makes her the delight of ' all who converse with her.'

This was what he was pleased to *say* thus, with the most graceful generosity, and a nobleness of mind *truly* peculiar to himself, was he pleased to *act*. And what, does your ladyship think, could Mrs Jervis or I say to him?—Why, indeed, nothing at all!—We could only look upon one another, with our eyes full, and our hearts full, of a gratitude that would not permit either of us to speak, but which expressed itself at last in a manner he was pleased to call more elegant than words, and that was, with uplifted folded hands, and tears of joy.

O my dear lady! how many opportunities have the beneficent *rich* to make *themselves*, as well as their *fellow creatures*, happy! All that I could think, or say, or act, was but my duty before; what a sense of obligation then must I lie under to this most generous of men!

But here let me put an end to this tedious subject, the principal part of which can have no excuse, if it may not serve as a proof of my chearful compliance with your ladyship's commands, that I recite *every* thing that is of concern to me, and with the same freedom as I was wont to do to my dear parents.

I have done it, and at the same time have offered what I had to plead in behalf of my conduct to the two housekeepers, which you expected from me, and I shall therefore close this my humble defence, if I may so call it, with the assurance that I am, *my dearest lady, your obliged and faithful servant*,

P. B.

LETTER XIX

FROM LADY DAVERS TO MRS B. IN ANSWER TO THE SIX LAST LETTERS.

' *WHERE she had it, I can't tell, ' but I think I never met with ' the fellow of her in my life, at any age,*' are, as I remember, my brother's words, speaking of his Pamela, in the * early part of your papers. In truth, thou art a surprizing creature, and every letter we have

* See Vol. I. page 34.

have from you, we have new subjects to admire you for. — Do you think, Lady 'Betty, said I, when I had read to the end of the subject about Mrs Jervis, 'I 'will not soon set out to hit this charm- 'ing girl a box of the ear or two?

'For what, Lady Davers? said she.

'For what! replied I — Why don't 'you see how many slaps of the face the 'bold slut gives me?—I'll Lady Airs 'her! I will —I'll teach her to reproach 'me, and so many of her betters, with 'her cottage excellences, and improve- 'ments, that shame our education.'

Why, you dear charming Pamela, did you only exceed me in words, I could forgive you; for there may be a knack and a volubility, as to words, that a natural talent may supply; but to be thus outdone in *thought* and in *deed*, who can bear it? And in so young an [illegible] too!

Well, Pamela, look to it, when I see you: you shall feel the weight of my hand, or—the pressure of my lip, one or t'other, depend on it, very quickly: for here, instead of my stooping, as I thought it would be, to call *you* sister, I shall be forced to think in a little while, that you ought not to own *me* as *yours*, till I am nearer your standard.

But to come to business. I will summarily take notice of the following particulars in all your obliging letters, in order to convince you of my friendship, by the freedom of my observations on the subjects you touch upon.

First, then, I am highly pleased with what you write of the advantages you received from the favour of my dear mother; and as you know many things of her by your attendance upon her, in the last three or four years of her life, I must desire you will give me, as opportunity shall offer, all you can recollect in relation to the honoured lady, and of her behaviour and kindness to you, and with a retrospect to your own early beginnings, the dawnings of this your bright day of excellence: and this not only I, but the countess, and Lady Betty, with whom I am going over your papers again, and her sister, Lady Jenny, request of you.

2. I am much pleased with your Kentish account, though we wished you had been more particular in some parts of it; for we are greatly taken with your descriptions, and your conversation pieces: yet I own, your honest father's letters, and yours, a good deal supply that de*fect*, as our pleasure in reading your relations makes us call it. Your parents are honest, discreet folks, I see that: I have a value for them: and you're the prudentest creature I ever knew, in all your ways, particularly in the advice you gave them about your more distant relations, and to aim at nothing beyond their natural sphere.—Every title is right, and as it should be. On these accounts it is, that all the world will allow, that you, and your parents too, merit the fortune you have met with.

3. I am highly delighted with the account you give me of my brother's breaking to you the affair of Sally Godfrey, and your conduct upon it. I had it from him as he brought it in, and as you relate it. The wretch has been very just in his account of it. But don't you think he was a sad young fellow? Well may you be thankful for *your* escape, *well* may you!—Your behaviour was what I admire; and so we do all, but none of us think we could have imitated it in all its parts. We are in love with your charitable reflections in favour of the poor lady, and the more, as she certainly deserved them, and a better mother too than she had, and a faithfuller lover than she met with.

4. You have exactly hit his temper, in your declared love of Miss Goodwin. I see, child, you know your man, and never fear but you'll hold him, if you can go on thus to act, and out-do your sex. But I should think you might as well not insist upon having her with you, for the girl may be pert, perhaps insolent (you know who is her father,) you'd not care to check her, for several reasons, and this may make you uneasy; for, if you *did*, he might take it amiss, let your motives be ever so good: so I think you'd better see her now-and then at the dairy-house, or at school, than have her with you. —But this I leave to your own discretion, and *his* good pleasure, to determine upon, for in the latter it must rest, let you, or me, or any body, say what we will.

5. You have fully, and to our satisfaction, answered our objections to your behaviour to Mrs Jewkes. We had not considered your circumstances quite so thoroughly as we ought to have done. You are a charming girl, and all your motives are so just, that we shall be a little more cautious for the future how we censure you. We are particularly pleased with

with the triumphs of your innocence over his and her guilt, and agree that they are the rightest and best-to be-defended motives for pride, that ever were set before us

In short, I say with the countess—'This good girl is not without her pride, 'but it is the pride that becomes, and can 'only attend, the innocent heart, and 'I'll warrant, said her ladyship, 'nobody will become her station so well, 'as one who is capable of so worthy a 'pride as this

But what a curtain-lecture hadst thou, Pamela! A noble one, dost thou call it! —Why, what a wretch hast thou got, to expect thou shouldst never expostulate against his lordly will, even when in the wrong, till thou hast obeyed it, and, of consequence, joined in the evil he imposes! He says, indeed, in *small* points but I suppose he is to judge which are and which are not small

Thus, I remember, my brother himself took notice once of a proposal in the House of Commons, to grant the crown a very great sum to answer civil list deficiencies, which being opposed by the minority, the minister found out an expedient, that they might give the money *first*, and examine into the merits of the demand *afterwards* So we read, that, in some countries, an accused person is put to death, and then tried, and all he has to hope for while he lives, is, that his relations, and his own family, will be released from obloquy if an acquittal ensues

Much good may such a husband do you, says Lady Betty!—Every body will *admire* you, but no one will have reason to *envy* you upon those principles Yet, I don't know how it is, but this is evident, that, at present, there is not a happier couple in the world than you two are

6 I am pleased with your promise of sending me what you think I shall like to see, out of those papers you choose not to *shew me collectedly* this is very obliging You're a good girl, and I love you dearly

7 We have all smiled at your paradox, Pamela, that his marrying you was an instance of his pride The thought, though, is pretty enough, and ingenious but whether it will hold or not, I won't just now examine

8 Your observation on the *forget* and *forgive* we are much pleased with, and think you have distinguished well on that head

9 You are a very good girl for sending me a copy of Miss Darnford's letter She is a charming young lady I always had a great opinion of her merit, her letter abundantly confirms me in it I hope you'll communicate to me every letter that passes between you, and pray send me in your next a copy of your answer to her letter I must insist upon it, I think

10 I am glad, with all my heart, to hear of poor Jewkes's reformation Your example carries all before it But pray oblige me with your answer to her letter, don't think me unreasonable [illegible] all for your sake You must needs know that, or you know nothing For I think you deserve all Miss Darnford says of you, and that's a great deal too

Pray—have you seen Jewkes's letter to your good friend?—Lady Betty wants to know (if you *have*) what he could say to it? For, she says, it cuts him to the quick And I think so too, if he takes it as he ought but, as you say, he's above loving virtue for *virtue's sake*, I warrant him He likes it in a wife, because 'tis a husband's security against the law of retaliation There's a great deal in that, I can tell you I once heard the wretch hold an argument that women had no souls I asked him, if he were to marry, whether he'd have his wife *act* as if she believed this doctrine to be good? That was another thing, he said he was for having his wife think she had, he must own such a belief could do her no harm Ah! Pamela, for theory and practice too, I doubt, never was such a rake, for one not quite a town debauchee!

11 Your manner of acting by Mrs Jervis, with so handsome a regard to my brother's interest, her behaviour upon it, and your relation of the whole, and of his generous spirit in approving, reproving, and improving your prudent generosity, make no inconsiderable figure in your papers And Lady Betty says—'Hang him, he has some excellent qua'lities too—It is impossible not to think 'well of him, and his good actions go 'a great way towards atoning for his 'bad' But you, Pamela, have the glory of all We desire, particularly, that you will never omit any of those moving scenes, which you so well describe, be the occasion what it will for they are nature,

ture, and that's your excellence. Keep to that, for one more learned, I verily think could not write so well, nor instruct and delight, and move all at once, so very engagingly.

I am glad you are learning French; thou art a happy girl in thy teacher, and he is a happy man in his scholar. We are pleased with the pretty account you give of his method of instructing and rewarding. 'Twould be strange, if you did not learn any language quickly under such methods, and with such encouragements, from the man you love, with your genius so apt than it is. But we wished you had enlarged on that subject; for such fondness of men to their wives, who have been any time married, is so rare, and so unexpected from my brother, that we thought you should have written a side upon that subject at least.

What a bewitching girl art thou! What an exemplar to wives now, as well as thou wast before to maidens! Thou canst tame lions, I dare say, if thou didst try.—Reclaim a rake in the meridian of his libertinism, and make such an one as my brother not only marry thee, but love thee better at several months end, than he did the first day, if possible! Wonderful girl! Yet usest thou no arts but honest ones, such as prudence directs, nature points out, and such as make duty delightful, even commanding most, when thou seemest most to submit.

It must be owned indeed, that thou hast no brutal mind to deal with: bad as he is, it must be said, that thou hast a sensible and a generous heart to work upon, one who takes no glory in the blind submission of a slave, but, like a true British monarch delights to reign in a free, rather than in an abject mind. Yet is he jealous as a tyrant of his prerogative; but you have found the way to lay that watchful dragon asleep, and so possess the golden fruits of content and true pleasure, the due reward of your matchless conduct.

Now, my dear Pamela, I think I have taken notice of the most material articles in your letters, and have no more to say to you, but, write on, and oblige us, and mind to send me the copy of your letter to Miss Darnford, of that you wrote to poor penitent Jewkes, and every article I have written about, and all that comes into your head, or that passes, and you'll oblige *yours*, &c.

B. DAVERS.

LETTER XX.

MY DEAR LADY,

I Read with pleasure your commands, in your last kind and obliging letter; and you may be sure of a ready obedience in every one of them, that is in my power.

That which I can most easily do, I will first do, and that is, to transcribe the answer I sent to Miss Darnford*, and that to Mrs. Jewkes, the former of which (and a long one it is) is as follows:

'DEAR MISS DARNFORD,

'I Begin now to be afraid I shall not 'have the pleasure and benefit I pro-'mised myself of passing a fortnight or 'three weeks at the Hall, in your sweet 'conversation, and that of your worthy 'family, as well as those others in your 'agreeable neighbourhood, whom I 'must always remember with equal ho-'nour and delight.

'The occasion will be principally, 'that we expect very soon a visit from 'Lord and Lady Davers, who propose 'to tarry here a fortnight at least, and 'after that, the advanced season will 'carry us to London, where Mr. B. has 'taken a house for his winter-residence, 'and in order to attend parliament; a 'service, he says, which he has been 'more deficient in hitherto, than he can 'either answer to his constituents, or to 'his own conscience; for though, he 'says, he is but one, yet if any good 'motion should be lost by *one*, every ab-'sent member, who is independent, has 'it to reproach himself with the conse-'quences that may follow on the loss of 'that good which might otherwise re-'dound to the commonwealth. And 'besides, he says, such excuses as *he* 'could make, *every one* might plead; 'and then publick affairs might as well 'be left to the administration, and no 'parliament be chosen.

'He observed further on this subject, 'that every absent member, in such cases, 'indirectly abets the minister, be he *who* 'he will, in all his designs, be they *what* 'they will; and is even less excusable

* See Miss Darnford's Letter, p. 324, of this Volume.

'to

'to his country, than the man, who, for 'a transitory benefit to his private family, takes a pension or reward for his 'vote, since the difference is only that 'the one passively ruins his country by 'neglect and indolence, which can do 'nobody good, and the other more actively for a bribe, which practice, though 'ruinous in the end to the whole publick, 'in which his own private is included, 'yet serves to answer some present turn 'or benefit to himself or family

'See you, my dear Miss Darnford, 'from the humble cottager, what a publick person your favoured friend is 'grown! And behold how easy it is 'for a bold mind to look forward, and, 'perhaps, forgetting what she was, now 'she imagines she has a stake in the 'country, takes upon herself to be as 'important, as significant, as if, like my 'dear Miss Darnford, she had been born 'to it! But if, nevertheless, I am censured for troubling my head with politicks, let me answer, that I am at liberty, I hope, to tell you Mr B s sentiments of these high matters and that 'is all I have done

'Well, but may I not presume to 'ask, whether, if the mountain cannot 'come to Mahomet, Mahomet will not 'come to the mountain? since Lady 'Davers s visit is so uncertain as to it's 'beginning and duration, and so great 'a favour as I am to look upon it, and 'really shall, it being her first visit to '*me*,—and since we must go and take 'possession of our London residence, 'why can t Sir Simon spare to us the dear 'lady, whom he could use hardly, and 'whose attendance (though he is indeed 'intitled to all her duty) he did not, just 'in that instance, quite so much deserve?

"Well, but after all, Sir Simon," 'would I say, if I had been in presence 'at his peevish hour, "you are a fine "gentleman, are you not? to take such "a method to shew your good daughter, "that because she did not come *soon* "*enough* to you, she came *too soon!* "And did ever papa before you, put a "*good book* (for such I doubt not it was, "*because* you were in affliction, though "so little affected by it's precepts) to "such a *bad use?* As parents examples are so prevalent, suppose your "daughter had taken this very book, "and flung it at her sister, Miss Nancy "at her waiting-maid, and so it had "gone through the family, would it "not have been an excuse for every one "to say, that the father and head of the "family had set the example?

"But again, Sir Simon, suppose you "had hurt the sweet dove-like eyes of "my dear Miss Darnford—Suppose you "had bruised or broken the fine skin of "any part of that fine face, which gives, "at first sight, so bright a promise of "her still finer mind, what, let me ask "you, Sir, could you have said for yourself? How would the dear lady s appearance, with one sweet eye, perhaps, "muffled up, with a plaistered forehead, "or a veiled cheek, hiding herself from "every body but you, and her grieved "mamma, and pitying sister, reproached you for so rash an act?—nay, reproached you more, by her unreproaching obligingness, and chearful duty, than if (were she capable of "it) she could have spoken in sharp complaints, and expostulatory wailings?

"You almost wish, my dear Miss "tells me, that I would undertake *you!* "—This is very good of you, Sir Simon," might I (would his patience 'have suffered me to run on thus) have 'added—"But I hope, since you are so "sensible that you *want* to be undertaken, (and since this peevish rashness "convinces me, that you *do*) that you "will undertake *yourself*, that you will "not, when your indisposition makes "the attendance and duty of your dear "lady and daughter necessary, make it "more uncomfortable to them, by *adding* a difficulty of being pleased, and "an impatience of spirit, to the concern "their duty and affection make them "have for you, and *at least*, resolve never "to take a book into your hand again, "if you cannot make a better use of it, "than you did then"

'Pray tell your papa, that I beg the 'favour of him, to present *me* with this 'book, and I will put a mark upon it, 'and it shall never more either give or 'receive such disgrace, I warrant it Be 'it what it will, I will present him with 'as good a one

'I will write in it, "Memorandum, "This book, reversing the author s good "intention, had like to have done mischief next to unpardonable"—Or, "This book, instead of subduing the "reader's passions, (I take it for granted, you see, Miss, it was Seneca s morals, or some such good book) "had "like to have been the cause of a vio-

" lend—Henceforth, unavailing instructor, be thou condemned to stand " by thyself on a lone shelf in my closet, " a shelf most out of mine or any other " person's reach, for pretending to prescribe rules for subduing the passions " in so inefficacious a manner! And, " consigned to dust and cobwebs, not " once presume (in hope to hide thy " conscious guilt) to squeeze thyself into " rank with better or at least with more " convincing teachers!

' But do you think, dear Madam, Sir Simon would be angry, if opportunity had offered, and I had been thus bold? If you think so, don't let him see I had such thoughts in my head. But after all, if he were to have been thus freely treated by me, and if he should have *blushed* with *anger* at my freedom, 'tis but what he ought to bear from me; for, more than once has he made me *blush* for *shame*, at much greater on his part; nay, and that too, in presence of his virtuous daughters. So, that I have but half my revenge upon him yet.—" And will you bear malice," will he say, " Mrs. B.?"— " Yes, Sir Simon, I will; and nothing " but your amending the evil can make " me forgive a gentleman, that is *really* " a gentleman, who can so sadly forego " his character, and before any company, not scruple to expose a modest virgin to the forward leer, and loud laugh, " of younger gentlemen, who durst not " make such inferences of speech, as they " would fancy they chuckle at, when coming from the mouth of one of Sir Simon's authority, though, but better promising time of life."

' But Sir Simon will say, I have *already undertaken* him, were he to see this. Yet my Lady Darnford once begged I would give him a hint or two on this subject, which she was pleased to say, would be better received from me than from any body: and if it be a little too severe, 'tis but a just reprisal made by one whose ears, he knows, he has cruelly wounded more than once, or twice or thrice times, besides by what he calls his *innocent* double entendres, and who, if she had not resented it, when an opportunity offered, must have been believed by him, to be neither more nor less than a hypocrite.—There's for you, Sir Simon! and so here ends all my malice; for now I have spoken my mind.

' Yet I hope your dear papa will not be so angry with me neither, as to deny me, for this my freedom, the request I make to *him*, to your *mamma*, and to your *dear self*, for your beloved company, for a month or two in Bedfordshire, and at London: and if you might be permitted to winter with us at the latter, how happy should I be! It will be half done the moment you desire it: Sir Simon loves you too well to refuse you, if you are earnest in it. Your honoured mamma is always indulgent to your requests: and Mr. B. as well in kindness to me, as for the great respect he bears you, joins with me to beg this favour of you, and of Sir Simon, and my lady.

' If it can be obtained, what pleasure and improvement may I not propose to myself, with so polite a companion, when we are carried by Mr. B. to the play, to the opera, and other of the town diversions! We will work together, visit together, read together, sing together, and improve one another; you *me*, in every word you shall speak, in every thing you shall do; I *you*, by my questions, and desire of information, which will make you open all your breast to me, and so unlocking that dear storehouse of virtuous knowledge, improve your own notions the more for communicating them. O my dear Miss Darnford! how happy is it in your power to make me!

' I am much affected with the account you give me of Mrs. Jewkes's reformation. I could have wished, had I not *other* and *stronger* inducements (in the pleasure of so agreeable a neighbourhood, and so sweet a companion) that on her account, I could have been down at the Hall, in hopes to have confirmed the poor woman in her newly assumed penitence. God give her grace to persevere in it!—To be an humble means of saving a soul from perdition! O my dear Miss Darnford, let me enjoy that heart ravishing hope!—To pluck such a brand as this out of the fire, and to assist to quench its flaming susceptibility for mischief, and make it useful to edifying purposes, what a pleasure does this afford one? How does it encourage one to proceed in the way one has been guided to pursue. How does it make me hope, that I am raised to my present condition, in order to be an humble instrument in

' the

'the hand of Providence to communicate 'great good to others, and so extend to 'many, those benefits I have received, 'which, were they to go no farther than 'myself, what a vile, what an ungrateful 'creature should I be!

'I see, my dearest Miss Darnford, how 'useful in every condition of life a virtuous and a serious turn of mind may 'be!

'*How have I seen some ladies in upper* life behave as if they thought good 'actions, and a pious demeanour, would 'be so unfashionable, as to make them 'the subjects of ridicule to the lighter-disposed world, and so they are shamed 'out of their duty! But let me make it 'my boast, that here is such a poor girl 'as I, raised from the cottage to the palace, as I may say, persevering in the 'good purposes which had been instilled 'into her, by worthy, though poor parents, and the best of ladies, her mistress, and resolving to be obstinate in 'goodness, having stood the tests of libertinism, has brought the world to 'expect good actions from her, to respect 'her for doing them, and has even found 'her example efficacious, through Divine 'grace, to bring over to penitence and 'imitation a poor creature who used to 'ridicule her for nothing so much as for 'her innocence and virtue, which, word 'and thing, were the constant subjects 'of her scorn, as well as the cause of her 'persecution

'But let me not too much dwell upon 'the thought, lest I fall into the snare, 'that, of all others, persons meaning 'well have reason to dread, that of *spiritual pride*, the most dangerous of all 'pride

'In hopes of seeing you with us, I 'will not enlarge on several agreeable 'subjects, which I could touch upon 'with pleasure, besides what I gave you 'in my former (of my reception here, 'and of the kindness of our genteel 'neighbours,) such, particularly, as the 'arrival here of my dear father and mother, and the kind, generous entertainment they met with from my best friend 'his condescension in not only permitting me to attend them to Kent, but 'accompanying us thither, and setting 'them in a most happy manner, beyond 'their wishes and my own, but yet so 'much in character, as I may say, that 'every one must approve his judicious 'benevolence. the favours of my good 'Lady Davers to me, who, pleased with 'my letters, has vouchsafed to become 'my correspondent, and a thousand, 'thousand things, which I want personally to communicate to my dear Miss 'Darnford

'Be pleased to present my humble respects to Lady Darnford, and to Miss 'Nanny, to good Madam Jones, and to 'your kind friends at Stamford, to Mr. 'and Mrs Peters likewise, and their 'kinswoman and beg of that good gentleman from me to encourage his new 'proselyte all he can and I doubt not, 'she will do credit, poor woman! to the 'pains he shall take with her In hopes 'of your kind compliance with my 'wishes for your company, I remain, '*dearest Miss Darnford, your faithful* '*and obliged friend and servant,*

'P B'

This, my good Lady Davers, is the long letter I sent to Miss Darnford, who, at parting, engaged me to keep up a correspondence with her, and put me in hopes of passing a month or two with us, at the Hall, if we came down, and if she could persuade Sir Simon and her mamma to spare her to my wishes Your ladyship will excuse me for so faintly mentioning the honours you confer upon me, but I would not either add or diminish in the communications I make to you

The following is the copy of what I wrote to Mrs Jewkes

'YOU give me, Mrs Jewkes, very 'great pleasure to find, that at 'length God Almighty has touched your 'heart, and let you see, while health and 'strength lasted, the error of your ways. 'Many an unhappy one has not been 'so graciously touched, till they have 'smarted under some heavy afflictions, 'or till they have been confined to the 'bed of sickness, when perhaps, they 'have made vows and resolutions, that 'have held them no longer than the discipline lasted but you give me much 'better hopes of the sincerity of your conversion, as you are so well convinced, 'before some sore evil has overtaken you 'and it ought to be an earnest to you of 'the Divine favour, and should keep you 'from despondency

'As to me, it became me to forgive 'you, as I most cordially did, since your 'usage of me, as it proved, was but a 'necessary means in the hand of Providence,

 'dence,

'dence, to exalt me to that state of hap-
'piness, in which I have every day more
'and more cause given me to rejoice, by
'the kindest and most generous of gen-
'tlemen.

'As I have often prayed for you, even
'when you used me the most unkindly,
'I now praise God for having heard my
'prayers, and [illegible] delight look
'upon [illegible] as a [illegible] given to
'[illegible] the Divine
'goodness [illegible] you to [illegible]
'[illegible] and
'when you can [illegible] repaling
'pleasure [illegible] worthy [illegible], on
'being [illegible] station, where your
'example may be of advantage to the
'[illegible] others, as well as to your own,
'[illegible] glories
'in, and none else can truly relish, then
'may you be assured, that nothing but
'your [illegible] e, and the consequen-
'[illegible] resulting from it is
'wanted to convince you, that you are
'in a right way, and that the woe, that
'is pronounced against the presumptuous
'sinner, belongs not to you.

'Let me therefore, dear Mrs Jewkes,
'(for now [illegible] you are dear to me)
'caution you against two things, the
'one, that you return not to your for-
'mer ways, and wilfully err after this
'repentance, for, in this case, the Di-
'vine goodness will look upon itself as
'mocked by you, and will withdraw it-
'self from you, and more dreadful will
'your future state be, than if you had ne-
'ver experienced the other, that you don't
'despair of the Divine mercy, which has
'[illegible] manifested itself in your
'[illegible], and has awakened you out of
'your deep [illegible], without those
'sharp [illegible] and operations, which
'[illegible], and perhaps not more faulty
'persons, have suffered. But go on
'cheerfully in the happy path which you
'have begun to tread. Depend upon it,
'you are now in the right way, and turn
'not either to the right-hand or to the
'left, for the reward is before you, in
'reputation and a good fame in this life,
'and everlasting felicity beyond it.

'Your letter is that of a sensible wo-
'man, as I always thought you, and of
'a truly contrite one, as I hope you will
'approve yourself to be, and I the rather
'hope it, because I shall be always de-
'sirous, then, of taking every opportu-
'nity that offers to me of doing you real
'service, as well with regard to your
'present as future life. For I am, good
'Mrs Jewkes, as I now hope I may
'call you, *your Loving friend to serve*
'*you*,

'P. B.

'Whatever good books the worthy Mr
'Peters will be so kind as to recom-
'mend to you, and for those under
'your direction, send for them either
'to Lincoln, or Stamford, or Gran-
'tham, as you can get them, and place
'them to my account. And may they
'be the effectual means of confirming
'you and them in the good way you
'are in! I have done as much for all
'here, and, I hope, to good effect.
'For I shall now tell them, by Mrs
'Jervis, if there be occasion, that I
'hope they will not be out done
'in Bedfordshire by Mrs Jewkes in
'Lincolnshire, but that the servants
'of both houses may do credit to the
'best of masters. Amen, *good* wo-
'man! as once more I take pleasure
'to call you.

Thus, my good lady, have I obeyed you, in transcribing these two letters. I will now proceed to your ladyship's twelve articles. As to the

1. I will oblige your ladyship, as I have opportunity, in my future letters, with such accounts of my dear lady's favour and goodness to me, as I think will be acceptable to you, and to the noble ladies you mention.

2. I am extremely delighted, that your ladyship thinks so well of my dear honest parents: indeed they are good people, and ever had minds that set them above low and sordid actions, and God and your good brother has rewarded them most amply in this world, which is more than they ever expected, after a series of unprosperousness in all they undertook.

Your ladyship is pleased to say, that people in upper life love to see how plain nature operates in honest minds, who have hardly any thing else for their guide, and if I might not be thought to descend too low for your ladyship's attention, (for as to myself, I shall, I hope, always look back with pleasure to what I *was*, in order to increase my thankfulness for what I *am*) I would give you a scene of resignation, and contented poverty, of which otherwise your ladyship can hardly have a notion. I *will* give it, because it will be a scene of nature, however low, which

your

Plate XVI. Published as the Act directs by Harrison & C. Jan.y 1. 1786

your ladyship loves, and it shall not tire you by its length

It was upon occasion of a great loss and disappointment which happened to my dear parents (for though they were never high in life, yet they were not always so low as my honoured lady found them, when she took me) my poor father came home, and as the loss was of such a nature, as that he could not keep it from my mother, he took her hand, I remember well, and said, after he had acquainted her with it—'Come, my dear, let us 'take comfort, that we did for the best. 'We left the issue to Providence, as we 'ought, and that has turned it as it pleas'ed, and we must be content, though 'not favoured as we wished All the 'business is, our lot is not cast for this 'life Let us resign ourselves to the Di'vine will, and continue to do our duty, 'and this short life will soon be past 'Our troubles will be quickly overblown, 'and we shall be happy in a better, I 'make no doubt

Then my dear mother threw her kind arms about his neck, and said with tears —'God's will be done, my dear love! 'All cannot be rich and happy I am 'contented, and had rather say, I have 'a poor honest husband, than a guilty rich 'one What signifies repining: let the 'world go as it will, we shall have our 'length and our breadth at last. And 'Providence, I make no doubt, will be 'a better friend to our good girl here, 'because she is good, than we could be, 'if this had not happened,' pointing to me, who, then about eleven years old, (for it was before my lady took me) sat weeping in the chimney-corner, over a few dying embers of a fire, at their moving expressions

I arose, and kissing both their hands, and blessing them, said—'And this length 'and breadth, my dear parents, will be 'one day, all that the rich and the great 'can possess, and, it may be, their un'gracious heirs will trample upon their 'ashes, and rejoice they are gone while 'such a poor girl as I, am honouring 'the memories of mine, who in their 'good names, and good lessons will have 'left me the best of portions

And then they both hugged their prating girl to their fond bosoms, by turns; and all three were so filled with comfort in one another, that after joining in a grateful hymn, we went to bed (what though supperless perhaps?) with such true joy, that very few of the rich and great can have any idea of it, I to my loft, and they to their rush-floor'd cleanly bed-room And we have had sweet sleep, and dreams so pleasant, that we have reaped greater pleasures, in repeating them one to another, at our next leisure-hour, than, possibly, we should have received, had we enjoyed the comforts we wanted

And, truly, I must needs say, that while the virtuous poor can be blessed with such sweet enjoyments as these, in contented minds all day, and in sound sleep at night, I don't know whether they have not more, even of *this* world's pleasures, than the abounding rich and while the hours of night bear so near a proportion to those of the day, may not such be said, even at the worst, to pass at least *half* their lives with more comfort than many times the *voluptuous* and *distempered* great can pretend to know?

For a farther proof that *honest poverty* is not such a deplorable thing as some people imagine, let me ask, what pleasure can those over happy persons know, who from the luxury of their tastes, and their affluent circumstances, always eat before they are hungry, and drink before they are thirsty? This may be illustrated by the instance of a certain eastern monarch, who, as I have read, marching at the head of a vast army through a wide extended desart, which afforded neither river nor spring, for the first time, found himself (in common with his soldiers) overtaken by a craving thirst, which made him wish for, and pant after a cup of water And when at last, after diligent and distant search, one of his soldiers found a little dirty puddle, and carried him some of the filthy water in his nasty helmet, the monarch, greedily swallowing it, cried out, that in all his life he never tasted so sweet a draught!

But when I talk or write of my worthy parents, how I run on!—Excuse me, my good lady, and don't think me, in this respect, too much like the cat in the fable*, turned into a fine lady, for methinks, though I would never forget what I was, yet I would be thought to know *how*, gratefully to enjoy my present happiness, as well with regard to my obligations to GOD, as to your dear brother. But let me proceed to your ladyship's third particular.

* See Æsop's Fables.

3. And

3. And you cannot imagine, Madam, how much you have set my heart at rest, when you tell me, that my dear Mr. B. gave me a just narrative of this affair with Miss Godfrey: for, when your ladyship desired to know how he had recounted that story, lest you should make a misunderstanding between us, madam, I did not know what to think. I was afraid some blood had been shed on the occasion by him: for the lady was ruined, and as to her, nothing could have happened worse. And the regard I have for Mr. B.'s future happiness, which in my constant supplications for him in private, costs me many a tear, gave me great apprehensions, and not a little uneasiness. But as your ladyship tells me that he gave me a just account, I am happy again.

What makes one, my dear lady, in our most prosperous condition, be always intermingling one's fears of what *may be*, whereby one robs one's self of the pleasure of one's best worldly enjoyments?—Is this apprehensiveness, does your ladyship think, implanted in our natures for wise and good ends, that we may not think ourselves so happy here, as to cause us to forget that there is a better, and more perfectly happy state, which we ought to aspire after? I believe it is: and if so, what an useful monitor do we carry about us, that shall make us consider and reflect, when in prosperity, and in adversity teach us to bear up to hopes of a happier lot! Thus it is said by Mr. Norris, in his translation of one of Horace's Odes,

Be life and spirit when fortune proves unkind,
And summon up the vigour of thy mind;
But when thou'rt driven by too officious gales,
Be wise, and gather in the swelling sails.

I now come to your ladyship's fourth particular.

And highly delighted I am for having obtained your approbation of my conduct to the child, as well as of my behaviour towards the dear gentleman, on the unhappy lady's score. Your ladyship's wise intimations about having the child with me, make due impression upon me; and I see in them, with grateful pleasure, your unmerited regard for me. Yet, I don't know how it is, but I have conceived a strange passion for this dear baby. I cannot but look upon her poor mamma as my sister in point of trial: and shall not the prosperous sister pity and love the poor dear sister, that, in so slippery a path, has *fallen*, while *she* had the happiness to keep her feet?

No doubt, Miss Godfrey loved virtue, and preferred it to all considerations. 'Tis plain she did even after her fall—when, as I have observed in the papers * I sent your ladyship, she could leave country, parents, friends, and the man of all others she loved best, and seek a new fortune, run the danger of the seas, and perhaps the hazards of meeting with worse men, rather than trust to her own strength, where it had once so unhappily failed her.—What a love of virtue for virtue's sake is this? I know not who could have acted up to this part of her character.

The rest of your ladyship's articles give me the greatest pleasure and satisfaction; and if I can but continue myself in the favour of your dear brother, and improve in that of his noble sister, how happy shall I be! I will do all I can to deserve both. And I hope your ladyship will take as an instance that I will, the cheerful obedience which I pay to your commands, in writing to so fine a judge, such crude and indigested stuff, as otherwise I ought to be ashamed to lay before you.

I am impatient for the honour, which your ladyship makes me hope for, of your presence here: and yet I perplex myself with the fear of appearing so unworthy in your eye when near you, as to suffer in your opinion; but I promise myself, that however this may be the case on your first visit, I shall be so much improved by the benefits I shall reap from your lessons and good example, that whenever I shall be favoured with a *second*, you shall have fewer faults to find with me; till, as I shall be more and more favoured, I shall in time be just what your ladyship will wish me to be, and, of consequence, more worthy than I am of the honour of styling myself *your ladyship's most humble and obedient servant*,

P. B.

LETTER XXI

FROM MISS DARNFORD. IN ANSWER TO MRS. B.'S, P. 334.

MY DEAR MRS. B.

YOU are highly obliging to me in expressing so warmly your wishes to have me with you. I know not any

* See Vol. II. p. 280.

body

body in this world, out of our own family, in whose company I should be happier but my papa won't part with me, I think, though I have secured my mamma in my interest, and I know Nancy would be glad of my absence, because the dear perversely envious thinks *me* more valued than *she* is, and yet, foolish girl, she don't consider, that if her envy be well-grounded, I should return with more than double advantages to what I now have, improved by your charming conversation

My papa affects to be in a fearful pet at your lecturing of him so justly, for my mamma would shew him the letter, and he says he will positively demand satisfaction of Mr B for your treating him so freely And yet he shall hardly think him, he says, on a rank with him, unless Mr B will, on occasion of the new commission, take out his Dedimus and then if he will bring you down to Lincolnshire, and join with him to commit you prisoner for a month at the Hall, all shall be well

It is very obliging in Mr B to join in your kind invitation but—yet I am loth to say it to you—the character of your worthy gentleman, I doubt, stands a little *in the way with my papa, for he will have* it, that he is just such a rake as is to be liked by a lady, one that saves common appearances, and that's all, and is too handsome, too witty, and too enterprising, for any *honest man*, that's Sir Simon's phrase, *to trust his daughter with*

My mamma pleaded his being married —'Ads dines, Madam,' said he, 'what of all that! What married man, 'when a pretty girl's in the way, minds 'his wife, except she has made him stand 'in fear of her? and that's far from the 'case here Why, I tell you,' added his peevish highness, 'if our Polly should 'happen to slip,' (I thank him for his supposition) 'he'd make his lady nurse 'both *her* and the *bastard*, (another of 'his polite expressions) if he had a mind 'to it, and she durst not refuse him And 'would you trust such a sprightly girl as 'Polly, in the house with such a fellow 'as that?'

These, it seems, were his words and his reasonings I thank him for his opinion of his daughter It becomes not me to say, by what rules my papa judges of mankind, rules, however, that are not much to the credit of his sex —but it made me put on very grave airs when I came to supper, (for after this repulse, and the reasons given for it, I pretended indisposition, not to dine with my papa, being half vexed, and half afraid of his rallery) and he said—'Why, how 'now, Polly! What! in the sullens, 'girl?' I said, I should have hoped, that I never gave my papa cause to suspect my conduct, and that he would have had a better opinion of the force which the example and precepts of my good mamma had upon me

'Not your papa's example then—'Very well, saucebox, I understand you'

'But, Sir,' said I, 'I hope, if I may 'not go to Bedfordshire, you'll permit 'me to go to London, when Mrs B. 'goes

'No,' said he, 'positively no!'

'Well, Sir, I have done I could hope, 'however, you would enable me to give 'a better reason to good Mrs B why I 'am not permitted to accept of the kind 'invitation, than that which I under'stand you have been pleased to assign'

He stuck his hands in his sides, with his usual humorous positiveness—'Why 'then tell her, she is a very saucy lady, 'for her last letter to you, and her lord 'and master *is not to be trusted, and it* 'is my absolute will and pleasure that 'you ask me no more questions about 'it'

'I will very faithfully make this re'port, Sir —'Do so'—And so I have —And your poor Polly Darnford is disappointed of one of the greatest pleasures she could have had

I can't help it—And if you truly pity me, I can put you in a way to make me easier under the disappointment, than otherwise I can possibly be, and that is, to favour me with an epistolary conversation, since I am denied a personal one, and this my mamma joins with me to request of you, and particularly, to let us know how Lady Davers's first visit passes, which Mrs Peters and Mrs Jones, who know my lady so well, likewise long to hear And this will make us the best amends in your power for the loss of your good neighbourhood, which we had all promised to ourselves

This denial of my papa comes out, since I wrote the above, to be principally owing to a proposal made him of an humble servant to one of his daughters he won't say which, he tells us, in his usual

humorous

humorous way, lest we should fall out about it.

' I suppose, I tell him, ' the young ' gentleman is to pick and choose which ' of the two he likes best But be he a duke tis all one to Polly, if he be not something above our common Lincolnshire class of fox hunters

I have shewn Mr and Mrs Peters your letter They admire you beyond expression, and Mr Peters says, he does not know, that ever he did any thing in his life, that gave him so much inward reproach, as his denying you the protection of his family, which Mr Williams * sought to move him to afford you, when you were confined at the Hall, before Mr B came down to you, with his heart bent on mischief, and all he comforts himself with is, that that very denial, as well as the other hardships you have met with, were necessary to bring about that work of Providence which was to reward your unexampled virtue.

Yet, he says, he doubts he shall not be thought excusable by you, who are so exact in *your own* duty, since he had the unhappiness to lose such an opportunity to have done honour to his function, had he had the fortitude to have done *his*, and he begged of me, some how or other, and at some time or other, to hint his concern to you on this head, and to express his hopes, that neither religion nor his cloth may suffer in your opinion, for the fault of one of it's professors, who never was wanting in his duty so much before

He had it often upon his mind, he says, to write to you on this very subject, but he had not the courage, and besides, did not know *how* Mr B might take it, if he should see that letter, as the case had such delicate circumstances in it, that in blaming himself, as he should very freely have done, he must, by implication, have cast still greater blame upon him

Mr Peters is certainly a very good man, and my favourite for that reason, and I hope *you*, who could so easily forgive the late wicked, but now penitent Jewkes, will overlook with kindness a fault in a good man, which proceeded more from pusillanimity and constitution, than from want of principle for once, talking of it to my mamma, before me, he accused himself on this score, to her, with tears in his eyes She, good lady, would have given you this protection at Mr Williams s desire, but wanted the power to do it

So you see, my dear Mrs B how your virtue has shamed every one into such a sense of what they ought to have done, that good, bad, and indifferent, are seeking to make excuses for past misbehaviour, and to promise future amendment, like penitent subjects returning to their duty to their conquering sovereign, after some unworthy defection

Happy, happy lady ! May you ever be so ! May you always convert your enemies, invigorate the lukewarm, and every day multiply your friends, wishes *your most affectionate*

POLLY DARNFORD

P S How I rejoice in the joy of your honest parents ! God bless em ! I am glad Lady Davers is so wise Every one I have named desire their best respects Let me hear from you oftener, and omit not the minutest thing for every line of yours carries instruction with it.

LETTER XXII

FROM SIR SIMON DARNFORD TO MR B.

SIR,

LITTLE did I think I should ever have occasion to make a formal complaint against a person very dear to you, and who I believe deserves to be so; but don t let her be so proud and so vain of obliging and pleasing you, as to make her not care how she affronts every-body else

The person is no other than the wife of your bosom, who has taken such liberties with me, as ought not to be taken, and sought to turn my own child against me, and make a dutiful girl a rebel

If people will set up for virtue, and all that, let em be uniformly virtuous, or I would not give a farthing for their pretences

Here I have been plagued with gouts, rheumatisms, and nameless disorders, ever since you left us, which have made me call for a little more attendance than ordinary, and I had reason to think

* See Vol I p. 86

myself

PAMELA
E.F. Burney del
Birrell sculp

[illegible]

myself slighted, where an indulgent father can least bear to be so, that is, where he most loves, and that by young upstarts, who are growing up to the enjoyment of those pleasures which have run away from me, fleeting rascals as they are! before I was willing to part with them. And I rung and rung, and—'Where's Polly?' (for I honour the slut with too much of my notice,) 'Where's 'Polly?' was all my cry, to every one who came up to ask what I rung for. And, at last, in burst the pert baggage, with an air of assurance, as if she thought all must be well the moment she appeared, with—'Do you want me, papa?'

'Do I want you, Confidence! Yes, I 'do. Where have you been these two 'hours, that you never came near me, 'when you knew 'twas my time to have 'my foot rubbed, which gives me mor-'tal pain?' For you must understand, Mr. B. that nobody's hand's so soft as Polly's.

She gave me a saucy answer, as I was disposed to think it, because I had just then a twinge, that I could scarce bear; for pain is a plaguy thing to a man of my lively spirits. Why with a pox to it, cannot it go and rouse up some stupid lethargick rascal, whose blood is ready to stagnate? There it might do some good, and not make an honest man miserable as it does me, who want none of its pungent helps to feeling.

She gave me, I say, a careless answer, and turned upon her heel; and not coming to me at my first word, I flung a book, which I had in my hand, at her head.

This the boldface (girls now-a-days make nothing of exposing their indulgent parents) has mentioned in a letter to your lady; and she has abused me upon it in *such* a manner!—Well, if you don't take some course with her, I must with you, that's positive; and, young as you are, and a cripple as I am, I'll stump to an appointed place, to procure to myself the satisfaction of a man of honour.

Your lady has written to Polly what *she* would have said to me on this occasion. She has reflected upon me for not reading a book of mortification, when I was labouring under so great a sense of it, and confined to my elbow chair in one room, whom lately half a dozen countries could hardly have contained. She has put it into Polly's head to fling this very book at her sister's head, in imitation of my example, and hopes Nancy will fling it at somebody's else, till it goes all round the house. She reproaches me for making no better use of a *good* book, as she calls Rabelais's Pantagruel, which I innocently was reading, to make me the more cheerfully bear my misfortune; and runs on a pack of stuff about my Polly's eyes, and skin, and I don't know what, on purpose to fill the girl with notions of what don't belong to her, in order to make her proud and saucy; and then, to inspire her with insolence to me, runs on with suppositions of what harm I might have done her, had the book bruised her face, or put out her eyes, and so forth: as if our daughters eyes were not our own eyes, their brazen faces our brazen faces, at least till we can find somebody to take them, and all the rest of their trumpery, off our hands. Saucy baggages! who have neither souls nor senses but what they have borrowed from us, and whose very bones, and the skin that covers them, so much their pride and their ornament, are so many parts of our own undervalued skin and bones; for our skins are only more wrinkled, by taking pains to make theirs smooth.

Nay, this fine lady of yours, this paragon of meekness and humility, in so many words, bids me, or, which is worse, tells my own daughter to bid me, never to take a book in my hands again, if I won't make a better use of it.—and yet, what better use can an offended father make of the best books, than to correct a rebellious child with them, and oblige a saucy daughter to jump into her duty all at once?

Then, pray, Sir, do you allow your lady to beg presents from gentlemen?—This is a tender point to touch upon, but you shall know all, I am resolved. For here she sends to desire me to make her a present of this very book, and promises to send me another as good.

Come, come, Sir, these are no jesting matters; for is it not a sad thing to think of, that ladies, let them be young or old, well married or ill married, cannot live without intrigue? And here, if I were not a very honest man, and your friend, and *resolved* to be a virtuous man too, in spite of temptation, one does not know what might be the consequence of such a correspondence as is here begun, or rather *desired* to be begun; for I have too much *honour* to give into it, for your ſake, and I hope you'll think yourſelf much obliged to me. I know the time that I have improved a more myſterious hint than this, into all that I had a mind to make of it. And it may be very happy for you, neighbour, that I *muſt* and *will* be virtuous, let the temptation be from whom it will; for the fineſt lady in the world is nothing to me now—in this my reformed ſtate.

But this is not all. Mrs. B. goes on to reflect upon me for making her bluſh formerly, and ſaying things before my daughters, that, truly, I ought to be aſhamed to ſay; and then avows malice and revenge, and all that. Why, Sir, why, neighbour, are theſe things to be borne?—Do you allow your lady to ſet up for a general corrector of every body's morals but your own?—Do you allow her to condemn the only inſtances of wit that remain to this generation, that dear polite *double entendre*, which keeps alive the attention, and quickens the apprehenſion, of the beſt companies in the world, and is the ſalt, the ſauce, which gives a poignancy to all our genteeler entertainments?

Very fine, truly! that more than half the world ſhall be ſhut out of ſociety, ſhall be precluded their ſhare of converſation amongſt the gay and polite of both ſexes, were your lady to have her will! Let her firſt find people who can ſupport a converſation with wit and good ſenſe like her own, and then ſomething may be ſaid: but till then, I poſitively ſay, and will ſwear upon occaſion, that *double entendre* ſhall not be baniſhed from our tables; and where this won't raiſe a bluſh, or create a laugh, we will be at liberty, if we pleaſe, for all Mrs. B. and her new-fangled notions, to force the one and the other by ſtill plainer hints, and let her help herſelf how ſhe can.

Thus, Sir, you find my complaints are of a high nature, regarding the quiet of a family, the duty of a child to a parent, the advances of a married lady to a gentleman who is reſolved to be virtuous, and the freedom and politeneſs of converſation; in all which points your lady has greatly offended; and I inſiſt upon ſatisfaction from you, or ſuch a correction of the fair tranſgreſſor, as is in your power to inflict, and which may prevent worſe conſequences from *your offended friend and ſervant*,

SIMON DARNFORD.

LETTER XXIII.

FROM MR. B. IN ANSWER TO THE PRECEDING ONE.

DEAR SIR SIMON,

YOU cannot but believe, that I was much ſurpriſed at your letter, complaining of the behaviour of my wife. I could no more have expected ſuch a complaint from ſuch a gentleman, than I could, that ſhe would have deſerved it: and I am very ſorry on *both* accounts. I have talked to her in ſuch a manner, that, I dare ſay, ſhe will never give you like cauſe to appeal to me.

It happened, that the criminal herſelf received your letter from her ſervant, and brought it to me in my cloſet; and, making her honours, (for I can't ſay but ſhe is very obliging to me, though ſhe takes ſuch ſaucy freedoms with my friends) away ſhe tript; and I, inquiring for her, when, with ſurpriſe, as you may believe, I had read your charge, found ſhe was gone to viſit a poor ſick neighbour, of which indeed ſhe had before apprized me, becauſe ſhe took the chariot, but I had forgot it in my wrath.

'Twas well for her, that ſhe was not in the way; perhaps I ſhould have taken more ſevere methods with her in my firſt emotions; and I longed for her return: and there is another *well-for-her* too, in her caſe; for one would be loth to ſpoil a ſon and heir, you know, Sir Simon, before we ſee whether the little varlet may deſerve one's conſideration.

I ment on theſe things, that you may obſerve, it was not owing to any regard for the offender herſelf, that I did not puniſh her as much as injured friendſhip required at my hands.

At laſt, in ſhe came, with that ſweet compoſure in her face which reſults from a conſciouſneſs of doing *generally* juſt and generous things, although in this inſtance ſhe has ſo egregiouſly erred, that it behoves me (as well in juſtice to my friend, as in policy to myſelf, for who knows whither firſt faults may lead, if not checked in time?) to nip ſuch boldneſs in the bud. And indeed the moment I beheld the charmer of my heart, (for I do love her too well, that's certain) all my anger was diſarmed, and had the offence regarded *myſelf*, I muſt have forgiven her, in ſpite of all my meditated wrath.

with. But it behoved me in a *friend's* cause not to be soon ſubdued by a too partial fondneſs. I reſumed therefore that ſternneſs and diſpleaſure which her entrance had almoſt diſſipated. I took her hand: her charming eye (you know what an eye ſhe has, Sir Simon) quivered at my over-clouded aſpect, and her lips, half drawn to a ſmile, trembled with apprehenſion of a countenance ſo changed from what ſhe left it.

And then, all ſtiff and ſtately as I could look, did I accoſt her—'Come along 'with me, Pamela, to my cloſet: I want 'to talk with you.'

'Dear Sir! good Sir! what's the 'matter? what have I done?'

We entered. I ſat down, ſtill holding her unſteady hand, and her pulſe fluttering under [illegible] finger, like a dying bird.

''T[illegible] well,' ſaid I, ''tis *well* your 'pre[illegible] [illegible]dition pleads for you, and 'I [illegible] carry what I have to ſay 't[illegible] [illegible] conſiderations leſs in your '[illegible] for once taken: but I have '[illegible] [illegible]ants againſt you.'

'[illegible] [illegible]n, Sir!—What have I [illegible] Let me know, dear good Sir!' lo[illegible] round with her half affrighted eyes, this way and that, on the books, and pictures, and on me, by turns.

'You ſhall know ſoon,' ſaid I, 'the '*crime* you have been guilty of.'

'*Crime*, Sir! Pray let me—This cloſet, I hoped, would not be a *ſecond* 'time witneſs to the flutter you put me 'in.'

There hangs a tale, Sir Simon, which I am not very fond of relating, ſince it gave beginning to the triumphs of this little* ſorcereſs.

I ſtill held one hand, and ſhe ſtood before me, as criminals ought to do before their judge; but ſaid—'I ſee, Sir, ſure 'I do, or what will elſe become of me! 'leſs ſeverity in your eyes, than you affect to put on in your countenance. 'Dear Sir, let me know my fault: I will 'repent, acknowledge, and amend: let 'me *but* know it.'

'You muſt have great preſence of 'mind, Pamela, ſuch is the nature of 'your fault, if you can look me in the 'face, when I tell it you.'

'Then let me,' ſaid the irreſiſtible charmer, hiding her face in my boſom, and putting her other arm about my neck, 'let me thus, my dear Mr. B. hide this 'guilty face, while I hear my fault told, 'and I will not ſeek to extenuate it, but 'by my tears, and my penitence.'

I could hardly hold out. What infatuating creatures are theſe women, when they can think it thus worth their while to ſoothe and calm the tumults of an angry heart! When, inſtead of *ſcornful* looks darted in return for *angry* ones, words of *defiance* for words of *peeviſhneſs*, perſiſting to defend *one* error by *another*, and returning *vehement wrath* for *ſlight indignation*, and all the hoſtile provocations of the marriage warfare, they can thus hide their dear faces in our boſoms, and wiſh but to *know* their faults, to *amend* them!

I could hardly, I ſay, reſiſt the ſweet girl's behaviour; nay, I believe I did, unawares to myſelf, and in defiance of my reſolved diſpleaſure, preſs her forehead with my lips, as the reſt of her face was hid on my breaſt: but, conſidering it was the cauſe of my *friend* that I was to aſſert, my *injured* friend, wounded and inſulted, in ſo various a manner, by the fair offender, thus haughtily ſpoke I to the trembling miſchief, in a pomp of ſtile theatrically tragick.

'I will not, too inadvertent and un'diſtinguiſhing Pamela, keep you long 'in ſuſpenſe, for the ſake of a circum'ſtance, that, on this occaſion, ought 'to give you as much joy, as it has, till 'now, given me—Since it becomes an 'advocate in your favour, when other'wiſe you might expect very ſevere treat'ment. Know then, that the letter you 'gave me before you went out, is a let'ter from a friend, a neighbour, a wor'thy neighbour, complaining of your 'behaviour to him,—no other than Sir 'Simon Darnford, (for I would not amuſe her too much) 'a gentleman I 'muſt always reſpect, and whom, as my 'friend, I expected *you* ſhould: ſince 'by the value a wife expreſſes for one 'eſteemed by her huſband, whether ſhe 'thinks ſo well of him herſelf, or not, a 'man ought always to judge of the ſin'cerity of her regards to himſelf.'

She raiſed her head at once on this. 'Thank Heaven,' ſaid ſhe, 'it is no 'worſe!—I was at my wits end almoſt, 'in apprehenſion: but I know how this 'muſt be.—Dear Sir, how could you 'frighten me ſo?—I know how all this 'is!—I can now look you in the face,

* See Vol. I p. 58.

'and hear all that Sir Simon can charge me with! For I am sure, I have not so affronted him, as to make him angry indeed. And truly, (ran she on, secure of pardon, as she seemed to think) I should respect Sir Simon not only as your friend, but on his own account, if he was not so sad a rake at a time of life—

Then I interrupted her, You must needs think, Sir Simon, for how could I bear to hear my worthy friend so freely treated? 'How now, Pamela!' said I, 'and is it thus, by repeating your fault, that you atone for it? Do you think I can bear to hear my friend so freely treated?'

'Indeed, said she, 'I do respect Sir Simon very much as your *friend*, permit me to repeat; but cannot for his wilful failings. Would it not be, in some measure, to approve of such conversation, if one can hear it, and not discourage it, when the occasion comes in one's power?—And indeed, I was glad of an opportunity, continued she, 'to give him a little rub. I must needs own, if what I have said provokes you, or has made him angry in earnest, I am sorry for it, and will be less bold for the future.'

'Read then, said I, 'the heavy charge, and I'll return instantly to hear your answer to it.' So I went from her, for a few minutes.

But, would you believe it, Sir Simon? she seemed on my return, very little concerned at your just complaints—What self-justifying minxes have we men to deal with!—Instead of finding her in repentant tears, as one might have expected, she attacked your angry letter for a peculiar one; and I had great difficulty to convince her of the heinousness of *her* fault, or the reality of your resentment. Upon which, being determined to have justice done to my friend, and a due sense of her own great error impressed upon her, I began thus:

'Pamela, Pamela, take heed that you do not, under the purity of your own mind, in breach of your charity, to make you so rigorous a censurer of other people's actions. Do not be so puffed up with your own perfections as to imagine, that, because other persons allow themselves liberties you cannot take, *therefore* they must be vile. Sir Simon's a gentleman who [illegible] in a pleasant vein, and, I believe, as well as you, has been a great rake and libertine. (You'll excuse me, Sir Simon, because I am taking your part.) 'But what then? You see it is all over with him now. You see, he says himself, that he *must*, and therefore he will be virtuous; and is a man for ever to hear of the faults of his youth, when he himself is so willing to forget them?'

'And, but, Sir, Sir,' said the bold slut, 'can you say he is *willing* to forget them?—Does he not repine, even in this very letter, that he *must* forsake them; and does he not plainly cherish the *inclination*, when he owns—' she hesitated.—'Owns what?'—'You know what I mean, Sir, and I need not speak it; and can there well be a more censurable character?—Then, dear Sir, *before* his maiden daughters! *before* his virtuous lady! *before* any body!—What a sad thing is this, at a time of life, which should afford a better example!'

'But, dear Sir,' continued the bold prattler, (taking advantage of a silence that was more owing to displeasure than approbation) 'let me, for I would not be too *censorious*, (No, not she! in the very act of censoriousness to say this!) 'let me offer but one thing: don't you think Sir Simon himself would be loth to be thought a reformed gentleman? Don't you see the delight he takes, when he speaks of his former pranks, as if he was sorry he could not play them over again? See but how he simpers, and *enjoys*, as one may say, the relations of his own rakish actions, when he tells a bad story!—And have you not seen how often he has been forced to take his handkerchief to wipe the outside of his mouth, though the inside was least cleanly, when he has wounded a lady's ears, and turned, as it were, his own faulty heart inside out?—Indeed, Sir, I am afraid, so bad in this way is your worthy neighbour, that he would account it no addition to him to be thought reformed. And, how then can I abuse the gentleman, by representing him in a light in which he loves to be considered?'

'But,' said I, 'were this the case, (for I profess, Sir Simon, I was at a grievous loss to defend you) 'for you to write all these things against a father to his daughter, is that right, Pamela?'

'O Sir! the *good* gentleman himself has taken care, that such a character as I presume to draw to Miss of her papa,

was

'was no strange one to her. You have 'seen yourself, Mr. B. whenever his 'arch leers, and the humourous attitude 'in which he puts himself on those occasions, have taught us to expect some 'shocking story, how his lady and daughters (used to him as they are) have suffered in their apprehensions of what he 'would say, before he spoke it: how, 'particularly, dear Miss Darnford has 'looked at me with concern, desirous, 'as it were, if possible, to save her papa 'from the censure, which his faulty expressions must naturally bring upon 'him. And, dear Sir, is it not a sad thing 'for a young lady, who loves and honours her papa, to observe, that he is 'discrediting himself, and *wants* the example he ought to *give*? And pardon 'me, Sir, for smiling on so serious an occasion, but is it not a fine sight, do you 'think, to see a gentleman, as we have 'more than once seen Sir Simon, when 'he has thought proper to read a passage 'or so, in some bad book, pulling off *his* '*spectacles*, to talk filthily upon it? 'Methinks I see him now,' added the bold slut, 'splitting his arch face with a 'broad laugh, shewing a mouth, with 'hardly a tooth in it, while he is making obscene remarks upon what he has 'read.'

And then the dear fancy-face laughed out, to bear *me* company; for I could not, for the soul of me, avoid laughing heartily at the figure she brought to my mind, which I have seen my old friend make, on two or three occasions of this sort, with his dismounted spectacles, his arch mouth, and gums of shining jet, succeeding those of polished ivory, of which he often boasts, as one ornament of his youthful days.—And I the rather in my heart, Sir Simon, gave you up, because, when I was a sad fellow, it was always a maxim with me, to endeavour to touch a lady's heart without wounding her ears. And, indeed, I found my account sometimes in observing it.

But resuming my gravity—'Hussy,' said I, 'do you think I will have my 'old friend thus made the subject of your 'ridicule?—Suppose a challenge should 'have ensued between us on your account—what might have been the issue 'of it? To see an old gentleman, stumping, as he says, on crutches, to fight a 'duel in defence of his wounded honour! 'A pretty sight this would have afforded, would it not? And what (had any 'one met him on the way) could he have 'said he was going to do? Don't you 'consider that a man is answerable for 'the faults of his wife? And, if my 'fondness for you would have made me 'deny doing justice to my friend, and, 'on the contrary, to resolve in your behalf to give him a meeting, and he had 'flung his crutch at my head, as he did 'the book at his daughter's, what might 'have been the consequence, think you?'

'Very bad, Sir, to be sure; I see that, 'and am sorry for it: for had you carried off Sir Simon's crutch, as a trophy, 'the poor gentleman must have lain sighing and groaning like a wounded soldier in the field of battle, till another 'had been brought him, to have stump'd 'home with.'

But, dear Sir Simon, I have brought this matter to an issue, that will, I hope, make all easy: and that is this—Miss Polly, and my Pamela, shall both be punished as they deserve, if it be not your own fault. I am told, that the sins of your youth don't sit so heavily upon your limbs, as they do in your imagination; and I believe change of air, and the gratification of your revenge, a fine help to such lively spirits as yours, will set you up. You shall then take coach, and bring your pretty criminal to mine, and when we have them together, they shall humble themselves before us, and it shall be in your power to absolve or punish them, as you shall see proper. For I cannot bear to have my worthy friend insulted in so heinous a manner, by a couple of saucy girls, who, if not taken down in time, may proceed from fault to fault, till there will be no living with them.

If (to be still more serious) your lady and you will lend Miss Darnford to my Pamela's wishes, whose heart is set upon the hope of her wintering with us in town, you will lay an obligation upon us both, which will be acknowledged with great gratitude by, dear Sir, *your affectionate and humble servant.*

LETTER XXIV.

FROM SIR SIMON DARNFORD, IN REPLY.

HARK ye me, Mr. B.—A word in your ear:—I like neither you nor your wife, to be plain with you, well enough to trust my Polly with you. What!

What! you are to shew her in your lady's case, all the game of a lying-in, I suppose, and, at least, set the girls a longing to make one in the dance, before I have found out the proper man for the partner.

But here's war declared against my poor gambols, it seems. Well, I will never open my mouth before your lady as long as I live, if I can help it. I have for these ten years avoided to put on my cravat, and for what reason, do you think?—Why, because I could not bear to see what ruins a few years have made in a visage, that used to inspire love and terror as it pleased. And here your—what-shall-I-call-her of a wife, with all the insolence of youth and beauty on her side, follows me with a glass, and would make me look in it, whether I will or not. I'm a plaguy good-humoured old fellow—If I am an old fellow—or I should not bear the insults contained in your letter. Between you and your lady, you make a wretched figure of me, that's certain—And yet this *taking my part*, with a pox to you, Mr. B. I would have had, but on your own account.—You see I have as much more charity than she, as she has prudery than me, or I should not have put in a single word for her herself.

But, what need—must I do?—I'd be glad ... to remain in your lady's graces, that I would; for now should I be the laughing-stock and diversion, if reformed by her example, which I suppose every one makes the fashion, if she goes on as she does. But here I am endeavouring to cut a joke and toss the squib about, and, as far as I know, it has helped to keep me alive in the midst of pains and aches, and with two women grown girls, and the rest of the mortifications that will attend on *old scarred years*, for I won't (hang me if I will) give it the name of *old age!*

I love, I own it, to make a pretty woman blush, 'tis a double unmasking a fine face, as it were; and till I saw your—Do, let me call her some free name or other. I always loved to be free with pretty women!—Till I saw your—methinks I like her Arcadian name, though I'm so old a swain, as not to merit any thing but rebuke at her hands—Well then, till I saw your—Pamela—I thought all ladies in their hearts loved a little bit of that kind. For why should they not, when it adds so much grace to their features, and improves their native charms?—And often have I tossed the joke about, as much in my intention, to oblige *them* as myself.—Yet no one can say, but that I always wrapt it up in clean linen, as the saying is—only suiting myself to my company, till I had made the dear rogues *sensible*, and then they could apprehend.

But now, it seems, I must leave all this off, or I must be mortified with a looking-glass held before me, and every wrinkle in my face must be made as conspicuous as if I were—And what, pray, is to succeed to this reformation?—I can neither fast nor pray, I doubt.—And besides, if my stomach and my jest depart from me, farewel Sir Simon Darnford!

But cannot I pass as one necessary character, do you think, as a foil (as, by-the-bye, some of your own actions have been to your lady's virtue) to set off some more edifying example, where variety of characters make up a feast in conversation?

I beseech you, Mr. B.'s Pamela, stick me into some posy among your finer flowers.—And if you won't put me into your bosom, let me stand in some gay flower-pot in your chimney-corner. I may serve for shew, if not for smell. Or, let me be the bass in your musick, or permit my humorous humdrum to serve as a pardonable kind of discord to set off your own harmony.—I verily think, I cannot be so good as you'd have me to be. So pray let your poor Anacreon go off with what he loves. It will be very cruel, if you won't.

Well, but after all, I believe I might have trusted you with my daughter, under your lady's eye, rake as you have been yourself; and fame says wrong, if you have not been, for your time, a bolder sinner than ever I was, (with your maxim of touching ladies hearts, without wounding their ears, which made surer work with them, that was all) though 'tis to be hoped you are now reformed, and if you are, the whole country round you, east, west, north, and south, owe great obligations to your fair reclaimer. But here is a fine prim young fellow coming out of Norfolk, with one estate in one county, another in another, and jointures and settlements in his hands, and more wit in his head, as well as more money in his pocket, than he can tell what to do with, to visit our Polly, though I tell her I much question the former quality, his wit, if he is for marrying.—And would you have her be attending your wife's nursery, when she may possibly be put into a way to have a raree show of her *own?*

Here then is the reason I cannot comply

ply with your kind Mrs B——'s request But if this matter should go off, if he should not like *her*, or she *him*, or if I should not like *his* terms, or he *mine*,—or still another *Or*, if he should like Nancy better—why, then, perhaps, if Polly be a good girl, I may trust to her virtue, and to your honour, and let her go for a month or two, for the devil's in you, if you attempt to abuse such a generous confidence—As to the superiority of beauty in your own lady, I depend nothing on that, for, with you young fellows, variety has generally greater charms

Now, when I have said this, and when I say further, that I can forgive your severe lady, and yourself too, (who, however, are less to be excused in the airs you assume, which looks like one chimney-sweeper calling another sooty rascal) I give a proof of my charity, which I hope with Mrs B—— will cover a multitude of faults, and the rather, since, though I cannot be a *follower* of her virtue in the strictest sense, I can be an *admirer* of it, and that is some little merit and indeed all that can be at present pleaded by *yourself*, I doubt any more than *your humble servant*,

SIMON DARNFORD

LETTER XXV

MY HONOURED AND DEAR PARENTS,

I Hope you will excuse my long silence, which has been owing to several causes, and having had nothing new to entertain you with and yet this last is but a poor excuse neither to you, who think every trifling subject agreeable from your daughter

I daily expect here my Lord and Lady Davers This gives me no small pleasure, and yet it is mingled with some uneasiness at times, lest I should not, when viewed so intimately near behave myself answerably to her ladyship's expectations But this I resolve upon, I will not endeavour to move out of the sphere of my own capacity, in order to emulate her ladyship She has, and must have, advantages, by conversation, as well as education, which it would be arrogance in me to assume, or to think of imitating

All that I will attempt to do, therefore, shall be, to shew such a respectful obligingness to my lady, as shall be consistent with the condition to which I am raised, that so her ladyship may not have reason to reproach me of pride in my exaltation, nor her dear brother to rebuke me for meanness in condescending and, as to my family management, I am the less afraid of inspection, because, by the natural bias of my own mind, I bless God, I am above dark reserves, and have not one selfish or sordid view, that should make me wish to avoid the most scrutinizing eye

I have begun a correspondence with Miss Darnford, a young lady of uncommon merit But you know her character from my former writings She is very solicitous to hear of every thing that concerns me, and particularly how Lady Davers and I agree together I loved her from the moment I saw her first, for she has the least pride, and the most benevolence and solid thought I ever knew in a young lady, and knows not what it is to envy any one I shall write to her often and as I shall have so many avocations besides to fill up my time, I know you will excuse me, if I procure from this lady, as I hope to do, the return of my letters to her, for your perusal, and for the entertainment of your leisure hours This will give you from time to time, the accounts you desire of all that happens here But as to what relates to our own particulars, I beg you will never spare writing, as I shall not answering, for it is one of my greatest delights that I have such dear, such worthy parents, (as I hope in God, I long shall) to bless me, and to correspond with me

The papers I send herewith will afford you some diversion, particularly, those relating to Sir Simon Darnford, and I must desire, that when you have perused them, (as well as what I shall send for the future) you will return them to me.

Mr Longman gave me great pleasure, on his last return from you, in his account of your health, and the satisfaction you take in your happy lot, and I must recite to you a brief conversation on this occasion, which, I dare say, will please you as much as it did me

After he had been adjusting some affairs with his dear principal, which took them up two hours, my best-beloved sent for me—' My dear,' said he, taking my hand, and seating me by him, and making the good old gentleman sit down, (for he will always rise at my approach) ' Mr Longman and I have settled in ' two hours some accounts, which would

' have

'have taken up as many months with some persons. For never was there an exacter or more methodical accomptant than Mr Longman. He gives me (greatly to my satisfaction, because I knew it would delight you) an account of the Kentish concern, and of the pleasure your father and mother take in it.— Now, my charmer,' said he, 'I see your lovely eyes begin to glisten. O how this subject swells your whole soul to the windows of it!—Never was so dutiful a daughter, Mr Longman, and never did parents better deserve a daughter's duty.'

I endeavoured before Mr Longman to restrain my gratitude, that my overflowing heart could not be brought [illegible], as I could perceive: but the good old gentleman could not hinder his from shewing itself at his worthy eyes, to see how much I was affected—*oppressed*, I should say—with the tenderest goodness to me and kind expressions.— 'Excuse me, Sir—excuse me, Madam,' said he, wiping his cheeks: 'my delight to see such merit so justly rewarded, will not be controuled, I think.' And so he arose, and walked to the window.

'Well, good Mr Longman,' said I, as he returned towards us, 'you give me the pleasure to know, that my father and mother are well, and happy, when they *must* be, in a goodness and honour [illegible] I, and many more rejoice in.'

'Well and happy, Madam,—ay, that they are, indeed! And a worthier couple never lived, I assure you. Most nobly do they go on in the farm. Your honour is one of the happiest gentlemen in the world. All the good you do, returns upon you in a trice. I may well be said *you cast your bread upon the waters*, for it presently comes to you again, richer and heavier than when you threw it in. All the Kentish tenants, Madam, are hugely delighted with their good landlord: every thing prospers under his management: the gentry love both him and my dame, and the poor people adore them. Indeed they do a power of good, in visiting their poor neighbours, and giving them cordials and such like, insomuch that the colicks, agues, and twenty ill tempers nipped in the bud, fly before them. And yet the doctors themselves can have nothing to say against them, for they administer help to those only who cannot be at the charge either of skill or physick.'

In this manner ran Mr Longman on, to my inexpressible delight, you may believe, and when he withdrew—'Tis an honest soul,' said my dear Mr B. 'I love him for his respectful love to my angel, and his value for the worthy pair. Very glad I am, that every thing answers *their* wishes. May they long live, and be happy!'

The dear man makes me spring to his arms, whenever he touches this string: for he speaks always thus generously and kindly of you, and is glad to hear, he says, that you don't live only to yourselves; and now and then adds, that he is as much pleased with your prudence, as he is with mine, that parents and daughter do credit to one another, and that the praises he hears of you from every mouth, make him take as great pleasure in you, as if you were his own relations. How delighting, how transporting, rather, my dear parents, must this goodness be to your happy daughter! And how could I forbear repeating these kind things to you, that you may see how well every thing is taken that you do?

When the expected visit from Lord and Lady Davers is over, the approaching winter will call us to London, and as I shall then be nearer to you, we may more frequently hear from one another, which, to be sure, will be a great heightening to my pleasures.

But I have such an account given me of the immoralities which persons may observe there, along with the publick diversions, that it takes off a little from the satisfaction I should otherwise have in the thought of going thither. For, they say, quarrels, and duels, and gallantries, as they are called, so often happen in London, that those enormities are heard of without the least wonder or surprise.

This makes me very thoughtful at times. But God, I hope, will preserve our dearest benefactor, and continue to me his affection, and then I shall be always happy, especially while your healths and felicity confirm and crown the delights of *your ever dutiful daughter*,

P B

LETTER XXVI

MY DEAREST CHILD,

IT may not be improper to mention to yourselves, what the nature of the benefits is, which we confer on our poor

poor neighbours, and the labouring people, leſt it ſhould be ſurmiſed by any body, that we are laviſhing away wealth that is not our own. Not that we fear either your honoured huſband or you will ſuſpect any ſuch matter, or that the worthy Mr. Longman would inſinuate as much; for he ſaw what we did, and was highly pleaſed with it, and ſaid he would make ſuch a report of it, as you write he did. What we do is in ſmall things, though the good we hope from them is not ſmall perhaps: and if a very diſtreſsful caſe ſhould happen among our poor neighbours, that would require any thing conſiderable, and the objects be deſerving, we would acquaint you with it, and leave it to you to do as God ſhould direct you.

But this, indeed, we have done, and continue to do: we have furniſhed ourſelves with ſimple waters and cordials of ſeveral ſorts; and when in a hot ſultry day I ſee poor labouring creatures ready to faint and drop down, if they are only fatigued, I order them a mouthful of bread or ſo, and a cup of good ale or beer; and this makes them go about their buſineſs with new ſpirits; and when they bleſs me for it, I tell them they muſt bleſs the good ſquire, from whoſe bounty, next to God, it all proceeds. If they are ill, I give them a cordial; and we have been the means of ſetting up ſeveral poor creatures who have laboured under cholicky and aguiſh diſorders, or have been taken with ſlight ſtomach ailments. And nothing is loſt by it, my dear child; for poor people have as grateful ſouls as any body; and it would delight your dear heart to ſee how many drooping ſpirits we have raiſed, and how, in an hour or two, ſome of them, after a little cordial refreſhment, from languiſhing under a hedge, or behind a hay ſtack, have ſkipped about as nimble as deer, whiſtling and ſinging, and purſuing with alacrity their ſeveral employments; and inſtead of curſing and ſwearing, as is the manner of ſome wicked wretches, nothing but bleſſings and praiſes poured out of their glad hearts upon his honour and you; calling me their father and friend, and telling me, they will live and die for me, and my wife, and that we ſhall never want an induſtrious ſervant to do his honour's buſineſs, or to cultivate the farm I am bleſſed in. And in like ſort, we communicate to our ſick or wanting neighbours, even although they be not tenants to the eſtate.

Come, my dear child, you are happy, very happy, to be ſure you are; and, if it *can* be, may you be yet happier and happier! But ſtill I verily think you cannot be more happy than your father and mother, except in this one thing, that all *our* happineſs under God, proceeds from you; and, as other parents bleſs their children with plenty and benefits, you have bleſs'd your parents (or your honoured huſband rather for your ſake) with all the good things this world can afford.

The papers you ſend us are the joy of our leiſure hours; and you are kind beyond all expreſſion, in taking care to oblige us with them. We know how your time is taken up, and ought to be very well contented, if but now-and then you let us hear of your health and welfare. But it is not enough with ſuch a good daughter, that you have made our lives *comfortable*, but you will make them *joyful* too, by communicating to us, all that befals you: and then you write ſo piouſly, and with ſuch a ſenſe of God's goodneſs to you, and intermix ſuch good reflections in your writings, that whether it be our partial love or not, I cannot tell, but, truly, we think, nobody comes up to you: and you make our hearts and our eyes ſo often overflow, as we read, that we join hand in hand together, and I ſay to her—'Bleſſed be God, and bleſſed be 'you, my dear,' and ſhe, in the ſame breath—'Bleſſed be God and you, my 'love.'—'For ſuch a daughter,' ſays the one—'For ſuch a daughter,' ſays the other.—'And ſhe has your own ſweet 'temper,' cry I.—'And ſhe has your 'own honeſt heart,' cries ſhe: and ſo we go on, bleſſing God, and bleſſing you, and bleſſing your ſpouſe, and bleſſing ourſelves!—Is any happineſs like our happineſs, my dear daughter!

Really and indeed we are ſo inraptured with your writings, that when our ſpirits flag through the infirmity of years which hath begun to take hold of us, we have recourſe to ſome of your papers.—'Come, my dear,' cry I, 'what ſay 'you to a banquet now?'—She knows what I mean. 'With all my heart,' ſays ſhe. So I read, although it be on a Sunday, ſo good are your letters; and you muſt know, I have copies of a many of them: and after a little while we are as much alive and briſk, as if we had no fa[illegible] at all, and return to the duties of the [illegible] [illegible] be [illegible]

Con[illegible] then, my dear child, what [illegible] writings give [illegible] and we [illegible] [illegible] [illegible], who have [illegible] [illegible] kinds, and we are [illegible], and you have found out a [illegible] to [illegible] yourself, and re[illegible] us [illegible] [illegible] worthy a young [illegible] Darnford, [illegible] I never [illegible] forget her dear good[illegible] to me, and the notice she took of me at the Hall *, and [illegible] pressing my rough hands with her fine hands, and looking [illegible] much kindness in her eyes —to be sure I never shall—What good people, as well as bad, there are in high stations!—Thank God there are, else our poor child would have had a sad time of it too often, when she was obliged to *[illegible] of herself*, as once I heard you praise it, into company you could not *[illegible]*.

Well, but what shall I say more? and yet now shall I end?—Only, with my prayers, that God will continue to you the blessing and comforts you are in possession of!—And pray now, be not over-thoughtful about what may happen at London, for why should you let the dread of future evils lessen your present joys? There is no [illegible] [illegible] in this life, that is true, but one would make one's self as easy as one could. 'Tis time enough to be troubled when troubles come.—' *Sufficient unto the day* ' *is the evil thereof.*'

Rejoice then, my dear child, as you have often said you would, in your present blessings, and leave the event of things to the Supreme Disposer of all events. And what have you to do but rejoice? *You*, who cannot see a [illegible], but [illegible] to bless you, and to raise up from the [illegible] numbers to join in the blessing? *You*, who [illegible] your high born friends, and your low born parents, and obscure relations! who can [illegible] the rich by your example, and the poor by your bounty, and bless besides so good and so brave a husband —O my dear child, what, I [illegible] [illegible], have *you* to do but rejoice? —*For many daughters have done [illegible], but you have excelled them all*.

I will only add, that every thing the 'squire ordered, is [illegible] upon the point of being finished. And when the good time comes, that we shall be again fa[illegible]voured with his presence and yours, what a [illegible] greater joy will this afford to the [illegible] overflowing hearts of *your ever loving father and mother*,

JOHN *and* ELIZ. A. DREWS!

LETTER XXVII

MY DEAREST MISS DARNFORD,

THE interest I take in every thing that concerns you, makes me very importunate to know how you approve the gentleman, whom some of his best friends and well wishers have recommended to your favour. I hope he will deserve your good opinion, and then he must excel most of the unmarried gentlemen in England.

Your papa, in his humorous manner, mentions his large possessions and riches: but, indeed, were he as rich as Crœsus, he should not have my consent, if he has no greater merit, though that is what the generality of parents look out for first: and indeed an easy fortune is so far from being to be disregarded, that, when attended with equal merit, I think it ought to have a *preference* given to it, supposing affections disengaged. For 'tis certain, that a man or woman may stand as good a chance for happiness in a marriage with a person of fortune, as with one who has not that advantage, and notwithstanding I had neither riches nor descent to boast of, I must be of opinion with those who say, that they never knew any Lady despise either, that had them. But to permit riches to be the *principal* inducement, to the neglect of superior merit, that is the fault which many a one smarts for, whether the choice be their own, or imposed upon them by those who have a title to their obedience.

Here is a saucy body, might some, who have not Miss Darnford's kind consideration for her friend, be apt to say, who being thus meanly descended, nevertheless presumes to give her opinion in these high cases unasked. But I have one thing, my dear Miss, to say, and that is, that I think myself so intirely divested of partiality to my own case, that, as far as my judgment shall permit, I will never have that in view, when I am presuming to hint my opinion of general rules. For, most surely, the honours I have received, and the debasement to which my best

* See Vol. I. p. 177.

friend

friend has subjected himself, have, for their principal excuse, that the gentleman was richly independent, had no questions to ask, and had a fortune sufficient to make himself, as well as the person he chose, happy, though she brought him nothing at all, and that he had, moreover, such a character for good sense, and knowledge of the world, that nobody could impute to him any other inducement, but that of a noble resolution to reward a virtue he had so frequently, and, I will say, so wickedly, tried, and could not subdue.

But why do I thus run on to Miss Darnford, whose partial friendship attributes to me merits I cannot claim? I will, therefore, quit this subject, as a needless one to her, and proceed to what was principally in my view, when I began to write, and that is, to complain of your papa, who has, let me say it, done his endeavours to set at variance a gentleman and his wife.

I will not enter into the particulars, because the appeal is to Cæsar, and it would look like invading his prerogative, to take it into my own hands. But I can tell Sir Simon, that he is the only gentleman, I hope, who, when a young person of my sex asked him to make her a present of a book, would put such a mischievous turn as he has done upon it, to her husband!—Indeed, from the *beginning*, I had reason to call him a * tell tale—But, no more of that—yet I must say, I had rather he should have flung his book at *my* head too, than to have made a so much worse use of it. But I came off tolerably, no thanks to Sir Simon, however!—And *out* tolerably neither; for Mr B. kept me in suspense a good while, and put me in great flutters, before he let me into the matter.

But I was much concerned, my dear Miss Darnford, at first, till you gave a reason I better liked afterwards, for Sir Simon's denying your company to me, after I had obtained the favour of your mamma's consent, and you were kindly inclined yourself to oblige me; and that was, that Sir Simon had a bad opinion of the honour of my dear Mr B. For, as to that part of his doubt, which reflected dishonour upon his dear daughter, it was all but the effect of his strange free humour, on purpose to vex you.

That gentleman must be the most abandoned of men, who would attempt any thing against the virtue of a lady, intrusted to his protection; and I am grieved, methinks, that the dear man, who is the better part of myself, and has, to his own debasement, acted so honourably by me, should be thought capable of so much vileness. But, forgive me, Miss, it is only Sir Simon, I dare say, who could think so hardly of him; and I am in great hope, for the honour of the present age, (quite contrary to the aspersion, that every age grows worse and worse) that the *last*, if it produced people capable of such attempts, was wickeder than this.

Bad as Mr B.'s designs and attempts were upon me, I can, now I am set above fearing them, and am enabled to reflect upon them with less terror and apprehension, be earnest, for his own dear sake, to think him not, even *then*, the worst of men, though bad enough in all conscience; for have we not heard of those who have had no remorse or compunction at all, and have actually executed all their vile purposes, when a poor creature was in their power?—Yet (indeed, after sore trials, that's true!) did not God turn his heart? And although I was still helpless, and without any friend in the world, and in the hands of a poor vile woman, who, to be sure, was worse than he, provoking him to ruin me, and so wholly in his power, that I durst not disobey him, whether he bade me come to him, or be gone from him, as he was pleased or displeased with me, yet, I say, for all this, did he not overcome his criminal passion, and entertain an honourable one, though to his poor servant girl, and brave the world, and the world's censures, and marry me?

And does not this shew that the seeds of honour were kept alive in his heart, though choaked or kept from sprouting forth, for a time, by the weeds of sensuality, pride, and youthful impetuosity? And by cutting down the latter, have not the former taken root, have they not shot out, and, in their turn, *kept down*, at least, the depressed weeds? And who now lives more virtuously than Mr B.?

Let me tell you, my dear Miss, that I have not heard of many instances of gentlemen, who, having designed vilely, have stopt short and acted so honourably, and who continue to act so nobly; and I have

* See Vol. I. p. 115.

great confidence, that he will, in time, be as pious, as he is now moral, for though he has a few bad notions, which he talks of now and then, as to gaming, and such like, which indeed, give me a little serious thought sometimes, because a man is too apt to practise what he has persuaded himself to believe is no crime, yet, I hope, they are owing more to the liveliness of his wit, (a wild quality, which does not always confine itself to proper exercises) than to his judgment And if I can but see the first three or four months residence over in that wicked London, (which, they say, is so seducing a place) without adding to my apprehensions, how happy shall I be?

So much, slightly, have I thought proper to say in behalf of my dear Mr B For a good wife cannot but hope for a sweeter and more elevated companionship, (if her presumptuous heart makes her look upward with hope herself) than this transitory state can afford us And what a sad case is hers, who being as exemplary as human frailty will permit her to be, looks forward upon the partner of her adverse, and of her prosperous estate, the husband of her bosom, the father of her children, the head of her family, as a poor unhappy soul, destined to a separate and a miserable existence for ever!—O my dear friend!—How can such a thought be supportable!—But what high consolation, what transport rather, at times, must hers be, who shall be blessed with the hope of being an humble instrument to reclaim such a dear, dear, thrice dear partner!—And that, heart in heart, and hand in hand, they shall one day issue forth from this incumbered state into a blessed eternity, benefited by each other's example!—I will lay down my pen, and enjoy the rich thought for a few moments

Now, my dear Miss Darnford, let me, as a subject very pleasing to me, touch upon your kind mention of the worthy Mr Peters's sentiments in relation to that part of his conduct to me, which (oppressed by the terrors and apprehensions to which I was subjected) once indeed I censured, and so much the rather, as I had ever so great an honour for his cloth, that I thought, to be a clergyman, and all that was compassionate, good and virtuous, was the same thing

But when I came to know Mr Peters, I had a high opinion of his worthiness, and as no one can be perfect in this life, thus I thought to myself How hard was then my lot, to be a cause of stumbling to so worthy a heart! To be sure, a gentleman, who knows so well, and practises so well, his duty, in every other instance, and preaches it so efficaciously to others, must have been *one day* sensible, that it would not have misbecome his function and character to have afforded that protection to oppressed innocence, which was requested of him, and how would it have grieved his considerate mind, had my ruin been compleated, that he did not!

But as he had once a name-sake, as one may say, that failed in a much greater instance, let not *my* want of charity exceed *his* fault, but let me look upon it as an infirmity, to which the most perfect are liable I was a stranger to him, a servant girl carried off by her master, a young gentleman of violent and lawless passions, who, in this very instance, shewed how much in earnest he was set upon effecting all his vile purposes, and whose heart although *God* might touch, it was not probable any lesser influence could

Then he was not sure, that though he might assist my escape, I might not afterwards fall again into the hands of so determined a violator, and that difficulty would not, with such a one, inhance his resolution to overcome all obstacles

Moreover, he might think, that the person, who was moving him to this worthy measure, might possibly be seeking to gratify a view of his own, and that while he was endeavouring to save, to outward appearance, a virtue in danger, he was, in reality, only helping another to a wife, at the hazard of exposing himself to the vindictiveness of a violent temper, and a rich neighbour, who had power as well as will to resent, for such was his * apprehension, groundless, intirely groundless as it was, though not improbable, as it might seem to him

Then again, the sad examples set by too many European sovereigns, in whom the *royal* and *priestly offices* are united (for are not kings the *Lord's anointed*?) and the little scruple which many persons, right reverend by their functions and characters, too generally make, to pay sordid courts and visits (far from bearing their testimony against such prac-

* Vol I p 26.

tices)

ters) *even to concubines, who have in*terest to promote them*, are no small discouragements to a private clergyman to do his duty, and to make himself enemies among his powerful neighbours, for the cause of virtue. And especially (forgive me, dear Sir Simon Darnford, if you should see this) when an eminent magistrate, one of the principal gentlemen of the county, of an independent *fortune*, who had *fine young ladies to* his daughters, (who had nothing but their superior conditions, not their sex, to exempt them from like attempts) a justice of peace, and of the *quorum*, refused to BE a † justice, though such a breach of the *peace* was made, and such a violation of *morals* plainly intended. This, I say, must add to the discouragement of a gentleman a little too diffident and timorous of himself; and who having no one to second him, had he afforded me his protection, must have stood alone in the gap, and made to himself, in an active gentleman, an enemy who had a thousand desirable qualities to make one wish him for a friend.

For all these considerations, I think myself obliged to pity, rather than too rigorously to censure, the worthy gentleman. And I must and will always respect him. And thank him a thousand times, my dear, in my name, for his *goodness in condescending* to acknowledge, by your hand, his infirmity, as such: for this gives an excellent proof of the natural worthiness of his heart, and that it is beneath him to seek to extenuate a fault, when he thinks he has committed one.

Indeed, my dear friend, I have so much honour for the clergy of all degrees, that I never forget in my prayers one article, that God will make them shining lights to the world, since so much depends on their ministry and examples, as well with respect to our publick as private duties. Nor shall the faults of a few make impression upon me to the disadvantage of the order. For I am afraid a very censorious temper, in this respect, is too generally the indication of an uncharitable and perhaps a profligate heart, levelling characters, in order to cover some inward pride, or secret enormities, which they are ashamed to avow, and *will not be instructed to amend*.

Forgive, my dear, this tedious scribble, I cannot for my life write short letters to those I love. And let me hope, that you will favour me with an account of your new affair, and how you proceed in it, and with such of your conversations, as may give me some notion of a polite courtship. For, alas! your poor friend knows nothing of this! All her courtship was sometimes a hasty snatch of the hand, a black and blue gripe of the arm, and—'Whither now?—Come to 'me when I bid you!' And Saucy face, and Creature, and such like, on his part—with fear and trembling on mine, and—'I will, I will!—Good Sir, have mer'cy!' At other times a scream, and nobody to hear or mind me, and with uplift hands bent knees, and tears in eyes—'For God's sake, pity your poor '*servant*!'

This, my dear Miss Darnford, was the hard treatment that attended my courtship—Pray, then, let me know, how gentlemen court their equals in degree, how they look when they address you, with their knees bent, sighing, supplicating, and *all that*, as Sir Simon says, with the words Slave, Servant, Admirer, continually at their tongues ends.

But after all, it will be found, I believe, that, be the language and behaviour ever so obsequious, it is all designed to end alike.—The English, the plain English, of the politest address, is—'I am now, 'dear Madam, your humble servant: 'pray be so good as to let me be your 'master.'—'Yes, and thank you too,' says the lady's heart, though not her lips, if she likes him. And so they go to church together: and, in conclusion, it will be happy, if these obsequious courtships end no worse than my frightful one.

But I am convinced, that with a man of sense, a woman of tolerable prudence *must* be happy.

That whenever you marry, it may be to such a man, who then must value you as you deserve, and make you happy as I now am, notwithstanding all that's past, wishes and prays *your obliged friend and servant*,

P. B.

N. B. Although Miss Darnford could *not receive the above letter so soon, as to*

* That these arguments were pleaded by Mr. Peters, see Vol. I. p. 86.

† Ibid.

answer, but before others were sent to her by her fair correspondent, yet we think it not amiss to dispense with the order of time, that the reader may have the letter and answer at one view; and shall on other occasions take the like liberty.

LETTER XXVIII.

IN ANSWER TO THE PRECEDING.

MY DEAR MRS. B.

YOU charm us all with your letters. Mr. Peters says, he never could go to bed, nor rest, but he will pray for you, and desires I will return his thankful acknowledgments for your favourable opinion of him, and kind allowances. If there be an angel on earth, he says you are one. My papa, although he has seen your stinging reflection upon his refusal to protect you, is delighted with you too, and says, when you come down to Lincolnshire again, he will be *undertaken* by you in good earnest, for he thinks it was wrong in him, to deny you his protection.

We are pleased with your apology for Mr. B. 'Tis so much the part of a good wife to extenuate her husband's faults, and make the best of his bad qualities, in order to give the world a good opinion of him, that, together with the affecting instances of your humility, in looking back with so much true greatness of mind, to what you were, make us all join to admire you, and own, that nobody can deserve what you deserve.

Yet I am sorry, my dear friend, to find, notwithstanding your defence of Mr. B. that you have any apprehensions about London. 'Tis pity any thing should give you concern. As to Mr. B.'s talking in favour of polygamy, you cannot expect, that he can shake off all his bad notions at once. And it must be a great comfort to you, that his *actions* do not correspond, and that his libertinisms have been reduced to *notions* only. In time, we hope that he will be every thing you wish him. If not, with such an example before him, he will be the more culpable.

We all smiled at the description of your own uncommon courtship. And, as they say, the days of courtship are the happiest part of life, if we had not known that your days of marriage are happier by far than any other body's courtship, we must needs have pitied you. But as the one were days of trial and temptation, the other are days of reward and happiness. May the last always continue to be so, and you'll have no occasion to think any body happier than Mrs. B.!

I thank you heartily for your good wishes as to the man of sense. Mr. Murray has been here, and continues his visits. He is a lively gentleman, well enough in his person, has a tolerable character, yet loves company, and will take his bottle freely; my papa likes him never the worse for that. He talks a good deal, dresses gay, and even richly, and seems to like his own person very well: no great pleasure this for a lady to look forward to, yet he falls far short of that genteel ease, and graceful behaviour, which distinguish your Mr. B. from any-body I know.

I wish Mr. Murray would apply to my sister. She is an ill-natured girl; but would make a good wife, I hope, and fancy she'd like him well enough. I can't say I do. He laughs too much, has something boisterous in his conversation, his complaisance is not a pretty complaisance: he is, however, well versed in country sports, and my papa loves him for that too, and says—'He is a most accomplished gentleman.'—'Yes, Sir,' cry I, 'as gentlemen go.'—'You *must* be saucy,' says Sir Simon, 'because the man offers himself to your acceptance. A few years hence, perhaps, if you remain single, you'll alter your note, Polly, and be willing to jump at a much less worthy tender.'

I could not help answering that, although I paid due honour to every thing that my papa was pleased to say, I could not but hope he would be mistaken in this.

But I have broken my mind to my dear, my indulgent mamma, who tells me, she will do me all the pleasure she can, but would be loth the youngest daughter should *go first*, as she calls it. But if I could come and live with you a little now-and-then, I did not care who married, unless such an one offered, as I never expect.

I have great hope, the gentleman will be easily persuaded to quit me for Nancy, for I see he has not delicacy enough to love with any great distinction. He says, as my mamma tells me by the-bye, that I am the handsomest, and best humoured, and he has found out, as he thinks, that I have some wit, and have ease and freedom

dom (and he tacks innocence to them) in my address and conversation. 'Tis well for me, *he* is of this opinion, for if he thinks justly, which I much question, *any-body* may think so still much more; for I have been far from taking pains to engage his good word, having been under more reserve to him, than ever I was before to any body.

Indeed, I can't help it, for the gentleman is forward without delicacy, and (pardon me, Sir Simon,) my papa has not one bit of it neither, but is for pushing matters on, with his rough raillery, that puts me out of countenance, and has already adjusted the sordid part of the preliminaries, as he tells me.

Yet I hope Nancy's three thousand pound fortune more than I am likely to have*, will give her the wished for preference with Mr Murray, and then, as to a brother in law, in prospect, I can put off all restraint, and return to my usual freedom.

This is all that occurs worthy of notice from us: but from you, we expect an account of Lady Davers's visit, and of the conversations that offer among you, and you have so delightful a way of making every thing momentous, either by your subject or reflections, or both, that we long for every post day, in hopes of the pleasure of a letter.—And your's I will always carefully preserve, as so many testimonies of the honour I receive in this correspondence: which will be always esteemed as it deserves, by, my dear Mrs B. *your obliged and faithful,*

POLLY DARNFORD.

Mrs Peters, Mrs Jones, my papa, mamma, and sister, present their respects. Mr Peters I mentioned before. He continues to give a very good account of poor Jewkes, and is much pleased with her.

LETTER XXIX.

MY DEAR MISS DARNFORD,

AT your desire, and to oblige your honoured mamma, and your good neighbours, I will now acquaint you with the arrival of Lady Davers, and will occasionally write what passes among us. I will not say worthy of notice; for were I only to do so, I should be more brief, perhaps, by much, than you seem to expect. But as my time is pretty much taken up, and I find I shall be obliged to write a bit now, and a bit then, you must excuse me, if I dispense with some forms, which I ought to observe, when I write to one I so dearly love, and so I will give it journal wise, as it were, and have no regard, when it would fetter or break in upon my freedom of narration, to inscription or subscription, but send it as I have opportunity: and if you please to favour me so far, as to lend it me, after you have read the stuff, for the perusal of my father and mother, to whom my duty and promise require me to give an account of my proceedings, it will save me transcription, for which I shall have no time, and then you will excuse blots and blurs, and I will trouble myself no farther for apologies on that score, but this once for all.

If you think it worth while, when they have read it, you shall have it again.

WEDNESDAY MORNING, SIX O'CLOCK.

FOR my dear friend permits me to rise an hour sooner than usual, that I may have time to scribble, for he is always pleased to see me so employed, or in reading, often saying, when I am at my needle, (as his sister once wrote†) 'Your 'maids can do this, Pamela, but they 'cannot write as you can.' And yet, as he tells me, when I choose to follow my needle, as a diversion from too intense study, as he is pleased to call it, (but, alas! I know not what study is, as may be easily guessed by my hasty writing, putting down every thing as it comes) I shall then do as I please. But you must understand I promised at setting out, what a good wife I'd endeavour to make‡, and every honest body should try to be as good as her word, you know, and such particulars as I then mentioned, I think I ought to dispense with as little as possible, especially as I promised no more than what was my duty to perform, if I had *not* promised.—But what a preamble is here? Judge by it what impertinencies you may expect as I proceed.

Yesterday about six in the evening arrived here my Lord and Lady Davers, their nephew, and the Countess of C.

* See Vol II page 198. † See this Vol p 310. ‡ Vol. II p 158.

mother

mother of Lady Betty, whom we did not expect, but took it for the greater favour. It seems her ladyship longed, as she said, to see *me*; and this was her principal inducement. The two ladies, and their two women, were in Lord Davers's coach and six; and my lord and his nephew rode on horseback, attended with a train of servants.

We had expected them to dinner, but they could not reach time enough; for the countess being a little incommoded with her journey, the coach travelled slowly. My lady would not suffer her lord, nor his nephew to come hither before her, though on horseback, because she would be present, she said, when his lordship first saw me, he having quite forgot *her mother's Pamela*; that was her word.

It rained when they came in, so the coach drove directly to the door, and Mr. B. received them there; but I was in a little sort of flutter, which Mr. B. observing, made me sit down in the parlour to compose myself. 'Where's Pamela?' said my lady, as soon as she alighted.

I stept out, lest she should take it amiss; and she took my hand, and kissed me. 'Here, my lady countess,' said she, presenting me to her—'here's the girl: see if I said too much in praise of her person.'

The countess saluted me with a visible pleasure in her eye, and said—'Indeed, Lady Davers, you have not. 'Twould have been strange, (excuse me, Mrs. B. for I know your story) if such a fine flower had not been transplanted from the field to the garden.'

I made no return, but by a low curtsey, to her ladyship's compliment. Then Lady Davers taking my hand again, presented me to her lord. 'See here, my lord, my mother's Pamela.'—'And see here, my lord,' said her generous brother, taking my other hand most kindly, 'see here your brother's Pamela too!'

My lord saluted me. 'I do,' said he to his lady. 'I do,' said he to his brother; 'and I see the first person in her, that has exceeded my expectation, when every mouth had *prepared* me to expect a wonder.'

Mr. H. whom every one calls Lord Jackey, after his aunt's example, when she is in good humour with him, and who is a very *young* gentleman, though about as old as my best friend, came to me next, and said—'Lovelier and lovelier, by my life!—I never saw your peer, Madam.'

Will you excuse me, my dear, all this seeming vanity, for the sake of repeating exactly what passed?

'Well, but,' said my lady, taking my hand, in her free quality way, which quite dashed me, and holding it at a distance, and turning me half round, her eye fixed to my waist, 'let me observe you a little, my sweet-faced girl!—I hope I am right: I hope you will do credit to my brother, as he has done you credit.—Why do you let her lace so tight, Mr. B.?'

I was unable to look up, as you may believe, Miss; my face, all over scarlet, was hid in my bosom, and I looked *so silly*!—

'Ay,' said my naughty lady, 'you may well look down, my good girl: for works of this nature will not be long hidden.—And, O! my lady, (to the countess) 'see now, like a pretty *thief* she looks!'

'Dear my lady!' said I—for still she kept looking at me; and her good brother, seeing my confusion, in pity to me, pressed my blushing face a moment to his generous breast, and said—'Lady Davers, you should not be thus hard upon my dear girl, the moment you see her, and before so many witnesses.—but look up, my best love, take your revenge of my sister, and tell her, you wish her in the same way.'

'It is so then,' said my lady! 'I'm glad of it with all my heart. I will now love you better and better;—but I almost doubted it, seeing her still so slender.—But if, my good child, you lace too tight, I'll never forgive you.' And so she gave me a kiss of congratulation, as she said.

Do you think I did not look very silly?—My lord, smiling, and gazing at me from head to foot; Lord Jackey grinning and laughing, like an oaf, as I then, in my spite, thought. Indeed the countess said, encouragingly to me, but severely on persons of birth—'Lady Davers, you are as much too teazing, as Mrs. B. is too bashful.—But you are a happy man, Mr. B. that your lady's bashfulness is the principal mark by which we can judge she is not of quality.' Lord Jackey, in the language of some character in a play, cried out—'*A palpable hit, by Jupiter!*' and laughed egregiously, running about from one to another, repeating the same words.

We talked only upon common topicks till supper-time, and I was all ear, as I

thought

thought it became me to be, for the countess had by her first compliment, and by an aspect as noble as intelligent, over-awed me, as I may say, into a respectful silence, to which Lady Davers's free, though pleasant raillery, (which she could not help carrying on now-and-then) contributed. Besides, Lady Davers's letters had given me still greater reason to revere her wit and judgment than I had before, when I reflected on her passionate temper, and such parts of the conversation I had had with her ladyship in your neighbourhood; which (however to be admired) fell short of her letters.

When we were to sit down at table, I looked, I suppose, a little diffidently, for I really then thought of my lady's anger at the Hall, when she would not have permitted me to sit at table with her*, and Mr B saying—'Take your place, my 'dear, you keep our friends standing,' I sat down in my usual seat. And my lady said—'None of your reproaching 'eye, Pamela, I know what you hint at 'by it: and every letter I have received 'from you, has helped to make me cen'sure myself for my *lady-airs*, as you 'call 'em, you saucebox you. I told you, 'I'd *lady-airs* you when I saw you, 'and you shall have it all in good time.'

'I'm sure,' said I, 'I shall have no'thing from your ladyship, but what will 'be very agreeable: but, indeed, I never 'meant any thing particular by that, or 'any other word that I wrote, nor could 'I think of any thing but what was 'highly respectful to your ladyship.'

Lord Davers was pleased to say, that it was impossible I should either write or speak any thing that could be taken amiss.

Lady Davers, after supper, and the servants were withdrawn, began a discourse on titles, and said—'Brother, I think you 'should hold yourself obliged to my Lord 'Davers, for he has spoken to Lord S. 'who made him a visit a few days ago, 'to procure you a baronet's patent. Your 'estate, and the figure you make in the 'world, are so considerable, and your fa'mily besides is so ancient, that, me'thinks, you should wish for some dis'tinction of that sort.'

'Yes, brother,' said my lord, 'I did 'mention it to Lord S. and told him, 'withal, that it was without your know'ledge or desire, that I spoke about it, 'and I was not very sure you would ac'cept of it, but 'tis a thing your sister 'has wished for a good while.'

'What answer did my Lord S. make 'to it?' said Mr B.

'He said—"We," meaning the mi'nisters, I suppose, "should be glad to "oblige a man of Mr B.'s figure in the "world, but you mention it so slightly, "that you can hardly expect courtiers "will tender it to any gentleman that is "so indifferent about it, for, Lord Da"vers, we seldom grant honours with"out a view, I tell you that,"' added he, 'smiling.'

'My Lord S. might mention this as a 'jest,' returned Mr B. 'but he spoke the 'truth. But your lordship said well, 'that I was indifferent about it. 'Tis 'true, 'tis an hereditary title: but the 'rich citizens, who used to be satisfied 'with the title of Knight, (till they made 'it so common, that it is brought into 'as great contempt almost as that of the† 'French knights of St Michael, and 'nobody cares to accept of it) now are 'ambitious of this, and, as I apprehend, 'it is hastening apace into like disrepute. 'Besides, 'tis a novel honour, and what 'the ancestors of our family, who lived 'at its institution, would never accept 'of. But were it a peerage they would 'give me, which has some essential pri'vileges and splendours annexed to it, 'that would make it desirable to some 'men, I would not enter into conditions 'for it. Titles at best,' added he, 'are 'but shadows, and he that has the sub'stance, should be above valuing them: 'for who that has the whole bird, would 'pride himself upon a single feather?'

'But,' said my lady, 'although I ac'knowledge, that the institution is of late 'date, yet, as abroad, as well as at home, 'it is regarded as a title of dignity, and 'it is supposed, that the best families 'among the gentry are distinguished by 'it, I should be glad you would accept 'of it. And as to citizens who have it, 'they are not many, and some of this 'class of people, or their immediate de'scendants however, have bought them'selves into the peerage itself of the one 'kingdom or the other.'

* See Vol II p 249

† This order was become so scandalously common in France, that, in order to suppress it, the hangman was vested with the ensigns of it, which effectually abolished it.

'As to what it is looked upon abroad,' said Mr B. 'this is of no weight at all; for when an Englishman travels, be he of what degree he will, if he has an equipage, and squanders his money away, he is a lord of course with foreigners; and therefore Sir Such-a-one is rather a diminution to him, as it fixes him down to a lower title than his vanity would perhaps make him aspire to be thought in the possession of. Then, as to citizens, in a trading nation like this, I am not displeased in the main, with seeing the overgrown ones, creeping into nominal honours, and we have so many of our first titled families who have allied themselves to trade, (whose inducements were riches only) that it ceases to be either a wonder as to the fact, or a disgrace to the honour.'

'Well, brother,' said my lady, 'I will tell you farther, the thing may be had for asking for: if you will but go to court, and desire to kiss the king's hand, that will be all the trouble you'll have; and pray now oblige me in it.'

'If a title would make me either a better or a wiser man,' replied Mr B. 'I would embrace it with pleasure. Besides, I am not so intirely satisfied with some of the measures now pursuing, as to owe any obligation to the ministers. Accepting of a small title from them, is but like putting on their badge, or listing under their banners, like a certain lord we all know, who accepted of one degree more of title to shew he was theirs, and would not have an higher, lest it should be thought a satisfaction for, or amount to half, the pension he demanded; and could I be easy to have it supposed, that I was an ungrateful man for voting as I pleased, because they gave me the title of a Baronet?'

The countess said, she had always thought Mr B. to be a man of steady principles, and not attached to any party, and it was her opinion, that it was far from being inconsistent with any gentleman's honour and independency, to accept of a title from a prince he acknowledged as his sovereign.

'Tis very true, Madam,' replied Mr B. 'that I am attached to no party, nor ever will, and I have a mean opinion of many of the heads of both; nay, I will say further, that I think in my heart, the gentlemen in the administration would pursue such measures, that I could give them every vote, as I am also with every one that I can, and I have no very high opinion of those who, right or wrong, would distress or embarrass a government. For this is certain, that our governors cannot be always in the wrong, and he therefore who never gives them a vote, must sometimes be in the wrong, as well as they, and must, moreover, have some view he will not own. But in a country like ours, where each of the legislative powers is in a manner independent, and where they are designed as mutual checks upon one another, I have, notwithstanding, so great an opinion of the necessity of an opposition sometimes, that I am convinced it is that which must preserve our constitution. I will therefore be a *country gentleman*, in the true sense of the word, and will accept of no favour that shall make any-one think I would *not* be of the opposition when I think it a necessary one, as, on the other hand, I should scorn to make myself a round to any man's ladder of preferment, or a caballer for the sake of my own.'

'You say well, brother,' returned Lady Davers, 'but you may undoubtedly keep your own principles and independency, and yet pay your duty to the king, and accept of this title, for your family and fortune will be a greater ornament to the title, than the title to you.'

'Then what occasion have I for it, if that be the case, Madam?'

'Why, I can't say, but I should be glad you had it, for your family's sake, as it is an hereditary honour. Then it would mend the style of your spouse here, for the good girl is at such a loss for an epithet when she writes, that I see the constraint she lies under. It is—"*My dear gentleman, my best friend, my benefactor, my dear Mr B.*" —whereas Sir William would turn off her periods more roundly, and no other soft epithets would be wanting.'

'To me,' replied he, 'who always delight to be distinguished as my Pamela's best friend, and think it an honour to be called *her dear Mr B.* and *her dear man*, this reason weighs very little, unless there were no other Sir William in the kingdom than *her* Sir William, for I am very emulous of her favour, I can tell you, and think it no small distinction.'

I blushed at this too great honour, before

fore such company, and was afraid my lady would be a little piqued at it But after a pause, she said—'Well then, 'brother, will you let Pamela decide 'upon this point?

'Rightly put, said the countess 'Pray let Mrs B choose for you, Sir 'My lady has hit the thing'

'Very good, very good, by my soul,' says Lord Jackey, 'let my *young aunt*, *that was his word*, 'choose for you, Sir

'Well then, Pamela, said Mr B 'give us your opinion, as to this point

'But, first, said Lady Davers, 'say 'you will be determined by it, or else 'she will be laid under a difficulty

'Well then, replied he, 'be it so.— 'I will be determined by your opinion, 'my dear give it me freely

Lord Jackey rubbed his hands together—'Charming, charming, as I hope 'to live! By Jove, this is just as I 'wished!

'Well, now Pamela,' said my lady, 'speak your true heart without disguise 'I charge you do

'Why then, gentlemen and ladies, said I, 'if I must be so bold as to speak 'on a subject, upon which, on several 'accounts, it would become me to be 'silent, I should be *against* the title, 'but perhaps my reason is of too private 'a nature, to weigh any thing, and if 'so, it would not become me to have any 'choice at all'

They all called upon me for my reason, and I said looking down a little abashed—'It is this Here my dear Mr 'B has disparaged himself by distinguishing, as he has done, such a low 'creature as I, and the world will be 'apt to say, he is seeking to repair *one* '*way* the honour he has lost *another*, 'and then, perhaps, it will be attributed 'to *my* pride and ambition "Here," 'they will perhaps say, "the proud cot "tager will needs be a lady, in hopes to "conceal her descent, whereas, had I 'such a vain thought, it would be but 'making it the more remembered against 'both Mr B and myself And indeed, 'as to my own part, I take too much 'pride in having been lifted up into this 'distinction, for the causes to which I 'owe it, your brother's *bounty* and *generosity*, than to be ashamed of what I '*was* only now and then I am concerned for his own sake, lest he should 'be too much censured But this would 'not be prevented, but rather be promoted by the title So I am humbly 'of opinion against the title'

Mr B had hardly patience to hear me out, but came to me, and folding his arms about me, said—'Just as I wished, 'have you answered, my beloved Pamela I was never yet deceived in you, '*no, not once*

'Madam, said he to the countess, Lord Davers, Lady Davers, 'do we 'want any titles, think you, to make 'us happy, but what we can confer upon 'ourselves?' And he pressed my hand to his lips, as he always honours me most in company, and went to his place highly pleased, while his fine manner drew tears from my eyes, and made his noble sister's and the countess's glisten too

'Well, for my part, said Lady Davers, 'thou art a strange girl where, as 'my brother once said*, gottest thou all 'this? Then, pleasantly humorous, as if she was angry, she changed her tone—'What signify thy *meek* words 'and *humble* speeches, when by thy *actions*, as well as *sentiments*, thou reflectest upon us all? Pamela, said she, 'have less merit, or take care to conceal 'it better I shall otherwise have no more 'patience with thee, than thy monarch 'has just now shewn

The countess was pleased to say— 'You're a happy couple indeed!—And 'I must needs repeat to you, Mr B 'four lines of Sir William Davenant, 'upon a lady who could not possibly deserve them so much as yours does

"She ne'er saw courts, but courts cou'd have
"outdone
"With untaught looks, and an unprac
"tis'd heart,
"Her nets, the most prepar'd could nev'r
"shun,
"For Nature spread them in the scorn
"of Art

But, my dear Miss Darnford, how lucky one sometimes is, in having what one says well accepted! Ay, that is all in all Since the reason for the answer I gave was so obvious, that one in my circumstances could not have miss'd it Yet what compliments had I upon it!

* See Vol. I. p. 34.

This a sign they were prepared to think well of me, and that is my great pleasure and happiness.

Such sort of entertainment as this you are to expect from your correspondent. I cannot do better than I can, and it may appear such a mixture of self-praise, vanity, and impertinence, that I expect you to tell me freely, as soon as this comes to your hand, whether it be tolerable to you. Yet I must write on, for my dear father and mother's sake, who require it of me, and are prepared to approve of every thing that comes from me, for no other reason but that: and I think you ought to leave me to write to them only, as I cannot hope it will be interesting to any body else, without expecting as much partiality and favour from others, as I have from my dear parents. Mean time I conclude here my first conversation piece, and am, and [illegible], *always your*, &c.

P. B.

LETTER XXX.

[illegible] MORNING, SIX O'CLOCK.

OUR breakfast conversation yesterday (at which only Mrs. Worden, my lady's woman, and my Polly attended) was so whimsically particular, (though I doubt some of it, at least, will appear too trifling) that I cannot help acquainting my dear Miss Darnford with it, who is desirous of knowing all that relates to Lady Davers's conduct towards me.

You must know then, that I have the honour to stand very high in the graces of Lord Davers, who on every occasion is pleased to call me his *good Sister*, his *dear Sister*, and sometimes his *charming Sister*, and he tells me, he will not be out of my company for an hour together, while he stays here, if he can help it.

My lady seems to relish this very well in the main, though she cannot quite so readily, yet, frame her mouth to the sound of the word *Sister*, as my lord does, of which this that follows is one instance.

His lordship had called me by that [illegible] times before, and saying—'I wish [illegible] dear, I [illegible], my good *Sister*'— My lady said—'Your lordship has got a word by the end, that [illegible] I have taken notice, that you have called Pamela, *Sister*, *Sister*, *Sister*, no less than three times in a quarter of an hour.'

My lord looked a little serious. 'I shall one day,' said he, 'be allowed to choose my own words and phrases, I hope—Your sister, Mr. B.' added he, 'often questions whether I am at age or not, though the House of Peers made no scruple of admitting me among them some years ago.'

Mr. B. said, severely, but with a smiling air—'Tis well she has such a gentleman as your lordship for a husband, whose affectionate indulgence to her makes you overlook all her saucy sallies.' I am sure, when you took her out of our family into your own, we all thought ourselves, I in particular, bound to pray for you.'

I thought this a great trial of my lady's patience: but it was from Mr. B. And she said, with a half pleasant, half serious air—'How now, Confidence!—None but my brother could have said this, whose violent spirit was always much more intolerable than mine: but I can tell you, Mr. B. I was always thought very good-humoured and obliging to every body, till your impudence came from college, and from your travels; and then, I own, your provoking ways made me now-and-then a little out of the way.'

'Well, well, sister, we'll have no more of this subject, only let us see, that my Lord Davers wants not his proper authority with you, although you used to keep *me* in awe formerly.'

'Keep *you* in awe!—That nobody could ever do yet, boy or man.—But, my lord, I beg your pardon; for this brother will make mischief betwixt us if he can—I only took notice of the word *Sister* so often used, which looked more like affectation than affection.'

'Perhaps, Lady Davers,' said my lord, gravely, 'I have two reasons for using the word so frequently.'

'I'd be glad to hear them,' said the domineering lady; 'for I don't doubt they're mighty good ones. What are they, my lord?'

'One is, because I love, and am fond of my new relation: the other, that you are so sparing of the word, that I call her so for us both.'

'Your lordship says well,' replied Mr. B. smiling; 'and Lady Davers can give two reasons why she does not.'

'Well,

'Well,' ſaid my lady, 'now we are 'in for't, let us hear *your* two reaſons 'likewiſe, I doubt not they are wiſe ones 'too.'

'If they are *yours*, Lady Davers, they 'muſt be ſo. One is, That every conde-'ſcenſion (to ſpeak in a proud lady's 'dialect) comes with as much difficulty 'from her, as a favour from the Houſe 'of Auſtria to the petty princes of Ger-'many. The ſecond, Becauſe thoſe of your ſex—(excuſe me, Madam, to the counteſs) 'who having once made 'ſcruples, think it inconſiſtent with them-'ſelves to be over haſty to alter their own 'conduct, chooſing rather to perſiſt in an 'error, than own it to be one.'

This proceeded from his impatience to ſee me in the leaſt ſlighted by my lady; and I ſaid to Lord Davers, to ſoften mat-ters—'Never, my lord, were brother and 'ſiſter ſo loving in earneſt, and yet ſo ſa-'tirical upon each other in jeſt, as my 'good lady and Mr. B. But your lord-'ſhip knows their way.'

My lady frowned at her brother, but turned it off with an air. 'I love the miſ-'treſs of this houſe,' ſaid ſhe, 'very well, 'and am quite reconciled to her: but 'methinks there is ſuch a hiſſing ſound 'in the word *Siſter*, that I cannot abide 'it. 'Tis a true Engliſh word, but a 'word I have not been uſed to, having 'never had a ſiſ-ſ-ſ-ter before, as you 'know.' Speaking the firſt ſyllable of the word with an emphatical hiſs.

Mr. B. ſaid—'Obſerve you not, Lady 'Davers, that you uſed a word (to avoid 'that) which had twice the hiſſing in it, 'that *ſiſter* has? And that was, miſ-ſ-ſ-'treſs, with two other hiſſing words to 'accompany it, of this-s-s houſ-ſe. 'but to what childiſh follies does not 'pride make one ſtoop!—Excuſe, Ma-'dam,' (to the counteſs) 'ſuch poor low 'converſation as we are dwindled in to.'

'O Sir,' ſaid her ladyſhip, 'the conver-'ſation is very agreeable,—and I think, 'Lady Davers, you're fairly caught.'

'Well,' ſaid my lady, 'then help me, 'good *ſiſter*,—there's for you!—to a 'little ſugar.—Will that pleaſe you, 'Sir?'

'I am always pleaſed,' replied her brother, ſmiling, 'when Lady Davers 'acts up to her own character, and the 'good ſenſe ſhe is miſtreſs of.'

'Ay, ay,' reſumed ſhe, 'my good 'brother, like other good men, takes it 'for granted, that it is a mark of good 'ſenſe to approve of whatever *he* does. '—And ſo, for this one time, I am a 'very ſenſible body with him.—And 'I'll leave off, while I have his good 'word. Only one thing I muſt ſay to 'you, my dear,' turning to me, 'that 'though I call you Pamela, and Pame-'la, as I pleaſe, I do aſſure you, I love 'you as well as if I called you *Siſter*, '*Siſter*, as Lord Davers does, at every 'word.'

'Your ladyſhip gives me great plea-'ſure,' ſaid I, 'in this kind aſſurance, 'and I don't doubt but I ſhall have the 'honour of being called by that tender 'name, if I can be ſo happy as to de-'ſerve it, and I'll loſe no opportunity 'that ſhall be afforded me, to ſhew how 'ſincerely I will endeavour to do ſo.'

She was pleaſed to riſe from her ſeat. 'Give me a kiſs, my dear girl, you de-'ſerve every thing: and permit me to 'ſay Pamela ſometimes, as the word oc-'curs; for I am not uſed to ſpeak in print, 'and I will call you *ſiſter* when I think 'of it, and love you as well as ever ſiſter 'loved another.'

'Theſe proud and paſſionate folks,' ſaid Mr. B. 'how good they can be, 'when they reflect a little on what be-'comes their characters!'

'So then,' rejoined my lady, 'I am 'to have no merit of my own, I ſee, do 'what I will. This is not quite ſo ge-'nerous in my brother, as one might ex-'pect.'

'Why, you ſaucy ſiſter—excuſe me, 'Lord Davers—what merit *would* you 'aſſume? Can people merit by doing 'their duty? And is it ſo great a praiſe, 'that you think fit to own for a ſiſter, 'ſo deſerving a girl as this, whom I take 'pride in calling my wife?'

'Thou art what thou always wert,' returned my lady, 'and were I in this 'my imputed pride to want an excuſe, 'I know not the creature living, that 'ought ſo ſoon to make one for me, as 'you.'

'I *do* excuſe you,' ſaid he, 'for *that* 'very reaſon, if you pleaſe; but it little 'becomes either your pride, or mine, to 'do any thing that wants excuſe.'

'Mighty moral! mighty grave, truly! '—Pamela, friend, ſiſter,—there's for 'you!—thou art a happy girl to have 'made ſuch a reformation in thy honeſt 'man's way of *thinking* as well as *act-*'*ing*. But now we are upon this topick, 'and none but friends about us, I am

'reſolved

'resolved to be even with thee, brother. '—Jackey, if you are not for another 'oath, I wish you'd withdraw.—Polly 'Barlow, we don't want you.—Beck, '[illegible] Mr H [illegible], and Polly [illegible]; for you must know, Miss, that my Lady Davers will have none of the [illegible], as she calls them, [illegible] And I [illegible] the right, [illegible] at night [illegible]

When they were [illegible], my lady [illegible]—'[illegible] of [illegible] 'or [illegible] reformation [illegible] me, 'that [illegible] you know I 'have [illegible] Pamela's 'papers, [illegible] take out the '[illegible] our door, '[illegible] in presence of '[illegible], as Mrs Jervis [illegible] '[illegible]—As to the other '[illegible], less wonder, 'although [illegible] *her* [illegible] the inno-'cence of *her* [illegible] work '[illegible] make [illegible] attempt before Mrs 'Jervis, and [illegible] *her* struggles 'and reproaches, was the very stretch 'of shameless wickedness.'

Mr B [illegible] concerted, and [illegible]—'Sure [illegible], Lady Davers, 'this [illegible] Look at Pamela's '[illegible], and [illegible]—and 'wonder at [illegible] question, 'as much as you do [illegible] for the action 'you [illegible].'

The countess [illegible]—'My dear 'Mrs B [illegible] I wonder not at this sweet 'confusion [illegible] affecting [illegible]—'but, indeed, since it has come in so 'naturally, I [illegible] Mr B that we '[illegible] of [illegible], won-'[illegible] part of '[illegible] ought '[illegible] men in 'England [illegible] could not [illegible], [illegible] appearances at '[illegible].'

'[illegible],' said Mr B, 'is to '[illegible] Pamela, the renewal of griefs, '[illegible] your dear face.—You may '—The [illegible] was yours—the shame 'and the blushes ought to be mine.—'And I will humour my [illegible] in '[illegible] would have me [illegible].'

Nay, said Lord Davers, 'you know the question [illegible] I [illegible] stronger.'

'That's very true, replied he.—'But would you expect I should give you a 'reason for an attempt that appears to '[illegible] shocking?'

'Nay, Sir, said the countess, 'don't 'say *appears to* Lady Davers, for (ex-'cuse me) it will appear so to every one 'who hears of it.'

'I think my brother is too hardly used, said Lord Davers. 'He has made all the 'amends he could make:—and *you*, my 'sister, who were the person offended, 'forgive him now, I hope, don't you?'

I could not answer, for I was quite confounded, and made a motion to withdraw; but Mr B said—'Don't go, 'my dear; though I ought to be ashamed 'of an action set before me in so full a 'glare, in presence of Lord Davers and 'the countess, yet I will not have you 'stir, because I forget how you repre-'sented it, and you must tell me.'

Indeed, Sir, I cannot, said I: 'pray, 'my dear ladies—pray, my good lord '—and, dear Sir, don't thus *renew my* '*griefs*, as you were pleased justly to 'phrase it.'

'I have the representation of that 'scene in my pocket, said my lady, 'for 'I was resolved, as I told Lady Betty, 'to shame the wicked wretch with it the 'first opportunity I had, and I'll read it 'to you—or, rather, you shall read it 'yourself, Bold-face, if you can.'

So she pulled those leaves out of her pocket, wrapped up carefully in a paper. 'Here,—I believe he who could act 'thus, must read it, and, to spare Pame-'la's confusion, read it to yourself, for 'we all know how it was.'

'I think, said he, taking the papers, 'I can say something that will abate the 'heinousness of this heavy charge, or 'else I should not stand thus at the in-'solent bar of my sister, answering her 'interrogatories.'

I send you, my dear Miss Darnford, a transcript of the charge, as follows.—To be sure, you'll say, he was a very wicked man.

[See Vol. I. p. 47, & seq.]

Mr B read this to himself, and said—'This is a dark affair, as it is here 'stated, and I can't say, but Pamela, and 'Mrs Jervis too, had a great deal of 'reason to apprehend the worst: but sure 'ly readers of it, who were less parties 'in the supposed attempt, and who were 'not determined at all events to condemn 'me, might have made a more favourable 'construction for me, than you, Lady 'Davers, have done in the strong light 'in which you have set this heinous mat-'ter before us.

'However, since my lady, bowing

to the counteſs, 'and Lord Davers ſeem to expect, that I ſhall particularly anſwer to this black charge, I will at a proper time, if it will be agreeable, give you a brief hiſtory of my paſſion for this dear girl, how it commenced and increaſed, and my own ſtruggles with it: and this will introduce, with ſome little advantage to myſelf perhaps, what I have to ſay, as to this ſuppoſed attempt, and at the ſame time enable you the better to account for ſome facts which you have read in my pretty accuſer's papers.'

This pleaſed every one, and they begged him to begin *then*: but, he ſaid, it was time we ſhould think of dreſſing: the morning being far advanced; and, if no company came in, he would, in the afternoon, give them the particulars they deſired to hear.

The three gentlemen rode out, and returned juſt time enough to dreſs before dinner; and my lady and the counteſs alſo took an airing in the chariot. Juſt as they returned, compliments came from ſeveral of the neighbouring ladies to our noble gueſts, on their arrival in theſe parts; and, to as many as ſent, Lady Davers deſired their companies for to-morrow in the afternoon, to tea: but Mr. B. having fallen in with ſome of the gentlemen likewiſe, he told me, we ſhould have moſt of our viſiting neighbours at dinner, and deſired Mrs. Jervis might prepare accordingly for them.

After dinner Mr. H. took a ride out, attended by Mr. Colbrand, of whom he is very fond, ever ſince he frighten'd Lady Davers's footman at the Hall, threatening* to chine them, if they offered to ſtop his lady; for, he ſays, he loves a man of courage, very probably knowing his own defects that way; for my lady often calls him a chicken-hearted fellow. And then Lord and Lady Davers, and the counteſs, revived the ſubject of the morning, and Mr. B. was pleaſed to begin in the manner I ſhall mention by-and-by. For here I am obliged to break off.

Now, my dear Miſs Darnford, I will proceed.

'I need not,' ſaid Mr. B. 'obſerve to any body who knows what love is, (or rather that violent paſſion which we mad young fellows are apt to miſcal love) what mean things it puts one upon, how it unmans, and levels with the duſt, the proudeſt ſpirit. In the ſequel of my ſtory you will obſerve ſeveral inſtances of this truth.

'I began very early to take notice of this lovely girl, even when ſhe was hardly thirteen years old; for her charms increaſed every day, not only in my eye, but in the eyes of every one who beheld her. My mother, as *you*, Lady Davers, know, took the greateſt delight in her, always calling her, her Pamela, her good child; and her waiting maid, and her cabinet of rarities, were her boaſts, and equally ſhewn to every viſitor: for, beſides the beauty of her figure, and the genteel air of her perſon, the dear girl had a ſurpriſing memory, a ſolidity of judgment above her years, and a docility ſo unequalled, that ſhe took all parts of learning which her lady, as fond of inſtructing her, as ſhe of improving by inſtruction, crowded upon her: inſomuch, that ſhe had maſters to teach her to dance, to ſing, and to play on the ſpinnet, whom ſhe every day ſurpriſed by the readineſs wherewith ſhe took every thing.

'I remember once, my mother praiſing her girl before me, and my aunt B. (who is ſince dead) I could not but take notice to her of her fondneſs for her, and ſaid—"What do you deſign, Madam, *to do with*, or to do *for*, this Pamela of yours? The accompliſhments you give her will do her more hurt than good: for they will ſet her ſo much above her degree, that what you intend as a kindneſs may prove her ruin."

'My aunt join'd with me, and ſpoke in a ſtill ſtronger manner againſt giving her ſuch an education, and added, as I well remember—"Surely, ſiſter, you do wrong. One would think, if one knew not my nephew's diſcreet pride, that you deſign her for ſomething more than your own waiting maid."

"Ah! ſiſter," ſaid the old lady, "there is no fear of what you hint at: his family pride, and ſtately temper, will ſecure my ſon: he has too much of his father in him.—And as for Pamela, you know not the girl. She has always in her thoughts, and in her mouth too, her parents mean condition, and I ſhall

* See Vol. II. p. 233.

" do nothing for *them*, at least at present, " though they are honest folks, and " deserve well, because I will keep the " girl humble."

' But what can I do with the little baggage?' continued my mother, "she conquers every thing so fast, and has such " a thirst after knowledge, and the more " she knows, I verily think, the humbler " she is, that I cannot help letting go, as " my son, when a little boy, used to do " to his kite, as fast as she pulls: and " to what height she'll soar I can't tell.

"I intended," proceeded the good lady, "at first, only to make her mistress " of some fine needle-work, to qualify " her, (as she has a delicacy in her person, that makes it a pity she should " ever be put to hard work) for a genteel " place: but she masters that so fast, that " now, as my daughter is married, and " gone from me, I am desirous to qualify her to divert and entertain me in " my thoughtful hours. and were *you*, " sister, to know what she is capable of, " and how diverting her innocent prattle " is to me, and her natural simplicity, " which I encourage her to preserve a-" midst all she learns, you would not, " nor my son neither, wonder at the pleasure I take in her.—Shall I call her in?

"I don't want," said I, "to have the " girl called in: if you, Madam, are " diverted with her, that's enough.—To " be sure Pamela is a better companion " for a lady, than a monkey or a harlequin: but I fear you'll set her above " herself, and make her vain and pert, " and that, at last, in order to support " her pride, she may fall into temptations which may be fatal to herself, and " others too."

' I'm glad to hear this from my *son*,' replied the good lady. "But the moment " I see my favour puffs her up, I shall " take other measures."

"Well," thought I to myself, "I only want to conceal my views from your " penetrating eye, my good mother, and " I shall one day take as much delight " in your girl, and her accomplishments, " as you now do. So, go on, and improve her as fast as you will: I'll " only now and then talk against her, to " blind you, and doubt not that all you " bestow upon her, will qualify her the " better for my purpose.—Only," thought ' I, "fly swiftly on, two or three more " tardy years, and I'll nip this bud by " the time it begins to open, and place " it in my bosom for a year or two at " least; for so long, if the girl behaves " worthy of her education, I doubt not, " she'll be new to me.—Excuse me, ladies,—excuse me, Lord Davers:—if I ' am not ingenuous, I had better be silent."

I will, as little as possible, interrupt this affecting narration, by mentioning my own alternate blushes, confusions, and exclamations, as the naughty man went on, nor the censures, and many *Out-upon-you's* of the attentive ladies, and *Fie, brother's*, of Lord Davers: nor yet with apologies for the praises on myself, so frequently intermingled—contenting myself to give you, as near as I can recollect, the very sentences of the dear relator. And as to our occasional exclaimings and observations, you may suppose what they were.

' So,' continued Mr. B. ' I went on ' dropping hints against her now-and-then; and whenever I met her in the ' passages about the house, or in the garden, avoiding to look at her, or to ' speak to her, as she passed me, curtseying, and putting on a thousand bewitching airs of obligingness and reverence, while I (who thought that the ' best way to demolish the influence of ' such an education, would be to avoid ' alarming her fears on one hand, or to ' familiarize myself to her on the other, ' till I came to strike the blow) looked ' haughty and reserved, and passed by ' her with a stiff nod at most: Or, if I ' spoke—"How does your lady this " morning, girl?—I hoped she rested " well last night:' then, covered with ' blushes, and curtseying at every word, ' as if she thought herself unworthy of ' answering my questions, she'd trip ' away in a kind of hurry and confusion, ' as soon as she had spoken. And once ' I heard her say to Mrs. Jervis—" Dear Sirs, my young master spoke to " me, and called me by my name, saying—"How slept your lady last night, " Pamela?" Was not that very good, " Mrs. Jervis, was it not?—"Ay," ' thought I, "I'm in the right way, I " find: this will do in proper time.—Go " on, my dear mother, improving as " fast as you will: I'll engage to pull " down

" down in three hours what you'll be " building up in as many years, in spite " of all the lessons you can teach her.'

'Tis enough for me, that I am establishing in you, ladies—and in you, ' my lord—a higher esteem for my Pamela (I am but too sensible I shall lose ' a good deal of my own reputation) in ' the relation I am now giving you. ' Every one but my mother, who however ' had no high opinion of her son's virtue, ' used to look upon me as a rake, and ' I got the name, not very much to my ' credit, you'll say, as well abroad as in ' England, of *The sober rake*,—some ' would say, *The genteel rake*, nay, for ' that matter, some pretty hearts, that ' have smarted for their good opinion, ' have called me *The handsome rake*— ' but whatever other epithet I was distinguished by, it all concluded in *rake* ' or *libertine*. nor was I very much offended at the character; for, thought I, 'if a lady knows this, and will ' come into my company, half the ceremony between us is over, and if she ' *calls* me so, I shall have an excellent ' excuse to punish her freedom, by greater of my own.

'So I dress'd, grew more and more ' confident, and became as insolent ' withal, as if, though I had not Lady ' Davers's wit and virtue, I had all her ' spirit—(excuse me, Lady Davers,) and ' having a pretty bold heart, which rather put me upon courting than avoiding a danger or difficulty, I had but ' too much my way with every body, ' and many a menac'd complaint have I ' *look'd down* with a haughty air, and a ' promptitude, like that of Colbrand's ' to your footmen at the Hall, to clap my ' hand to my side which was of the ' greater service to my bold enterprizes, ' as two or three gentlemen had found ' I knew how to be in earnest.'

'Ha!' said my lady, 'thou wast ever ' an impudent fellow, and many a vile ' roguery have I kept from my poor mother.—Yet, to my knowledge, she ' thought you no saint.'

'Ay, poor lady,' continued he, 'she ' used now and then to catechize me, ' and was *sure* I was not so good as I ' ought to be.—"For, son, she would ' cry, "these late hours, these all-night " works, and to come home so *sober*, " cannot be right.—I'm not sure, if I " were to know all, (and yet I'm afraid " of inquiring after your ways) whether I should not have reason to wish " you were brought home in wine, rather than to come in so sober, and so " late, as you do.'

'Once, I remember, in the summer-time, I came home about six in the ' morning, and met the good lady unexpectedly by the garden back-door, ' of which I had a key to let myself in ' at all hours. I started, and would have ' avoided her, as soon as I saw her; but ' she called me to her, and then I approached her with an air: "What " brings you, Madam, into the garden " at so early an hour? turning my face ' from her, for I had a few scratches on ' my forehead,—with a thorn, or so,— ' which I feared she would be more inquisitive about than I cared she should.'

" And what makes you,' said she, " so early here, Billy?—What a rakish " figure dost thou make!—One time or " other these courses will yield you but " little comfort, on reflection. would " to God thou wast but happily married!"

" So, Madam, the old wish!—I'm " not so bad as you think me.—I hope " I have not merited so great a punishment.'

'These hints I give, not as matter of ' glory, but shame. yet I ought to tell ' you all the truth, or nothing. "Mean-" time, thought I, (for I used, as I ' mentioned in the morning, to have ' some compunction for my vile practices, when cool reflection, brought ' on by satiety, had taken hold of me) " I wish this sweet girl was grown to " years of susceptibility, that I might " reform this wicked course of life, and " not prowl about, disturbing honest " folks peace, and endangering myself." And as I had, by a certain ' very daring and wicked attempt, in ' which however I did not succeed, set ' a hornet's nest about my ears, which ' I began to apprehend would sting me ' to death, having once escap'd an ambush, by dint of mere good luck, I ' thought it was better to remove the ' seat of my warfare into another kingdom, and to be a little more discreet ' for the future in my amours. So I ' went to France a second time, as you ' know, sister, and passed a twelvemonth 'there in the best of company, and with 'some improvement both to my morals 'and understanding, and had a very few 'sallies, considering my love of intrigue, 'and the ample means I had to prose-'cute successfully all the desires of my 'heart.

'When I returned, several matches 'were proposed to me, and my good mo-'ther often requested me to make her so 'happy, as she called it, as to see me 'married before she died: but I could 'not endure the thoughts of the state, 'for I never saw a lady whose temper 'and education I liked, or with whom I 'thought I could live tolerably.* She 'used in vain therefore to plead family 'reasons to me: like most young fellows, 'I was too much a self-lover, to pay so 'great a regard to posterity; and, to say 'truth, had very little solicitude at that 'time, whether my name were continued 'or not, in my own descendants. How-'ever, upon my return, I looked upon 'my mother's Pamela with no small 'pleasure, and I found her so much im-'proved, as well in person as behaviour, 'that I had the less inducement either to 'renew my intriguing life, or to think of 'a married state.

'Yet, as my mother had all her eyes 'about her, as the phrase is, I affected 'great shyness, both before her, and to 'the girl; for I doubted not, my very 'looks would be watched by them both, 'and what the one discovered would not 'be a secret to the other; and laying my-'self open to too early a suspicion, I 'thought would but set the girl over, 'and make her lady more watchful.

'So I used to go into my mother's 'apartment, and come out of it, without 'taking the least notice of her; but put 'on stiff airs; and, as she always with-'drew when I came in, I never made 'any pretence to keep her there.

'Once indeed, my mother, on my look-'ing after her, when her back was turn-'ed, said—"My dear son, I don't like "your eye following my girl so intent-"ly. Only I know that sparkling lustre "natural to it, or I should have some "fear for my Pamela, as she grows "older."

"*I* look after her, Madam!—*My* eyes "sparkle at such a girl as that! No in-'deed!—She may be your favourite as "a waiting-maid, but I see nothing but "clumsy curtsies in her, and aukward "airs about her. A little rustick af-"fectation of innocence, that, to such as "cannot see into her, may pass well "enough."

"Nay, my dear," replied my mother, "don't say that of all things. She has "no affectation, I am sure."

"Yes, she has, in my eye, Madam, "and I'll tell you how it comes about: "you have taught her to assume the airs "of a gentlewoman, to dance, and to "enter a room with a grace, and yet bid "her keep her low birth and family in "view; and between the one character, "which she wants to get into, and the "other she dares not get out of, she trips "up and down mincingly, and knows "not how to set her feet; so 'tis the same "in every gesture; her arms she knows "not whether to swim with, or to hold "before her, nor whether to hold her "head up, or down, and so does neither, "but hangs it on one side: a little auk-"ward piece of one-and-t'other, I think "her.—And, indeed, Madam, you'd do "the girl more kindness to put her into "your dairy, than to keep her about your "person; for she'll be utterly spoiled, I "doubt, for any useful purpose."

"Ah, son!" said she, "I fear by "your description, you have minded her "too much in one sense, though not "enough in another. 'Tis not my in-"tention to recommend her to your no-"tice, of all men: and I doubt not, if "it please God I live, and she continues "to be a good girl, but she will make a "man, of some middling, genteel busi-"ness, very happy."

'Pamela came in just then, with an air 'so natural, so humble, and yet so much 'above herself, that I was forced to turn 'my head from her, lest my mother 'should watch my eye again, and lest I 'should be inclined to do her that justice, 'which my heart assented to, but which 'my lips had just before denied her.

'All my difficulty, in apprehension, was 'my good mother: the effect of whose 'lessons to her girl, I was not, however, 'so much afraid of, as her vigilance. "For," thought I, "I see by the delicacy "of her person, the brilliancy of her eye, "and the sweet apprehensiveness that "plays about every feature of her face,

* See, to the particular reasons against marrying, Vol. II. p. 255, &c.

'that

'that she must have tinder enough in her "constitution, to catch a well struck "spark, and I'll warrant I shall know "how to set her in a blaze, in a few "months more

'Yet I wanted, as I passed, to catch 'her attention too I expected her to turn 'after me, and look so, as to shew a be-'ginning liking towards me, for, you 'must know, I had a great opinion of 'my person and air which had been for-'tunately distinguished by the ladies, 'whom, of course, my vanity made me 'allow to be very good judges of these 'outward advantages

'I'll give your ladyships an instance of 'this my vanity in a catch I made *ex-'tempore*, to a lady whom I had been 'urging to give me some proofs of a love, 'that I had the confidence to tell her, I 'was sure she had in her heart for me 'she was a lively lady, and, laughing, 'said, whoever admired me, it must be 'for my confidence, and nothing else 'but urging her farther—"Why," said 'she, "brazen man," (for she called 'names, like Lady Davers) "what "would you have me say? I would love "you, if I *could* —But— Here inter-'rupting her, and putting on a free air, 'I half said and half sung—

"You'd love me, you say, if you *cou'd*!
"Why, thou mak'st me a very odd crea-
"ture;
"I prythee survey me again
"What canst thou object to my *fea-
'ture?*"

'This shewed my vanity and I an-'swered for the lady—

"*Why nothing*—Very well—Then I'm sure
"you'll admit,
"That the *choice* I have made, is a sign of
"my WIT.'

'But, to my great disappointment, Pa-'mela never, by any favourable glance, 'gave the least encouragement to my va-'nity "Well," thought I, "this girl "has certainly nothing ethereal in her "mould all unanimated clay!—But "the dancing and singing airs my mo-"ther is teaching her, will make her "better qualified in time, and another "year will ripen her into my arms, no "doubt of it Let me only go on in my "present way, and make her *fear* me "that will inhance in her mind, every 'favour I shall afterwards vouchsafe to "shew her, and never question, old "*humdrum* Virtue, thought I, "but "the tempter *without*, and the tempter "*within*, will be too many for the per-"versest nicety that ever the sex boasted"

'Yet, though I could not once attract 'her eye towards me, she never failed to 'draw mine after her, whenever she went 'by me, or where-ever I saw her, except, 'as I said, in my mother's presence, and 'particularly, when she had passed me, 'and could not see me look at her, with-'out turning her head, as I expected 'so often from her in vain

'You will wonder, Lord Davers, 'who, I suppose, was once in love, or 'you'd never have married such an hostile 'spirit as my sister's there—'

'Go on, sauce-box, said she,' I won't 'interrupt you.'

'You will wonder how I could be-'have so coolly as to escape all discovery 'so long from a lady so watchful as my 'mother, and from the apprehensiveness 'of the girl, for, high or low, every in-'dividual of the sex is quick as light-'ning to imaginations of this kind and 'besides, well says the poet—

"Men without love, have oft so cunning
"grown,
"That something *like* it, they have
"shown,
"But none who had it, e'er seem'd to have
"none
"Love's of a strangely open, simple kind,
"Can no arts or disguises find;
"But thinks none sees it, cause itself is
"blind"

'But to say nothing of her tender 'years, and that my love was not of this 'bashful sort, I was not absolutely de-'termined, so great was my pride, that 'I ought to think her worthy of being 'my *mistress*, when I had not much rea-'son, as I thought, to despair of pre-'vailing upon persons of higher birth '(were I disposed to try) to live with me 'upon my own terms My pride there-'fore kept my passion at bay, as I may 'say so far was I from imagining I 'should ever be brought to what has 'since happened! But to proceed

'Hitherto my mind was taken up with 'the beauties of her person only My 'EYE had drawn my HEART after it, 'without giving myself any trouble 'about that sense and judgment, which 'my mother was always praising in her Pamela, as exceeding her years and opportunities: but an occasion happened, which, though slight in itself, took the HEAD into the party, and made me think of her, young as she was, with a distinction, that before I had not for her. It was thus:

'Being with my mother in her closet, who was talking to me on the old subject, *matrimony*, I saw Pamela's common-place book, as I may call it, in which, by her lady's direction, from time to time, she had transcribed from the Bible, and other good books, such passages as made most impression upon her, as she read.—A method, I take it, my dear, *turning to me*, 'that was of great service to you, as it initiated you into writing with that freedom and ease, which shine in your saucy letters and journals, and to which my present fetters are not a little owing: just as pedlars catch monkeys in the baboon kingdoms, provoking the attentive fools, by their own example, to put on shoes and stockings, till the apes of imitation, trying to do the like, entangle their feet, and so cannot escape upon the boughs of the tree of liberty, on which *before they were wont to hop and skip* about, and play a thousand puggish tricks.

'I observed the girl wrote a pretty hand, and very swift and free; and affixed her points or stops with so much judgment, (her years considered) that I began to have an high opinion of her understanding. Some observations likewise upon several of the passages were so just and solid, that I could not help being greatly surprised at them.

'My mother watched my eye, and was silent: I seemed not to observe that she did, and after a while, laid down the book, shutting it with great indifference, and talking of another subject.

'Upon this, my mother said—"Don't you think Pamela writes a pretty hand, son?"

'"I did not mind it much," said I, with a careless air. 'This is her writing, is it?' taking the book and opening it again, at a place of Scripture. 'The girl is mighty pious!' said I.

"I wish *you* were so, child."

"I wish so too, Madam, if it would please *you*."

"I wish so, for your *own* sake, child."

"So do I, Madam," and down I laid the book again very carelessly.

"Look once more in it," said she, "and see if you can't open it upon some place that may strike you."

'I opened it at—"*Train up a child in the way it should go*, &c." "I fancy," said I, "when I was at Pamela's age, I was pretty near as good as she."

"Never, never," said my mother, "I'm sure I took great pains with you; but, alas! to very little purpose. You had always a violent headstrong will."

"Some allowances for boys and girls, I hope, Madam: but you see I am as good for a man as my sister for a woman."

"No indeed, you are not, I do assure you."

"I am sorry for that, Madam: you give me a sad opinion of myself."—

'Brazen wretch!' said my lady: 'but go on.'

"Turn to one of the girl's observations on some text," said my mother.

'I did, and was pleased with it more than I would own. "The girl's well enough," said I, "for what she is; but let's see what she'll be a few years hence. Then will be the trial."

"*She'll be always good, I doubt not.*"

"So much the better for her.—But can't we talk of any other subject? You complain how seldom I attend you, Madam; and indeed, when you are always talking of matrimony, or of this low-born, raw girl, it must needs lessen the pleasure of approaching you."

'But now, as I hinted to you, ladies, and my lord, I had a still higher opinion of Pamela, and esteemed her more worthy of my attempts. "For," thought I, "the girl has good sense, and it will be some pleasure to watch by what gradations she may be made to rise into love, and into an higher life, than that to which she was born." And so I began to think she would be worthy in time of being my *mistress*, which till now, as I said before, I had been a little scrupulous about.

'I took a little tour soon after this, in company of some friends, with whom I had contracted an intimacy abroad, into Scotland and Ireland, they having a curiosity to see those countries; and we spent six or eight months on this expedition; and when I had landed them in France, I returned home, and found

'my

‘my good mother in a very indifferent state of health, but her Pamela arrived to a height of beauty and perfection, which exceeded all my expectations. I was ſo much taken with her charms the firſt time I ſaw her, after my return, which was in the garden, with a book in her hand, juſt come out of a little ſummer-houſe, that I then thought of obliging her to go back again, in order to begin a parley with her: but while I was reſolving, ſhe tript away, with her curtſies and reverences, and was out of my ſight before I could determine.

‘I was reſolved, however, not to be long without her; and Mrs Jewkes having been recommended to me a little before, by a brother rake as a woman of tried fidelity, I aſked her, if ſhe would be faithful, if I ſhould have occaſion to commit a pretty girl to her care.

‘She hoped, ſhe ſaid, it would be with the lady's own conſent, and ſhe ſhould make no ſcruple in obeying me.

‘So I thought I would way-lay the girl, and carry her firſt to a little village in Northamptonſhire, to an acquaintance of Mrs Jewkes's. And when I had brought her to be eaſy and pacified a little, I deſigned that Jewkes ſhould attend her to * Lincolnſhire: for I knew there was no coming at her here, under my mother's wing, by her own conſent, and that to offer terms to her, would be to blow up my project all at once. Beſides, I was ſenſible, that Mrs Jervis would ſtand in the way of my proceedings, as well as my mother.

‘The method I had contrived was quite eaſy, as I imagined, and ſuch as could not have failed to anſwer my purpoſe, as to carrying her off; and I doubted not of making her well ſatisfied in her good fortune very quickly; for, having a notion of her affectionate duty to her parents, I was not diſpleaſed, that I could make the terms very eaſy and happy to them all.

‘What moſt ſtood in my way, was my mother's fondneſs for her: but on the ſuppoſition, that I had got her favourite in my hands, which appeared to me, as I ſaid, a taſk very eaſy to be conquered, I had actually formed a letter for her to tranſcribe, acknowledging a love-affair, and laying her withdrawing herſelf ſo privately, to the implicit obedience ſhe owed to her huſband's commands, to whom ſhe was married that morning, and who, being a young gentleman of a genteel family, and dependant on his friends, was deſirous of keeping it all a profound ſecret, and begging, on that account, her lady not to divulge it, ſo much as to Mrs Jervis.

‘And to prepare for this, and make her eſcape the more probable, when matters were ripe for my plot, I came in one night, and examined all the ſervants, and Mrs Jervis, the latter in my mother's hearing, about a genteel young man, whom I pretended to find with a pillion on the horſe he rode upon, waiting about the back door of the garden, for ſomebody to come to him, and who rode off, when I came up to the door, as faſt as he could.

‘Nobody knew any thing of the matter, and they were much ſurpriſed at what I told them: but I begged Pamela might be watched, and that no one would ſay any thing to her about it.

‘My mother ſaid, ſhe had two reaſons not to ſpeak of it to Pamela; one to oblige me, the other and chief, becauſe it would break the poor innocent girl's heart, to be ſuſpected. ‘Poor “dear child!” ſaid ſhe, “whither can ſhe go, to be ſo happy as with me? Would it not be inevitable ruin to her to leave me? There is nobody comes after her; ſhe receives no letters, but now and then one from her father and mother, and thoſe ſhe ſhews me.”

“Well,” replied I, “I hope ſhe can have no deſign; 'twould be ſtrange if ſhe had formed any to leave ſo good a miſtreſs: but you can't be *ſure* all the letters ſhe receives are from her father: and her ſhewing to you, Madam, thoſe he writes, looks like a cloak to others ſhe may receive from another hand. But it can be no harm to have an eye upon her. You don't know, Madam, what tricks there are in the world.”

“Not I, indeed; but only this I know, that the girl ſhall be under no reſtraint, if ſhe is reſolved to leave me, well as I love her.”

‘Mrs Jervis ſaid, ſhe would have an eye upon Pamela, in obedience to my command; but ſhe was ſure there was

* See Vol I. p. 73.

‘no

no need, nor would ſhe ſo much wound the poor child's peace, as to mention the matter to her.

'This I ſuffered to blow off, and ſeemed to my mother to have ſo good an opinion of her Pamela, that I was ſorry, as I told her, I had ſuch a ſurmiſe: ſaying, that though the fellow and the pillion were odd circumſtances, yet I dared to ſay, there could be nothing in it: for I doubted not, the girl's duty and gratitude would hinder her from doing a fooliſh or a raſh thing.

'This my mother heard with pleaſure: although my motive to it, was but to lay her Pamela on the thicker to her, when ſhe was to be told ſhe had eſcaped.

'She ſaid, ſhe was glad I was not an enemy to the poor child. "Pamela has no friend but me," continued the good lady; "and if I don't provide for her, I ſhall have done her more harm than good, (as you and your aunt B. have often ſaid) in the accompliſhments I have given her: and yet the poor girl, I ſee that," added ſhe, "would not be backward to turn her hand to any thing for the ſake of an honeſt livelihood, were ſhe put to it; which, if it pleaſe God to ſpare me, and ſhe continues good, ſhe never ſhall be."

'I wonder not, Pamela, at your tears on this occaſion. Your lady was an excellent woman, and deſerved this tribute to her memory. All my pleaſure now is, that ſhe knew not half my wicked pranks, and that I did not vex her worthy heart in the proſecution of this ſcheme; which would have given me a ſevere ſting, inaſmuch as I might have apprehended, with too much reaſon, that I had ſhortened her days by the knowledge of the one and the other.

'I had thus in readineſs every thing neceſſary for the execution of my project: but my mother's ill ſtate of health gave me too much concern, to permit me to proceed. And, now and then, as my frequent attendance upon her in her illneſs gave me an opportunity of obſerving more and more of the girl, and her affectionate duty, and continual tears, (finding her frequently on her knees, praying for her miſtreſs) I was moved to pity her; and even did I, while thoſe ſcenes of my mother's illneſs and [illegible] before me, reſolve to conquer, if poſſible, my guilty paſſion, as thoſe ſcenes taught me, while their impreſſions held, juſtly to call it; and I was much concerned I found it a more difficult taſk than I imagined: for, till now, I thought it principally owing to my uſual enterpriſing temper, and a love of intrigue, and that I had nothing to do but to reſolve againſt it, and to ſubdue it.

'But I found I was greatly miſtaken, for I had inſenſibly brought myſelf to admire her in every thing ſhe ſaid or did; and there was ſo much gracefulneſs, humility, and innocence in her whole behaviour, and I ſaw ſo many melting ſcenes between her lady and her, that I found I could not maſter my eſteem for her.

'My mother's illneſs increaſing beyond hopes of recovery, and having ſettled all her greater affairs, ſhe talked to me of her ſervants. I aſked her what ſhe would have done for Pamela and Mrs. Jervis?

"Make Mrs. Jervis, my dear ſon," ſaid ſhe, "as happy as you can: ſhe is a gentlewoman born, you know, let her always be treated as ſuch: but, for your own ſake, don't make her independent; for then you'll want a faithful manager. Yet, if you marry, and your lady ſhould not value her as ſhe deſerves, allow her a competency for the reſt of her life, and let her live as ſhe pleaſes.

"As for Pamela, I hope you will be her protector, I hope you will!—She is a good girl: I love her next to you and your dear ſiſter. She is juſt arriving at a trying time of life. I don't know what to ſay for her. What I had deſigned was, that if any man of a genteel calling ſhould offer, I would have given her a little pretty portion, had God ſpared my life till then. But if ſhe ſhould be made independent, ſome idle fellow perhaps might ſnap her up; for ſhe is very pretty: or if ſhe ſhould carry what you give her to her poor parents, as her duty would lead her to do, they are ſo unhappily involved, that a little matter would be nothing to them, and the poor girl might be to ſeek again. Perhaps Lady Davers will take her. But I wiſh ſhe was not ſo pretty! She will be likely to be the bird for which ſome wicked fowler will ſpread his ſnares; or, it may be, every lady will not chooſe to 'have such a waiting maid You are "a young gentleman, and, I am sorry "to say it, not better than I wish you 'to be—Though I hope my Pamela "would not be in danger from her ma "ster, who owes to all his servants "protection, as much as a king does to "his subjects Yet I don't know how "to wish her to stay with you,—for your "own reputation s sake, my dear son, "—for the world will censure as it lists "—Would to God!" said she, "the "dear girl had the small pox in a mor- "tifying manner she d be lovely enough "in the genteelness of her person, and "the excellencies of her mind, and more "out of danger of suffering from the tran- "sient beauties of countenance Yet I "think, added she, "she might be safe "and happy under Mrs Jervis s care, "and if you marry, and your lady parts "with Mrs Jervis, let 'em go together, "and live as they like.—I think that will "be the best for both.—And you have "a generous spirit enough I will not "direct you in the *quantum* But, my "dear son, remember that I am the less "concerned, that I have not done for "the poor girl myself, because I depend "upon you the manner how fitly to "provide for her, has made me defer it "till now, that I have so much more im- "portant concerns on my hands, life "and strength ebbing so fast, that I am "hardly fit for any thing, or to wish for "any thing, but to receive the last re- "leasing stroke

Here he stopped, being under some concern himself, and we in much more. At last he resumed the subject

'You will too naturally think, my 'lord—and you, my good ladies—that 'the mind must be truly diabolical, that 'could break through the regard due to 'the solemn injunctions and recommen- 'dations of a dying parent They *did* 'hold me a good while indeed, and as 'fast as I found any emotions of a con- 'trary nature rise in my breast, I en- 'deavoured for some time to suppress 'them, and to think and act as I ought 'but the dear bewitching girl every day 'rose in her charms upon me: and find- 'ing she still continued the use of her pen 'and ink, I could not help entertaining 'a jealousy, that she was writing to some- 'body who stood well in her opinion; 'and my love for her, and my own spi- 'rit of intrigue, made it a sweetheart of 'course And I could not help watch- 'ing her motions, and seeing her once 'putting a letter she had just folded up, 'into her bosom, at my entrance into my 'mother s dressing-room, I made no 'doubt of detecting her, and her cor- 'respondent, and so I took the letter 'from her stays*, she trembling and 'curtseying with a sweet confusion, and 'highly pleased I was to find it contained 'nothing but innocence and duty to the 'deceased mistress, and the loving pa- 'rents, expressing her joy, that in the 'midst of her grief for losing the one, 'she was not obliged to return to be a 'burden to the other and I gave it her 'again, with words of encouragement, 'and went down much better satisfied, 'than I had been with her correspond- 'ents

'But when I reflected upon the inno- 'cent simplicity of her style, I was still 'more in love with her, and formed a 'stratagem, and succeeded in it, to come 'at her other letters †, which I sent for- 'ward, after I had read them, all but 'three or four, which I kept back, when 'my plot began to ripen for execution, 'although the little slut was most abo- 'minably free with my character to her 'father and mother

'You will censure me, no doubt, that 'my mother s injunctions made not a 'more lasting impression upon me But 'really I struggled hard with myself to 'give them their due force, and the dear 'girl, as I said, every day grew lovelier, 'and more accomplished. Her letters 'were but so many links to the chains in 'which she had bound me, and though 'once I had resolved to part with her ‡ 'to Lady Davers, and you, Madam, 'had an intention to take her, I could 'not for my life give her up, and think- 'ing at that time more honourably of 'the state of a mistress than I have done 'since, I could not persuade myself, '(since I intended to do as handsomely 'by her as ever man did to a lady in that 'situation) but that I should do better 'for her than my mother had wished me 'to do, and so *more* than answer all her 'injunctions, as to the providing for her. 'and I could not imagine I should have 'met with a resistance from her, that I

* See Vol I p. 20. † Ibid p. 59, 63. ‡ Ibid p. 22.

'had

'had seldom encountered from persons 'much her superiors as to descent, and 'was amazed at it, for it confounded 'all the notions I had of her sex, 'which, like a true libertine I supposed 'wanted nothing but *importunity* and '*opportunity*, a bold tempter, and a 'mind not ungenerous.

'Sometimes I admired her for her 'virtue, at other times, impetuous in my 'temper, and unused to controul, I could 'have beat her. She will, I remember, 'describes the tumults of my soul, when 'she repeats what once passed between 'us, in words like these.* "Take the 'little villain from me, Mrs Jervis — 'I can neither bear, nor forbear her — "But stay—you shan't go—Yet be 'gone—No, come back again." — 'She thought I was mad, I remember, 'she says in her papers. Indeed I was 'little less.

'She says, I took her arm, and griped 'it black and blue, to bring her back 'again, and then sat down and looked 'at her as if I was such a poor girl as she!'

Well could the dear slut describe the 'passion I struggled with, and no one 'can conceive how much my pride made 'me despise myself at times, or [illegible] the 'affronts my love for her put me upon, 'and yet to find the [illegible] increasing 'every day, as her charms and her re-'sistance increased!

'I have called myself a ranging fly, 'sometimes vowing I would have the 'girl, at others [illegible] 'herself from my attempts, she would 'throw herself into the arms of some 'menial or inferior, whom otherwise she 'would not have thought of.

'Sometimes I soothed her, sometimes 'threatened her, but never was such 'courage, when she apprehended her 'virtue was in danger, mixed with so 'much humility, when her fears gave 'way to her hopes of a juster treatment.

'Then I would think it impossible, '(so slight an opinion had I of woman's 'virtue) that such a girl as this cottage-'born, who owed every thing to my fa-'mily, and had an absolute dependence 'upon my pleasure, myself not despi-'cable in person or mind, as I supposed, '[illegible] any man's favour, 'at an age susceptible of impressions, 'and a virtue and constitution not ice 'nor snow. "Surely, thought I, "all "this frost must be owing to the want "of fire in my attempts to thaw it. I "used to dare more, and succeed better. "Shall such a girl as *this* awe me by 'her rigid virtue? No, she shall not."

Then I would resolve to be more 'in earnest. Yet my love was a traitor 'to me: that was more faithful to *her* 'than to *me*: it had more honour in it 'at bottom, than I had designed it should 'have. Awed by her unaffected inno-'cence, and a virtue I had never before 'encountered, so uniform and unmove-'able, the moment I *saw* her I was 'half disarmed, and I courted her con-'sent to that, which, though I was not 'likely to obtain, yet it went against me 'to think of extorting by violence. Yet 'marriage was never in my thoughts; I 'scorned so much as to promise it.

'To what numberless mean things 'did not this unmanly passion subject 'me!—I used to watch for her letters, 'though mere pretty prattle and chit-'chat, received them with burning im-'patience, and read them with delight, 'though myself was accused in them, 'and stigmatized as I deserved.

'I would listen meanly at her cham-'ber door, try to over-hear her little 'conversations, in vain attempted to 'suborn Mrs Jervis to my purposes, 'inconsistently talking of honour, when 'no one step I took, or action I attempt-'ed, shewed any thing like it, lost my 'dignity among my servants, made a 'party in her favour against me, of every 'body, but whom my money corrupt-'ed, and that hardly sufficient to keep 'my partisans steady to my interest, so 'greatly did the virtue of the servants 'triumph over the vice of the master, 'when confirmed by such an example!

'I have been very tedious, ladies, and 'my Lord Davers, in my narration: but 'I am come within view of the point 'for which I now am upon my trial at 'your dread tribunal (*bowing to us all*.)

'After several endeavours of a smooth 'and a rough nature, in which my devil 'constantly failed me, and her good an-'gel prevailed, I had talked to Mrs Jer-'vis to induce the girl (to whom, in 'hopes of frightening her, I had given 'warning, but which she rejoiced to take, 'to my great disappointment) to desire 'to stay†, and suspecting Mrs Jervis 'played me booty, and rather confirmed

* See Vol. I. p. 44. † Ibid.

'her

her in her coyneſs, and her deſire of leaving me, I was mean enough to conceal myſelf in the cloſet in Mrs Jervis's room, in order to hear their private converſation; but really not deſigning to make any other uſe of my concealment, than to teaze her a little, if ſhe ſhould ſay any thing I did not like, which would give me a pretence to treat her with greater freedoms than I had ever yet done, and would be an introduction to take off from her unprecedented apprehenſiveneſs another time: and I had the leſs ſcruple as to Mrs Jervis's preſence, becauſe I was ſenſible, ſhe knew as bad of me as ſhe could know, from Pamela's apprehenſions, as well as her own, and would find me, if I kept within any decent bounds, better than either of them expected. But I had no deſign of proceeding to extremities, although I had little hope of making any impreſſion upon her by gentleneſs.

'So, like a benighted traveller, who having ſtrayed out of his knowledge, and deſpairing to find his way, throws the reins upon his horſe's neck, to be guided at it's uncertain direction, I reſolved to take my chance for the iſſue which the adventure ſhould produce.

'But the dear prattler, not knowing I was there, as ſhe undreſſed herſelf, began ſuch a bewitching chit-chat with Mrs Jervis, who, I found, but ill kept my ſecret, that I never was at ſuch a loſs in my life what to reſolve upon. One while I wiſhed myſelf unknown to them, out of the cloſet, into which my inconſiderate paſſion had meanly led me; another time I was incenſed at the freedom with which I heard myſelf treated; but then, rightly conſidering, that I had no buſineſs to hearken to their private converſation, and that it was ſuch as became *them*, while I ought to have been aſhamed to give occaſion for it, I excuſed them both, and admired ſtill more and more the dear prattler.

'In this ſuſpenſe, the undeſigned ruſtling of my night-gown from changing my poſture as I ſtood, giving alarm to the watchful Pamela, ſhe in a fright came towards the cloſet to ſee who was there, ſo that I could be no longer concealed.

'What could I then do, but bolt out upon the apprehenſive charmer; and having ſo done, and ſhe running to the bed, ſcreaming to Mrs Jervis, would not any man have followed her thither, detected as I was? But yet, I ſaid, if ſhe forbore her ſcreaming, I would do her no harm; but if not, ſhe ſhould take the conſequence.

'I found by their exclamations, that this would paſs with both for an attempt of the worſt kind; but really I had no ſuch intentions as they feared. When, indeed, I found myſelf detected, when the dear frightened girl ran to the bed, when Mrs Jervis threw herſelf about her, when they would not give over their hideous ſquallings, when I was charged by Mrs Jervis with the worſt deſigns, it was enough to make me go farther than I deſigned, and could I have prevailed upon Mrs. Jervis to go up, and quiet the maids, who were riſing, as I heard by the noiſe they made over head, upon the other ſcreaming; I believe, had Pamela kept out of her fit, I ſhould have been a little freer with her, than ever I had been; but, as it was, I had no thought but of making as honourable a retreat as I could, and to ſave myſelf from being expoſed to my whole family, and I was not guilty of any freedoms, that her modeſty, unaffrighted, could reproach herſelf with having ſuffered, and the dear creature's fainting fits gave *me* almoſt as great apprehenſions as I could give *her*.

'Thus, ladies—and, my lord—have I tediouſly, and little enough to my own reputation, given you a character of myſelf, and told you more againſt myſelf than any *one* perſon could accuſe me of. Whatever redounds to the credit of my Pamela, redounds in part to my own, and ſo I have the leſs regret to accuſe myſelf, ſince it exalts her. But as to a formed intention to hide myſelf in the cloſet, in order to attempt the girl by violence, and in the preſence of a good woman, as Mrs. Jervis is, which you impute to me, indeed, bad as I was, I was not ſo vile, ſo abandoned as that.

'Love, as I ſaid before, ſubjects it's inconſiderate votaries to innumerable meanneſſes, and unlawful paſſion to many more. I could not live without this dear girl. I hated the thoughts of matrimony with any body, and to be brought to the ſtake by my mother's waiting maid—"Forbid it, pride!" thought I, "forbid it, example! forbid "it, all my past sneers, and constant ridicule, both on the estate, and on those who descended to inequalities in it! and, lastly, for giving my family, to whom, in Lady Davers, as well as in myself, to whose insults, and those of all the world, I shall be obnoxious, if I make such a step!'

'All this tends to demonstrate the strength of my passion. I could not conquer my love, so I conquered a pride, which every one thought unconquerable; and since I could not make an innocent heart vicious, I had the happiness to follow so good an example, and by this means, a vicious heart is become virtuous, and I have the pleasure of rejoicing in the change, and hope I shall still more and more rejoice in it; for I really look back with contempt upon my past follies, and it is now a greater wonder to me how I could act as I did, than that I should detest those actions, which made me a curse, instead of a benefit to society. Indeed, I am not yet so pious as my Pamela, but that is to come, and it is one good sign, that I can truly say, I delight in every instance of her piety and virtue. And now I will conclude my tedious narration with the poet —

"Our passions gone, and Reason in her throne,
"Amaz'd we see the mischiefs we have done:
"After a tempest, when the winds are laid,
"The calm sea wonders at the wrecks it made."

Thus ended my dear Mr B. his affecting relation, which in the course of it gave me a thousand different emotions, and made me often pray for him, (as I constantly do) that God will surely convert a heart so generous and worthy, as his is on most occasions. And if I can but find him once delicate, when we go to London, I shall have great hopes, that nothing will affect his morals again.

I'll next read over again the foregoing account of myself. As near as I remember [illegible] was [illegible] beautiful [illegible] and spoke in a more [illegible] I [illegible]. Ye don't you think, says [illegible] that I have not come in [illegible] that the beginning of it, [illegible] of a man too much above [illegible] notions? For so the ladies observed in his narration—Is it very like the style of a true penitent?—But indeed he went on better, and concluded best of all.

But don't you observe what a near good lady I had? Blessings, a thousand blessings, on her beloved memory! Were I to live to see my children's children, they should be all taught to lisp her praises before they could speak. *My* gratitude should always be renewed in *their* mouths, and GOD, and my dear father and mother, my lady, and my master that was, my best friend that is, but principally, as most due, the FIRST, who inspired all the rest, should have their morning, their noon-tide, and their evening praises, as long as I lived!

I will only observe further, as to this my third conversation piece, that my Lord Davers offered to extenuate some parts of his dear brother-in-law's conduct, which he did not himself vindicate, and Mr B. was pleased to observe, that my lord was always very kind to him, and kind in his allowances for the sallies of an ungovernable youth. Upon which my lady said, a little tartly,—'Yes, and for a very good reason, I doubt not: for who cares to condemn himself?'

'Nay, said my lord, pleasantly, 'don't put us upon a foot neither: for what sallies I made before I knew your ladyship, were but like those of a fox, which now-and-then runs away with a straggling pullet, when nobody sees him: whereas those of my brother were like the invasions of a lion, breaking into every man's fold, and driving the *shepherds*, as well as the *sheep*, before him.'—'Ay, said my lady, 'but I can look around me, and have reason perhaps to think the invading lion has come off, little as he deserved it, better than the creeping fox, who, with all his cunning, sometimes suffers for his pilfering theft.'

O, my dear, these gentlemen are strange creatures!—What can they think of themselves for my sex? here is not one virtuous man in five, but I hope for our sex's sake, as well as for the world's sake, it is not true that evil fame reports; for, you know, every man that offers must *find* or *make* a woman trespasser!—And is this what it is then?—And now must the innocent suffer from the guilty! Yet, how much better is it to suffer one's self, than to be the cause of another's sufferings?

I'cg

I long to hear of you And must shorten my future accounts, or I shall do nothing but write, and tire *you* into the bargain, though I cannot my dear father and mother I am, my dear Miss, *always yours*,

P B

LETTER XXXI

FROM MISS DARNFORD TO MRS B

DEAR MRS B

EVERY post you more and more oblige us to admire and love you and let me tell you, I will gladly receive your letters upon your own terms* only when your worthy parents have perused them, see that I have every line of them again

Your account of the arrival of your noble guests, and their behaviour to you, and yours to them, your conversation, and noble determination, on the offered title of Baronet, the just applauses conferred upon you by all, particularly the good countess, your breakfast conversation, and the narrative of your saucy abominable *master*, though amiable *husband*, all delight us beyond expression

Do, go on, dear excellent lady, with your charming journals, and let us know all that passes

As to the state of matters with us, I have desired my papa to allow me to decline Mr Murray's addresses The good man loved me most violently, nay, he could not live without me, life was no life, unless I favoured him but yet, after a few more of these flights, he is trying to sit down satisfied without my papa's foolish perverse girl, as Sir Simon calls me, and to transpose his affections to a worthier object, my sister Nancy, and it would make you smile to see how, a little while before he *directly* applied to her, she screwed up her mouth to my mamma, and, truly, she'd have none of Polly's leavings, no, not she!—But no sooner did he declare himself in form, than the *gaudy wretch*, as he was before with her, became a *well dressed* gentleman;—the *chattering magpye*, (for he talks and laughs much) *quite conversible*,—and has something *agreeable* to say upon *every subject* Once, he would make a good master of the buck-hounds, but now, really, the *more* one is in his company, the *more polite* one finds him

Then, on his part,—indeed, he happened to see Miss Polly first! and, truly, he could have thought himself very happy in so agreeable a young lady, yet there was always something of majesty (what a stately name is that for ill-nature!) in Miss Nanny, something so awful, that while Miss Polly engaged the affections at first sight, Miss Nanny struck a man with reverence, insomuch, that the one might be loved as a woman, but the other revered as something more. a goddess, no doubt?

I do but think, that when he comes to be lifted up to her celestial sphere, as her fellow constellation, what a figure Nancy and her *ursus major* will make together, and how will they glitter and shine to the wonder of all beholders!

Then she must make a brighter appearance by far, and a more pleasing one. too, for why? She has three thousand *satellites*, or little stars, in her train more than poor Polly can pretend to Won't there be a fine twinkling and sparkling, think you, when the greater and lesser bear-stars are joined together?

But excuse me, dear Mrs B, this saucy girl has vexed me just now, by her ill natured tricks, and I am even with her, having thus vented my spite, though she knows nothing of the matter

So, fancy, my dear friend, you see Polly Darnford abandoned by her own fault, her papa angry at her, her mamma pitying her, and calling her silly girl, Mr Murray, who is a rough lover, growling over his mistress, as a dog over a bone he fears to lose, Miss Nancy, putting on her prudish pleasantry, and snarling out a kind word, and breaking through her sullen gloom, for a smile now and then in return and I laughing at both in my sleeve, and thinking, that in a while I shall get leave to attend you in town, and that will be better than twenty humble servants of Mr Murray's cast or, if I can't, that I shall have the pleasure of your correspondence here, and shall enjoy, unrivalled, the favour of my dear papa and mamma, which this ill tempered girl is always envying me

Forgive all this nonsense I was w[illegible] ling to write something, though wo[illegible] than nothing, to shew how desiro[illegible] would be to oblige you, had I a cap[illegible]

* See p 357.

or subject, as you have. But nobody can love you better, or admire you more, of this you may be assured, (however unequal in all other respects) than *your*

POLLY DARNFORD.

I send you up some of your papers for the good couple in Kent. Pray my respects to them, and beg them to let me have 'em again as soon as they can, by your conveyance.

Our Stamford friends desire their kindest respects: they mention you with delight in every letter.

LETTER XXXII.

THE JOURNAL CONTINUED.

THURSDAY, FRIDAY EVENING.

MY DEAR MISS DARNFORD,

I Am retired from a very busy day, having had no less than fourteen of our neighbours, gentlemen and ladies, to dinner with us: the occasion, principally, to welcome our noble guests into these parts, Mr. B. having, as I mentioned in a former, turned the intended visit into an entertainment, after his usual generous manner.

Mr. B. and Lord Davers are gone part of the way with them home, and Lord Jackey, mounted with his favourite Colbrand, as an escorte to the countess and Lady Davers, who are gone to take an airing in the chariot. They offered to take the coach, if I would have gone, but being fatigued, I desired to be excused. So I retired to my closet, and Miss Darnford, who is seldom out of my thoughts, coming into my mind, I had a new recruit of spirits, which enabled me to resume my pen, and thus I proceed with my journal.

Our company was*, the Earl and Countess of D. who are so fashionable a married couple, that the earl made it his boast, and his countess bore it like one accustomed to such treatment, that he had not been in his lady's company an hour abroad before for seven years. You know his lordship's character, as every body does; and there is not a worse, as report says, in the peerage.

Sir Thomas Atkyns, a single gentleman, not a little finical and ceremonious, and a mighty beau, though of the tawdry sort, and affecting foreign airs, as if he was afraid it would not be judged by any other mark, that he had travelled.

Mr. Arthur and his lady, a moderately happy couple, who seem always when together to behave as if they were upon a compromise, that is, that each would take it in turn to say free things of the other, though some of their freedoms are of so cutting a nature, that it looks as if they intended to divert the company at their own expence. The lady, being of a noble family, takes great pains to let every one know that she values herself not a little upon that advantage; but otherwise has many good qualities.

Mr. Brooks and his lady. The gentleman is a free joker on serious subjects, but a good-natured man, and says sprightly things with no ill grace: the lady is a little reserved, and of a haughty turn, though to day she happened to be freer than usual, as was observed at table by

Lady Towers, who is a maiden lady of family, noted for her wit and repartee, and who says many good things, with so little doubt, and really so good a grace, that one cannot help being pleased with her. This lady is generally gallanted by

Mr. Martin of the Grove, as he is called, to distinguish him from a rich citizen of that name, who is settled in these parts, but being covetous and proud, is seldom admitted among the gentry in their visits or parties of pleasure. Mr. Martin is a shrewd gentleman, but has been a little too much of the libertine cast, and has lived freely as to women; and for that reason has not been received by Lady Towers, who hates free actions, though she'll use free words, modestly free, as she calls them, that is to say, the double entendre, in which Sir Simon Darnford, a gentleman you are not unacquainted with, takes great delight, though by the way, what that worthy gentleman calls innocent, Lady Towers would blush at.

Mr. Dormer, a gentleman of a very courteous demeanour, a widower, was another, who always speaks well of his deceased lady, and of all the sex for her sake.

Mr. Chapman and his lady, a well be-

* For the characters of most of these gentlemen and ladies, see Vol. I. p. 41, 51, and Vol. II. p. 275, 276, and 283 to 28[illegible].

haved

haved couple, who are not ashamed to be very tender and obliging to one another, but without that censurable fondness which sits so ill upon some married folks in company

Then there was the dean, our good minister, whom I name last, because I would close with one of the worthiest, and his daughter, who came to supply her mamma's place, who was indisposed, a well-behaved prudent young lady And here were our fourteen guests

The Countess of C Lady Davers, Lord Davers, Mr H my dear Mr B and your humble servant, made up the rest of the company So we had a capacious and brilliant circle, you may imagine, and all the avenues to the house were crowded with their equipages

The subjects of discourse at dinner were various, as you may well suppose, and the circle was too large to fall upon any regular or very remarkable topicks A good deal of sprightly wit, however, flew about, between the Earl of D Lady Towers, and Mr Martin, in which that lord suffered as he deserved, for he was by no means a match for the lady, especially as the presence of the dean was a very visible restraint upon him, and upon Mr Brooks too so much awe will the character of a good clergyman always have upon even forward spirits, where he is known to have had an inviolable regard to it himself

Besides, the good gentleman has, naturally, a genteel and inoffensive vein of raillery, and so was too hard for them at their own weapons

But after dinner was over, and the servants were withdrawn, Mr Martin singled me out, as he loves to do, for a subject of encomium, and made some high compliments to my dear Mr B upon his choice, and wished (as he often does) he could find just such another person for himself

Lady Towers told him, that it was a thing as unaccountable as it was unreasonable, that every rake who loved to destroy virtue, should expect to be rewarded with it and if his *brother* B had come off so well, she thought no one else ought to expect it

Lady Davers said, it was a very just observation and she thought it was pity there was not a law, that every man who made a harlot of an honest woman, should be obliged to marry one of another's making

That would be too severe, Mr B. said, it would be punishment enough, if he was to marry his own, and especially if he had not seduced her under promise of marriage

'Then you'd have a man be obliged 'to stand to his promise, I suppose, 'Mr B ?' replied Lady Davers. 'Yes, 'Madam '

'But, said she, 'the proof would 'be difficult perhaps and the most unguilty heart of our sex might be least 'able to make it out.—But what say 'you, my Lord D ' continued her ladyship, 'will you, and my Lord Davers, 'join to bring a bill into the House of 'Peers, for the purposes I mentioned? 'I fancy my brother would give it all 'the assistance he could in the Lower 'House '

'Your ladyship, said Mr Martin, 'is highly unreasonable, I think, to 'propose that it would be enough, 'surely, that a man should be obliged, 'as Mr B says, to marry the woman 'he himself seduced.'

The earl said, that he thought neither the one nor the other should be imposed upon any man for that when women's virtue was their glory, and they were brought up with that notion, and to avoid the snares of men, he thought, if they yielded, they ought to pay the forfeit, and take the disgrace of it to themselves

'May I ask your lordship, said I, 'how it comes to pass, that a woman's 'virtue is her glory, and that a man's 'shall not be his?—Or, in other words, 'why you think virtue in a man is not as 'requisite as in a woman?'

'Custom, Madam,' replied the earl, 'has made it very different, and those 'things which are scandalous in a lady, 'are not so in a gentleman

'Will your lordship argue, that it 'should be so, because it is so? Does not 'the gentleman call himself the head of 'his family? Is it not incumbent upon 'him, then, to set a good example? And 'will he plead it as a fashion, that he may 'do by the dearest relatives of another 'man's family, what, if any one should 'attempt to do by his, he would mortally 'resent?'

'Very well observed, Madam,' said the dean 'there is not a free liver in 'the world, I believe, who can answer 'that argument

'Mr. B ' said the earl, 'pray speak 'to

'to your lady: she is too close upon us. And where sentiments have been so well supported by a conduct so uniform and exemplary, I choose not to enter the lists with such an antagonist.'

'Well, well,' said Mr B. 'since your lordship will speak in the plural number, US, let me say, we must not pretend to hold an argument on this subject—But, however, I think, my lord, you should not call upon a man to defend it, who, bad as he has been, never committed a fault of this nature, that he was not sorry for, though the sorrow generally lasted too little a while.'

'Mr B.' said Lady Towers, 'has some merit with me for that confession; and he has still a greater on another account, and that is, that he has seen his error so early, and has left his vices before they left him.'

She looked, as every one did, on the earl, who appeared a little disconcerted, as one conscious that he deserved the reflection. And the dean said—'Lady Towers observes very well: for, although I presume not to make personal applications, yet I must say, that the gentleman who sees his error in the prime of life, before he is overtaken by some awakening misfortune, may be called one of the happiest of those who have erred.'

'Ay, Mr Dean,' said Lady Towers, 'I can tell you one thing, that such another buttress as you know who, taken away from libertinism, and such another example as a certain lady every day gives, would go near in a few years to ruin the devil's kingdom in Bedfordshire.'

The gentlemen looked round upon one another upon this home push, and the lady would not let them recover. 'See,' said she, 'how the gentlemen look upon one another, as who should say, each to his companion—"I'm not so bad as you."'

'Ay,' said Lady Davers, 'I see, my Lord Davers, and the Earl of D. and Mr Martin, look most concerned.'

'Faith, ladies,' said Mr Martin, 'this is too severely personal. A man who contends with a lady has a fine time of it, for we are under restraint, while you say any thing you please. But let me tell you, there's not a man of us all, 'tis my opinion, that could have attempted what a certain renegado has attempted, though he is so readily acquitted.'

'Not so hasty, my good friend,' said Mr B. 'You don't consider well what you say, nor of whom: for did I take upon myself to censure *you*? But though I may challenge you to say the worst you can, because I always dealt upon my own stock, while other people I could name, entered into a society, and clubb'd for mischief, yet I see you deal with a brother rake, when he reforms, as highwaymen with one of their gang, who would fain withdraw and be honest: but is kept among them by fear of an impeachment.'

'But is not this, ladies,' said Mrs Arthur, 'a sad thing, that so many fine gentlemen, as think themselves concerned in this charge, should have no way to clear themselves but by recrimination?'

'Egad, gentlemen,' said Sir Thomas Atkyns, 'I know not what you're about! You make but sorry figures, by my faith.—I have heard of many *queer* pranks among my Bedfordshire neighbours, but I bless my stars, I was in France and Italy all the time.'

Said Mr Martin—'Mrs Arthur spoke the words *fine gentleman*, and Sir Thomas thought himself obliged to enter upon his own defence.'

'Ay,' said the earl, 'and the best of it is, Sir Thomas pleads not his *virtue* neither, that he did not join in these *queer* pranks with his Bedfordshire neighbours, but his *absence*.'

'Gad take me,' returned he, taking a pinch of snuff with an air, 'you're plaguy sharp, gentlemen. I believe in my conscience you're in a confederacy, as Mr B. says, and would swear an honest man into the plot, that would not care for such company.—What say you, Mr H.? Which side are you of?'

'Every gentleman,' replied he, 'who is not of the ladies side, is deem'd a criminal, and I was always of the side that had the power of the gallows.'

'That shews,' returned Lady Towers, 'that Mr H. is more afraid of the *punishment*, than of deserving it.'

''Tis well,' said Mr B. 'that any consideration deters a man of Mr H.'s time of life. What may be *fear* now, may improve to *virtue* in time.'

'Ay,' said Lady Davers, 'Jackey is 'one

one of his uncle's *foxes*, he'd be glad to ſnap up a ſtraggling pullet, if he was not well looked after, perhaps.

‘Pray, my dear,’ ſaid Lord Davers, ‘forbear: you ought not to introduce two different converſations into different companies.’

‘I think, truly,’ ſaid Mr B. ‘you ſhould take the dean's hint, my good friends, elſe you'll be leſs *polite* than *perſonal*.’

‘Well, but, gentlemen,’ ſaid Lady Arthur, ‘ſince you ſeem to have been ſo hard put to it, as *ſingle* men, what's to be done with the married man who ruins an innocent body?—What puniſhment, Lady Towers, ſhall we find out for ſuch an one? and what reparation to the injured?’ This, it ſeems, was ſaid with a particular view to the earl, on a late ſcandalous occaſion; but I knew it not till afterwards.

‘As to the puniſhment of the gentleman,’ replied Lady Towers, ‘where the law has not provided for it, it muſt be left, I believe, to his conſcience. It will then one day be heavy enough. But as to the reparation to the woman, ſo far as it can be made, it will be determinable as the unhappy perſon *may* or may *not* know, that her ſeducer is a married man. If ſhe knows he is, I think ſhe neither deſerves redreſs nor pity, though it alleviates not *his* guilt. But if the caſe be otherwiſe, and *ſhe* had no means of informing herſelf that he was married, and he promiſed to make her his wife, to be ſure, though *ſhe* cannot be acquitted, *he* deſerves the ſevereſt puniſhment that can be inflicted.—What ſay you, Mrs B.?’

‘If I muſt ſpeak my mind,’ replied I, ‘I think, that ſince cuſtom, as the earl ſaid juſt now, exacts ſo little regard to virtue from men, and ſo much from women, and ſince the deſigns of the former upon the latter are ſo flagrantly avowed and known, the poor creature, who ſuffers herſelf to be ſeduced, either by a *ſingle* or *married* man, *with* promiſes, or *without*, has nothing to do, but to ſequeſter herſelf from the world, and devote the remainder of her days to penitence and obſcurity. As to the gentleman,’ added I, ‘he muſt, I doubt, be left to his conſcience, as you ſay, Lady Towers, which he will one day have enough to do to pacify.’

‘Every young lady has not your angelick *perfection*, Madam,’ ſaid Mr Dormer. ‘And there are caſes in which the fair ſex deſerve compaſſion, ours execration. Love may inſenſibly ſteal upon a ſoft heart; when once admitted, the oaths, vows, and proteſtations of the favoured object, who perhaps, on all occaſions, declaims againſt the deceivers of his ſex, confirm her good opinion of him, till, having lull'd aſleep her vigilance, in an unguarded hour he takes advantage of her unſuſpecting innocence. Is not ſuch a poor creature to be pitied? And what puniſhment does not ſuch a ſeducer deſerve?’

‘You have put, Sir,’ ſaid I, ‘a moving caſe, and in a generous manner. What, indeed, does not ſuch a deceiver deſerve?’

‘And the more,’ ſaid Mrs Chapman, ‘as the moſt innocent heart is generally the moſt credulous.’

‘Very true,’ ſaid my counteſs, ‘for ſuch an one as would do no harm *to* others, ſeldom ſuſpects any *from* others: and her lot is very unequally caſt, admired for that very innocence, which tempts ſome brutal ravager to ruin it.’

‘Yet, what is that virtue,’ ſaid the dean, ‘which cannot ſtand the teſt?’

‘But,’ ſaid Lady Towers, very ſatirically, ‘whither, ladies, are we got? We are upon the ſubject of virtue and honour. Let us talk of ſomething, in which the *gentlemen* can join with us. This is ſuch an one, you ſee, that none but the dean and Mr Dormer can diſcourſe upon.’

‘Let us then,’ retorted Mr Martin, ‘to be even with *one* lady at leaſt, find a ſubject that will be *new* to her: and that is CHARITY.’

‘Does what I ſaid concern Mr Martin more than any other gentleman,’ returned Lady Towers, ‘that he is diſpoſed to take offence at it?’

‘You muſt pardon me, Lady Towers,’ ſaid Mr B. ‘but I think a lady ſhould never make a motion to wave ſuch ſubjects as thoſe of virtue and honour, and leſs ſtill, in company, where there is ſo much occaſion, as ſhe ſeems to think, for enforcing them.’

‘I deſire not to wave the ſuject, I'll aſſure you,’ replied ſhe. ‘And if, Sir, you think it may do good, we will continue it for the ſakes of all *you* gentlemen, (looking round her archly) who are of opinion you may be benefited by it.’

‘We

'We are going into personals again, 'gentlemen and ladies,' said the earl

'And that won't bear, my lord, you 'seem to think,' retorted Lady Davers.

A health to the king and royal family brought on publick affairs, and politicks, and the ladies withdrawing to coffee and tea, I have no more to say as to this conversation, having repeated all that I remember was said to any purpose, for such large companies, you know, my dear, don't always produce the most agreeable and edifying talk. But this I was the more willing to recite, because I thought the characters of some of our neighbours would be thereby made more familiar to you, if ever I should have the happiness to see you in these parts.

I will only add, that Miss L. the dean's daughter, is a very modest and agreeable young lady, and a perfect mistress of musick, in which the dean takes great delight also, and is a fine judge of it. The gentlemen coming in, to partake of our coffee and conversation, as they said, obtained of Miss to play several tunes on the harpsichord, and would have me play too. But really Miss L. so very much surpassed me, that had I regarded my reputation for playing, above the desire I had (as I find, and truly said) to satisfy the good company, I ought not to have pretended to touch a key after such a mistress of it. Miss has no voice, which is great pity, and, at the request of every one, I sung to her *accompanyment*, twice or thrice, as did Lady Towers, whose voice exceeds her taste. But here, Miss, will I end my fourth conversation-piece.

SATURDAY MORNING.

THE countess being a little indisposed, Lady Davers and I took an airing this morning in the chariot, and had a great deal of discourse together. Her ladyship was pleased to express great favour and tenderness towards me, gave me a great deal of good advice, as to the care she would have me take of myself; and told me, that her hopes, as well as her brother's, all centered in my welfare; and that the way I was in made her love me better and better.

She was pleased to tell me, how much she approved of the domestick management, and to say, that she never saw such regularity and method in any family in her life, where was the like number of servants: every one, she said, knew their duty, and did it without speaking to, in such silence, and with so much apparent chearfulness and delight, without the least hurry or confusion, that it was her surprize and admiration: but kindly would have it, that I took too much care upon me. 'Yet, said she, 'I don't 'see but you are always fresh and lively, 'and never seem tired or fatigued, and 'are always dressed and easy, so that 'no company find you unprepared, or 'unfit to receive them, come when they 'will, whether it be to breakfast or dinner.'

I told her ladyship, I owed all this, and most of the conduct for which she was pleased to praise me, to her dear brother, who at the beginning of my happiness, gave me several cautions * and instructions for my behaviour, which had always been the rule of my conduct ever since, and I hoped ever would be. 'To 'say nothing,' added I, 'which yet 'would be very unjust, of the assistance 'I receive from worthy Mrs Jervis, 'who is an excellent manager.'

Good Creature, *Sweet Pamela*, and *Charming Girl*, were her common words, and she was pleased to attribute to me a graceful and unaffected ease, and would have it, that I have a natural dignity in my person and behaviour, which command love and reverence at the same time, so that, my dear Miss Darnford, I am in danger of being as proud as any thing. For you must believe, that her ladyship's approbation gives me great pleasure, and the more, as I was afraid, before she came, I should not have come off near so well in her opinion.

As the chariot passed along, she took great notice of the respects paid me by people of different ranks, and of the blessings bestowed upon me, by several, as we proceeded, and said, she should fare well, and be rich in good wishes for being in my company.

'The good people who know us, *will* 'do so, Madam,' said I, 'but I had rather have their silent prayers than their 'audible ones, and I have caused some 'of them to be told so.'

'What I apprehend, Madam,' continued I, 'is, that you will be more uneasy 'to-morrow, when at church you'll see

* See Vol. II. p. 261, 262.

'a good

'a good many people in the ſame way. 'Indeed,' added I, 'my ſtory, and your dear brother's tenderneſs to me, are ſo much talked of, that many ſtrangers are brought hither to ſee us. 'Tis the only thing,' continued I, (and ſo it is, Miſs) 'that makes me deſirous to go to London; for by the time we return, the novelty, I hope, will ceaſe.'

Then I mentioned ſome verſes of Mr. Cowley, which had been laid under my cuſhion in our ſeat at church, two Sundays ago, by ſome unknown hand, and how uneaſy they have made me. I will tranſcribe them, my dear, and give you the particulars of our converſation on that occaſion. The verſes are theſe:

'Thou robb'ſt my days of bus'neſs and de-
'lights,
'Of ſleep thou robb'ſt my nights.
'Ah! lovely thief! what wilt thou do?
'What! rob me of heav'n too!
'Thou ev'n my pray'rs doſt ſteal from me,
'And I, with wild idolatry,
'Begin to GOD, and end them all to thee.

'No, to what purpoſe ſhould I ſpeak?
'No, wretched heart, ſwell till you break.
'She cannot love me, if ſhe would;
'And, to ſay truth, 'twere pity that ſhe
'ſhould.
'No, to the grave thy ſorrows bear,
'As ſilent as they will be there.
'Since that lov'd hand this mortal wound
'does give,
'So handſomely the thing contrive,
'That ſhe may guiltleſs of it live;
'So periſh, that her killing thee
'May a chance medley, and no murder be!'

I had them in my pocket, and read them to my lady, who aſked me, if her brother had ſeen them? I told her, it was he that found them under the cuſhion I uſed to ſit upon, but did not ſhew them to me till I came home, and that I was ſo vexed at them, that I could not go to church in the afternoon.

'What ſhould you be vexed at, my dear?' ſaid ſhe: 'how could you help it?—My brother was not diſturbed at them, was he?'

'No, indeed,' replied I: 'he chid *me* for being ſo, and was pleaſed to make me a fine compliment upon it, that he did not wonder that every body who ſaw me loved me.—But I ſaid, this was all that wicked wit was good for, to inſpire ſuch boldneſs in bad hearts, which might otherwiſe not dare to ſet pen to paper to affront any one.

'But pray, Madam,' added I, 'don't own I have told you of them, leſt the leaſt ſhadow of a thought ſhould ariſe, that I was prompted by ſome vile, ſecret vanity, to tell your ladyſhip of them: when, I am ſure, they have vexed me more than enough. For is it not a ſad thing, that the church ſhould be profaned by ſuch actions, and ſuch thoughts, as ought not to be brought into it?

'Then, Madam, to have any wicked man *dare* to think of one with impure notions! It gives me the leſs opinion of myſelf, that I ſhould be ſo much as *thought of* as the object of any wicked body's wiſhes. I have called myſelf to account upon it, whether any levity in my looks, my dreſs, my appearance, could embolden ſuch an affrontive inſolence. And I have thought upon this occaſion better of Julius Cæſar's delicacy than I did, when I read of it, who, upon an attempt made on his wife, to which, however, it does not appear ſhe gave the leaſt encouragement, ſaid, to thoſe who pleaded for her againſt the divorce he was reſolved upon, *that the wife of Cæſar ought not to be ſuſpected.*

'Indeed, Madam,' continued I, 'it would extremely ſhock me, but to know, that any wicked heart had conceived a deſign upon me, upon *me*, give me leave to repeat, whoſe only glory and merit is, that I have had the grace to withſtand the greateſt of trials and temptations, from a gentleman more worthy to be beloved, both for perſon and mind, than any man in England.'

'Your obſervation, my dear, is truly delicate, and ſuch as becomes your mind and character. And I really think, if any lady in the world is ſecure from vile attempts, it muſt be you, not only from your ſtory ſo well known, and the love you bear to your man, and his merit to you, but from the prudence, and natural *dignity*, I will ſay, of your behaviour, which, though eaſy and chearful, is what would ſtrike dead the hope of any preſumptuous libertine, the moment he ſees you.'

'How can I enough,' returned I, and kiſſed her hand, 'acknowledge your ladyſhip's polite goodneſs in this compliment! But, my lady, you ſee by the very inſtance I have mentioned, that a liberty *is* taken, which I cannot think of without pain.

'Tis such a liberty,' replied my lady, 'as shews more despair than hope, and is a confirmation of my sentiments on the prudence and dignity which not only I, but every body attributes to you.'

'Kind, kind, Lady Davers!' said I, again pressing her hand with my lips. 'But, I think, I will turn my quarrel, since I know not, and hope I never shall, the vile transcriber, upon the author of the verses; for had they not been written, I should not have been thus insulted, perhaps.'

'Cowley,' replied my lady, 'is my favourite poet. He has a beautiful imagination, a vast deal of brilliant wit, and a chastity too in most of his pieces, that hardly any of the tribe can boast.'

'I once liked him better too,' said I, 'than I have done since this; for he was one of the poets that my lady would permit me to read sometimes, and his pieces in praise of the country-life, and those charming lines against ambition, used to delight me much.

"If e'er ambition should my fancy cheat,
With any wish so mean as to be great,
Continue, heav'n, still from me to remove
The humble blessings of that life I love!"

'I have taken notice of these lines often,' said my lady, 'and been pleased with them. But I think you have no reason to be out of conceit with Cowley, for the ill use made of his verses. It but too naturally describes the influence of love, which frequently interferes with our best duties. And there is something very natural, and easy, and witty, in the first lines; and shews that the poet's *laments* are too engaging impressions which love made upon his mind, even on the most solemn occasions — "*What! rob me of Heaven too!*" — A bad heart, Pamela, could not have so lamented, or so written.'

'Ah! but, Madam,' returned I, 'I have seen in your dear brother's collection of manuscripts, a poem in which this very point, nice as it is, is touched with much greater propriety.'

'Can you repeat it, my dear?'

'The lines I *mean*, I can. Your ladyship must know it was upon a quarrel between a beloved couple, where the gentleman had been wild, and the lady's ill-natured uncle, who wanted to break the match, (although it was designed by her deceased parents) had fomented it, so that she would not look upon her lover, nor see him, nor receive a letter of excuse from him, though they were betrothed, and she loved him dearly. This obliged him to throw himself in her way at church, and thus he writes:

"But, O! forgive me, Heav'n, if oft my fair
Robs thee of my devoir, disturbs my pray'r,
Confounds my best resolves, and makes me prove,
Tho' she's too much a rival in thy love."

'These now, Madam,' continued I, 'are the lines I admire:

"But better thoughts my happier hopes engage,
When once this stormy doubt's expell'd my breast,
When once this *agitated flame* shall turn
To *steadier* heat, and more *intensely* burn,
My dear *Maria* then, thought I, will join,
And we, *one heart*, *one soul*, shall *all* be THINE!"

'Ay, Pamela, these are very pretty lines. But you must not think ill of my favourite Cowley, however; for I say with a gentleman, whose judgment and good heart have hardly any equal, that though Cowley was going out of fashion with some, yet he should always suspect the head or the heart of him or her, who could not taste, and delight in his beauties.

'The words—

"She *were* love me, if she would,
"And, *to say* truth, twere pity that she should,

shew the *goodness* of the *poet's heart*; and even, that the transcriber himself, be he who he will, had not the *worst*, that he could single out *these*, when, if he would be shining with borrowed rays, he might have chosen a much worse poet to follow.'

'O Madam!' replied I, 'say not one word in behalf of the wicked transcriber. For a wretch to entertain the shadow of a wish for a married person is a degree of impurity that ought not to be excused: but to commit such 'thoughts to writing, to put that writing under the seat of the married person at church, where her heart should be engaged *wholly* in her first duties, where too it might be more likely to be seen by the pew-keepers than her, and so be spread over the whole parish, to the propagation of bad ideas, whenever I appeared, and, moreover, might come to the hands of one's husband, who from his own free life formerly, and high passions, as far as the transcriber knew, might be uneasy at, and angry with, the innocent occasion of the insult.—Besides the apprehension it must give one, that the man who could take this vile step might proceed to greater lengths, which my busy fears could improve to duelling and murder—Then the concern it must fill me with, to the diverting of my mind from my first regards, when *any one* looked at me wistfully, that he might be the transcriber! which must always give me confusion of thought.—dearest Madam, can one forbear being vexed, when all these imaginations dart in upon a mind apprehensive as mine? Indeed, this action has given me great uneasiness, at times, ever since, and I cannot help it.'

'I am pleased with your delicacy, my dear, as I said before.—You can never err, while thus watchful over your conduct: and I own you have the more reason for it, as you have married a mere Julius Cæsar, an open-eyed rake,' that was her word, 'who would, on the least surmises, though ever so causeless on your part, have all his passions up in arms, in apprehension of liberties that might be offered like those he has not scrupled to take.'

'O but, Madam,' said I, 'your dear brother has given me great satisfaction in one point; for you must think I should not love him as I ought, if I had not a concern for his future happiness, as well as for his present, and that is, he has assured me, that in all the liberties he has taken, *he never attempted a married lady*, but always abhorred the thought of so great an evil.'

''Tis pity,' said her ladyship, 'that a man who could conquer his passions *so far*, could not subdue them entirely. This shews it was in his own power to do so, and encreases his crime: and what a wretch is he, who scrupling, under pretence of conscience or honour, to attempt ladies *within* the pale, boggles not to ruin a poor creature *without*; although he knows, he thereby, most probably, for ever deprives her of that protection, by preventing her marriage, which even among such rakes as himself, is deemed, he owns, inviolable, and so casts the poor creature headlong into the jaws of perdition?'

'Ah! Madam,' replied I, 'this was the very inference I made upon the occasion.'

'And what could he say?'

'He said, my inference was just, but called me *pretty preacher*,—and once having cautioned me* not to be over-serious to him, so as to cast a gloom, as he said, over our innocent enjoyments, I never dare to urge matters farther, when he calls me by that name.'

'Well,' said my lady, 'thou'rt an admirable girl! God's goodness was great to our family, when it gave thee to it.'

'No wonder,' continued her ladyship, 'as my brother says, every body that sees you, and has heard your character, loves you. And this is some excuse for the inconsiderate folly even of this unknown transcriber.'

'Ah! Madam,' replied I, 'but is it not a sad thing, that people, if they must take upon them to like one's behaviour in general, should have the *worst*, instead of the *best* thoughts upon it? If I were as good as I *ought* to be, and as some *think* me, must they wish to make me bad for that reason? And so to destroy the cause of that pleasure which they pretend to take in seeing a body set a good example? For what, my dear lady, could a wretch mean, even by the words your ladyship think most innocent?

"She cannot love me, if she would,
"And, to say truth,—(as if this truth
'were extorted rather by his *fears* than his
'*wishes*)
"—— 'twere pity that she should."

'But why, then, if this be the case, and that he would bear his *sorrows*, as the poet calls them, to the grave,

* See Vol. II. p. 196.

'ſhould he not keep them to *himſelf?* 'Make that very myſtery their grave, which 'gave them their *birth?* If the bold 'creature, whoever he be, had not 'thought this might be a hint that 'might ſome-how be improved, and a 'vile foundation for ſome viler ſuper-'ſtructure, would he have tranſcribed 'them, and cauſed them to be placed 'where they were found?—Then, in 'my humble opinion, the thought that 'is contained in theſe lines—

"Since thus I love a hand this mortal wound
"does give,
"So handſomely the thing contrive,
"That ſhe may guiltleſs of it live!
'So periſh, that her killing thee
"May a chance-medley, and no murder be,"

'is rather a *conceit* or *prettineſs*, that 'won't bear examination, than that true 'wit in which this fine poet excels: 'for if ſhe cannot love him if *ſhe would*, 'and it were *pity* that ſhe *ſhould* love 'him, this implies ſhe was a lady under 'previous obligation, whether marriage 'or betrothment, is the ſame thing to 'him: then, need the thing to be ſo '*handſomely contrived*, need any pains 'be taken (if her repulſe *had killed*, 'as poetical licence makes him ſay, this 'invader of another's right) to bring it 'in *chance medley*,—ſince no jury could 'have brought it in *murder*, except that 'ſort of murder which is called *felo de* '*ſe*, you know, my lady, what a ſcho-'lar your brother has made me: ſo that 'I preſume to think, the poet himſelf 'is not ſo blameleſs in this, as he has 'taken care to be in moſt of his pieces. 'And permit me to make one obſerva-'tion, my good lady, that if the chaſteſt 'writers (ſuppoſing Cowley meant ever 'ſo well) may have their works, and 'their thoughts, turned to be panders 'and promoters of the wickedneſs of 'coarſe minds, whoſe groſſer ideas could 'not be clothed in a dreſs fit to appear 'in decent company, without *their* aſ-'ſiſtance, how careful ought a good 'author to be, whoſe works are likely 'to live to the end of time, how he pro-'pagates the worſt of miſchiefs to ſuch 'a duration, when he himſelf is dead 'and gone, and incapable of antidoting 'the poiſon he has ſpread?'

Her ladyſhip was pleaſed to kiſs me as we ſat. 'My charming Pamela, my '*more than ſiſter*,—(Did ſhe ſay)—Yes, ſhe did ſay ſo! and made my eyes overflow with joy to hear the ſweet epithet! 'How your converſation 'charms me!—I charge you, when 'you get to town, let me have your re-'marks on the diverſions you will be 'carried to by my brother. Now I 'know what to expect from *you*, and *you* 'know how acceptable every thing will 'be *to me* that comes from you. I pro-'miſe great pleaſure, as well to myſelf 'as to my worthy friends, particularly 'to Lady Betty, in your unreſtrained 'free correſpondence.

'Indeed, Pamela, I muſt bring you 'acquainted with Lady Betty: ſhe is one 'of the worthies of our ſex, and has a 'fine underſtanding.—I'm ſure you'll 'like her.—But (for the world ſay it 'not to my brother, nor let Lady Betty 'know I tell you ſo, if ever you ſhould 'be acquainted—) I had carried the 'matter ſo far by my officious zeal to 'have my brother married to ſo fine a 'lady, not doubting his joyful approba-'tion, that it was no ſmall diſappoint-'ment to *her*, I can tell you, when he 'married you: and this is the beſt ex-'cuſe I can make for my furious beha-'viour to you at the Hall. For though 'I am naturally very haſty and paſſion-'ate, yet then I was almoſt mad.—In-'deed my diſappointment had given me 'ſo much indignation both againſt you 'and him, that it is well I did not do 'ſome violent thing by you. * I be-'lieve you did feel the weight of my 'hand.—but what was that?—'Twas 'well I did not *kill you dead.*——theſe were her ladyſhip's words—'For how 'could I think the wild libertine capa-'ble of being engaged by ſuch noble 'motives, or thee what thou art?—So 'this will account to thee a little for my 'violence then.'

'Your ladyſhip, ſaid I, 'all theſe 'things conſidered, had but too much 'reaſon to be angry at your dear bro-'ther's proceedings, ſo well as you al-'ways lov'd him, ſo high a concern as 'you always had to promote his honour 'and intereſt, and ſo far as you had gone 'with Lady Betty.

* Compare this part of the converſation with Lady Davers's behaviour to Pamela, Vol. II. p. 222, to 233.

'I tell

'I tell thee, Pamela, ſaid ſhe, 'that 'the old ſtory of Eleanor and Roſamond 'run in my head all the way of my 'journey, and I almoſt wiſhed for a po-'tion to force down thy throat: and 'when I came, and found thy lewd 'paramour abſent, (for little did I 'think thou waſt married to him, though 'I expected thou wouldſt endeavour to 'perſuade me to believe it) apprehend-'ing that his intrigue with thee would 'effectually fruſtrate my hopes as to 'Lady Betty and him: "Now, thought I, "all happens as I wiſh!—Now will "I confront this brazen girl!—Now "will I try her innocence, as I pleaſe, "by offering to take her with me out of "his hands, if ſhe refuſes, take that re-"fuſal for a demonſtration of her guilt, "and then, thought I, "I will make "the creature provoke me, in the pre-"ſence of my nephew and my woman, '(and I hoped to have got that woman 'Jewkes to teſtify for me too,) and I 'cannot tell what I might have done, if 'thou hadſt not got out of the window 'as thou didſt, eſpecially after thou 'hadſt told me thou waſt as much mar-'ried as I was, and hadſt ſhewn me his 'tender letter to thee, which had a quite 'different effect upon me than thou 'hadſt hoped for. But if I had com-'mitted any act of violence, what 'remorſe ſhould I have had, when I 'came to reflect, and had known what 'an excellence I had injured? Thank 'God thou didſt eſcape me! thank God 'thou didſt!" And then her ladyſhip folded her arms about me, and kiſſed me.

This was a ſad ſtory, you'll ſay, my dear: and I wonder what her lady-ſhip's paſſion would have made her do! Surely ſhe would not have *killed me dead* indeed! ſurely ſhe would not!—Let it not however, Miſs Darnford—nor you, my dear father and mother,—when you ſee it,—go out of your own hands, nor be read, for my Lady Davers's ſake, to any body elſe—No, not to your own mamma.—It made me tremble a little, even at this diſtance, to think what a ſad thing paſſion is, when way is given to it's ungovernable tumults, and how it deforms and debaſes the nobleſt minds.

We returned from this agreeable air-ing but juſt time enough to dreſs before dinner, and then I attended my lady, and we went together into the counteſs's apartment, where I received abundance of compliments from both. As this brief converſation will give you ſome notion of that management and œcono-my for which they heaped upon me their kind praiſes, I will recite to you what paſſed in it, and hope you will not think me too vain, and the leſs, becauſe what I underwent formerly from my lady's indignation, half entitles me to be proud of her preſent kindneſs and favour.

Lady Davers ſaid—'Your ladyſhip 'muſt excuſe us, that we have loſt ſo 'much of your company, but here, this 'ſweet girl has entertained me in ſuch a 'manner, that I could have ſtaid out 'with her all day, and ſeveral times 'did I bid the coachman prolong his cir-'cuit.'

'My good Lady Davers, Madam,' ſaid I, 'has given me inexpreſſible plea-'ſure, and has been all condeſcenſion 'and favour, and made me as proud as 'proud can be.'

'You, my dear Mrs. B. ſaid ſhe, 'may have given great pleaſure to Lady 'Davers, for it cannot be otherwiſe— 'But I have no great notion of her lady-'ſhip's condeſcenſion, as you call it— '(pardon me, Madam, ſaid ſhe to her, ſmiling) 'when ſhe cannot raiſe her 'ſtyle above the word *girl*, coming off 'from a tour you have made ſo delight-'ful to her.'

'I proteſt to you, my Lady C. re-plied her ladyſhip, with great goodneſs, 'that that word, which once indeed I 'uſed through pride, as you'll call it, I 'now uſe for a very different reaſon. I 'begin to doubt, whether to call her 'Siſter, is not more honour to myſelf 'than to her, and to this hour am not 'quite convinced. When I am, I will 'call her ſo with pleaſure.'

I was quite overcome with this fine compliment, but could not anſwer a word: and the counteſs ſaid—'I could 'have ſpared you longer, had not the 'time of day compelled your return. 'For I have been very agreeably enter-'tained, as well as you, although but 'with the talk of your woman and 'mine. For here they have been giving 'me ſuch an account of Mrs. B.'s œco-'nomy, and family management, as 'has highly delighted me. I never 'knew the like, and in ſo young a lady 'too.—We ſhall have ſtrange reforma-'tions to make in our families, Lady 'Davers, when we go home, were we 'to follow ſo good an example.'

'Why,

'Why, my dear Mrs B' continued her ladyship, 'you out-do all your 'neighbours And indeed I am glad 'I live so far from you—for were I to 'try to imitate you, it would still be *but* 'imitation, and you'd have the honour 'of it.

'Yet you hear, and you see by yes-'terday's conversation, said Lady Da-vers, 'how much her best neighbours, 'of both sexes admire her they all yield 'to her the palm, unenvying

'Then, my good ladies, said I, 'it 'is a sign I have most excellent neigh-'bours, full of generosity, and willing 'to encourage a young person in doing 'right things so it makes, considering 'what I was, more for their honour 'than my own For what censures 'should not such a one as I deserve, who 'have not been educated to fill up my 'time like ladies of condition, were I 'not to employ myself as I do? I, who 'have so little other merit, and who 'brought no fortune at all?'

'Come, come, Pamela, none of your 'self-denying ordinances, that was Lady Davers's word, 'you must know 'something of your own excellence If 'you do not, I'll tell it you, because 'there is no fear you will be proud or 'vain upon it I don't see then, that 'there is the lady in your neighbour-'hood, or *any* neighbourhood, that be-'haves with more decorum, or better 'keeps up the part of a lady, than you 'do How you manage it, I can't tell, 'but you do as much by a look, and 'a pleasant one too, that's the ra-'rity! as I do by high words, and pas-'sionate exclamations I have often no-'thing but blunder upon blunder, as if 'the wretches were in a confederacy to 'try my patience'

'Perhaps, Madam, said I, 'the awe 'they have of your ladyship, because of 'your high qualities, makes them com-'mit blunders, for I myself have always 'been more afraid of appearing before 'your ladyship, when you have visited 'your honoured mother, than of any 'body else, and have been the more sen-'sibly aukward through that very aw-'ful respect

'Psha, psha, Pamela, that is not it 'tis all in yourself I used to think 'my mamma, and my brother too, had 'as aukward servants as ever I saw any 'where—except Mrs Jervis.—Well 'enough for a batchelor, indeed!—But, 'here!—thou hast not parted with one 'servant—Hast thou?

'No, Madam

'How! said the countess, 'what 'excellence is here!—All of them, 'pardon me, Mrs B your fellow-ser-'vants, as one may say, and all of them 'so respectful, so watchful of your eye, 'and you, at the same time, so gentle to 'them, so easy, so cheerful!

Don't you think me, my dear, insuf-ferably vain? But tis what they were pleased to say 'Twas their goodness to me, and shewed how much they can excel in generous politeness So I will proceed

'Why this, continued the countess, 'must be *born* dignity—*born* discretion—'Education cannot give it—if it could, 'why should not *we* have it?

The ladies said many more kind things of me then, and after dinner they men-tioned all over again, with additions, be-fore my best friend, who was kindly de-lighted with the encomiums given me by two ladies of such distinguishing judg-ment in all other cases They told him, how much they admired my family manage-ment then would have it, that my genius was universal, for the employments and accomplishments of my sex, whether they considered it, they were pleased to say, as employed in penmanship, in needle-work, in paying or receiving visits, in musick, and I can't tell how many other qualifications, which their goodness made them attribute to me, over and above the family management, saying, that I had an understanding which comprehended every thing, and an eye that penetrated into the very bottom of matters in a mo-ment, and never was at a loss for the *should be*, the *why* or *wherefore*, and the *how*, these were their comprehensive words—that I did every thing with ce-lerity, clearing all as I went, and left no-thing, that was their observation, to re-cur, or come over again, that could be dispatched at once by which means, they said, every hand was clear to undertake a new work, as well as my own head to direct it, and there was no hurry nor confusion, but every coming hour was fresh and ready, and unincumbered (so they said,) for it's new employment, and to this they attributed that ease and plea-sure with which every thing was per-formed and that I could *do*, and *cause* to be done, so much business without hur-ry either to myself or servants

These

These things, they would have it, they observed in part themselves, and in part were beholden for to the observations of their women, who looked, they said, so narrowly into every part of the management, as if they were spies upon it, but were such faithful ones, that it was like a good cause brought to a strict scrutiny, the brighter and fairer for it

Thus, my dear Miss Darnford, did their ladyships *praise me for what I ought to be*, and I will endeavour to improve more and more by their kind admonitions, which come clothed in the agreeable and flattering shape of praise, the noblest incitement to the doing of one's duty

Judge you how pleasing this was to my best beloved, who found, in their kind approbation, such a justification of his own conduct, as could not fail of being pleasing to him, especially as Lady Davers was one of the kind praisers

Lord Davers was so highly delighted, that he rose once, begging his brother's excuse, to salute me, and remained standing over my chair, with a pleasure in his looks that cannot be expressed, now-and-then lifting up his hands, and his good-natured eye glistening with joy, which a pier-glass gave me the opportunity of seeing, as sometimes I stole a bashful glance towards it, not knowing how or which way to look Even Mr H seemed to be touched very sensibly, and recollecting his behaviour to me at the Hall, he once cried out—'What a sad whelp 'was *I*, to behave as I formerly did, to 'so much excellence!—Not, Mr B that 'I was any thing uncivil, neither,—but 'in unworthy sneers, and nonsense— 'You know me well enough.—P-x on 'me for a Jackanapes!—You called me, '* *Tinsell'd toy*, though, Madam, don't 'you remember that? and said, *twenty 'or thirty years hence, when I was at 'age, you'd give me an answer* Egad! 'I shall never forget your looks, nor 'your words neither!—They were 'd—n'd severe speeches, were they not, 'Sir?'

'O you see, Mr H' replied my dear Mr B 'Pamela is not quite perfect — 'We must not provoke her, for she'll 'call us both so, perhaps, for I wear a 'laced coat, sometimes, as well as you'

'Nay, faith, I can't be angry,' said he 'I deserved it richly, that I did, had it 'been worse

'Thy silly tongue,' said my lady, 'runs on without fear or wit What's 'past is past

'Why, i'faith, Madam, I was plaguily wrong, and I said nothing of any 'body but *myself*—and have been ready to hang myself since, as often as I 'have thought of my nonsense'

'*My nephew*,' *said my lord*, '*must* 'bring in hanging, or the gallows, in 'every speech he makes, or it will not 'be he'

Mr B smiling, said, with severity enough in his meaning, as I could see by the turn of his countenance—'Mr H 'knows, that his birth and family intitle him more to the *block*, than the 'rope, or he would not make so free with 'the latter.'

'Good! very good, by Jupiter!' said Mr H laughing The countess smiled Lady Davers shook her head at her brother, and said to her nephew—'Thou'rt 'a good-natured foolish fellow, that thou 'art'

'For what, Madam? Why the word '*foolish*, aunt? What have I said now?'

'Nothing to any purpose, indeed,' said she, 'when thou dost, I'll write it 'down'

'Then, Madam,' said he, 'have your 'pen and ink always about you, when 'I'm present.—The devil's in't if you 'won't put that down, to begin with!'

This made every one laugh 'What 'a happy thing is it, thought I, 'that 'good nature generally accompanies this 'character, else, how would some people be supportable?

But here I'll break off 'Tis time, you'll say —But you know to whom I write, as well as to yourself, and they'll be pleased with all my silly scribble.— So excuse one part for that, and another for friendship's sake, and then I shall be wholly excusable to you

Now the trifler again resumes her pen. I am in some pain, Miss, for to-morrow, because of the rules we observe of late in our family on Sundays, and of going through a crowd to church, which will afford new scenes to our noble visitors either for censure or otherwise but I

will

* See Vol II p. 228.

will ſooner be cenſured for doing what I think my duty, than for the want of it, and so will omit nothing that we have been accuſtomed to do.

I hope I ſhall not be thought ridiculous, or as one who aims at works of ſupererogation, for what I think is very ſhort of my duty.—Some order, ſurely, becomes the heads of families, and beſides, it would be discrediting one's own practice, if one did not appear at one time what one does at another. For that which is a reaſon for diſcontinuing a practice for ſome company, would ſeem to be a reaſon for laying it aſide for ever, eſpecially in a family viſiting and viſited as ours.

And I remember well a hint given me by my deareſt friend once on another ſubject*, That it is in every one's power to preſcribe rules to himſelf, after a while, and perſons ſee what is one's way, and that one is not to be put out of it.

But my only doubt is, that to ladies, who have not been accuſtomed perhaps to the *neceſſary* ſtrictneſs, I ſhould make myſelf cenſurable, as if I aimed at too much perfection: for, however one's duty is one's duty, and ought not to be diſpenſed with; yet, when a perſon, who uſes to be remiſs, ſees ſo hard a taſk before them, and ſo many great points to get over, all to be no more than tolerably regular, it is rather apt to frighten and diſcourage, than to allure, and one muſt proceed, as I have read ſoldiers do, in a difficult ſiege, inch by inch, and be more ſtudious to intrench and fortify themſelves, as they go on gaining upon the enemy, than by ruſhing all at once upon an attack of the place, be repulſed, and perhaps obliged with great loſs to abandon a hopeful enterprize.

And permit me to add, that young as I am, I have often obſerved, that overgreat ſtrictneſſes all at once injoined and inſiſted upon, are not fit for a beginning reformation, but for ſtronger Chriſtians only, and therefore generally do more harm than good, in ſuch a circumſtance.

'What a miſerable creature am I, ſaid a neighbouring widow gentlewoman, (whom I viſited in her illneſs, at her own deſire, though a ſtranger to me but by name) 'if all the good *you* do, and the 'ſtrict life *you* live, is no more than abſolutely neceſſary to ſalvation!'

I ſaw the poor gentlewoman, through illneſs and low ſpirits, was ready to deſpond, and, to comfort her, I ſaid—'Dear Madam, don't be caſt down. 'God Almighty gives us all a light to 'walk by in theſe our dark paths, and 'tis my humble opinion, he will judge 'us according to the *unforced* and *unbiaſſed* uſe we make of that light: I 'think it my duty to do ſeveral things, 'which, perhaps, the circumſtances of 'others will not permit *them* to do, or 'which they, on ſerious and diſintereſted 'reflection, may not think abſolutely 'neceſſary to be done: in each caſe our 'judgments are a law to each, and I 'ought no more to excuſe myſelf from 'doing ſuch parts as I think my duty, 'than you to condemn yourſelf for not 'doing what does not appear to you ſo 'ſtrictly neceſſary: and beſides, Madam, 'you may do as much good one way, 'as I another, and ſo both may be equally uſeful in the general ſyſtem of Providence.'

But ſhall I not be too grave, my dear friend?—Excuſe me, for this is Saturday night, and as it was a very good method which the ingenious authors of the Spectators took, generally to treat their more ſerious ſubjects on this day, ſo I think one ſhould, when one can, conſider it as the preparative eve to a ſtill better.

SUNDAY.

NOW, my dear, by what I have already written, it is become in a manner neceſſary to acquaint you briefly with the method my dear Mr. B. not only permits, but encourages me to take, in the family he leaves to my care, as to the Sunday *duty*.

The worthy dean, at my requeſt, and by my beloved's permiſſion, recommended to me, as a ſort of family chaplain, for Sundays, a young gentleman of great ſobriety and piety, and ſound principles, who having but lately taken orders, has at preſent no other proviſion. And this gentleman comes, and reads prayers to us about ſeven in the morning, in the leſſer hall, as we call it, a retired apartment, next the little garden, for we have no chapel with us here, as in your neighbourhood: and this generally, with ſome ſuitable exhortation, or meditation out of

* See Vol. II. p. 217.

of ſome good book, which the young gentleman is ſo kind as to let me chooſe now-and-then, when I pleaſe, takes up little more than half an hour

We have a great number of ſervants of both ſexes and myſelf, my good Mrs Jervis, and my Polly Barlow, are generally in a little cloſet, which, when we open the door, is but juſt a ſeparation, and that's all, from the hall.

Mr Adams (for that is our young clergyman's name) has a deſk, at which ſometimes Mr Jonathan makes up his running accounts to Mr Longman, who is very ſcrupulous of admitting any body to the uſe of his office, becauſe of the writing in his cuſtody, and the order he values himſelf upon having every thing in

About ſeven in the evening the young gentleman comes again, and I generally, let me have what company I will, find time to retire for about another half-hour, and my dear Mr B connives at, and excuſes my abſence, if enquired after, though, for ſo ſhort a time, I am ſeldom miſſed

To the young gentleman I ſhall preſent, every quarter, five guineas, and Mr B preſſes him to accept of a place at his table at his pleaſure but, as we have generally a good deal of company, his modeſty makes him decline it, eſpecially at thoſe times

Mr Longman is ſo kind as to join with us very often in our Sunday office, and Mr Colbrand ſeldom miſſes, and they tell Mrs Jervis, that they cannot expreſs the pleaſure they have to meet me there, and the edification they receive, as they are ſo kind to ſay, from my example, and from the cheerful temper I am always in, which does em good to look upon me and they will have it, that I do credit to religion But if they do but think ſo, it muſt have been of ſervice to me in the order I have now eſtabliſhed, as I hope, and that through leſs difficulties than I expected to meet with, eſpecially from the *cookmaid, but ſhe ſays, ſhe comes with double delight to have the opportunity to ſee her bleſſed lady, as it ſeems ſhe calls me at every word

My beſt beloved diſpenſes as much as he can with the ſervants, for the evening part, if he has company, or will be attended only by John or Abraham, perhaps by turns, and ſometimes looks upon his watch, and ſays—'Tis near 'ſeven, and if he ſays ſo, they take it for a hint they may be diſpenſed with for half an hour, and this countenance which he gives me, has not contributed a little to make the matter eaſy and delightful to me, and to every one.

I am ſure, were only policy to be conſidered, this method muſt be laudable, for ſince I begun it, there is not a more diligent, a more ſober, nor more courteous ſet of ſervants in any family in a great way we have no broils, no hard words, no revilings, no commandings nor complainings, and Mrs Jervis's government is made ſo eaſy, as ſhe ſays, that ſhe need not ſpeak twice, and all the language of the ſervants is—'Pray, 'John,' or, 'Pray, Jane, do ſo or ſo, and they ſay, their maſter's ſervice is a heaven upon earth

When I part from them, on the breaking up of our aſſembly, they generally make a little row on each ſide of the hall-door, and when I have made my compliments, and paid my thanks to Mr Adams, one whiſpers, as I go out—'God bleſs you, Madam!' and ſo ſays another, and another, and indeed every one, and bow and curt'ſy with ſuch pleaſure in their honeſt countenances as greatly delights me and I ſay, (if it ſo happens)—'So, my good friends!—I 'am glad to ſee you—Not one abſent!' or but one—(as it falls out)—'This is 'very obliging, I cry and thus I ſhew them, that I take notice, if any body be not there And back again I go to pay my duty to my earthly benefactor and he is pleaſed to ſay ſometimes, that I come to him with ſuch a radiance in my countenance, as gives him double pleaſure to behold me', and often he tells me afterwards, that but for appearing too fond before company, he could meet me, as I enter, with embraces as pure as my own heart

I hope in time, I ſhall prevail upon the dear man to give me his company —But, thank God, I am enabled to go thus far already!—I will leave the reſt to his providence For I have a point very delicate to touch upon in this particular, and I muſt take care not to loſe the ground I have gained, by too precipitately puſhing at too much at once. This is my comfort, that next to being uniform *himſelf*,

* See Vol I p 69 Vol. II p. 272.

is that permission and encouragement he gives *me*, to be so, and the pleasure he takes in seeing me so delighted—and besides, he always gives me his company to church. O how happy should I think myself, if he would be pleased to accompany me to the Divine office, which yet he has not done, though I have urged him as much as I durst! 'One thing after 'another, he says; we shall be better and 'better, I hope; but nobody is good all 'at once.' But, my dear Miss Darnford, as I consider this as the seal of all the rest, and he himself has an awful notion of it, I shall hardly think my dear Mr B— morally secured till then.

Mrs Jervis asked me, on Saturday evening, if I would be concerned to see a larger congregation in my little chapel next morning, than usual. I answered—'No, by 'no means.' She said, Mrs Worden, and Mrs Lesley, (the two ladies women) and Mr Sydney, my Lord Davers's gentleman, and Mr H.'s servant, and the coachmen and footmen belonging to our noble visitors, who are, she says, all great admirers of our family management and good order, having been told our method, begged to join in it. I knew I should be a little dashed at so large an appearance, but the men being orderly, for lords servants, and Mrs Jervis assuring me, that they were very earnest in their request, I consented to it.

When I came at the usual time, (attended by my Polly,) I came down, I found Mr Adams there, (to whom I made my first compliments) and every one of our own people waiting for me, Mr Colbrand excepted, (whom Mr H. had kept up late the night before) together with Mrs Worden and Mrs Lesley, and Mr Sydney, with the servants of our guests, who, as also worthy Mr Longman, and Mrs Jervis, and Mr Jonathan, paid me their respects, and I said— 'This is early rising, Mrs Lesley and 'Mrs Worden, you are very kind to 'countenance us with your companies 'in this our family order.—Mr Sydney, I am glad to see you.—How do 'you, Mr Longman?' and looked round with complacency on the servants of our noble visitors. And then I led Mrs Worden and Mrs Lesley to my little retiring place, and Mrs Jervis and my Polly followed, and throwing the door open, Mr Adams began some select prayers, and as the young gentleman reads with great emphasis and propriety, and as if his heart was in what he read, all the good folks were exceedingly attentive.

After prayers, Mr Adams read a meditation, from a collection made for private use, which I shall more particularly mention by-and-by, and ending with the usual benediction, I thanked the worthy gentleman, and gently chid him, in Mr B.'s name, for his modesty in declining our table, and thanking Mr Longman, and Mrs Worden, and Mrs Lesley, received their kind wishes, and hastened, blushing through their praises, to my chamber, where being alone, I pursued the subject for an hour, till breakfast was ready, when I attended the ladies, and my best beloved, who had told them of the verses placed under my cushion at church.

We set out, my Lord and Lady Davers, and myself, and Mr H. in our coach, and Mr B. and the countess in the chariot, both ladies, and the gentlemen, splendidly dressed, but I avoided a glitter as much as I could, that I might not seem to vie with the two peeresses.—Mr B. said—'Why are you not full-'dressed, my dear?' I said, I hoped he would not be displeased: if he was, I would do as he commanded. He kindly answered—'As you like best, my love. 'You are charming in every dress.'

The chariot first drawing up to the church-door, Mr B. led the countess into the church. My Lord Davers did me that honour, and Mr H. handed his aunt through a crowd of gazers, many of whom, as usual, were strangers. The neighbouring gentlemen and their ladies paid us their silent respects, but the thoughts of the wicked verses, or rather, as Lady Davers will have me say, wicked action of the transcriber of them, made me keep behind in the pew: but my lady, with great goodness, sat down by me, and whisperingly talked a good deal, between whiles, to me, with great tenderness and freedom in her aspect, which I could not but take kindly, because I knew she intended by it, to shew every one she was pleased with me.

Among other things she said softly— 'Who would wish to be a king or queen, 'Pamela, if it is so easy for virtue and 'beauty (so she was pleased to say) 'to 'attract so many sincere admirers, with-'out any of their grandeur?—Look 'round, my dear girl, and see what a 'solemn respect, and mingled delight,

'appears

'appears in every countenance' and pressing my hand—'Thou art a charming creature! Such a natural modesty, 'and such a becoming dignity, in thy 'whole appearance—no wonder that 'every one's eyes are upon thee, and that 'thou bringest to church so many booted 'gentlemen, as well as neighbours, to 'behold thee!'

Afterwards she was pleased to add, taking my hand, and Mr B and the countess heard her, (for she raised her voice to a more audible whisper) 'I am 'proud to be in thy company, and in 'this solemn place, I take thy hand, and 'acknowledge with pride, my *sister*' I looked down, and indeed here at church, I can hardly at any time look up, for who can bear to be gazed at so?—and softly said—'Oh! my good lady! how 'much you honour me, the place, and 'these surrounding eyes, can only hinder 'me from acknowledging as I ought'

My best friend, with pleasure in his eyes, said, pressing his hand upon both ours, as my lady had mine in hers—'You 'are two beloved creatures both excellent in your way, God bless you 'both'—'And you too, my dear brother,' said my lady

The countess whispered—'You should 'spare a body a little! You give one, 'ladies, and Mr B too much pleasure 'all at once. Such company, and such 'behaviour, adds still more charms to 'devotion, and were I to be here a 'twelvemonth, I would never miss once 'accompanying you to this good place'

Mr H thought he must say something, and addressing himself to his noble uncle, who could not keep his good-natured eye off me, 'I'll be *hang'd*, my lord, if I 'know how to behave myself! Why this 'outdoes the chapel!—I'm glad I put 'on my new suit!' And then he looked upon himself, as if he would support, as well as he could, his part of the general admiration

But think you not, my dear Miss Darnford, and my dearest father and mother, that I am now at the height of my happiness in this life, thus favoured by Lady Davers!

The dean preached an excellent sermon, but I need not have said that, only to have mentioned, that *he* preached, was saying enough

My lord led me out, when divine service was over (and being a little tender in his feet, from a gouty notice, walked very slowly) Lady Towers and Mrs Brooks joined us in the porch, and made us their compliments, as did Mr Martin 'Will you favour us with your 'company home, my old acquaintance' said Mr B to that gentleman 'I 'can't, having a gentleman my relation 'to dine with me, but if it will be agreeable in the evening, I will bring him 'with me to taste of your Burgundy, 'for we have not any such in the country'—'I shall be glad to see you, or 'any friend of yours,' replied Mr B

Mr Martin whispered—'It is more, 'however, to admire your lady, I can 'tell you that, than your wine'—Get 'into your coaches, ladies, said he, with his usual freedom, 'our maiden 'and widow ladies have a fine time of it, 'wherever you come by my faith, *they* 'must every one of them quit this neighbourhood, if you were to stay in it 'but all the hopes they have, are, that 'while you are in London, they'll have 'the game in their own hands'

'*Sister*, said Lady Davers, most kindly to me, in presence of many, who (in a respectful manner) gathered near us, 'Mr Martin is the same gentleman he 'used to be, I see'

'Mr Martin, Madam, said I, smiling 'has but one fault, he is too apt to 'praise whom he favours, at the expence 'of his absent friends'

'I am always proud of your reproofs, 'Mrs B' replied he

'Ay, said Lady Towers, 'that I be 'here'—And therefore, I wish, for all 'our sakes, you'd take him oftener to 'task, Mrs B'

Lady Towers, Lady Arthur, Mrs Brooks, and Mr Martin, all claimed visits from us, and Mr B making excuses, that he must husband his time, because of being obliged to go to town soon, proposed to breakfast with Lady Towers the next morning, dine with Mrs Arthur, and sup with Mrs Brooks, and as there cannot be a more social and agreeable neighbourhood any-where, his proposal, after some difficulty, was accepted, and our usual visiting neighbours were all to have notice accordingly, at each of the places

I saw Sir Thomas Atkyns coming towards us, and fearing to be stifled with compliments, I said—'Your servant, ladies and gentlemen,' and giving my hand to Lord Davers, stept into the chariot, instead of the coach, for people that would avoid buſtle, ſometimes make it. Finding my miſtake, I would have come out, but my lord ſaid— 'Indeed you ſhan't and I'll ſtep in, 'becauſe I'll have you all to myſelf.'

Lady Davers ſmiled—'Now, ſaid ſhe, (while the coach drew up) 'is my 'Lord Davers pleaſed,—but I ſee, ſiſter, 'you were tired with part of your com'pany in the coach.

'Tis well contrived, my dear, ſaid Mr B 'as long as you have not de'prived me of this honour,' taking the counteſs's hand, and leading her into the coach.

Will you excuſe all this impertinence, my dear —I know my father and mother will be pleaſed with it, and you will have the goodneſs to bear with me on that account, for their kind hearts will be delighted to hear every minute thing in relation to Lady Davers and myſelf.

When Mr Martin came in the evening, with his friend, (who is Sir William G a polite young gentleman of Lincolnſhire) he told us a deal of the praiſes laviſhed away upon me by ſeveral genteel ſtrangers, one ſaying to his friend, he had travelled twenty miles to ſee me.

My Lady Davers was praiſed too for her goodneſs to me, and the gracefulneſs of her perſon, the counteſs for the noble ſerenity of her aſpect, and that charming eaſe and freedom, which diſtinguiſh her birth and quality my dear Mr B he ſaid, was greatly admired too but he would not make *him* proud, for he had ſuperiorities enough already, that was his word, over his neighbours 'But 'I can tell you, ſaid he, 'that for moſt 'of your praiſes you are obliged to your 'lady, and for having rewarded her ex'cellence as you have done for one 'gentleman' added he, 'ſaid, he knew 'no one but *you* could deſerve her, and 'he believed *you* did, from that tender'neſs in your behaviour to her, and 'from that grandeur of air, and majeſty 'of perſon, that ſeemed to ſhew you 'formed for her protector, as well as re'warder —Get you gone to London, 'both of you,' ſaid he 'I did not 'intend to tell you, Mr B what was 'ſaid of you —

The women of the two ladies had acquainted their ladyſhips with the order I obſerved for the day, and the devout behaviour of the ſervants And about ſeven, I was withdrawing as ſilently and as unobſerved as I could, was ſurpriſed, as I was going through the great hall, to be joined by both.

'I ſhall come at all your ſecrets, Pa'mela, ſaid my lady, 'and be able, in 'time, to cut you out in your own way. 'I know whither you are going.'

'My good ladies, ſaid I, 'pardon 'me for leaving you I will attend you 'in half an hour.

'No, my dear, ſaid Lady Davers, 'the counteſs and I have reſolved to at'tend you for that half-hour, and we 'will return to company together.

'Is it not deſcending too much, my 'ladies, as to the company?'

'If it is for us, it is for you, ſaid the counteſs, 'ſo we will either act up to 'you, or make you come down to us, 'and we will judge of all your proceed'ings.

Every one, but Abraham, (who attended the gentlemen) and all their ladyſhips ſervants, and their two women, were there, which pleaſed me, however, becauſe it ſhewed, that even the ſtrangers, by this their ſecond voluntary attendance, had no ill opinion of the ſervice But they were all ſtartled, ours and theirs, to ſee the ladies accompanying me.

I ſtept up to Mr Adams.—'I was 'in hopes, Sir,' ſaid I, 'we ſhould have 'been favoured with your company at 'our table.'

He bowed.

'Well, Sir,' ſaid I, 'theſe ladies come 'now to be obliged to you for your 'good offices, and you'll have no better 'way of letting them return their obli'gation, than to ſup, though you would 'not dine with them.

'Mr Longman, ſaid my lady, 'how 'do you?—We are come to be witneſſes 'of the family decorum.'

'We have a bleſſed lady, Madam, ſaid he 'and your ladyſhips preſence 'augments our joys.

I ſhould have ſaid, we were not at church in the afternoon.—And when I do not go, we have the evening ſervice read to us, as it is at church, which Mr Adams performed now, with his uſual diſtinctneſs and fervour.

When all was concluded, I ſaid— 'Now, my deareſt ladies, excuſe me for 'the ſake of the delight I take in ſeeing 'all my good folks about me in this de'cent and obliging manner —Indeed, 'I have no oſtentation in it, if I know 'my own heart.

The

The countess and Lady Davers, delighted to see such good behaviour in every-one, sat a moment or two looking upon one another in silence, and then my Lady Davers took my hand 'Beloved, deservedly beloved of the kindest of husbands, what a blessing art thou to this family!'

'And to every family, said the countess, 'who have the happiness to know, and the grace to follow, her example!' —'But where,' said Lady Davers, 'collectedst thou all this good sense, and fine spirit in thy devotions?'

'The Bible, my dear ladies, said I, is the foundation of all but this, and the Common Prayer Book, and the Duty of Man, our worthy folks have every one of them, and are so good as to employ themselves in them at all leisure opportunities on other days For which reason, that I may diversify their devotions, I have, with the assistance of Mr Adams, and by advice of the dean, made extracts from several good pieces, which we read on these days —'Mr Adams,' said my Lady Davers, 'will you oblige me with a copy of my sister's book, at your leisure?' He readily engaged to do this, and the countess desired another copy, which he also promised

Lady Davers then turning herself to Mrs Jervis—'How do you, good woman?' said she —'Why you are now made ample amends for the love you bore to this dear creature formerly!'

'You have an angel, and not a woman, for your lady, my good Mrs Jervis,' said the countess

Mrs Jervis, folding her uplifted hands together—'O my good lady! you know not our happiness, no, not one half of it We were before blessed with plenty, and a bountiful indulgence, by our good master, but our plenty brought on wantonness and wranglings but now we have peace as well as plenty, and peace of mind, my dear lady, in doing all in our respective powers, to shew ourselves thankful creatures to God, and to the best of masters and mistresses'

'Good soul!' said I, and was forced to put my handkerchief to my eye 'your heart is always overflowing thus with gratitude and praises, for what you so well merit from us'

'Mr Longman,' said my lady, assuming a sprightly air, although her eye twinkled, to keep within its lids the precious water, that sprang from a noble and well affected heart, 'I am glad to see you here, attending your pious young lady —Well might you love her, honest man! Well might you!— I did not know there was so excellent a creature in any rank

'Madam, said the other worthy heart, unable to speak but in broken sentences, you don't know—indeed you don't, what a—what a—hap—happy—family we are!—Truly, we are like unto Alexander's soldiers, every one fit to be a general, so well do we all know our duties, and *practise* them too, let me say —Nay, and please your ladyship, we all of us long till morning comes, thus to attend my lady, and after that is past, we long for evening, for the same purpose for she is *so* good to us—You cannot think how good she is! But permit your honoured father's old servant to say one word more, that though we are always pleased and joyful on these occasions, yet we are in transports to see our master's noble sister thus favouring us—with your ladyship too, (to the countess)—'and approving our young lady's conduct and piety

'Blessing on you all! said my lady. Let us go, my lady,—let us go, sister, —for I can't stay no longer!'

As I slid by, following their ladyships—'How do you, Mr Colbrand?' said I, softly —'I feared you were not well in the morning' He bowed— 'Par-don me, Ma dame—I vas leetel indispose, dat ish true!'

Now, my dear friend, will you forgive me all this self praise, as it may seem?—Yet when you know I give it you, and my dear parents, as so many instances of my Lady Davers's reconciliation and goodness to me, and as it will shew what a noble heart that good lady has at bottom, when her pride of quality and her passion have subsided, and her native good sense and excellence taken place, I flatter myself, I may be the rather excused, and especially, as I hope to have my dear Miss Darnford's company and countenance one day, in this my delightful Sunday employment.

I should have added, for I think a good clergyman cannot be too much respected, that I repeated my request to Mr Adams, to oblige us with his company at supper, but he so very earnestly begged

begged to be excused and with so much concern of countenance, that I thought it would be wrong to insist upon it, though I was sorry for it, because I am sure, as of any thing, that modesty is always a sign of merit

We returned to the gentlemen as soon as supper was ready, and as cheerful and easy, as Lady Davers observed, as if we had not been present at so solemn a service. 'And this, said she, after the gentlemen were gone, 'makes religion 'so pleasant and delightful a thing, that 'I profess I shall have a much higher 'opinion of those who make it a regular 'and constant part of their employment, 'than ever I had But I have seen, added her ladyship, 'perhaps, such characteristic wry faces, and such gloomy 'countenances, among some of your 'pious folks, in and after a solemn office, 'as was enough to dishearten such an 'one as me, and make one think that 'it would be a sin to go to bed with a 'smile upon one's face, or without sighing and groaning

'Then, said she, 'I was once, I remember, when a girl, at the house of 'a very devout man, for a week, with 'his grand daughter, my school-fellow, and there were such preachments '*against* vanities, and *for* self-denials, 'that were we to have followed the good 'man's precepts, (though indeed not 'his practice, for well did he love his 'belly) half God Almighty's creatures 'and works would have been useless, 'and industry would have been banished 'the earth

'Then, added her ladyship, 'have I 'heard the good man confess himself 'guilty of such sins, as, if true, (and by 'his hiding his face with his broad 'brimmed hat, it looked a little bad 'against him) he ought to have been 'hanged on a gallows fifty feet high

These reflections, as I said, fell from my lady, after the gentlemen were gone, when she recounted to her brother, the entertainment, as *she was pleased to call it*, I had given her On which she made high encomiums, as did the countess, and they praised also the natural dignity which they imputed to me, saying I had taught them a way they never could have found out, to descend to the company of servants and yet to secure, and even augment, the respect and veneration of inferiors at the same time 'And, Pamela, said my lady, 'you are certainly very 'right to pay so much regard to the young 'clergyman, for that makes all he reads, 'and all he says, of greater efficacy with 'the auditors, facilitates the work you 'have in view to bring about, and in 'your own absence (for your monarch 'may not always dispense with you, perhaps) strengthens his influences, and 'encourages the young gentleman, besides'

MONDAY

I Am to thank you, my dear Miss Darnford, for your kind letter, approving of my scribble* When you come to my Saturday's and Sunday's accounts, I shall try your patience But no more of that, for as you can read them, or let them alone, I am the less concerned, especially as they will be more indulgently received somewhere else, than they may merit, so that my labour will not be wholly lost

I congratulate you with all my heart, on your dismissing Mr Murray, for, besides that some of his qualities are not to be approved by a lady of your taste and judgment, I will never give my consent, that any gentleman shall have the honour of calling you his, who can so easily resign his pretensions to you, and address your sister

You are extremely diverting, my dear, with your greater and lesser Bear stars, and I could not help shewing your letter to Mr B And what do you think the free gentleman said upon it? I am half afraid to tell you but do, now you are so happily disengaged, get leave to come, and let us two contrive to be even with him for it You are the only lady in the world that I would join with against him

He said, that your characters of Mr Murray and Miss Nanny, which he called *severe*, (*but I won't call them so, without your leave*) looked a little like pretty spite, and as if you were sorry the gentleman took you at your word —That was what he said—Pray let us punish him for it Yet, he called you charming lady, and said a great deal in your praise, and joined with me, that Mr Murray, who

* See Letter XXVIII of this Volume.

was

was so easy to part with you, could not possibly deserve you

'But, Pamela,' said he, 'I know 'the sex well enough Miss Polly may 'not love Mr Murray, yet, to see her 'sister addressed and complimented, and 'preferred to herself, by one whom she 'so lately thought it was in her power to 'choose or to refuse, is a mortifying 'thing And young ladies cannot bear 'to sit by neglected, while two lovers are 'playing pugs tricks with each other

'Then, said he, 'all the preparations 'to matrimony, the cloaths to be bought, 'the visits to be paid and received, the 'compliments of friends, the busy no-'velty of the thing, the day to be fixed, 'and all the little foolish humours 'and nonsense attending a concluded 'courtship, when *one sister* is to ingross 'all the attention and regard, the new 'equipages, and so forth, these are all 'subjects of mortification to the *other*, 'though she had no great value for the 'man perhaps

'Well, but, Sir,' said I, 'a lady of 'Miss Darnford s good sense, and good 'taste, is not to be affected by these pa 'rades, and has well considered the mat-'ter, no doubt and I dare say, rejoices, 'rather than repines at missing the gen 'tleman

I hope you will leave the happy pair, for they are so, if they think themselves so, together, and Sir Simon to rejoice in his accomplished son in law elect, and give us your company to London For who would stay to be vexed by that ill natured Miss Nanny, as you own you were, at your last writing?

But I will proceed with my journal, and the rather, as I have something to tell you of a conversation, the result of which has done me great honour, and given me inexpressible delight of which in it s place

We pursued Mr B 's proposal, returning several visits in one day, for we have so polite and agreeable a neighbourhood, that all seem to concur in a desire to make every thing easy to one another and, as I mentioned before, hearing Mr B 's intention to set out for London, as soon as our company should leave us, they dispensed with formalities, being none of them studious to take things amiss, and having a general good opinion of one another s intentions not to disoblige

We came not home till ten in the evening, and then found a letter from Sir Jacob Swynford, uncle by the half-blood to Mr B acquainting him, that hearing his niece, Lady Davers, was with him, he would be here in a day or two, (being then upon his journey) to pay a visit to his nephew and niece at the same time

This gentleman is very particularly odd and humoursome, and his eldest son being next heir to the maternal estate, if Mr. B should have no children, has been exceedingly dissatisfied with his debasing himself in marrying me, and would have been better pleased had he not married at all, perhaps

There never was any cordial love between Mr B s father and him, nor between the uncle, and nephew and niece, for his positiveness, roughness, and self-interestedness too, has made him, though very rich, but little agreeable to the generous tempers of his nephew and niece, yet when they meet, which is not above once in four or five years, they are always very civil and obliging to him

Lady Davers wondered what could bring him hither now, for he lives in Herefordshire, and seldom stirs ten miles from home Mr B. said, he was sure it was not to compliment him and me on our nuptials 'No, rather,' said my lady, 'to satisfy himself if you are in a way to 'cut out his own cubs —'Thank God, 'we are,' said my dearest friend 'When-'ever I was strongest set against matri-'mony, the only reason I had to weigh 'against my dislike to it was, that I was 'unwilling to leave so large a part of my 'estate * to that family

'My dear, said he to me, 'don t be 'uneasy, but you ll see a relation of 'mine much more disagreeable than you 'can imagine but no doubt you have 'heard his character '

'Ah, Pamela,' said Lady Davers, 'we 'are a family that value ourselves upon 'our ancestry, but upon my word, Sir 'Jacob, and all his line, have nothing 'else to boast of And I have been often 'ashamed of my relation to them '

'No family, I believe, my lady, has 'every body excellent in it,' replied I 'but I doubt I shall stand but poorly 'with Sir Jacob.

* See Vol. II p. 162, 286.

He

'He won't dare to affront you, my 'dear,' said Mr B 'although he'll say to 'you, and to me, and to my sister too, 'blunt and rough things. But he'll not 'stay above a day or two, and we shall 'not see him again for some years to 'come; so we'll bear with him'

I am now, Miss, coming to the conversation I hinted at.

TUESDAY

ON Tuesday, Mr Williams came to pay his respects to his kind patron I had been to visit the widow gentlewoman I mentioned before, and on my return, went directly to my closet, so knew not of his being there till I came to dinner, for Mr. B and he were near two hours together in discourse in the library.

When I came down, Mr B presented him to me. 'My friend Mr Williams, 'my dear, said he.

'Mr Williams, how do you do?' said I, 'I am glad to see you

He rejoiced, he said, to see me look so well, and had longed for an opportunity to pay his respects to his worthy patron and me before but had been prevented twice when he was upon the point of setting out.

Mr B said—'I have prevailed upon 'my old acquaintance to take up his residence with us, while he stays in these 'parts Do you, my dear, see that every 'thing is made agreeable to him'

'To be sure, Sir, I will

Mr Adams being in the house, Mr B. sent to desire he would dine with us, if it were but in respect to a gentleman of the same cloth, who gave us his company.

Mr B when dinner was over, and the servants were withdrawn, said—'My 'dear, Mr. Williams's business, in part, 'was to ask my advice as to a living that 'is offered him, by the Earl of ——, 'who is greatly taken with his preaching 'and conversation

'And to quit yours, I presume, Sir, said Lord Davers?

'No, the earl's is not quite so good as 'mine, and his lordship would procure 'him a dispensation to hold both What 'would you advise, my dear?

'It becomes not me, Sir, to meddle 'with such matters as these.'

'Yes, my dear, it does, when I ask 'your opinion

'I beg pardon, Sir—My opinion then 'is, that Mr Williams will not care to 'do any thing that *requires* a dispensation, and which would be unlawful 'without it'

'Your ladyship,' said Mr Williams, 'speaks exceedingly well'

'I am glad, Mr Williams, that you 'approve of my sentiments You see 'they were required of me by one who 'has a right to command me in every 'thing otherwise this matter is above 'my sphere, and I have so much good-'will to Mr Williams, that I wish him 'every thing that will contribute to make 'him happy

'Well, my dear,' said Mr B 'but 'what would you advise in this case? 'The earl proposes, that Mr Williams's 'present living be supplied by a curate, 'to whom, no doubt, Mr Williams will 'be very genteel, and, as we are seldom 'or never there, his lordship thinks we 'shall not be displeased with it, and insists upon it, that he will propose it to 'me, as he has done'

Lord Davers said—'I think this may 'do very well, brother.—But what, pray, 'Mr Williams, do you propose to allow 'to your curate? Excuse me, Sir, but I 'think the clergy do so hardly by one 'another generally, that they are not to 'be surprised, that some of the laity treat 'them as they do'

'Indeed, said Mr H 'that's well 'observed, for I have heard it said twenty 'and twenty times—"If you would know "how to value a clergyman, and what he "deserves for spending his whole life in "the duties of his function, you need but "form your opinion upon the treatment "they give to one another, and forty or "fifty pounds a year would be thought "too much, even for him who does all "the labour"

'Who says my nephew speaks not 'well,' said my lord?

'O,' said my lady, 'no wonder! This 'is Jackey's peculiar He has always 'something to say against the clergy For 'he never loved them, because his tutors 'were clergymen, and since,' said her ladyship, (very severely) 'he never got 'any good from them, why should they 'expect any from him?

'Always hard upon my poor nephew,' said Lord Davers

'Think

'Thank you, aunt,' said Mr H

Mr Williams said, Mr H 's observation was but too true, that nothing gave greater cause of scandal than the usage some even of the dignified clergy gave their brethren that he had always lamented it, as one of the greatest causes of the contempt with which the clergy are too generally treated

He was proceeding, but Lady Davers said—'I am not at all surprised at their 'treatment of one another, for if a gen-'tleman of education and learning can so 'far forget what belongs to his function, 'as to accept of two livings, when one 'would afford him a handsome main-'tenance, it is no wonder, that such a 'one would make the most of it, for does 'he not as good as declare, that he takes 'it for that very purpose?'

'I must not let this argument proceed,' said Mr B 'without clearing my worthy 'friend He is under no difficulty about 'holding the two He proposes *not* to 'do it, and, like a good man, as I al-'ways thought him to be, is of opinion 'he *ought not* to do it but here is the 'difficulty, and all his difficulty, he is 'desirous to oblige his good friend the 'earl, who is very pressing to have him 'near him but apprehending that I may 'take it amiss, if he relinquishes my liv-'ing, he came to ask my advice; and 'after we had talked a good deal of the 'matter, I told him we would refer it to 'Pamela, who was a kind of casuist in 'such matters of equity and good order 'as fell within the compass of her ob-'servation and capacity —and so, my 'dear, give us your free opinion, for this 'is a subject you have spoken your mind 'to me upon once before

'I am very glad, Sir,' replied I, 'that 'Mr Williams's own resolution was so 'conformable to what I wished it to be, 'and, indeed, expected from his cha-'racter, and I can therefore more freely 'speak my mind upon the occasion, 'though I am but a poor casuist neither'

'You remember, my dear,' said Mr. B 'what you observed to me in favour 'of the clergy, and their maintenance, 'when we fell occasionally upon that 'subject a while ago I found you had 'considered the point, and thought your 'spoke well upon the occasion Let us 'hear your opinion now upon it

'Indeed,' replied I, 'I say now, as I 'then took the liberty to say, that I have 'so general a good will to the order, that 'if my wishes could have effect, there is 'not one of it, but should have a hand-'some competency, at least such a one 'as to set him above contempt And 'this, I am persuaded, would be a great 'furtherance to the good we expect from 'them, in teaching the lower rank of 'people (as well as the higher) their 'duties, and making them good servants, 'and useful members of the common-'wealth'

'But, my dear, you took notice of 'some things, which would, if you can 'recollect them, be very *à propos* to the 'subject we are now upon'

'I remember, Sir, we were talking of 'impropriations I took the liberty to 'express myself a little earnestly against 'impropriations, and I remember you 'stopped my mouth at once upon that 'head'

'As how, sister?' said Lady Davers

'Ay, as how, Mrs B?' said the countess

'Why, Madam, Mr B was pleased 'to say, that when the clergy would come 'into a regulation for the more equal 'and useful disposition of the revenues 'which at present were in the church, he 'would be the first who would bring in 'a bill for restoring it to all that it had 'lost by impropriations and other secu-'larizations, and leave it upon the pub-'lick to make satisfaction to such of the 'laity as would be sufferers by the re-'storation

'That was not, my dear, what I 'meant,' returned Mr B 'You are par-'ticularly against dispensations, which 'is the point before us now'

'I remember, Sir, I did say, that as 'there are so many gentlemen of the 'function, who have no provision at all, I 'could not wish any one of it should hold 'two livings, especially if they cannot 'perform the duties of both, and where 'one would afford a tolerable competence 'Much less, (I remember I took the li-'berty to add) could I think it excusa-'ble, that a gentleman should rate the 'labours of his brother, who does *every* 'thing, so low, as is too frequently the 'case, and pay himself so well, for do-'ing *nothing* at all'

'This is what I mean,' returned Mr B 'and I thought you observed very 'well upon it, my dear For my own 'part, I have always been of opinion, 'that the clergy who do thus, make the 'best excuse that can be made for impro-

'impropriators and lay patrons. For here is 'a gentleman, the son of a lay-man, (I 'speak to general cases) is sent to the 'university, and takes orders. He has 'interest, perhaps, to get two or more 'livings, and hires a person, who is as 'deserving as himself, but destitute of 'friends, at a low rate, to do the duties 'of one of them. We will suppose in 'his instance, that he has several children 'to provide for out of these, and makes 'that his pretence for oppressing the per-'son he employs to do his own duty. Some 'of these children are males, some fe-'males, and not one in five of the former 'is brought up to the church, and all 'that he saves for them, and gives them 'out of what he squeezes from his un-'happy brother, is it not secularizing, as 'it were, at least as far as he can do it, 'the revenue appropriated to the church? 'And can he, while he does this, plead 'an impropriator for applying that por-'tion of the produce of church-lands to 'his lay-family, which the other intends 'for the lay-family he is endeavouring 'to build up? Some one or two of which 'impropriators sons may possibly too, 'in order to possess the living in their 'father's gift, be brought up to the 'church: what is the difference, I would 'fain know?'

'If the clergy were always to have 'done thus, continued Mr B. 'should 'we not have wanted many endowments, 'and charitable foundations, which we 'now have? And I am very sorry to have 'reason to say, that we owe such sort of 'works more to the piety of the clergy 'of past times than to the present; for 'now, let us cast our eye upon the prac-'tices of some of our prelates, for who 'is it that looks not up first for examples 'to that venerable order? And we shall 'find, that too many among them turn 'more intent upon making a family, as 'it is called, and thereby secularizing, as 'I observed, as much as they can, the 'revenues of the church, than to live up 'either to the ancient hospitality, or with 'a view to those acts of munificence, 'which were the reason for endowing the 'church with such ample revenues as it 'once had, and still has, were it not so 'unequally distributed, and in so few 'hands.'

'But, dear Sir, said I, 'what a sad hard-'ship do the inferior clergy labour under 'all this time!—To be oppressed and 'kept down, by their brethren, and by 'the laity too? This is hard indeed—'Tis pity, methinks, this, at least, could 'not be remedied.'

'It will hardly ever be done, my dear. 'The evil lies deep, 'tis in human na-'ture, and when that can be mended, it 'will be better, but I see not how it can 'be expected, while those who have most 'influence to procure the redress, are 'most interested to prevent it; and the 'views of others, aspiring to the same 'power and interest, make too many wish 'to have things left as they are, although 'they have no present benefit by it. And 'those would join in a cry of the church's 'danger, were the legislature to offer at 'a redress.'

'Tis pity, Sir, said I, 'the convoca-'tion are not permitted to sit. They 'would, perhaps, undertake this pro-'vince, and several others, for the benefit 'of the whole body of the clergy, and I 'should think such regulations would 'come best from them.'

'So it is, my dear, would they employ 'themselves, and their deliberations, in 'such good works. But 'tis a sad thing 'to consider, that there is little good to 'be expected from bodies of men in ge-'neral; for although an individual cares 'not to pull down upon himself the 'odium of a bad or unpopular action, 'yet when there are many to share it 'among them, I see not, that they scruple 'doing things which very little become 'them to do. But, far be it from me to 'say this with a view to convocations *as* 'convocations. I speak what is but too 'generally the case in all bodies of men 'whatever, whether clergy or laity. And 'let us look into the greater or lesser 'corporations and societies throughout 'the kingdom, and we shall find, if a 'poor witticism may be excused, that 'bodies are really *bodies*, and act too 'often as if they had no *souls* among 'them.'

'I hope, Sir, said the countess, 'when 'you judge thus hardly of bodies, you 'include the two supreme bodies.'

"*Thou shalt not*, said Mr B.—'I 'know these reverend gentlemen, (look-ing at Mr Williams and Mr Adams) 'will tell me, "*speak evil of the rulers* "*of thy people*.—But I wish I could al-'ways defend, what I am loth at any 'time to censure. But were you to read, 'or attend to the debates in both houses, 'which sometimes happen in cases almost '*self evident*, you would find it *impossible*

'not

'not to regret, that you are now-and-then under a necessity to join with the minority,—as well in your house, Lord Davers, as in ours.'

'I wish, brother,' replied his lordship, 'I could differ from you with reason: but this always *was*, and, I fear, always *will be* so, more or less in every session.'

'But, to return to our first subject,' said Mr B. 'You know, my dear, how much pleasure I take to hear your opinion in cases of natural equity: and you must tell us freely, what you would advise your friend Mr Williams to do.'

'And must I, Sir, speak my mind on such a point, before so many better judges?'

'Yes, *sister*,' said her ladyship, (a name she is now pleased to give me freely before strangers, after her dear brother's example, who is kindest, though always kind, at such times) 'you *must*, if I may be allowed to say *must*.'

'Why then,' proceeded I, 'I beg leave to ask Mr Williams one question, that is, whether his present parishioners do not respect and esteem him, in that particular manner, which I think every body must, who knows his worth?'

'I am very happy, Madam, in the good will of all my parishioners, and have great acknowledgments to make for their civilities to me.'

'I don't doubt,' said I, 'but it will be the same where-ever you go, for bad as the world is, a prudent and good clergyman will never fail of respect. But, Sir, if you think your ministry among them is attended with good effects; if they esteem your person with a preference, and listen to your doctrines with attention, methinks, for *their* sakes, 'tis pity to leave them, were the living of *less* value, as it is of *more*, than the other. For, how many people are there who can benefit by one gentleman's preaching, rather than by another's, although, possibly, the one's abilities may be no way inferior to the other's? There is a great deal in a *delivery*, as it is called, in a way, a manner, a deportment, to engage people's attention and liking, and as you are already in possession of their esteem, you are sure to do much of the good you aim and wish to do. For where the flock loves the shepherd, all his work is easy, and more than half done, and without that, let him have the tongue of an angel, and let him live the life of a saint, he will be heard with indifference, and, oftentimes, as his subject may be, with disgust.'

I paused here, but every one being silent—'As to the earl's friendship, Sir,' continued I, 'you can best judge, what force that ought to have upon you, and what I have mentioned would be the only difficulty with me, were I in Mr Williams's case. To be sure, it will be a high compliment to his lordship, and so he ought to think it, that you quit a better living to oblige him. And he will be bound in honour to make it up to you. For I am far from thinking, that a prudent regard to worldly interest misbecomes the character of a good clergyman, and I wish all such were set above the world, for their own sakes, as well as for the sakes of their hearers, since independency gives a man respect, besides the power of doing good, which will enhance that respect, and, of consequence, give greater efficacy to his doctrines.'

The countess mentioned hereupon, the saying of Dr Fisher, Bishop of Rochester, who was beheaded in the reign of Henry VIII. because he would not own the King's supremacy: this prelate, being offered a richer bishoprick, would not accept of it, saying, he looked upon his bishoprick as his wife, and he should not think it excusable to part with his wife because she was poor. This brought so many reflections upon frequent translations, and the earnestness with which richer bishopricks were sought after, that I was very sorry to hear, or to think, there were occasion for them. And I did take the liberty to say, that as Mr B. had observed the fault was in human nature, and though it was an inexcusable one, perhaps we that censured them, might find it hard, in their circumstances, to resist the temptation.

Mr B. said, he wished, for the sake of the clergy in general, that there was a law against translations, and that all the bishopricks in England were made equal in revenue. 'For, do we not see,' said he, 'that the prelates, almost to a man, vote on the side of power? And by this means, contribute not a little to make themselves and the whole body of the clergy, (so numerous, and so deserving too, as those of the *Church of*

'*England* are) a by-word to freethinkers of all denominations, who are ever ready to take occasion to malign them, and their venerable order.'

'Would you not, asked Lord Davers, have the two primacies distinguished in revenue?'

'No, said Mr B. 'the distinction of dignity and precedence would be enough, if not too much; for where there is but one pope, the whole college of cardinals, seventy in number, are always looking up to, and gaping after the chair: and I would have no temptations laid in the way of good men to forfeit their characters, and weaken their influences, which are of so much consequence for example-sake, to the publick weal.'

'I think, said Lord Davers, 'there was some reason for the celibacy of the clergy in the Roman church at first, although the inconveniencies arising from it are too many and too obvious, to wish the restraint so general. For the provision for families and children, furnishes so natural and so laudable a pretence to clergymen to lay up all they can for them, that their characters suffer not a little on that account.'

'If we look round us, said Mr B. 'and see how many good and worthy families are sprung from the clergy, and look abroad, and see what are too often the effects of celibacy in the Roman church, and the scandal, worse than what we complain of, thrown upon them, even by bigots of their own communion, we shall have sufficient reason to condemn the celibacy which that church enjoins. Besides, a bad mind, an oppressive or covetous nature, will be the same, whether married or single: for have we not seen to what a scandalous height nepotism has been carried in that church? And has not a pope of a private and narrow spirit done as much for his nephews and nieces (and perhaps nearer relations under those names) as he could have done for sons and daughters? So still *here* too, we must resolve all into that common sewer of iniquity, human nature, and conclude, that a truly good man will not do a bad thing upon any the nearest and most affecting considerations, and that a bad man will never want a pretence to display his evil qualities, nor flatterers neither (if he has power) to defend him, in the worst he can do.

'I well remember the argument, when I was at Rome, used to the pope, on such an occasion. His holiness declared against nepotism, saying, that he would never look upon the revenues of the church, as the patrimony of his private family; and forbad his numerous relations, who, on his promotion, swarmed about him, with looks as hungry as if they were so many North Britons, travelling southward for preferment, — (that was Mr B.'s word, spoken pleasantly) 'to think of him in any other light, than that of the common father of all his people, and as having no other relation but Merit.

'This was setting out well, you'll say: but what was the event?—Why, two thirds of his relations rushed into orders directly, and it was not long, before parasites were found, to represent to the holy father, that it was a sin to deprive the church of so many excellent props and buttresses, and that for the good of the publick, he ought to prefer them to the first dignities, so that the good man, overcome with their reasons, and loth to continue in so great a sin, graced the cardinalate with one, the episcopate with half a dozen, and the richest abbacies with a score or two, and the emperor having occasion to make interest with his holiness, found merit enough in some of the lay relations to create them princes and counts of the Holy Roman Empire.'

'But, Sir, said I, (for I am always sorry to hear things said to the discredit of the clergy, because I think it is of publick concern that we reverence the function, notwithstanding the failings of particulars) 'have I not been a silent witness, that you have made the same observations on a minister of state, who, though he shall be perhaps the first to blame this disposition in a clergyman, will be equally ready to practise it himself, to relations and children, full as worthless, to the exclusion of the worthy?—So that, Sir, this is all human nature still, and should we not be tender in our censures of the one, when we are so ready to acquit the other?'

'There's this difference, Mrs B.' said the countess: 'from the one we expect a better example, from the other, no example fit to be followed. And this is one reaſon that makes the firſt miniſter generally ſo hated a thing in all nations, becauſe he uſually reſolves all conſiderations into ſelf, and is beloved by nobody, but thoſe to whom he gives the overflowings of ſuch benefits, as he has not relations enough to heap them upon.'

‘Well, Mr Adams,' ſaid I, ‘if I may be allowed to be ſo ſerious, does not this ſhew the excellency of the prayer we are taught by the Supreme Teacher, and that part of it—“*Lead us not into temptation?*” For it ſeems too natural a conſequence, that no ſooner are we tempted, but we *deliver ourſelves up to evil*.'

‘Right, ſiſter,' ſaid Lord Davers, ‘and this ends in Mr B's *human nature* again.'

‘What remains, then,' obſerved Lady Davers, ‘but that we take the world as we find it? Give praiſe to the good, diſpraiſe to the bad, and every one try to mend *one?*'

‘Yet I wiſh,' ſaid Mr B. ‘ſo over tender are many good clergymen of the failings in their brethren, which they would not be guilty of themſelves, that we might avoid diſpleaſing them, if they were to know the freedom of this converſation, when we are ſo well-diſpoſed to reverence their function.'

‘I hope otherwiſe,' returned Mr Williams, ‘for it is but giving *due* praiſe and diſpraiſe, as my lady ſays, and were evil actions to go uncenſured, good ones would loſe their reward; and vice, by being put upon a foot with virtue in this life, would meet with too much countenance.'

‘But give me leave,' reſumed Lady Davers, ‘to interpoſe a little in the matter we have departed from, that of the curate and diſpenſation; and when I have delivered my ſentiments, I inſiſt upon it, that Mrs B will as freely give us hers, as if I had been ſilent.

‘Diſpenſations are uſual things. Mr Williams may pay a young gentleman *handſomely*, and the cenſure we have paſſed is only upon ſuch as do *no*. To a young man at firſt ſetting out, a good curacy will be very acceptable. If he has merit, it will put him in a way of ſhewing it, and he may raiſe himſelf by it. If he has not, he will not deſerve more. And Mr Williams may marry, perhaps, and have a family to provide for. His opportunities may not always be the ſame: the earl may die, and he ſhould be excuſed if he makes the beſt uſe of his intereſt and favour, for the very reaſon Mrs B gave, that as he is a good man, it will ſtrengthen his influences.—And, come, brother, you know I am always for preſcribing: here is a worthy young gentleman in my eye, who won't take it amiſs to begin with a curacy; and you ſhall give *your* diſpenſation, previous to the legal one, on condition, that Mr Williams will permit you to preſent his curate; and thus all will be reſolved.'

Both the gentlemen bowed, and Mr Williams was going to ſpeak; but Mr B ſaid—‘Take my ſiſter at her word, Pamela, and if you have any thing to ſay to this ſcheme, ſpeak it freely, as if her ladyſhip had been ſilent; for, I perceive, by your downcaſt eye and ſilence, you could ſay ſomething if you would.'

‘Ay, pray do,' ſaid my lady. ‘I love to hear you ſpeak. You always make me think of ſomething I had not conſidered before.'

‘I am very loth to ſay any thing on ſo nice a ſubject. Indeed it would not become me. There is ſo much generoſity and benevolence in my good lady's ſcheme, that I ought not.'

‘*Ought not!*' repeated my deareſt friend, interrupting me, ‘none of your *ought nots*, I know you are always forming in your mind notions of right and wrong, in the common caſes of life. Let us therefore have your opinion in this matter more fully than you have hitherto given it; and deliver it too without heſitation, and with that eaſe and freedom, which are born with you; for, I can tell you, that were we, through the corruption of human nature, to loſe the diſtinctions of right and wrong, I know not where we could apply ourſelves, but to ſuch as you, to recover them.'

I bowed, and ſaid—‘If you will have it ſo, Sir, it muſt be ſo; and I will then beſpeak all your kind allowances, (caſting my eye around me, to each perſon) and tell you all I think upon this matter; and when I have done, ſubmit my poor ſentiments, as becomes me, to your ſuperior judgments.

‘Thus then, I would ſay—Pardon me, Madam, for taking your ladyſhip's words for my theme, as I re-

'member them, and hardly any thing 'falls from our ladyſhip that I do *not* 'remember—*That diſpenſations are* '*uſual things*—I am ſure I am going to 'diſplay my ignorance, becauſe, know'ing nothing of their original or deſign, 'I muſt preſume them to be very ancient 'in this kingdom and introduced only 'when there were fewer clergymen than 'benefices Was there ever ſuch a 'time?'

They ſmiled—'Nay, now, you *would* 'command me, Sir, to ſpeak, when I 'need to do nothing elſe, to expoſe my'ſelf There was a time, as I have 'read, that there were ſo few ſcholars, 'that the benefit of clergy was allowed 'to ſome ſort of criminals who could do 'no more than read, becauſe the com'monwealth could ill ſpare learned men, 'and thought it right to encourage the 'love of letters—And might there not 'be a time, then, when diſpenſations 'were allowed to worthy men, becauſe 'it was difficult to find enow of ſuch as 'deſerved that character, to fill the 'church preferments?'

'Tell us, Pamela, ſaid Mr B 'whe'ther you do not intend this, as a ſatire 'upon the practice Or, is it really your 'pretty ignorance, that has made you 'pronounce one of the ſevereſt cenſures 'upon it that could be thought of?'

I ſmiled, and ſaid—'Indeed, Sir, I 'think only ſome ſuch reaſon, or a 'worſe, muſt be the original of diſpen'ſations, for, is it right, that one gen'tleman ſhall have two or three livings, 'the duties of no more than one of which 'he can perſonally attend, while ſo many 'are deſtitute of bread, almoſt, and ex'poſed to contempt, the too frequent 'companion of poverty? And what 'though cuſtom may have ſanctified it, 'to be ſure that is all that can, and a 'good man will not do all he may do 'without incurring a penalty, becauſe 'there is in every thing a right and a 'wrong, and becauſe, be the cuſtom 'what it will, a man ſhould regulate his 'actions by his conſcience and the 'golden rule.

'My good lady ſays, Mr Williams 'may pay a gentleman handſomely I 'don't doubt but Mr. Williams would 'do ſo, and this, I am ſorry to ſay it, 'would be doing what is not ſo often 'done as one would wiſh But I may 'be permitted to aſk, For *what* would 'he pay the gentleman handſomely?— 'Why, for doing that duty for him, 'which in conſcience and honour he 'ought to do himſelf, and which, when 'he takes inſtitution and induction, he 'engages ſolemnly to do?—And pray, 'excuſe me, my dear Every-body—that was my fooliſh word, which made them ſmile—'to what end is all this?—Only, 'that the gentleman who does all the 'labour in the vineyard, ſhall live upon 'thirty, forty, or fifty pounds per an'num, more or leſs, while the gentle'man who has *beſt* nothing but *beſt* in'tereſt,' (another of my fooliſh phraſes) 'ſhall receive twice, and perhaps three 'times the ſum for doing nothing at all? 'Can any diſpenſation, my dear friends, 'make this a juſt or equitable thing 'Indeed, if the living be ſo poor, as too 'many of them are, that a man cannot 'comfortably and creditably ſubſiſt with'out putting two poor ones together to 'make one tolerable one, that is another 'thing—But pray now, my good Mr 'Williams, excuſe me, if Mr Adams 'can live upon a curacy of forty or fifty 'pounds a year, cannot another gentle'man live, unleſs his rectory or vicarage 'bring him two or three hundred? Mr 'Adams may marry as well as Mr 'Williams, and both, I believe, will 'find God's providence a better reli'ance than the richeſt benefice in Eng'land

'A good curacy, no doubt, conti'nued I, 'may be a comfortable thing at 'ſetting out to a young gentleman but 'if there be a rectory or vicarage, of two 'hundred pounds a year, for example, '(for if it be of no more value than a good 'curacy, he *muſt* be content) is not that 'two hundred pounds a year the reward 'for doing ſuch and ſuch labour? And if 'this be the ſtated hire for this labour, to 'ſpeak in the Scripture phraſe, *Is not* '*the labourer worthy of his hire?* Or 'is he that does *not* labour to go away 'with the greateſt part of it?'

'If the gentleman, my lady is pleaſed 'to ſay, has merit, this curacy may put 'him in a way of ſhewing it But does 'the manifeſtation of merit, and the re'ward of it, always go together?

'My lady is ſo good as to obſerve— 'But may I, Madam, be excuſed?'

'Proceed, proceed, child!—I ſhall 'only have a care of what I ſay before 'you for the future, that's all'

'And I too, ſaid Mr H which made them ſmile

'Nay,

'Nay, now, my lady—

'Proceed, I tell you—I only wonder, 'as my brother has said, on another oc- 'casion, where thou gottest all these equi- 'table notions

'My lady is so good as to observe,' proceeded I, (for they were pleased to be attentive) 'that Mr Williams should 'make use of his opportunities I know 'her ladyship speaks this rather in ge- 'nerous indulgence to the usual prac- 'tice, than what always *ought* to be the 'chief consideration, for if the earl 'should die, may not some other friend 'arise to a gentleman of Mr Williams's 'merit?

'As to strengthening of a good man's 'influence, which is a point always to 'be wished, I would not say so much as 'I have done, if I had not heard Mr 'Longman say, and I am sure I heard it 'with great pleasure, that the benefice 'Mr Williams so worthily enjoys, is 'a clear two hundred and fifty pounds 'a year

'But after all, does happiness to a 'gentleman, a scholar, a philosopher, 'rest in a greater or lesser income?—On 'the contrary, is it not oftener to be 'found in a happy competency or me- 'diocrity? Suppose my dear Mr B 'had five thousand pounds a year added 'to his present large income, would that 'increase his happiness? That it would 'add to his cares, is no question, but 'could that addition give him one single 'comfort which he has not already? And 'if the dear gentleman had two or three 'thousand less, might he be less happy 'on that account? No, surely, for it 'would render a greater prudence on 'my humble part necessary, and a nearer 'inspection, and greater frugality, on 'his own, and he must be contented (if 'he did not, as now, perhaps, lay up 'every year) so long as he lived within 'his income—And who will say, that the 'obligation to greater prudence and 'œconomy is a misfortune?

'The competency, therefore, the gold- 'en mean is the thing, and I have of- 'ten considered the matter, and endea- 'voured to square my actions by the re- 'sult of that consideration For a per- 'son, who being not born to an estate, 'is not satisfied with a competency, will 'probably not know any limits to his 'desires One whom an acquisition of 'one hundred or two hundred pounds a 'year will not satisfy, will hardly sit 'down contented with any sum For 'although he may propose to himself at 'a distance, that such and such an ac- 'quisition will be the height of his am- 'bition, yet he will, as he approaches to 'that, advance upon himself farther and 'farther, and know no bound, till the 'natural one is forced upon him, and 'his life and his views end together

'Now let me humbly beg pardon of 'you all, ladies and gentlemen, turning my eye to each, 'but most of you, my 'good lady, whose observations I have 'made so free with If *you* can forgive 'me, it will be an instance of your good- 'ness, that I may wish for, but hardly 'can promise to myself Will you, my 'dear lady?' said I, and laid my hand upon her ladyship's, in a supplicatory manner, for she sat next me

'I think *not*, said her ladyship 'I 'think I *ought* not —Should I, brother? '—Can I, my lord?—Ought I, my 'lady countess?—Brother, brother, if 'you have been in any degree contribut- 'ing to the excellency of this—what shall 'I call her? How cunningly do you act, 'to make her imbibe your notions, and 'then utter them with such advantage, 'that you have the secret pride to find 'your own sentiments praised from her 'mouth? But I will forgive you both, 'be it as it will, for I am sure, outdone 'as I am, in thought, word, and deed, 'and by so young a gipsey, —that was her word, 'it is by one that would out- 'do every body else, as well as me 'only I would except your ladyship

'None of your exceptions, Lady Da- 'vers, replied the countess—'I know 'not, in so young a lady, whether I 'should most envy or admire her excel- 'lence

'Well, but since I have the pleasure,' resumed I, 'to find myself forgiven, may 'I be indulged a few moments prattle 'more? Only just to observe, that the 'state of the case I have given, is but '*one* side of the question, that which a 'good clergyman, in my humble opi- 'nion, would choose to act. But when 'we come to the *other* side, what it 'would be kind we of the laity should 'think fit and act by them, that is an- 'other thing For, when we think of 'the hardships the clergy lie under, more 'than almost any other body of men, we 'shall see they are intitled to better usage 'than they often meet with

'Here, in the first place, a youth is 'sent

'sent to the university, after a painful 'course, to qualify him for it. He endangers his health, and impairs his 'constitution, by hard study, and a sedentary life: and after he has passed 'such a number of years, he is admitted 'into orders, perhaps gets a small fellowship, turns tutor, a painful employment, and his education having been 'designed for all his portion, and that 'expended in it, he at last, by interest or 'favour, gets a curacy or little living of 'forty, fifty, or sixty pounds a year; if 'less, so much the worse, and is obliged 'to maintain himself in a genteel appearance out of that, and be subject, 'not seldom, to the jests of buffoons and 'rakes at a great man's table, where the '*parson* is too often the butt to receive 'the supposed witty shafts of such as can 'allow themselves to say any thing. If 'he marries, which possibly too he is 'kept from, contrary to his wishes, of 'all men he is the least to follow his own 'liking, since prudence too often obliges 'him to take the person his inclination 'would not.

'If children follow, what melancholy 'views has he of providing for them, did 'not his strong reliance on Providence 'exercise his faith against worldly appearance?

'Then he has too often to contend for 'his dues, the produce of his poor income, with churlish and ignorant spirits, 'whom his function would make him 'wish to smooth and instruct; who though 'they farm and pay to the landlord for 'no more than nine tenths of the lands 'they occupy, hardly think it a sin to 'cheat the parson of his tythe, who, 'however, has the same right to it by the 'laws of the land, as the gentleman has 'to the estate, or the tenant to the produce of his farm.

'This obliges the poor gentleman to 'live in a state of war among a people, 'with whom both his duty and inclination would make him desirous to cultivate a good understanding. And what 'benefits can result from his ministry in 'such a situation, when the people to be 'instructed look upon him as an invader 'of their substance, at the very time that 'they are robbing him of what is legally 'his?

'In the next place, I presume to think, 'that the clergy are too much looked 'upon by some as a detached body, as I 'may say, from the rest of the people, 'and as persons acting upon a separate 'interest, quite opposite to that of the 'laity: when, possibly, that very churl, 'who refuses them their right, or would 'cheat them of it, has a view to bring 'up one of his family to the church, and 'hopes to get him provided for out of 'its revenues. And are not the clergy, 'moreover, the fathers, the sons, the 'uncles, the brothers of the laity, who 'shall set themselves against their maintenance? And must their education 'debar them of those comforts, which 'it better qualifies them to enjoy, and 'which it incapacitates them any other 'way to procure?

'Forgive me, looking all round me, and curt'sying when I cast my eye on Mr B. 'for entering so deeply into this 'subject. I have often heard my excellent lady, who had a great veneration 'for good clergymen, talk to this purpose with a lady who had very different 'sentiments from hers; and I have not 'been used to forget any thing that fell 'from her lips. Mr B. and Lady Davers bid me proceed; I could not, my lady said, have had a better instructress.

'What opportunity, resumed I, 'have 'not the laity in general, of all degrees 'and ranks, to make their lives easy and 'happy, to what the clergy have? Here 'is a middling family, with three or four 'sons: suppose the father's circumstances 'will allow him to bring up one to the '*law*: what opportunities has *he*, unenvied, to make a fortune? Another is 'brought up to *trade*; if he has but tolerable success in the world, in what 'ease and affluence does he support himself, and provide for his family? And 'as to the *physick line*, what fortunes are 'raised in that? And nobody envies any 'of these. But the son, whose inclination shall lead him perhaps *best* to deserve, and *most* to require an easy 'and comfortable subsistence, and who 'ought wholly to devote himself to the '*duties of his function*, is grudged every 'thing, and is treated as if he were not 'a son of the same family, and had not a 'natural right and stake in the same 'commonwealth.

'There are, 'tis true, preferments, and 'some great ones, and honours too, in 'the church; but how few, compared to 'the numbers of the clergy, or to those 'livings which are so poor, as can hardly

'set

'set a man above penury and contempt? '—And how are those few ingrossed by 'the descendants or dependants of the 'rich and powerful? And, what by 'commendams, dispensations, and such-'like contrivances, how does one man of 'interest and address swallow up the pro-'vision which was designed for several, 'as deserving, perhaps, at least, as him-'self? For, my good lady, (you *have* 'forgiven me, and must not be displeas-'ed) a man's friends *may die off*, and he 'must, you know, *make the best of his* '*opportunities*.

'O you dear sauce-box, as my bro-'ther calls you!—How dare you, by 'that arch pretty look, triumph over me 'thus?—Let me, brother, give her a slap 'for this!—I'm sure she deserves it.'

'I think she *is* a little insolent, indeed, 'Lady Davers. But to the case in hand: 'There is so much truth in what Pamela 'says, of the hardships to which the 'clergy, the inferior clergy particularly, 'are subjected, that I wonder any gen-'tleman who can choose for himself, and 'has no probable prospect, should enter 'into orders, under such discourage-'ments.'

'I humbly conceive, Sir,' said I, 'that 'there can be but one *good* inducement, 'and this is what the Apostle hints at in 'these words—"*If in* this life *only we* "*have hope, we are of all men most* "*miserable*."'

'Well,' said Mr B. 'by how much 'this is their motive, by so much are 'they intitled to that better hope; and 'may it never deceive them!'

'But I have the pleasure to acquaint 'this company, that I had a mind only 'to hear what Pamela, who, as I hinted, 'talked to me learnedly on this very sub-'ject a few days ago, would say, when 'she came face to face, to her two worthy 'friends, Mr Williams and Mr Adams, '(and so I desired Mr Williams would 'let her run on, if I could set her into 'the subject)—else my old acquaintance 'was resolved not to hold both livings, 'since *either*, he was so good as to say, 'would afford him as handsome a pro-'vision as he wished for; his only diffi-'culty being about obliging the earl, or 'whether he should not disoblige me, if 'he complied with that nobleman's re-'quest.'

'Indeed, Madam,' said Mr Wil-'liams, 'this is the very case, and after 'what I have heard from you, I would 'not, for the world, have been of another 'mind, nor have put it upon any other 'foot than I did.'

'You are a good man,' said I, 'and 'I have such an opinion of your worthi-'ness, and the credit you do your 'function, that I can never suspect either 'your judgment or your conduct. But 'pray, Sir, may I ask, what have you 'determined to do?'

'Why, Madam,' replied he, 'I am 'staggered in that too, by the observa-'tion your ladyship made, that where a 'man has the love of his parishioners, he 'ought not to think of leaving them.'

'Else, Sir, I find you was rather in-'clined to oblige the earl, though the 'living be of *less* value! This is very 'noble, Sir, it is more than generous.'

'My dear,' said Mr B. 'I'll tell you, '(for Mr Williams's modesty will not 'let him speak it before all the company) 'what *is* his motive; and a worthy one 'you'll say it is. Excuse me, Mr. Wil-'liams,—for the reverend gentleman blushed.

'The earl has of late years—we all 'know his character—given himself up 'to carousing, and he will suffer no man 'to go from his table sober. Mr Wil-'liams has taken the liberty to expostu-'late, as became his function, with his 'lordship on this subject, and upon some 'other irregularities, in so agreeable a 'manner, that the earl has taken a great 'liking to him, and promises, that he will 'suffer his reasonings to have an effect 'upon him, and that he shall reform his 'whole household, if he will come and 'live near him, and regulate his table by 'his own example.

'The countess is a very good lady, 'and privately presses Mr. Williams to 'oblige the earl: and this is our worthy 'friend's main inducement; with the 'hope, which I should not forget to men-'tion, that he has, of preserving untaint-'ed the morals of the two young gen-'tlemen, the earl's sons, who, he fears, 'will be carried away by the force of 'such an example: and he thinks, as the 'earl's living has fallen, mine, proba-'bly, will be better supplied than the 'earl's, if he, as he kindly offers, gives 'it me back again; otherwise the earl, 'as he apprehends, will find out for his, 'some gentleman, if such a one can 'be found, as will rather further, than 'obstruct his own irregularities, as was 'the unhappy case of the last incumbent.'

'Well,' said Lady Davers, (and so said the countess) 'I shall always have the 'highest respect for Mr Williams, for 'a conduct so genteel and so prudent.— 'But, brother, will you—and will you, 'Mr Williams—put this whole affair, 'in all its parts, into Mrs B's hands, 'since you have such testimonies, *both* of 'you, of the rectitude of her thinking 'and acting?'

'With all my heart, Madam,' replied Mr Williams, 'and I shall be proud of 'such a direction.'

'What say *you*, brother? You are to 'suppose the living in your own hands 'again, will you leave the whole matter 'to my *sister* here?'

'Come, my dear,' said Mr B. 'let us 'hear how you'd wish it to be ordered. 'I know you have not need of one moment's consideration, when once you 'are a mistress of a point.'

'Nay,' said Lady Davers, 'that is not 'the thing. I repeat my demand. Shall 'it be as Mrs B. lays it out, or not?'

'This is a weighty matter, my good 'sister, and bad as I have been, I think 'patrons are accountable, in a great 'measure, for the characters of the per-'sons they prefer; and I do assure you, 'that had I twenty livings in my gift, I 'should think, I ought not to prefer my 'brother to any one of them, if his mo-'rals and character were not likely to do 'honour to the church, as well as to my 'presentation. And I expected to hear 'from Pamela, when she was enume-'rating the hardships of the clergy, of 'that scandalous practice of some patrons 'who rob the regularly-bred clergymen, 'by pushing into orders some kinsman, 'or friend, or friend's kinsman or friend, 'when a living falls in, let his character 'or qualifications be ever so faulty and 'defective. I could name several such 'instances, that ought to make the or-'dainers, as well as the ordained, *blush*, 'as (were I to borrow one of Pamela's 'serious inferences, I would say) it will 'one day make them both *tremble*, when 'they come to give an account of the 'trusts committed to them.'

'Well,' said my lady, 'I have a noble 'brother, that's true. What pity you 'ever were wicked at all! But, come,' and with her hand upon mine, 'this same 'good girl will be a blessing to you. nay, 'why said I, *will* be? she *is*, and the 'greatest that man can receive.—But 'still I must have you put this matter into 'Mrs B.'s hands.'

'Conditionally I will—Provided I can-'not give satisfactory reasons, why I '*ought not* to conform to her opinion, for 'this, as I said, is a point of conscience 'with me, and I made it so, when I pre-'sented Mr Williams to the living, and 'have not been deceived in that pre-'sentation.'

'To be sure,' said I, 'that is very 'reasonable, Sir, and on that condition, 'I shall the less hesitate to speak my 'mind, because I shall be in no danger 'to commit an irreparable error.'

'I know well, Lady Davers,' added Mr B. 'the power your sex have over 'ours, and their subtle tricks, and so 'will never, in my weakest moments, be 'drawn in to make a blindfold promise. 'There have been several instances, 'both in sacred, and profane story, of 'mischiefs done by such surprizes. So 'you must allow me to suspect myself, 'when I know the dear slut's power over 'me, and have been taught, by the in-'violable regard she pays to her own 'word, to value mine—And now, Pa-'mela, speak all that's in your heart to 'say.'

'With your *requisite* condition in my 'eye, I will, Sir. But let me see, that 'I state the matter right. And, prepara-'tive to it, pray, Mr Williams, though 'you have not been long in possession of 'this living, yet may-be you can com-'pute what it is likely, by what you 'know of it, to bring in clear?'

'Madam,' said he, 'by the best cal-'culation I can make, (I thank *you* for 'it, good Sir) it may, one year with ano-'ther, be reckoned at three hundred 'pounds per annum. It is the best living 'within twenty miles of it, having been 'improved within these two last years.'

'If it was five hundred pounds, and 'would make you happier,—(for *that*, 'Sir, is the thing) I should wish it you,' said I, 'and think it short of your merits. 'But pray, Sir, what is the earl's living 'valued at?'

'At about two hundred and twenty 'pounds, Madam.'

'Well then,' replied I, very pertly, 'I believe now I have it.

'Mr Williams, for motives most ex-'cellently worthy of his function, in-'clines to surrender up to Mr B. his 'living

'living of three hundred pounds per an-' num, and to accept of the earl's living of 'two hundred and twenty pounds per an' num Dear Sir, I am going to be very 'bold; but under *your* condition never-'theless.—let the gentleman to whom 'you shall present the living of F allow 'eighty pounds per annum out of it to 'Mr Williams, till the earl's favour 'shall make up the difference to him, 'and no longer —And—but I dare not 'name the gentleman —for, how, dear 'Sir, were I to be so bold, shall I part 'with my chaplain?'

'Admirable! most admirable!' said Lord and Lady Davers, in the same words The countess praised the decision too, and Mr H with his 'Let me be hang'd, and his ''Fore Gads,' and such exclamations natural to him, made his plaudits

Mr Williams said, he could wish with all his heart it might be so, and Mr Adams was so abashed and surprised, that he could not hold up his head,—but joy danced in his silent countenance for all that

Mr B having hesitated a few minutes, Lady Davers called out for his objection, or consent, according to condition, and he said—'I cannot so soon determine as 'that prompt slut did. I'll withdraw 'one minute

He did so, as I found afterwards, to advise, like the considerate and genteel spirit he possesses, with Mr Williams, whom he beckoned out, and to examine whether he was in *earnest* willing to give it up, or had any body he was very desirous should succeed him, telling him, that if he had, he thought himself obliged, in return for his worthy behaviour to him, to pay a particular regard to his recommendation And so being answered as he desired, in they came together again

But, I should say, that his withdrawing with a very serious aspect, made me afraid I had gone too far and I said, before they came in—'What *shall* I do, 'if I have incurred Mr. B's anger by 'my over-forwardness!—Did he not 'look displeased?—Dear ladies, if he be 'so, plead for me, and I'll withdraw, 'when he comes in, for I cannot stand 'his anger I have not been used to it'

'Never fear, Pamela,' said my lady, 'he can't be angry at any thing you say 'or do But I wish, for the sake of 'what I have been witness to of Mr 'Adams's behaviour and modesty, that 'such a thing could be done for him'

Mr Adams bowed, and said—'O my 'good ladies! 'tis too, too considerable 'a thing —I connot expect it—I do 'not—it would be presumption if I 'did'

Just then re entered Mr B and Mr. Williams, the first with a stately air, the other with a more peace portending smile on his countenance

But Mr B sitting down—'Well, 'Pamela,' said he, very gravely, 'I see, 'that power is a dangerous thing in any 'hand —'Sir, Sir!' said I,—'My dear 'lady,' whispering to Lady Davers, 'I 'will withdraw, as I said I would And I was getting away as fast as I could but he arose, and coming up to me, took my hand—'Why is my charmer 'so soon frightened?' said he, most kindly, and still more kindly, with a noble air, pressed it to his lips. 'I must not 'carry my jest too far upon a mind so 'apprehensive, as I otherwise might be 'inclined to do And leading me to Mr Adams and Mr Williams, he said, taking Mr Williams's hand with his left, as he held mine in his right—'Your 'worthy brother clergyman, Mr Adams, 'gives me leave to confirm the decision 'of my dear wife, and you are to thank 'her for the living of F upon the * con-'dition she proposed, and may you give 'but as much satisfaction *there*, as you 'have done in *this* family, and as Mr 'Williams has given to his flock, and 'they will then, after a while, be pleased 'as much with your ministry, as they 'have hitherto been with his'

Mr Adams trembled with joy, and said, he could not tell how to bear this excess of goodness in us both and his countenance and his eyes gave testimony of a gratitude that was too high for further expression

As for myself, you, my honoured and dear friends, who know how much I am always raised (even out of myself, as I may say) when I am made the dispenser of acts of bounty and generosity to the deserving, and who now, instead of incurring blame, as I had apprehended, found myself applauded by every one, and most by the gentleman whose ap-

* This condition Mr Williams generously renounced afterwards, lest it should have a simoniacal appearance. See Vol. IV. Letter XLI.

probation I chiefly coveted to have you, I say, will judge how greatly I must be delighted

But I was still more affected, when Mr B directing himself to me, and to Mr Williams, at the same time, was pleased to say—'Here, my dear, you 'must thank this good gentleman for 'enabling you to give such a shining 'proof of your excellence and whenever 'I put power into your hands for 'the future, act but as you have now 'done, and it will be impossible that I 'should have any choice or will but 'yours'

'O Sir,' said I, pressing his hand with my lips, forgetting how many witnesses I had of my grateful fondness, 'how 'shall I, oppressed with your goodness, 'in such a signal instance as this, find 'words equal to the gratitude of my heart! '—But here, parting my bosom, 'just 'here, they stick,—and I cannot—

And, indeed, I could say no more, and Mr B in the delicacy of his apprehensiveness for me, led me into the next parlour, and placing himself by me on the settee, said—'Take care, my best 'beloved, that the joy, which overflows 'your dear heart, for having done a beneficent 'action to a deserving gentleman, 'does not affect you too much'

My Lady Davers followed us 'Where 'is my angelick sister' said she. 'I 'have a share in her next to yourself, 'my noble brother' And clasping me to her generous bosom, she ran over with expressions of favour to me, in a style and words, which would suffer, were I to endeavour to repeat them.

Coffee being ready, we all three returned to the company My Lord Davers was pleased to make me a great many compliments, and so did Mr H. after his manner But the countess exceeded *herself* in goodness

Mr Williams seemed so pleased, or, rather, so elated, with the deserved acceptation his worthy conduct had met with, that it shewed he was far from repenting at the generous turn the matter had taken in favour of Mr Adams on the contrary, he congratulated him upon it, telling him, he would introduce him, when his generous patron thought proper, to his new parishioners, and would read prayers for him at his first preaching 'And I think, Mr Adams,' said he, 'since this happy affair has been 'brought about from the conversation 'upon dispensations, you and I, both by 'our example and our arguments, must, 'on all occasions, discredit that practice, 'since, as my lady has observed, 'God's providence is a better reliance 'than the richest benefice in England, 'and since, as her ladyship has also observed, 'we ought not to look beyond a 'happy competency, as if in *this life* '*only we had hope*'

'My lady,' said Mr Adams, 'has 'given me many lessons relating to different 'parts of my duty, both as a 'Christian and a clergyman, that will 'not only furnish me with rules for my 'future conduct, but with subjects for 'the best sermons I shall ever be able to 'compose'

Mr B was pleased to say—'It is a 'rule with me, not to leave till to-morrow 'what can be done to day—and '*when*, my dear, do you propose to dispense 'with Mr Adams's good offices 'in your family? Or did you intend to 'induce him to go to town with us?

'I had not proposed any thing, Sir, 'as to that, for I had not asked your kind 'direction but the good dean will supply 'us, I doubt not, and when we set 'out for London, Mr Adams will be 'at full liberty, with his worthy friend, 'Mr Williams, to pursue the happy 'scheme, which your goodness has permitted 'to take effect

'Mr Adams, my dear, who came 'so lately from the university, can, perhaps, 'recommend such another young 'gentleman as himself, to perform the 'functions *he* used to perform in your 'family'

I looked, it seems, a little grave, and Mr B said—'What have you to offer, 'Pamela?—What have I said amiss?'

'Amiss! dear Sir!—'

'Ay, and dear Madam too! I see 'by your bashful seriousness, in place of 'that smiling approbation which you 'always shew when I utter any thing 'you *entirely* approve, that I have said 'something which would rather meet 'with your acquiescence, than choice 'So, as I have often told you, none of 'your reserves and never *hesitate* to me 'your consent in any thing, while you 'are sure I will conform to your wishes, 'or pursue my own liking, as *either* 'shall appear reasonable to me, when I 'have heard *your* reasons.'

'Why,

'Why then, dear Sir, what I had presumed to think, but I submit it to your 'better judgment, was, whether, since 'the gentleman who is so kind as to assist us in our family devotions, in some 'measure acts in the province of the 'worthy dean, it were not right, that 'our own parish minister, whether here 'or in London, should name, or at least 'approve *our* naming, the gentleman?'

'Why could not I have thought of 'that, as well as you, sauce-box?—Lady 'Davers, I am intirely on your side I 'think she deserves a slap now from us 'both'

'I'll forgive her,' said my lady, 'since 'I find her sentiments and actions as 'much a reproof to others as to me

'Mr Williams, did you ever think,' said Mr B 'it would have come to 'this?—Did you ever know such a saucy 'girl in your life?—Already to give herself these reproaching airs?'

'No, never, if your honour is pleased 'to call the most excellent lady in the 'world by such a name, nor any body 'else'

'Pamela, I charge you,' said the dear gentleman, 'if you *study* for it, be sometimes in the wrong, that one may not 'always be taking lessons from such an 'assurance; but, in our turns, have 'something to teach *you*

'Then, dear Sir,' said I, 'must I not 'be a strange creature? For how, when 'you, and my good ladies, are continually giving me such charming examples, can I do a wrong thing?

Mr H said, let *him be hang'd* if he would not marry, as soon as ever he could get any body to have him'

'Foolish fellow!' said Lady Davers, 'do'st think that thou'lt meet with such 'a wife as that, when thou marriest?'

'Why not, Madam?—For if I am 'not so good as Mr B now is, I have 'not been so bad neither as he was formerly,—excuse me, Sir—and so I 'may stand a chance'

'A chance!' said my lady—'that's 'like thee—Didst ever hear of such an 'one as she?'

'I never,' said he, and fell a laughing, '*saw* such an one, I own, And take '*that*, my good lady, for calling me '*foolish fellow*'

'There's not the reproach in thy answer that thou intendest, except to thy 'own grinning insolence,' said her ladyship, (severe enough, but smiling) 'that 'makes thee think *that* a reflection, 'which is none in this case

'Egad, Madam, you're always hard 'upon me! I can say nothing to please 'you While every body else gives and 'receives compliments, I can come in 'for nothing but *foolish fellow* with your 'ladyship'

'Nephew,' said my lord, laughing, 'I think you come in for a large part, 'and a facetious one too for when you represent, and conversation takes a serious turn, you make an excellent character to set us all a laughing.

He got up, and bowed very low 'I 'thank your lordship—You might as 'well have called me a jack-pudding in 'plain words,—but then I would have 'looked upon you all as so many mountebanks!—There I have you, said he, and fell a laughing

The countess, shuddering, said—'Dear, dear Mr H be silent, I beseech 'you, whenever we are serious for you 'tear one from the feast of souls to the 'froth of bodies.

I hope you will forgive me, my dear, for being so tedious on the aforegoing subject, and its most agreeable conclusion It is an important one, because *several persons*, as conferrers or receivers, have found their pleasure and account in it, and it would be well, if conversation were often attended with like happy consequences I have one merit to plead in behalf even of my prolixity, that in reciting the delightful conferences I have the pleasure of holding with our noble guests and Mr B I am careful not to write twice upon one topick, although several which I omit, may be more worthy of your notice than those I give, so that you have as much variety from me, as the nature of the facts and cases will admit of

But here I will conclude, having a very different subject, as a proof of what I have advanced, to touch in my next Till when, I am *your most affectionate and faithful*

P B.

LETTER XXXIII

MY DEAR MISS DARNFORD,

I Now proceed with my journal, which I brought down to Tuesday evening; and of course I begin with

WEDNESDAY.

WEDNESDAY.

Towards the evening came Sir Jacob Swynford, on horseback, attended by two servants in liveries. I was abroad; for I had got leave for a whole afternoon, attended by my Polly; which time I passed in visiting no less than four several poor sick families, whose hearts I made glad. But I should be too tedious, were I to give you the particulars; and besides, I have a brief list of cases, which when you'll favour me with your company, I may shew you; for I have obliged myself*, though not desired, to keep an account of what I do with no less than two hundred pounds a year, that Mr. B. allows me to expend in acts of charity and benevolence.

Lady Davers told me afterwards, that Sir Jacob carried it mighty stiff and formal, when he alighted. He strutted about the court-yard in his boots, with his whip in his hand; and though her ladyship went to the great door, in order to welcome him, he turned short, and, whistling, followed the groom into the stable, as if he had been at an inn; only, instead of taking off his hat, pulling its broad brim over his eyes, for a compliment. In she went in a pet, as she says, saying to the countess—'A surly brute he always was! *My* uncle! He's more of an hostler, than a gentleman; I'm resolved I'll not stir to meet him again. And yet the wretch loves respect from others, though he never practises common civility himself.'

The countess said, she was glad he was come, for she loved to divert herself with such old characters now and then.

And now let me give you a short description of him as I found him, when I came in, that you may the better conceive what sort of a gentleman he is.

He is about sixty-five years of age, a coarse, strong, big-boned man, with large irregular features; he has a haughty supercilious look, a swaggering gait, and a person not at all bespeaking one's favour in behalf of his mind; and his mind, as you shall hear by-and-bye, not clearing up these prepossessions in his disfavour, with which his person and features at first strike one. His voice is big and surly; his eyes little and fiery; his mouth large, with a yellow and blackish stumps of teeth, what are left of which being broken off to a tolerably regular height, looked as if they were ground down to his gums, by constant use. But with all these imperfections, he has an air that sets him somewhat above the mere vulgar, and such as makes one think, that half his disadvantages are rather owing to his own haughty humour, than to nature; for he seems to be a perfect tyrant at first sight, a man used to prescribe, and not to be prescribed to; and has the advantage of a shrewd penetrating look, which yet, methinks, seems rather acquired than natural.

After he had seen his horses well served, and put on an old fashioned gold-buttoned coat, which by its freshness shewed he had been very chary of it, a better wig, but in stiff buckle, and a long sword, stuck stiffly, as if through his coat lappets, in he came, and with an imperious air entering the parlour—'What, nobody come to meet me!' said he, and saluting her ladyship—'How do you do, niece?' and looked about haughtily, she says, as if he expected to see me.

My lady, presenting the countess, said—'The Countess of C. Sir Jacob.'—'O, cry mercy!' said he, 'your most obedient humble servant, Madam. I hope his lordship is well.'

'At your service, Sir Jacob.'

'I wish he was,' said he, bluntly; 'he should not have voted as he did last sessions, I can tell you that.'

'Why, Sir Jacob,' said she, '*servants*, in this free kingdom, don't always do as their *masters* would have 'em.'

'*Mine* do, I can tell you that, Madam.'

'Right or wrong, Sir Jacob?'

'It can't be wrong if I command them.'

'Why, truly, Sir Jacob, there's many a private gentleman carries it higher to a servant, than he cares his *prince* should to him: but I thought, 'till now, 'twas the king only could do no wrong.'

'But, Madam, I always take care to be right.'

'A good reason—because, I dare say, you never think you *can* be in the wrong.'

'Your ladyship should spare me: I'm but just come off a journey. Let me

* See Vol. II. p. 274.

'turn

Plate VIII

Published as the Act directs, by Harrison & C° Nov.r 26, 178[illegible]

'turn myself about, and I'll be up with 'you, never fear, Madam —But where's 'my nephew, Lady Davers? And 'where's your lord? I was told you 'were all here, and young H too, upon 'a very extraordinary occasion, so I 'was willing to see how causes went 'among you, and what you were about 'It will be long enough before you come 'to see me'

'My brother, and Lord Davers, and 'Mr H are all rid out together'

'Well, niece,' strutting with his hands behind him, and his head held up—'Ha! '—He has made a fine kettle on't—'han't he!—'Sblood, (that was his profligate word) 'that ever such a rake 'should be so caught!—They tell me, 'she's plaguy cunning, and quite smart 'and handsome —But I wish his father 'were living —Yet what could he have 'done? Your brother was always un-'manageable I wish he'd been my 'son,—by my faith I do!—What! I 'hope, niece, he locks up his baby, while 'you're here! You don't keep her com-'pany, do you?'

'Yes, Sir Jacob, I do, and you'll 'not scruple to do so too, when you see 'her'

'Why, thou countenancest him in his 'folly, child; I'd a better opinion of 'thy spirit? Thou married to a lord, 'and thy brother to a—Canst tell me 'what, Barbara? If thou canst, pr'ythee 'do

'To an angel, and so you'll say pre-'sently

'What, dost think I shall look through '*his* foolish eyes?—What a disgrace to 'a family ancienter than the Conquest! '—*O Tempora! O Mores!* What will 'this world come to!'

The countess was diverted with this odd gentleman, but ran on in my praise, for fear he should say some rude things to me when I came in; and Lady Davers seconded her But all, it seems, signified nothing He would tell us both his mind, let the young whelp, that was his word, take it as he would 'And 'pray, said he, 'can't I see this fine 'body before he comes in? Let me but 'turn her round two or three times, and 'ask her a question or two, and by her 'answers I shall know what to think of 'her in a twinkling'

'She is gone to take a little airing, Sir 'Jacob, and won't be back till supper-'time'

'Supper time! Why, she is not to sit 'down at table, is she? If she does, I 'won't, that's positive —But now you 'talk of supper, what have you?—I must 'have a boiled chicken, and shall eat it 'all myself —Who's house keeper now? 'I suppose all's turned up-side down.'

'No, there is not one new servant, 'except a girl that waits upon her own 'person all the old servants are conti-'nued'

'That's much! These creatures ge-'nerally take as great state upon them 'as a born lady and they're in the 'right If they can make the man stoop 'to the great point, they'll hold his nose 'to the grind stone, never fear, and all 'the little ones come about in course'

'Well, Sir Jacob, when you see her, 'you'll alter your mind'

'Never, never! that's positive'

'Ay, Sir Jacob, I was as positive as 'you once; but I love her now as well 'as if she was my own sister

'O hideous, hideous!—Tell it not in 'Gath, for thou'lt make the daughters 'of Philistia triumph! All the fools that 'he has made wherever he has travelled, 'will clap their hands at him, and at you 'too, if you talk at this rate.—But let 'me speak to Mrs Jervis, if she be here 'I'll order my own supper

So he went out, saying, he knew the house, though in a better mistress's days

The countess said, if Mr B kept his temper, as she hoped he would, there would be good diversion with the old gentleman

'O yes,' said my lady, 'my brother 'will, I dare say He despises the surly 'brute too much to be angry with him, 'let him say what he will'

He went, and talked a great deal against me to Mrs Jervis You may guess, my dear, that she launched out in my praises, and he was offended at her, and said—'Woman, woman! forbear these 'ill-timed praises: her birth's a disgrace 'to our family. What! my sister's 'waiting-maid, taken upon charity! I 'cannot bear it'

I mention all these things, as the ladies afterwards told them to me, because it shall prepare you to judge what a fine time I was likely to have of it

When Mr B and my Lord Davers, and Mr H came home, which they did about half an hour after six, they were told who was there, just as they entered the parlour, and Mr B. smiled at Lord Davers,

Davers and entering—' Sir Jacob, said he, ' welcome to Bedfordshire! and ' twice welcome to this house! I rejoice ' to see you.'

My lady says, never was so odd a figure as the old baronet made, when thus accosted. He stood up indeed, but as Mr. B. offered to take his hand, he put 'em both behind him—' Not that ' you know of, Sir!—And then looking up at his face, and down at his feet, three or four times successively—' Are ' you my brother's son?' That very individual son, that your good father ' used to boast of, and say, that for handsome person, true courage, noble mind, ' was not to be matched in any three ' counties in England?'

' The very same, dear Sir, that my ' honoured father's partiality used to ' think he never praised enough.'

' And what is all of it come to at last! ' —He paid well, did he not, to teach you ' to know the world?—Ad's life, nephew! hadst thou been born a fool, or ' a raw greenhead, or a doating grey-' head—'

' What then, Sir Jacob?'

' What then? Why then thou wouldst ' have done just as thou hast done!'

' Come, come, Sir Jacob, you know ' not my inducements. You know ' not what an angel I have in person and ' mind. Your eyes shall by and-bye ' be blest with the sight of her: your ears ' with hearing her speak: and then you'll ' call all you have said, profanation.'

' What is it I hear!—What is it I ' hear!—You talk in the language of ' romance; and from the house-keeper ' to the head of the house, you're all ' stark-staring mad.—By my soul, nephew, I wish, for thy own credit, thou ' wert—But what signifies wishing!— ' I hope you'll not bring your syren into ' my company.'

' Yes, I will, Sir, because I love to ' give you pleasure. And say not a ' word more, for your own sake, till you ' see her.—You'll have the less to unsay, ' Sir Jacob, and the less to repent of.'

' The devil!—I'm in an inchanted ' castle, that's certain. What a plague ' has this little witch done to you all?— ' And how did she bring it about?'

The ladies and Lord Davers laughed, it seems; and Mr. B. begging him to sit down, and answer him some family questions, he said—(for it seems he is very captious at times) ' What, a devil! am ' I to be laughed at!—Lord Davers, I ' hope *you're* not bewitched too, are ' you?'

' Indeed, Sir Jacob, I am. My sister ' B. is my doating-piece.'

' Whew, whistled he, with a wild stare ' and how is it with *you*, youngster?'

' With me, Sir Jacob?' said Mr. H. ' I'd give all I'm worth in the world, ' and ever shall be worth, for such another wife.'

He ran to the window, and throwing up the sash, looking into the court-yard, said—' Hollo—So-ho—Groom—Jack ' —Jonas—Get me my horse!—I'll ' keep no such company!—I'll be gone! ' Why, Jonas!' calling again.

' You're not in earnest, Sir Jacob, said Mr. B.

' I am, by my soul!—I'll away to the ' village this night! Why, you're all ' upon the high game!—I'll—But who ' comes here?' For just at that instant, the chariot brought me into the court-yard—' Who's this? who is she?'

' One of *my* daughters,' started up the countess, ' my youngest daughter ' Jenny!—She's the pride of my family, ' Sir Jacob!'

' By my soul,' said he, ' I was running, for I thought it was the grand ' inchantress.'

Out stept Lady Davers to me. ' Dear ' Pamela, said she, ' humour all that's ' said to you. Here's Sir Jacob come. ' You're the Countess of C——'s youngest daughter Jenny—That's your cue.'

' Ah! but, Madam,' said I, ' Lady ' Jenny is not married,'—looking (before I thought) on a circumstance that I think too much of sometimes, though I carry it off as well as I can.'

She laughed at my exception. ' Come, ' Lady Jenny,' said she, (for I just entered the great door) ' I hope you've ' had a fine airing?'

' A very pretty one, Madam,' said I, as I entered the parlour. ' This is a ' pleasant country, Lady Davers,— ' (*Wink when I'm wrong, whispered I*) ' Where's Mrs. B.?'—Then, as seeing a strange gentleman, I started half back, into a more reserved air; and made him a low curt'sy.

Sir Jacob looked as if he did not know what to think of it, now at me, now at Mr. B.—But the dear gentleman put him quite out of doubt, by taking my hand. ' Well, Lady Jenny, did you meet ' my fugitive in your tour?'

' No,

'No, Mr. B.' replied I. 'Did she go my way? I told you I would keep the great road.'

'Lady Jenny C——,' said Mr B. presenting me to his uncle. 'A charming creature!' added he. 'Have you not a son worthy of such an alliance?'

'Ay, marry, nephew, this is a lady indeed! Why, the plague,' whispered he, 'could you not have pitched your tent here?—Miss, by your leave!' and saluting me, turned to the countess.—'By my soul, Madam, you've a charming daughter! Had my rash nephew seen this lovely creature, and you'd have condescended, he'd never have stooped to the cottage, as he has done.'

'You're right, Sir Jacob,' returned Mr B., 'but I always ran too fast for my fortune. yet, these ladies of family never bring out their jewels into bachelors company; and when, too late, we see what we've missed, we are vexed at our precipitation.'

'Well said, however, boy. By my soul, I wish thee repentance, though 'tis out of thy power to amend. Be that one of thy curses, when thou seest this lady, as I make no doubt it is.'

Again taking my hand, and surveying me from head to foot, and turning me round, which, it seems, is a mighty practice with him to a stranger lady, (and a modest one too, you'll say, Miss)—'Why, truly, you're a charming creature, Miss—Lady Jenny, I would say—By your leave, once more!—Upon my soul, my Lady Countess, she is a charmer—But—but—' staring at me, 'Are you married, Madam?'

I looked a little silly, and my new mamma came up to me, and took my hand.—'Why, Jenny, you are dressed oddly to-day!—What a hoop you wear! It makes you look I can't tell how!'

'Upon my soul, Madam, I thought so, what signifies lying?—But 'tis only the hoop, I see—Really and truly, Lady Jenny, your hoop is enough to make half a hundred of our sex despair, for fear you should be married. I thought it was something! Few ladies escape my notice. I always kept a good look-out, for I have two daughters of my own. But 'tis the hoop, I see plainly enough. You are so slender every where but *here*,' putting his hand upon my hip, which quite dashed me, and I retired behind my Lady Countess's chair.

'Fie, Sir Jacob!' said Mr B.; 'before us young gentlemen, to take such liberties with a maiden lady!—You give a bad example.'

'Hang him that sets you a bad example, nephew. But I see you're right, I see Lady Jenny's a maiden lady, or she would not have been so shamefaced. I'll swear for her on occasion. Ha, ha, ha,—I'm sure,' repeated he, 'she's a maiden—For our sex give the married ladies a freer air in a trice.'

'How, Sir Jacob!' said Lady Davers.

'O fie,' said the countess! 'Can't you praise the maiden ladies, but at the expence of the married ones? What do you see of freedom in me?'

'Or in me?' said Lady Davers.

'Nay, for that matter, you are very well, ladies, I must needs say.—But will you pretend to blush with that virgin rose?—Will ye?—Od's my life, Miss—Lady Jenny, I would say,' taking my hand, 'come from behind your mamma's chair, and you two ladies stand up now together.—There, so you do—Why now, blush for blush, and Lady Jenny shall be three to one, and a deeper crimson by half. Look you there, look you there else! An hundred guineas to one against the field.'—Then stamping with one foot, and lifting up his hands and eyes—'O Christ! Lady Jenny has it all to nothing—By my soul she has—Ha, ha, ha,—You may well sit down both of you, but you're a blush too late, I can tell you that.—Well hast thou done, Lady Jenny,' tapping my shoulder with his rough paw.

I was hastening away, and he said—'But let's see you again, Miss, for now I will stay, if they bring nobody else'—And away I went, for I was quite out of countenance—'What a strange creature,' thought I, 'is this!'

Supper being near ready, he continued calling out for Lady Jenny, for the sight of her, he said, did him good, but he was resolved he would not sit down at table with *somebody else*.

The countess said, she would fetch her daughter, and stepping out, returned, saying—'Mrs B. understands that Sir Jacob is here, and that he does not 'choose to see her, so she begs to be excused, and my Jenny and she desire to sup together.'

'The very worst tidings I have heard this twelvemonth. Why, nephew, let your girl sup with any body, so we may have Lady Jenny back with us.'

'I know,' said the countess, (who was desirous to see how far he would carry it) 'Jenny won't leave Mrs B, so if you see *one*, you must see *t'other*.'

'Nay, then, if it must be so, I must sit down contented.—But yet, I should be glad to see Lady Jenny, that I should. But I will not sit down at table with Mr B's girl—that's positive.'

'Well, well, let 'em sup together, and there's an end of it,' said Mr B. '—I see my uncle has as good a judgment as any body of fine ladies.—' —'(*That I have, nephew.*)' 'But he can't forego his humour, in compliment to the finest lady in England.'

'Consider, nephew, consider—'Tis not thy doing a foolish thing, and calling a girl wife, shall cram a niece down my throat, that's positive. The moment thy girl comes down to take place of these ladies, I am gone, that's most certain.'

'Well then, shall I go up, and oblige Pamela to sup by herself, and persuade Lady Jenny to come down to us?'

'With all my soul, nephew—a good motion.—But, Pamela—did you say? —A *queer* sort of name! I've heard of it somewhere!—Is't a Christian or a Pagan name?—Linsey-wolsey—half one, half t'other—like thy girl—Ha, ha, ha.'

'Let me be *hang'd*,' whispered Mr H to his aunt, 'if Sir Jacob has not a power of wit, though he's so whimsical with it. I like him much.'

'But hark ye, nephew,' said Sir Jacob, as Mr B was going out of the parlour, 'one word with you. Don't fob upon us your girl with the Pagan name for Lady Jenny. I have set a mark upon her, and should know her from a thousand, although she had changed her hoop.' Then he laughed again, and said, he hoped Lady Jenny would come—and come without any body with her—'But I smell a plot,' said he—'By my soul I won't stay, if they both come together. I won't be put upon—But here comes one or both—Where's my whip?—I'll go.'

'Indeed Mr B I had rather have staid with Mrs B,' said I, as I entered—as he had bid me.

''Tis she! 'tis she!—You've nobody behind you?—No, she han't.—Why now, nephew, you're right. I was afraid you'd have put a trick upon me. —You'd *rather*,' repeated he to me, 'have staid with Mrs B!—Yes, I warrant.—But you *shall* be placed in better company, my dear child.'

'Sister,' said Mr B, 'will you be pleased to take that chair, for Pamela does not choose to give my uncle disgust, who so seldom comes to see us.'

My lady took the upper end of the table, and I sat next below my new mamma. 'So, Jenny,' said she, 'how have you left Mrs B?'

'A little concerned—but she was the easier, as Mr B himself desired I'd come down.'

My Lord Davers sat next me, and Sir Jacob said—'Shall I beg a favour of you, my lord, to let me sit next to Lady Jenny?'

Mr B said—'Won't it be better to sit over-against her, uncle?'

'Ay, that's right. I faith, nephew, thou know'st what's right. Well, so I will.'—He accordingly removed his seat, and I was very glad of it, for though I was sure to be stared at sufficiently by him, yet I was afraid, if he sat next me, he would not keep his hands off my hoop.

He run on a deal in my praises, after his manner, but so rough at times, that he gave me pain, and I was under a difficulty too, lest he should observe my ring, but he stared so much in my face, that that escaped his notice.

After supper, the gentlemen sat down to their bottle, and the ladies and I withdrew, and about twelve they broke up, Sir Jacob talking of nothing but Lady Jenny, and wished Mr B had married so happily as with such a charming creature, one, he said, that carried tokens of her high birth in her face, and whose every feature, and look, shewed her to be nobly descended.

They let him go to bed with his mistake, but the countess said next morning, she thought she never saw a greater instance of stupid pride and churlishness, and she should be sick of the advantage of birth or ancestry, if this was the natural fruit of it. 'For a man,' said her ladyship,

ladyship, 'to come to his nephew's house, 'and to suffer the mistress of it to be closetted up, (as he thinks) and not permitted to appear, in order to humour 'his absurd and brutal insolence, and to 'behave as he has done, is such a ridicule upon the pride of descent, that I 'shall think of it as long as I live.—O 'Mrs B. said she, 'what advantages 'have you over every one who sees you, 'but most over those who pretend to 'treat you unworthily!'

I expect to be called to breakfast every minute, and shall then, perhaps, see how this matter will end. I wish, when it is revealed, he is not in a fury, and don't think himself imposed on. I fear it won't go off so well as I wish, for every body seems to be grave, and angry at Sir Jacob.

THURSDAY.

I Now proceed with my tale. At breakfast-time, when every one was sat, and a chair left for me, Sir Jacob began to call out for Lady Jenny. 'But,' said he, 'I'll have none of your girl, nephew, 'although the chair at the tea-table is 'left for somebody.'

'No,' said Mr B. 'we'll get Lady 'Jenny to supply Mrs B.'s place, since 'you don't care to see her.'

'With all my heart,' replied he.

'But, uncle, said Mr B. 'have you 'really no desire, no curiosity to see the 'girl I have married?'

'No, none at all, by my soul.'

Just then I came in, and paying my compliments to the company, and to Sir Jacob—'Shall I, said I, 'supply Mrs 'B.'s place in her absence?' And down I sat.

After breakfast, and the servants were withdrawn—'Lady Jenny,' said Lady Davers, 'you are a young lady, who have 'all the advantages of birth and descent, 'and some of the best blood in the kingdom runs in your veins, and here Sir 'Simon Swynford is your great admirer: 'cannot *you*, from whom it will come 'with a double grace, convince him that 'he does an unkind thing, at my brother's house, to keep the person my 'brother has thought worthy of making 'the mistress of it, out of company? 'And let us know your opinion, whether my brother himself does right, to 'comply with such an unreasonable distaste?'

'Why, how now, Lady Davers! This 'from you! I did not expect it!'

'My uncle, said Mr B. 'is the only 'person in the kingdom that I would 'have humoured thus: and I made no 'doubt, when he saw how willing I was 'to oblige him in so high a point, he 'would have acted a more generous part 'than he has yet done.—But, Lady Jenny, 'what say you to my sister's questions?'

'If I must speak my mind,' replied I, 'I should take the liberty to be very serious with Sir Jacob, and to say, that 'when a thing is done, and cannot be 'helped, he should take care how he 'sows the seeds of indifference and animosity between man and wife: and 'how he makes a gentleman dissatisfied 'with his choice, and perhaps unhappy 'as long as he lives.'

'Nay, Miss, said he, 'if all are against 'me, and you, whose good opinion I value more than all, you may e'en let the 'girl come, and sit down, if you will.—'If she is but half as pretty, and half as 'wise, and modest, as you, I shall, as it 'cannot be helped, as you say, be ready 'to think better of the matter. For, 'tis 'a little hard, I must needs say, if she 'has hitherto appeared before all the 'good company, to have her kept out of 'the way on my account.'

'Really, Sir Jacob, said the countess, 'I have blushed for you *more* than once 'on this occasion. But the mistress of 'this house is more than half as wise, 'and modest, and lovely: and in hopes 'you will return me back some of the 'blushes I have lent you, see *there*, in 'my daughter Jenny, whom you have 'been so justly admiring, the mistress of 'the house, and the lady with the Pagan 'name.'

Sir Jacob sat aghast, looking at one, and at another, and at me, each in turn, and then cast his eyes on the floor.—At last, up he got, and swore a sad oath; 'And am I thus trick'd and bamboozled,' that was his word, 'am I?—There's no 'bearing this house; nor her presence 'now, that's certain, and I'll be gone.'

Mr B. looking at me, and nodding his head towards Sir Jacob, as he was in a flutter to be gone, I rose from my chair, and went to him, and took his hand. 'I 'hope, Sir Jacob, you will be able to 'bear *both*, when you shall see, that there 'is no other difference but that of descent, between the supposed Lady Jenny, whom you so kindly praised, and the girl your dear nephew has so much exalted.

'Let me go,' said he, 'I'm most confoundedly bit.—I cannot look you in the face!—By my soul, I cannot!—For 'tis impossible you should forgive me.'

'Indeed it is not, Sir, you have done nothing but what I can forgive you for, if your dear nephew can, for to him was the wrong, if any, and I'm sure he can overlook it.—And for his sake, to the uncle of so honoured a gentleman, to the brother of my late good lady, I can, with a bent knee, *thus*, ask your blessing, and desire your excuse for joining to keep you in this suspence.'

'Bless you!—O Christ!' said he, and stamped—'Who can choose but bless you?' And he kneeled down, and wrapped his arms about me.—'But, curse me, that was his strange word, 'if ever I was so touched before!'

My dear Mr B. for fear my spirits should be too much affected, (for the rough baronet, in his transport, had bent me down lower than I kneeled) came to me, and held me by my arm, but permitted Sir Jacob to raise me, only saying—'How does my angel? Now she has made this conquest, she has completed all her triumphs.'

'Angel did you call her!—By my soul, I'm confounded with her goodness, and her sweet carriage!—Rise, and let me see if I can stand myself!—And, believe me, I am sorry I have acted so much like a bear as I have done, and the more I think of it, the more I shall be ashamed of myself.'—And the tears, as he spoke, ran down his rough cheeks, which moved me a good deal, for to see a man with so hard a countenance weep, was a touching sight.

Mr H. putting his handkerchief to his eyes, his aunt said—'What's the matter, Jackey?'—'The matter!' answered he, 'I don't know how the d—l 'tis—But here's strange doings, as ever I knew—For here, day after day, one's ready to cry, without knowing whether it be for joy or sorrow!—What a plague's the matter with me, I wonder!'—And out he went, the two ladies, whose charming eyes, too, glistened with pleasure, smiling at the effect the scene had upon Mr H. and at what he said.

'Well, Madam, said Sir Jacob, approaching me, for I had sat down, but then stood up—'You will forgive me, and from my heart I wish you joy. By my soul I do,'—and saluted me—'I could not have believed there had been such a person breathing. I don't wonder at my nephew's loving you!—And you call her Sister, Lady Davers, don't you?—If you do, I'll own her for my niece.'

'Don't I!—Yes, I do, said her ladyship, coming to me, 'and am proud so to call her. And this I tell you, for *your* comfort, though to *my own* shame, that I used her worse than you have done, before I knew her excellence, and have repented of it ever since.'

I bowed to her ladyship—and kissed her hand—'My dearest lady, said I, you have made me such rich amends since, that I am sure I may say—"*It was good for me that I was afflicted!*"'

'Why, nephew, she has the fear of God, I perceive, before her eyes too! I'm sure, I've heard those words. They are somewhere in the Scripture, I believe!—Why, who knows but she may be a means to save your soul!—Hay, you know!'

'Ay, Sir Jacob, she'll be a means to save an hundred souls, and might go a great way to save yours, if you were to live with her but one month.'

'Well, but nephew, I hope *you* forgive me, too, for, now I think of it, I never knew you take any matter so patiently in my life.'

I knew, said the dear gentleman, that every extravagance you insisted upon, was heightening my charmer's triumph, and increasing your own contrition, and, as I was not *indeed* deprived of her company, I could bear with every thing you said or did—Yet, don't you remember, that I cautioned you, that the less you said against her, the less you'd have to unsay, and the less to repent of?'

'I do, and let me ride out, and call myself to account for all I have said against her, in her own hearing, and when I can think of but one half, and how she has taken it, by my soul, I believe 'twill make me *more* than half-mad.'

At dinner (when we had Mr Williams's company) the baronet told me, he admired me now, as much as he did when he thought me Lady Jenny, but complained of the trick put upon him by us all, and seemed now and-then a little serious upon it

He took great notice of the dexterity which he imputed to me, in performing the honours of the table And every now-and-then, he lifted up his eyes—'God take me! Very clever, by my soul!—Why, Madam, you seem to me to be born to these things!—I will be helped by nobody but you—And you'll have a task of it, I can tell you, for I have a whipping stomach, and were there fifty dishes, I always taste of every one' And, indeed, John was in a manner wholly employed in going to and fro between the baronet and me, for an half hour together

He went from us afterwards to Mrs. Jervis, and made her answer him abundance of questions about me, and how all these matters had *come about*, as he phrased it, and returning, when we drank coffee, said—'I have been *confabbing*,' that was his word, 'with Mrs Jervis, about you, niece By my soul, I never heard the like! She tells me, you can play on the harpsichord, and sing too will you let a body have a tune or so? My Mab can play pretty well, and so can Dolly —I'm a judge of musick, and would fain hear you I said, if he was a judge, I should be afraid to play before him, but I would not be asked twice, when we had taken our coffee

Accordingly, he repeating his request, I gave him a tune, and, at his desire, sung to it, 'Od's my life,' said he, 'you do it purely!—But I see where it is—My girls have got *my* fingers! And then he held both hands out, and a fine pair of paws shewed he!—'Plague on't, they touch two keys at once, but those slender and nimble fingers, how they sweep along! My eye can't follow 'em—Whew, whistled he, 'they are here and there, and every where at once!—Why, nephew, I believe you have put another trick upon me My niece is certainly of quality! And report has not done her justice.—One more tune,, one more song—By my faith, your voice goes sweetly to your fingers 'Slife—I'll thrash my jades,' that was his polite phrase, 'when I come home —Lady Davers, you know not the money they have cost me to qualify them, and here's a mere baby to them, outdoes em by a bar's length, without any expence at all bestowed upon her Go over that again—Confound me for a puppy! I lost it by my prating —Ay, there you have it!—That's it! By my soul, it is! Oh! that I could but dance as well as thou sing'st! I'd give you a saraband, as old as I am'

After supper, we fell into a conversation, of which I must give you some account, because it was upon a topick that Mr B has been blamed for in his marrying me, and which has stuck by some of his friends, even after they have in kindness to me, acquitted him in every other respect, and that is,, *the example that he has set to young gentlemen of family and fortune to marry beneath them*.

It was begun by Sir Jacob, who said —'I am in love with my new niece, that I am but still one thing sticks with me in this affair, and that is, what will become of degree or distinction, if this practice of gentlemens marrying their mothers waiting-maids, (excuse me, Madam) should come into vogue? Already, young ladies and young gentlemen are too apt to be drawn away in this manner, and to disgrace their families We have too many instances of this You'll forgive me, both of you

'That,' said Lady Davers, 'is the *only* thing!—I must needs say, Sir Jacob has hit upon the point, that would make one wish this example had not been set by a gentleman of such an ancient family, till one comes to be acquainted with this dear creature, and then every body thinks it ought not to be otherwise than it is'

'Ay, Pamela,' said Mr B 'what can you say to this? Cannot you defend me from this charge? This is a point that has been often objected to me try for one of your pretty arguments in my behalf

'Indeed, Sir, replied I, looking down,' it becomes not me to say any thing to this'

'But indeed it does, if you can: and I beg you'll help me to some excuse, if you have any at hand.'

'Won't you, Sir, dispense with me on this occasion? Indeed I know not what to say Indeed I should not, if

'I may

'I may judge for myſelf, ſpeak one 'word to this ſubject.—For it is my 'abſolute opinion, that degrees in ge- 'neral ſhould be kept up, although I 'muſt always deem the preſent caſe an 'happy exception to the rule

Mr B looking as if he ſtill expected I ſhould ſay ſomething—'Won't you, 'Sir, diſpenſe with me? repeated I 'I liked I ſhould not ſpeak to this point, 'if I may be my own judge

'I always intend, my dear, you ſhall 'judge for yourſelf, and you know, I 'ſeldom urge you farther, when you 'uſe thoſe words But if you have any 'thing upon your mind to ſay, let's have 'it for your arguments are always new 'and unborrowed

'I would then, if I *muſt*, Sir, aſk, if 'there be not a nation, or if there has 'not been a law in ſome nation, that, 'whenever a young gentleman, be *his* 'degree what it would, has ſeduced a 'poor creature, be *her* degree what it 'would, obliges the gentleman to marry 'that unhappy perſon?'

'I think there is ſuch a law in ſome 'country, I can't tell where, ſaid Sir Jacob

'And do you think, Sir, whether it 'be ſo or not, that it is equitable it ſhould 'be ſo

'Yes, by my troth—Though I muſt 'needs own, if it were ſo in England, 'many men, that I know, would not 'have the wives they now have.'

'You ſpeak to your knowledge, I 'doubt not, Sir Jacob? ſaid Mr B

'Why, indeed—Why, truly—I don't 'know but I do

'All then, ſaid I, 'that I would in- 'fer, is, whether another law would not 'be a ſtill more juſt and equitable one, 'that the gentleman who is repulſed, 'from a principle of virtue and honour, 'ſhould not be cenſured for marrying a 'perſon he could *not* ſeduce? And whe- 'ther it is not more for both their ho- 'nours, if he does, inaſmuch as it is 'nobler to reward a virtue, than to re- 'pair a ſhame; were that ſhame to be 'repaired by matrimony, which I take 'the liberty to doubt. But I beg par- 'don, you commanded me, Sir—Elſe 'this ſubject ſhould not have found a 'ſpeaker to it, in me

'This is admirably ſaid—by my ſoul 'it is, ſaid Sir Jacob

'But yet this comes not up to the 'objection, ſaid Mr B 'The ſetting 'an example to waiting maids to aſpire, 'and to young gentlemen to deſcend 'And I will enter into the ſubject my- 'ſelf, and the rather, becauſe, as I go 'along, I will give Sir Jacob a faint 'ſketch of the merit and character of my 'Pamela, of which he cannot be ſo well 'informed, as he has been of the diſ- 'grace, which he imagined I had brought 'upon myſelf by marrying her

'In order to this, give me leave to 'ſay, that I think it neceſſary, that as 'well thoſe perſons who are afraid the 'example ſhould be taken, as thoſe who 'are inclined to follow it, ſhould take '*all* the material parts of it into their 'conſideration otherwiſe, I think the 'precedent may be juſtly cleared, and 'the fears of the one be judged ground- 'leſs, and the plea of the other but 'a pretence, in order to cover a folly, 'into which they would have fallen, 'whether they had this example or not

'For inſtance in order to lay claim 'to the excuſes which my conduct, if I 'may ſuppoſe it of force enough to do 'either good or hurt, will furniſh, it is 'neceſſary,

'That the object of their wiſh ſhould 'be a girl of exquiſite beauty, (and that 'not only in their own blinded and par- 'tial judgments, but in the opinion of '*every one*, who ſees her, friend or foe) 'in order to juſtify the force which the '*firſt* attractions have upon him,

'That ſhe be deſcended of honeſt and 'conſcientious, though poor and obſcure 'parents, who having preſerved their 'integrity, through great trials and af- 'flictions, have, by their examples, as 'well as precepts, laid deep in the girl's 'mind the foundations of piety and vir- 'tue

'It is neceſſary, that to the charms of 'perſon, this waiting maid ſhould have 'an humble, teachable mind, fine natu- 'ral parts, a ſprightly, yet inoffenſive 'wit, a temper ſo excellent, and a judg- 'ment ſo ſolid, as ſhould promiſe for her, '(by the love and eſteem theſe qualities 'ſhould attract to herſelf from her fel- 'low ſervants, ſuperior and inferior) 'that ſhe would become an higher ſta- 'tion, and be reſpected in it

'It is neceſſary, that after ſo good a 'foundation laid by her parents, ſhe 'ſhould have all the advantages of fe- 'male education conferred upon her 'the example of an excellent lady, im- 'proving and building upon ſo worthy

'a foun-

'a foundation a capacity surprisingly 'ready to take in all that is taught her 'an attention, assiduity, and diligence 'almost peculiar to herself, at her time 'of life, insomuch as, at fifteen or six-'teen years of age, to be able to vie with 'any young ladies of rank, as well in 'the natural genteelness of her person, 'as in her acquirements and that in 'nothing but her *humility* she should 'manifest any difference between herself 'and the high-born

'It will be necessary, moreover, that 'she should have a mind above tempta-'tion, that she should resist the *offers* 'and *menaces* of one upon whom all her 'worldly happiness seemed to depend, 'the son of a lady to whom she owed 'the greatest obligations, a person whom 'she did not *hate*, but greatly *fear-ed*, and whom her grateful heart would 'have been *glad* to oblige, and who 'sought to prevail over her virtue, by 'all the inducements that could be 'thought of, to *attract* a young unex-'perienced virgin, at one time, or to '*frighten* her at another, into his pur-'poses, who offered her high, very high 'terms, her circumstances considered, 'as well for herself, as for parents she 'loved better than herself, whose cir-'cumstances at the same time were low 'and distressful

'Yet to all these *offers* and *menaces*, 'that she should be able to answer in such 'words as these, which will always dwell 'upon my memory—"*I reject your "proposals with all my soul —May "GOD desert me, whenever I make "worldly grandeur my chiefest good! "I know I am in your power, I dread "your will to ruin me is as great as your "power —Yet, will I dare to tell you, "I will make no free-will offering of "my virtue All that I *can* do, poor "as it is, I *will* do, to shew you, that "my will bore no part in the violation "of me.' And when future marriage 'was intimated to her, to induce her to 'yield, to be able to answer—"The "moment I yield to your proposals, "there is an end of all merit, if now I "have any —And I should be so far "from *expecting* such an honour, that "I will pronounce, I should be most *un-"worthy* of it."

'If, I say, my dear friends, such a 'girl can be found, thus beautifully at-'tractive in *every one's* eye, and not 'partially so only in a young gentle-'man's *own*, and after that, (what 'good persons would infinitely prefer 'to beauty) thus piously principled, thus 'genteelly educated and accomplished; 'thus brilliantly witty; thus prudent, 'modest, generous, undesigning, and 'having been thus tempted, thus tried, 'by the man she hated not, pursued, '(not intriguingly pursuing) be thus in-'flexibly virtuous, and proof against 'temptation let her reform her liber-'tine, and let him marry her, and were 'he of princely extraction, I dare an-'swer for it, that no *two* princes in *one* 'age, take the world through, would be 'in danger For, although I am sen-'sible it is not to my credit, I will say, 'that I never met with a repulse, nor a 'conduct like this, and yet I never sunk 'very low for the subjects of my at-'tempts, either at home or abroad.

'These are obvious inferences,' added the dear gentleman, 'and not refine-'ments upon my Pamela's story, and if 'the gentleman were capable of thought 'and comparison, would rather make 'such an example, as is apprehended, '*more*, than *less* difficult than *before*.

'But if, indeed, added he, 'the young 'fellow be such a booby, that he cannot '*reflect* and *compare*, and take the case '*with all it's circumstances* together, I 'think his good papa or mamma should 'get him a wife to their own liking, as 'soon as possible, and the poorest girl in 'England, who is honest, would rather 'have reason to bless herself for escaping 'such a husband, than to glory in the 'catch she would have of him For 'such a young fellow as that, would 'hardly do honour to his family in any '*one* instance '

'Indeed,' said the countess, 'it would 'be pity, after all, that such an one 'should marry any lady of prudence and 'birth, for 'tis enough in conscience, 'that he is a disgrace to *one* worthy fa-'mily, it would be pity he should make '*two* unhappy '

'Why, really, nephew,' said Sir Jacob, 'I think you have said a great deal to 'the purpose There is not so much 'danger from the example, as I appre-'hended, from *sensible* and *reflecting* 'minds I did not consider this matter 'thoroughly, I must needs say '

* See Vol. I. p. 116.

'All

'All the business is, said Lady Davers—' You'll excuse me, sister—There 'will be more people hear that Mr B 'has married his mother's waiting-maid, 'than will know his inducements

'Not many, I believe, sister—For 'when 'tis known, I have some character 'in the world, and am not quite an idiot, '(and my faults, in having not been one 'of the most virtuous of men, will stand 'me in some stead in *this* case, though 'hardly in *any other*) they will naturally 'inquire into my inducements

'But see you not, when we go abroad 'to church, or elsewhere, what numbers 'of people her character draws to admire 'the dear creature? Does not this shew, 'that her virtue has made her more conspicuous, than my fortune has made 'me? For I passed up and down quietly 'enough before, (handsome as my equipage always was) and attracted not 'any body's notice and indeed I had as 'lieve these honours were not so publickly 'paid *her*, for even, were I fond of shew 'and parade, what are they, but a reproach to me?—And can I have any 'excellence, but a secondary one, in having, after all my persecutions of her, 'done but common justice to her merit?

'This answers your objection, Lady 'Davers, and shews, that *my* inducements and *her* story must be equally 'known. And, upon my conscience, 'I think, (every thing I have said considered, and every thing that might still 'farther be urged, and the conduct of 'that dear creature in the station she 'adorns, so much exceeding all I hoped, 'or could flatter myself with, from the 'most promising appearances) that she 'does *me* more honour than I have done '*her*; and if I am capable of putting 'myself in a third person's place, I think 'I should be of the same opinion, were 'I to determine upon such another pair, 'exactly circumstanced as we are

You may believe, my friend, how much this *generous defence* of the *step* he had taken, attributing every thing to me, and deprecating his worthy self, affected me I played with a cork one while, with my rings another, turning them round my fingers, looked down, and on one side, and every way I looked, but on the company, for they gazed too much upon me all the time, so that I could only glance a tearful eye now-and then upon the dear man, and when it would overflow, catch in my handkerchief the escaped fugitives, that would start unbidden beyond their proper limits, though I often endeavoured, by a twinkling motion, to disperse the gathering water, before it had formed itself into drops too big to be restrained

All the company praised the dear generous speaker, and he was pleased to say farther—' Although, my good friends, 'I can truly say, that with all the pride 'of family, and the insolence of fortune, 'which once made me doubt whether I 'should not sink too low, if I made my 'Pamela my mistress, (for I should then 'have treated her not ungenerously, and 'should have suffered her, perhaps, to 'call herself by my name) I have never 'once repented of what I have done on 'the contrary, I have always rejoiced in 'it, and it has been, from the first day 'of our marriage, my pride and my 'boast, (and shall be, let others say what 'they will) that I can call such an excellence, and such a purity, which I so 'little deserve, mine, and I look down 'with contempt upon the rashness of 'all such as reflect upon me, for they 'can have no notion of my happiness, or 'her merit'

'O dear Sir,' said I, 'how do you 'over-rate my poor merit!—Some persons are happy in a life of *comforts*,' but 'mine's a life of *joy*!—One rapturous 'instance follows another so fast, that I 'know not how to bear them.'

'Whew!—whistled Sir Jacob—'Whereabouts am I?—I hope, by-and-by, you'll come down to our pitch, 'that one may put in a word or two with 'you

'May you be long thus blest, and thus 'happy together!' said Lady Davers 'I 'know not which to admire most, the 'dear girl that never was bad, or the 'dear gentleman, that, having been bad, 'is now so good!'

Said my Lord Davers—' There is 'hardly any bearing these moving scenes, '*following one another so quick*, as my 'sister says

The countess was pleased to say, that till now, she had been at a loss to form any notion of the happiness of the first pair before the Fall but now, by so fine an instance as this, she comprehended it in all it's force—' God continue you to 'one another,' added her ladyship, 'for 'a credit to the state, and to human nature

M. H, having his elbows on the table,

table, folded his hands, shaking them, and looking down—'Egad, this *is* uncommon life, that it is!—Your two souls, I can see that, are like well tuned instruments but they are too high-set for me a vast deal.'

'The best things, said Lady Davers, (always severe upon her poor nephew) thou ever saidst. The musick must be equal to that of Orpheus, which can make such a savage as thee dance to it. I charge thee, say not another word to-night.'

'Why, indeed, aunt,' returned he, laughing, 'I believe it *was* pretty well said for your foolish fellow though it was by chance, I must confess. I did not think of it.'

'That I believe, replied my lady,—if thou hadst, thou dit not have spoken so well.'

Sir Jacob and Mr B afterwards fell into a family discourse, and Sir Jacob gave us an account of two or three courtships *by* his three sons, and *to* his two daughters, and his reasons for disallowing them and I could observe, he is an absolute tyrant in his family, though they are all men and women grown, and he seemed to please himself how much they stood in awe of him.

One odd piece of conversation I must tell you, Miss, because of the inference that followed it.

Sir Jacob asked Mr B if he did not remember John Wilkins, his steward? 'He was an honest fellow,' said he, 'as ever lived.—But he's dead. Alas for him, poor Jack!—He physick'd himself out of his life.—He would be always taking slops. had I done so, I should have gone to the dogs long ago.—But whom do you think, nephew, I have got in his place?—Nay, you can't know him, neither. Why, 'tis Jerry Sherwood, a boy I took upon charity, and taught to write and read, or paid for't, and that's the same thing—Hay, you know!—And now Jerry's a gentleman's fellow, and is much respected by all our hunters, for he's a keen sportsman, I'll assure you. I brought him up to that myself, and many a jerk has the dog had from me, before I could make any thing of him. Many and many a good time have I thwack'd the rascal's jacket, and he owes all he is, and will be, to me. And I now suffer him to sit down at table with me, when I have no guests.'

'*But is not this a bad example*,' said Mr B 'to promote so low a servant to *the command of the family*, under you? What do *gentlemen* say to this?'

'Gentlemen say to it!—Why, what gentlemen have any thing to do with my family management?—Surely, I may do as I will in my own house, and in my own family, or else it would be very hard.'

'True, Sir Jacob, but people will be meddling where they have least business. But are not all the gentlemen uneasy, for fear their *lowest servants*, from the example set by so leading a man as you, a chairman of the sessions, a colonel of militia, a deputy lieutenant, and a justice of quorum, should want to be made their *stewards*?'

'Why, I can't say that any body has taken it into their heads to question me upon this subject. I should think them plaguy impertinent, if they had, and bid them mind their own business.'

'But you'll allow, Sir Jacob, that every one who knows you have raised your foot-boy to be your steward, will not know your *inducements*, although, I doubt not, they are very good ones.'

Lady Davers shook her head at her brother, saying—'Very well, Sir, very well!'

Sir Jacob cried out—'O ho, nephew! are you thereabouts with your bears? Why, I can't say, but you're in with me now.—Let's see, what have I said?—Ay, by my soul, you have nabb'd me cleverly. Faith and troth, you have convinced me, by an example of my own, that I was impertinent to trouble my head about the management of your family. Though near kindred makes some excuse for me too.—And, besides, a *steward* and a *wife* are two things.'

'So I'd have 'em be, Sir Jacob. But good wives are but stewards to their husbands in many cases, and mine is the best that ever man had.'

'Pretty expensive ones, nephew, for all that, as the world runs. Most gentlemen find, I believe, stewards of this sort run them out more than they save. but that's not your case, I dare say.—I faith, though, you have nick'd me cleverly, that you have.'

'But, my witty brother,' said my lady, 'I believe you'd better, for all your fling at me, as to *inducements*, stick to your first defence, as to the example sake, for, who stands upon birth or degree in the office of a steward?'

'It will answer several purposes, sister, and come nearer the point in what you object, than you are aware of, were we to dispute upon it. But I have gained my end in the observation. Sir Jacob takes the force of the comparison, and is convinced, I dare say, there is some justice in it.'

'Ay, ay, a great deal, said Sir Jacob, for a wife is, or ought to be, her husband's steward. I'm sure, when mine was living, I made her so, and had no other; for she made memorandums, and I digested them into a book, and yet she brought me a noble fortune too, as you all know.'

Here, Miss, I conclude my tedious narrations.—Be so good as to skim them over lightly, that you may not think the worse of me, and *then return* them, (with some of your charming penmanship) that I may send them on to Kent. To be sure I would not have been so tediously trifling, but for the sake of my dear parents: and there is so much self-praise, as it may seem, from a person repeating the fine things said of herself, that I am half of opinion I should send them to Kent only, and to think you should be obliged *to me for saving you so much trouble* and impertinence.

Do, dear Miss, be so free as to forbid me to send you any more long journals, but common letters only, of how you do? and who and who's together, and of respects to one, and to another, and so forth.—Letters that one might dispatch, as Sir Jacob says, in a *twinkling*, and perhaps be more to the purpose than the tedious scrawl, which kisses your hands, from *yours most sincerely*,

P. B.

Do, dear good Sir Simon, let Miss Polly add to our delights, by her charming company. Mr. Murray, and the new affair, will divert *you*, in her absence.—So pray, since my good Lady Darnford has consented, and she is willing, and her sister can spare her, don't be so cross as to deny me.

LETTER XXXIV.

FROM MISS DARNFORD TO MRS. B.

MY DEAR MRS. B.

YOU have given us great pleasure in your accounts of your conversations, and of the verses put so boldly and wickedly under your seat, and in your just observations on the lines, and the occasion.

I am quite shocked, when I think of Lady Davers's passionate intentions, at her first coming down to you to the Hall, but have let nobody into the worst of the matter, in compliance with your desire. We are delighted with your account of your family management, and your Sunday's service—What an excellent lady you are! And how happy and how good, you make every one who knows you, is seen by the ladies joining in your evening service, as well as their domesticks.

We go on here swimmingly with our courtship. Never was there a fonder couple than Mr. Murray and Miss Nancy. The moody girl is quite alive, easy, and pleased, except now-and then with me.—We had a sad falling-out t'other day. Thus it was:

She had the assurance, on my saying, they were so fond and so free beforehand, that they would leave nothing for improvement afterwards, to tell me, she had for some time perceived, that my envy was very disquieting to me. This she said before Mr. *Murray, who had the* good manners to retire, seeing a storm rising between us.

'Poor foolish girl, cried I, when he was gone, provoked to great contempt by her expression before him, 'thou wilt make me despise thee in spite of my heart.—But, pr'ythee, manage thy matters with common decency, at least.'

'Good lack! *Common decency*, did you say? When my sister Polly is able to shew me what it is, I shall hope to be better for her example.'

'No, thou'lt never be better for any body's example! Thy ill-nature and perverseness will keep thee from that, as it has always hitherto done.'

'My ill-temper, you have often told me, is *natural* to me, so it must become *me*; but upon such a sweet-tempered young lady as Miss Polly, her late assumed petulance fits but ill!'

'I must have had no bad temper, and that every one says, to bear with thy sullen and perverse one, as I have done all my life.'

'But why can't you bear with it a little longer, sister?—Does any thing provoke you *now* (with a sly leer, and affected drawl) 'that did not *formerly*?'

'Provoke me!—What should provoke me?—I gave thee but a hint of thy fond

'folly,

'folly, which makes thee behave so be'fore company, that every one smiles at 'thee, and I'd be glad to save thee 'from contempt for thy *new* good hu'mour, as I used to try to do, for thy '*old* bad nature'

'Is that it?—What a kind sister have 'I!—But perhaps I see it vexes you, 'and *ill-natured* folks love to teize, you 'know—But, dear Polly, don't let the '*affection* Mr Murray expresses for me, 'put such a good-tempered body out of 'humour, pray don't!—Who knows, (continued the provoker, who never says a tolerable thing that is not ill-natured, that being her talent) 'but the gentleman 'may think himself happy, that he has 'found a way, with so much ease, to 'dispense with the difficulty that elder'ship laid him under?—But as he did 'you the favour to let the repulse come 'from you, don't be angry, sister, that 'he took you at the *first* word'

'Indeed, indeed,' said I, with a contemptuous smile, 'thou'rt in the right, 'Nancy, to take the gentleman at *his* 'first word. Hold him fast, and play 'over all thy monkey tricks with him, 'with all my heart: who knows but it 'may engage him more? For should *he* 'leave thee, I might be too much pro'voked at thy ingratitude, *to turn over* 'another gentleman to thee—And let 'me tell thee, without such an introduc'tion, thy temper would keep any body 'from thee, that knows it'

'Poor Miss Polly!—Come, be as 'easy as you can! Who knows but we 'may find out some cousin or friend of 'Mr Murray's between us, that we 'may persuade to address you? Don't 'make us your enemies: we'll try to 'make you easy, if we can—'Tis a little 'hard, that you should be so cruelly 'taken at your word, that it is'

'Dost think,' said I, 'poor stupid, ill'judging Nancy, that I can have the 'same regret for parting with a man I 'could not like, that thou had'st, when 'thy vain hopes met with the repulse 'they deserved from Mr B?'

'Mr B come up again! I have not 'heard of Mr B a great while'

'No, but it was necessary that one 'nail should drive out another, for 'thou didst been repining still, had not 'Mr Murray been *turned over* to thee'

'*Turned over*! You used that word 'once before, sister: such great wits as 'you, methinks, should not use the same 'word twice'

'How dost *thou* know what wits '*should*, or should *not* do? Thou hast 'no talent but ill-nature, and 'tis enough 'for thee, that *one* view takes up thy 'whole thought. Pursue that—But I 'would only caution thee, not to *satiate* 'where thou wouldst *oblige*, that's all: 'or, if thy man can be so gross, as to 'like thy fondness, to leave something 'for *hereafter*'

'I'll call him in again, sister, and you 'shall acquaint us how you'd have it.—'Bell,' (for the maid came in just then) 'tell Mr Murray I desire him to walk 'in'

'I'm glad to see thee so teachable all 'at once!—I find now what was the 'cause of thy constant perverseness: for 'had the unavailing lessons my mamma 'was always inculcating into thee, come 'from a *man* thou couldst have had 'hopes of, they had succeeded better'

In came Sir Simon, with his crutch-stick—But can you bear this nonsense, Mrs B? 'What, sparring, jangling 'again, you sluts!—O what fiery eyes 'on one side! and contemptuous looks 'on t'other!'

'Why, papa, my sister Polly has '*turned over* Mr Murray to me, and 'she wants him back again, and he 'won't come—That's all the matter!'

'You know your daughter Nancy, 'papa—she never could *bear* reproof, 'and yet would always *deserve* it!—I 'was only gently remarking for her in'struction, on her fondness before com'pany, and she is as she *used to be*!—'Courtship, indeed, is a new thing to the 'poor girl, and so she knows not how to 'behave herself in it'

'So, Polly, because you have been 'able to run over a long list of humble 'servants, you must insult your sister, 'must you?—But are you really con'cerned, Polly?—Hey!'

'Sir, this or any thing, is very well 'from you—But these imputations of 'envy, before Mr Murray, must make 'the man very considerable with him'self. Poor Nancy don't consider that '—But, indeed, how should she? How 'should *she* be able to reflect, who 'knows not what reflection is, ex'cept of the spiteful sort? But, papa, 'should the poor thing add to *his* vanity, 'which wants no addition, at the ex-

'pence of that pride, which can only 'preserve her from contempt [illegible]

I saw her affected, and was resolved to pursue my advantage

'Prythee, Nancy, continued I, 'can't thou not have a *little* patience child— 'My papa will set the day as soon as he shall think it proper And don't let thy man to[illegible] to keep pace with thy fondness, for I have pitied him many a time, when I have seen him first hold on the tenters to keep thee in countenance'

This set the ill-natured girl into tears and fretfulness, till her old temper came upon her, as I designed it should, for she had kept me at a[illegible] longer than usual, and I left her under the dominion of it, and because I would not come into a fresh dispute, got my mamma's leave, and the chariot, and went and begged a dinner at Lady Jones's, and then came home as cool and as easy as I used to be, and found Nancy as sullen and [illegible], as was her custom, before Mr Murray tendered himself to her ready acceptance But I went to my spinnet, and suffered her to swell on

We have had nothing but No, and Yes, ever [illegible] and I wish I was with you for a month, and all this nonsense [illegible] me I am, my dear, obliging[illegible] Mrs B *your faith[illegible]* [illegible]

POLLY D[illegible]RNFORD

[illegible] the or der of time, [illegible] mentioned [illegible]

LETTER XXXV

FROM [illegible] D[illegible]RNFORD TO [illegible]RS B

[illegible]Y DEAR [illegible]

PRAY give my [illegible] to your Mr B [illegible] very unpolite [illegible] reflections* upon me, in relation to Mr Murray, [illegible] supposes I re[illegible] You are much [illegible] too, I will say, to your P[illegible] Darnford These gentle[illegible] men, [illegible] of them, are such [illegible] They think so highly of their [illegible], and confident sex as if a lady [illegible] from *her* heart despise them but if she turns them off, as they deserve, and happens to continue her dislike, what should be interpreted in her favour, as a just and *regular* piece of conduct, is turned against her, and it must proceed from spite

Mr B may think he knows a good deal of the sex But, perhaps, were I as malicious as he is reflecting, (and yet, if I have any malice, he has raised it) I could say, that his acquaintance was not with the most unexceptionable, till he had the happiness to know you and he has not long enough been happy in you, I find, to do justice to those who are proud to emulate your virtues

But I can't bear, *it seems*, to see my sister addressed and complimented, and preferred by one whom I had thought in my own power! But he may be mistaken with all his sagacity, he *has been* often Nor is it so mortifying a thing to me as he imagines, to sit and see two such anticks playing their pugs tricks, as he calls them, with one-another

But you hardly ever saw *such* pugs tricks played as they play, at so early a time of courtship The girl hangs upon his arm, and receives his empty head on her shoulder, already, with a freedom that would be censurable in a bride, before folks A stiff, sullen, proud, scornful girl, as she used to be, she now puts on airs that are not natural either to her features or her character, and judge then how it must disgust one, especially when one sees her man so proud and vain upon it, that, like a *true* man, he treats her with the less ceremony for her condescensions, putting on airs of consequence, while her easiness of behaviour makes him secure of acceptance, and a kind reception, let him be as *negligent* or as *forward* as he pleases

I say, Mrs B there can be no living with these men upon such beginnings.— They ought to know their distance, or be taught it, and not to think it in their power to confer that as a favour, which they should esteem it an honour to receive

But neither can I bear, it seems, the preparatives to matrimony, the fine clothes, the compliments, the *busy novelty*, as he calls it, the new equipages, and so forth That's his mistake again, tell him for one who can look forward[illegible]

* See this Vol p 396.

than

than the nine days of wonder, can easily despise so flashy and so transient a glare And were I fond of compliments, it would not, perhaps, be the way to be pleased, in that respect, if I were to marry

Compliments in the single state are a lady s due, whether courted or not, and she receives them, or ought always to receive them, as such but in courtship they are poured out upon one, like a hasty shower, that one knows will soon be over —A mighty comfortable consideration this, to a lady who *loves to be complimented* !—Instead of the refreshing April like showers, which beautify the sun shine, she shall stand a deluge of complaisance, be wet to the skin with it, and then—What then !—Why be in a Lybian desart ever after,—Experience a constant parching drought, and all her attributed excellencies will be swallowed up in the quicksands of matrimony

It may be otherwise with you, and it *must* be otherwise, because there is such an infinite variety in your excellence — But does Mr B think it must be so in *every* matrimony ?

Tis true, he improves every hour, as I see in your kind papers, in his fine speeches to you But it could not be Mr B if he did not your merit *extorts* it from him and what an ingrateful, as well as absurd churl, would he be, who should seek to obscure a meridian lustre, that dazzles the eyes of every one else ?

But let me observe, moreover, that you had so few of these fine speeches *before hand*, that you have all the reason in the world to expect them *now* and this lessens his merit a good deal, as the most he can say, is but common justice, on *full proof*, for, can the like generosity be attributed to him, as might to a gentleman who praises *on trust*?

You promise, if I will come to you, you will join with me against Mr B on this subject 'Tis very kindly offered but when Mr B is in the question, I expect very little assistance from you, be the argument what it will

But 'tis not *my* fault, I don t come, I am quite tired with the perverse folly of this Nancy of ours She every day behaves *more* like a fool to Mr Murray, and *less* like a sister to me, and takes delight to teize and vex me, by all the little ways in her power And then surliness and ill temper are so natural to her, that I, who can but throw out a spiteful word, by way of flourish, as I may say, and tis over, and I am sorry for it as soon as spoken, am no match for her —for she *perseveres* so intolerably, and comes back to the attack, though never so often repulsed, rising like Antæus, with fresh vigour for every fall, or like the Lernæan hydra, which had a new head sprouting up, as fast as any one of the seven was lopt off, that there is no bearing her. Wedlock, in fine, must be her Hercules, and will furnish me, I doubt, with a revenge I wish not for

But let me thank you for your delightful narratives, and beg you to continue them I told you how your Saturday's conversation with Lady Davers, and your Sunday employments, charm us all so regular, and so easy to be performed— That s the delightful thing —What every body may do !—And yet so beautiful, so laudable, so uncommon in the practice, especially among people in genteel life !

Your conversation and decision in relation to the two parsons (more than charm) transport us Mr B let me tell you, judges right, and acts a charming part, to throw such a fine game into your hands And so excellently do you play it, that you do as much credit to your partner s judgment as to your own — Never, surely, was so happy a couple

He has a prodigious merit *with* me I can tell him, though he thinks not so well *of* me as I would have him To *see*, to *praise*, and to *reward* a virtue, is *next* to having it *one s self* and, in time, he will make as good a *man* (these fine appearances encourage one to hope so) as he is a *husband*

Your notions of dispensations, and double livings, are admirably just Mr Williams is more my favourite than ever !—And the amply rewarded Mr Adams, how did that scene affect us !

Again, and again, I say, (for what can I say else, or more—since I can't find words to speak all I think ?) you are a charming lady! Yet, methinks, poor Mr H makes but a sorry figure among you

We are delighted with Lady Davers, but still more, if possible, with the countess she is a fine lady, as you have drawn her but your characters, though truth and nature, are the most shocking, or the most amiable, that I ever read

We are full of impatience to hear of the

the arrival of Sir Jacob Swynford We know his character pretty well but when he has sat for it to your pencil, it must be an original indeed

I will have another trial with my papa, to move him to let me attend you I am rallying my forces for that purpose I have got my mamma on my side again, who is concerned to see her girl vexed and insulted by her younger sister, and who yet minds no more what *she* says to her, than what I say, and Sir Simon loves at his heart to make mischief between us, instead of interposing to silence either and truly, I am afraid, the delight of this kind, which he takes, will make him deny his Polly what she so ardently wishes for

I had a good mind to be sick, to be with you I could fast two or three days, to give it the better appearance but then my mamma, who loves not deceit, would blame me, if she knew my stratagem, and be grieved, if she thought I was really ill.—I know, fasting, when one has a stomach to eat, gives one a very gloomy and mortified air.

What would I not do, in short, to procure to myself the inexpressible pleasure that I should have in your company and conversation - But continue to write to me till then, however, and that will be *next best*. I am *your most obliged and obedient*

POLLY DARNFORD

LETTER XXXVI

FROM THE SAME

MY DEAREST MRS B

I Am all over joy and rapture My good papa has given me leave to tell you, that he will put his Polly under your protection, when you go to London If you have but a *tenth part* of the pleasure I have on this occasion, I am sure, I shall be as welcome as I wish But he will insist upon it, he says, that Mr B signs some acknowledgment, when I am to carry along with *me*, that I am intrusted to his honour and yours, and to be returned to him *heart whole* and *dutiful*, and with a reputation as unsullied as he receives me

But do, dearest Mrs B continue your journals till then, for I have promised to take them up where you leave off, to divert our friends in these parts There will be presumption! But yet I will write nothing but what I will shew you, and have your consent to send! For I was taught early not to tell tales out of school, and a school, the best I ever went to, will be your charming conversation

We have been greatly diverted with the trick put upon that *barbarian* Sir Jacob His obstinacy, repentance, and amendment, followed so irresistibly in one half hour, from the happy thought of the excellent lady countess, that I think no plot was ever more fortunate It was like springing a lucky mine in a siege, that blew up twenty times more than was expected from it, and answered all the besiegers ends at once

Mr B s defence of his own conduct towards you is quite noble, and he judges with his usual generosity and good sense, when, by adding to your honour, he knows he inhances his own Mr Pitt's fine diamond met with a world of admirers, but all turned upon this reflection—'What a happy man is Mr Pitt, 'who can call such a jewel his own!' How greatly do you excel this diamond, and how much does Mr B outdo Mr Pitt!—Who has contributed to give so rich a jewel a polish so admirable, and then has set it in so noble a light, as makes it's beauty conspicuous to every eye!

You bid me skim over your writings lightly, but tis impossible I will not flatter you, my dear Mrs B nor will I be suspected to do so, and yet I cannot find words to praise, so much as I think you deserve so I will only say, that your good parents, for whose pleasure you write, as well as for mine, cannot receive or read them with more delight than I do —Even my sister Nancy (judge of their effect by this!) will at any time leave Murray, and forget to frown or be ill-natured, while she can hear read what you write.—And, angry as she makes me sometimes, I cannot deny her this pleasure, because possibly, among the innumerable improving reflections they abound with, some one may possibly dart in upon her, and illuminate her, as your conversation and behaviour did Sir Jacob

But your application in P S. to my papa, pleased him, and confirmed his resolution to let me go—He snatched the sheet that contained this—'That's to me,' said he 'I must read this myself' He did, and said—'I faith she's a sweet one'

"Do,

" *Do, dear good Sir Simon,*' repeated he aloud, " *let Miss Polly add to our de-" lights!*"—So she shall then,—if that ' will do it!—And yet this same Mrs ' B has so many delights already, that ' I should think she might be contented ' But, Dame Darnford, I think I'll let ' her go These sisters then, you'll see, ' how they'll love at a distance, though ' always quarrelling when together He read on—" *The new affair will divert " you—Lady Darnford has consented— " Miss is willing, and her sister can " spare her*— Very prettily put, faith —" *And don't you be so cross*—" Very ' sweet!—" *to deny me!*

' Why, dear Mrs B I won't be so ' cross, then, indeed I won't!—And so, ' Polly, let 'em send word when they set ' out for London, and you shall join ' 'em there with all my heart but I'll ' have a letter every post, remember that, ' girl'

' Any thing, any thing, dear papa,' said I, ' so I can but go!' He called for a kiss, for his compliance I gave it most willingly, you may believe

Nancy looked envious, although Mr Murray came in just then—She looked almost like a great glutton, whom I remember, one Sir Jonathan Smith, who killed himself with eating: he used, while he was heaping up his plate from one dish, to watch the others, and follow the knife of every body else, with such a greedy eye, as if he could swear a robbery against any one who presumed to eat as well as he This is a gross simile but all greedy and envious folks look alike about the eyes, and, thinking of Nancy on this occasion, (who envied a happiness she knew I preferred to that she has in prospect) I could not but call to mind Sir Jonathan at the same time

Well, let's know when you set out, and you shan't have been a week in London, if I can help it, but you shall be told by my tongue, as now by my pen, how much I am *your obliged admirer and friend,*

POLLY DARNFORD

LETTER XXXVII.

MY DEAR FRIEND,

I Now proceed with my journal, which I had brought down to Thursday night,

FRIDAY

The two ladies resolving, as they said, to inspect all my proceedings, insisted upon it, that I would take them with me in my *benevolent round*, (as they, after we returned, would call it) which I generally take once a week among my poor and sick neighbours, and finding I could not get off, I set out with them, my lady countess proposing Miss Worden to fill up the fourth place in the coach

We talked all the way of charity, and the excellency of that duty, and my Lady Davers took notice of the text, that it would hide a *multitude of faults*. ' And if, she was pleased to say, ' there ' was to be any truth in the popish doc- ' trine of supererogation, what abundance ' of *such* merits would arise from the life ' and actions of our dear friend here!' kindly looking at me

I said, that when we had the pleasure to reflect that we served a Master, who exacted no hard terms from us, but in every case almost that could be thought of, only required of us to do justice, and shew mercy, to one another, and gave us reason to think He would judge us by those rules, it must be a mighty inducement to acts of charity and benevolence. ' But indeed,' added I, ' were there not ' that inducement, the pleasure that at- ' tends such acts is a high reward, and ' I am sure the ladies I have the honour ' to speak to, must have found it in an ' hundred instances

The countess said, she had once a much better opinion of herself, than she found she had reason for, within these *few* days past ' And indeed, Mrs B' said she, ' when I get home, I shall make ' a good many people the better for your ' example And so said Lady Davers, which gave me no small inward pleasure, and I acknowledged, in suitable terms, the honour they both did me

The coach set us down by the side of a large common, about five miles distant from our house, and we alighted, and walked a little way, choosing not to have the coach come nearer, that we might be taken as little notice of as possible, and they entered with me into two mean cots with great condescension and goodness; one belonging to a poor widow and five children, who had been all down in agues and fevers, the other to a man and his

wife

wife bed-rid with age and infirmities, and two honeſt daughters, one a widow with two children, the other married to an huſbandman, who had alſo been ill, but now, by comfortable cordials, and good phyſick, were pretty well, to what they had been.

The two ladies were well pleaſed with my demeanour to the good folks; to whom I ſaid, that as I ſhould go ſoon to London, I was willing to ſee them before I went, to wiſh them better and better, and to tell them, that I ſhould leave orders with Mrs Jervis concerning them, to whom they muſt make known their wants; and that Mr Barrow would take care of them, I was ſure, and do all that was in the power of phyſick for the reſtoration of their healths.

Now you muſt know, Miſs, that I am not ſo good as the old ladies of former days, who uſed to diſtil cordial waters, and prepare medicines, and diſpenſe them themſelves. I knew, if I were ſo inclined, my dear Mr B. would not have been pleaſed with it; becauſe, in the approbation he has kindly given to my preſent method, he has twice or thrice praiſed me, that I don't carry my charity to extremes, and make his houſe a diſpenſatory. I would not, therefore, by aiming at doing too much, loſe the opportunity of doing any good at all in theſe reſpects; and beſides, as the vulgar ſayings is, One muſt creep before one goes. But this is my method:

I am upon an agreement with this Mr Barrow, who is deemed a very ſkilful and honeſt apothecary, and one Mr Simmonds, a ſurgeon of like character, to attend all ſuch caſes and perſons as I ſhall recommend; Mr Barrow to adminiſter phyſick and cordials as he ſhall judge proper; and even, in neceſſary caſes, to call in a phyſician. And now and then, by looking in upon them one's ſelf, or ſending a ſervant to aſk queſtions, all is kept right.

Beſides, one can take this method without the oſtentation, as ſome would deem it, which would attend the having one's dear friend's gate always crouded with unhappy objects, and with ſome who deſerve no countenance, perhaps, and yet would poſſibly be the moſt clamorous; and then one does not ſubject the poor neither to the inſolence of ſervants, who ſometimes in one's abſence, might, were they ſome ſervants, ſhew, that they were far from being influenced by the ſame motives as their principals. Beſides, the advantage the poor have from the ſkill and experience which conſtant practice gives to the gentlemen I employ, and with whom I agree but by the quarter, becauſe, if there were a juſt foundation of complaint, for negligence, or hardneſs of heart, I would not be tied down from changing; for, in ſuch caſes, in a criſis, the poor people depending on the aſſiſtance of thoſe gentlemen, might look no farther, and ſo my good intentions might not only be fruſtrated, but do harm.

My Lady Davers obſerved a Bible, a Common Prayer Book, and a Whole Duty of Man, in each cot, in leathern outſide caſes, to keep them clean, and a Church Catechiſm or two for the children; and was pleaſed to ſay, it was right; and her ladyſhip aſked one of the children, a pretty girl, who learnt her her catechiſm? And ſhe curtſy'd, and looked at me; for I *do* aſk the children queſtions, when I come, to know how they improve. 'Tis as I thought,' ſaid my lady, 'my ſiſter provides for both parts.—God bleſs you, my dear!' ſaid ſhe, and tapped my neck.

My ladies left tokens of their bounty behind them to both families, and all the good folks bleſſed and prayed for us at parting; and as we went out, my Lady Davers, with a ſerious air, was pleaſed to ſay to me—'Take care of your health, my dear ſiſter, and God give you, when it comes, a happy hour; for how many real mourners would you have, if you were to be called early to reap the fruits of your piety!'

'God's will muſt be done, my lady,' ſaid I. 'The ſame Providence that has ſo wonderfully put it in my power to do a little good, will raiſe up new friends to the honeſt hearts that rely upon Him.'

This I ſaid, becauſe ſome of the good people heard my lady, and ſeemed troubled, and began to redouble their prayers for my ſafety and preſervation.

We walked thence to our coach, and ſtretched a little farther, to viſit two farmers families, about a mile diſtant from each other. One had the mother of the family, with two ſons, juſt recovering, the former from a fever, the latter from tertian agues; and I aſked, when they ſaw Mr Barrow? They told me, with great commendations of him, that he had but juſt left them. So having congratulated their hopeful way, and wiſhed them to

take

take care of themſelves, and not go too early to buſineſs, I ſaid I ſhould deſire Mr Barrow to watch over them, for fear of a relapſe, and ſhould hardly ſee em again for ſome time, and ſo under the notion of my ſoy, I ſlid a couple of guineas into the good woman's hand for I had had an hint given me by Mrs Jervis, that their illneſs had made it low with them

We proceeded then to the other farm, where the caſe was a married daughter, who had had a very dangerous lying-in, and a wicked huſband, who had abuſed her, and run away from her but ſhe was mending apace, by good comfortable things, which from time to time I had cauſed to be ſent her Her old father had been a little unkind to her, before I took notice of her, for ſhe married againſt his conſent, and indeed the world went hard with the poor man, and he could not do much, and, beſides, he had a younger daughter, who had loſt all her limbs, and was forced to be tied in a wicker chair, to keep her up in it, which (having expended much to relieve her) was a great *pull back*, as the good old woman called it And having been a year in arrear to a harſh landlord, who finding a good ſtock upon the ground, threatened to diſtreſs the poor family and turn them out of all I advanced the money upon the ſtock, and the poor man has already paid me half of it, (for, Miſs, I muſt keep within compaſs too) which was fifty pounds at firſt, and is in a fair way to pay me the other half, and make as much more for himſelf

Here I found Mr Barrow, and he gave me an account of the ſucceſs of two other caſes I had recommended to him, and told me, that John Smith, a poor man, who, in thatching a barn, had tumbled down, and broken his leg, and bruiſed himſelf all over, was in a fair way of recovery

This poor creature had like to have periſhed by the cruelty of the pariſh officers, who would have paſſed him away to Eſſex, where his ſettlement was, though in a burning fever, occaſioned by his misfortune but hearing of the caſe, I directed Mr Simmonds to attend him, and provide for him, at my expence, and gave my word, if he died, to bury him

I was glad to hear he was in ſo good a way, and told Mr Barrow, I hoped to ſee him and Mr Simmonds together at Mr B s, before I ſet out for London, that we might adviſe about the caſes under their direction, and that I might acquit myſelf of ſome of my obligations to them

'You are a good man, Mr Barrow,' added I 'God will bleſs you for your 'care and kindneſs to theſe poor deſti- 'tute creatures They all praiſe you, 'and do nothing but talk of your hu- 'manity to them'

'O my good lady,' ſaid he, 'who 'can forbear following ſuch an exam- 'ple as you ſet? Mr Simmonds can 'teſtify, as well as I, (for now and 'then a caſe requires us to viſit together) 'that we can hardly hear any complaints 'from our poor patients, let em be ever 'ſo ill, for the praiſes and bleſſings they 'beſtow upon you

'It is good Mr B that enables and 'encourages me to do what I do Tell 'them, they muſt bleſs God, and bleſs 'him, and pray for me, and thank you 'and Mr Simmonds we all join to- 'gether, you know, for their good

The counteſs and Lady Davers aſked the poor lying-in woman many queſtions, and left with her, and for her poor ſiſter, a miſerable object indeed!—(God be praiſed, that I am not ſuch an one!) marks of their bounty in gold, but I ſaw not how much, and looking upon one another, and then upon me, and lifting up their hands, could not ſay a word till they were in the coach and ſo we were carried home, after we had juſt looked in upon a country ſchool, where I pay for the learning of eight children

And here (—I hope I recite not this with pride, though I do with pleaſure) is a curſory account of my *benevolent weekly round*, as my ladies will call it

I know you will not be diſpleaſed with it, but it will highly delight my worthy parents, who, in their way, do a great deal of diſcreet good in their neighbourhood for, indeed, Miſs, a little matter, *prudently* beſtowed, and on true objects of compaſſion, (whoſe caſes are ſoon at a criſis, as are thoſe of moſt labouring people) will go a great way, and eſpecially if laid out properly for em, according to the exigencies of their reſpective caſes —For ſuch poor people, who live generally low, want very ſeldom any thing but reviving cordials at firſt, and good wholeſome kitchen phyſick afterwards, and then the wheels of nature being unclogged, new oiled, as it were, and ſet right, they will go round again with pleasantness and ease, for a good while together, by virtue of that exercise which their labour gives them, while the rich and voluptuous are forced to undergo great fatigues to keep theirs clean and in order

This is well remarked in a manuscript poem in Mr B s possession, written in answer to a friend, who recommended a poor man of genius to the favour of the author, in order to induce the benevolent gentleman to lift him into a higher life than that to which he was born and as I am sure you will be pleased with the lines, I will transcribe them for your entertainment

' WARMLY, once more, this r ; k s
' ca fe you press,
' Whom genius dignifies, amidst distress
' All, that you wish, my f iendship renders dear,
' And weeping Industry demands a tear
' Ease we his pangs,—but let the *means* be
' weigh'd,
' Let anguish meet him, in the form of aid
' —Where-e'er kind Help can Want s bleak
' waste repair
' Whate'er touch d pity owes to chill despair,
' *The.* shall be his —For he who claims *your*
' grief,
' To *me* brings title, that commands relief.

' Premising this, permit me to maintain,
' That, wishing happiness, you purpose pain
' What, tho he sweats along the scorching soil,
' Till ev'ry aching sinew burns, with toil?
' Health, and contempt of spleen—and
' sleep s soft call—
' And unobstructed spirits—balance all.

' Nor let fatigue, like his, presume com-
' plaint,
' Where exercise, of choice, out works con-
' straint
' What length ning furrow, turn d with tor-
' t ring fall,
' Heats like the *racket*, when it bunts the *ball*?
' What lab'rer toils like him, o er hill or dale,
' Whose triumph is the *f x*'s ear or tail?
' All un-mur d to *bear*—in lite sweat *d wn*,
' Boy-sportsmen tire and shame those sons
' of brawn.

" But shall a fire, like his, want room to
" flame?
" And what is *peace*, to one who pants for
" *fame*?"

' Bless'd in his low-born quiet, would he
' dare
' Adopt distinction, to induce despair?
' Would he, for envy give up safe neglect?
' And hazard calumny, to gain respect?
' Blow up ambition s storm, to blast his race?
' And scorn obscurity, to court disgrace?

' True, he is poor,—and so are *kings* no less:
' *They* want, whate'er they wish, and not pos-
' sess
' While *swains*, who scorn to feel by others
' sense,
' Are rich in their own right, of competence
' Bread and self-satisfy'd, is wealth, *within*,
' Nor call that *gain*—which wisdom shuns to
' win.

' From what proud root cou'd this vain
' error grow,
' That poverty is *want*, and rest is *woe*!
' Weigh—but let reason hold th impartial
' scale,
' When peace is purpos'd, what does rank
' avail?
' Is it, to live in noise, that makes us *bless'd*?
' Is it to hear our flatter'd faults caress'd?
' Is it, in idle ease, to yawn untaught,
' And, fatt'ning *folly*, pine the famish d
' *thought*?
' True happiness, disdaining all *extreme*,
' Is measur'd continence—and reas'ning
' phlegm
' This if your rustick knows, confess him
' *great*,
' Beyond the proudest slave, that guides a
' *state*
' This if he knows not, should he empire
' gain,
' 'Twere sharpen'd appetite, for strengthen d
' pain

" But wit like his, you say, by nature grac d
" To charm in cities, is in shades *misplac'd*"

' Shines he so bright, within his rural
' sphere?
' There let him still shine out—and still shine
' *clear*!
' Superior genius, *there*, may gain him weight,
' To polish rudeness, civilize debate,
' Warm the too *easy* heart, excite the *cold*,
' Impel the backward, and repulse the bold,
' Compose small *jars*, ere bitterness increase,
' And smile the factious cottage into peace
' Wipe out each spot that fades the flow'ry
' plain,
' And reign, pacifick father of the swains

' Remote from cities, peaceful nature
' dwells,
' There, exil d Justice sits, in silent cells
' There, Truth, in naked plainness, dares be
' seen
' There, Pride provokes no envy,—Shame
' no spleen
' There, unsupported Worth can rev'rence
' draw,
' And Probity disdains the help of Law

' There,

'There, maids no caution need—for man is
'just
'There, love is tenderness, and friendship
'trust
'There, unfelt flushes tinge the conscious
'*heart*,
'And modest semblance is not, yet, an *art*

'How weak a judge, dear friend, is hu-
'man pride!
'To loath known good, and long for ills un-
'try'd!
'Stretching our greedy eye to distant height,
'The bliss, beneath us, lies too low for
'sight,
'Impatient thirst of pow'r but little thinks,
'What troubled waters fev'rish greatness
'drinks
'Nor dreams distrustless *Vanity*, what cares,
'What weights, what torments, rash dis
'tinction bears
'Hence, fears no aukward actor to sustain
'*His part of danger in those scenes of pain*
'Yet, out of character, mistakes his *cue*,
'And hiss'd, unheard bawls on—and blun-
'ders through

'Or, grant him safe, behind some guardian
'skreen,
'Some patron's transient int'rest, push'd be-
'tween,
'Grant, that his suppliant soul can sense de-
'stroy,
'Can bear dependence, with unfeeling joy
'Yet comes a time, when all his props decay,
'And each dishonour o ruin drops away
'Then the bl ak tott'rer shakes, in ev'ry blast,
'Dreads the d m future, wishes for the past
'Finds his first loss and, with corrected view,
'Envies the humble *cot*, from which he flew

'And yet, perhaps, 'twas Heav'n's com-
'mission'd plan,
'That passion's restless whirl shou'd actuate
'man,
'That pride, by envy plagu'd, should *pity*
'know;
'And wealth, and joy, take birth, from want,
'and woe,
'Were hush'd content to stop the busy swing,
'The stagnant virtues all might lose their
'spring
'One tideless lake of life engulph mankind
'And the still mass corrupt—for want of
'*wind*.

'Th Almighty, then,—who sees beyond
'our sense,
'Did various parts, for various minds, dispense.
'The meanest slave, who lives, to hedge and
'ditch,
'Is useful, in his rank, to feed the rich.
'The rich, in retribution, wastes his store,
'And streams refreshful floods, to float the
'poor;
'Nor let the *peer* the *peasan*'s lot disdain,
'Each link, howe'er remote, connects the
'*chain*
'Both but two diff'rent marks, in one great
'view,
'Extend God's landscape, and adorn it, too;
'And both, without distinction,—*king* and
'*slave*,
'At last lie levell'd, in the silent grave

'This known, *your* choice directs my ready
'will
'Say,—Shall your rustick be a rustick still?
'With ease augmented, hold his safe degree?
'Live, and grow old, in pangless poverty?
'Or, shall he tread the world's great *wild* of
'*hope*?
'Despise his danger—and enlarge his scope?—

'Choose for his wish whate'er his virtues
'claim
'And tax *my* fortune—or restrain *his* aim'

I don't remember ever to have read any thing of this subject placed in these natural, easy, and, I therefore think, uncommon lights, and belive you'll allow them to be right lights for there are certainly no cases in the world, that require more judgment and distinction, than charitable ones And except a casual distress among those who make a trade of begging, such persons (especially if I see them often and so much in the same place as if they were as tenacious of their stand, as others of their freehold,) move not my compassion or notice They cannot be lower in spirit, nor (being frequently brought up to it) do they often wish to be higher in calling, or to change their idle state for a laborious one but the poor industrious souls, who are reduced by sickness, or misfortune, or even mistake, not wilful or persisted in, who sigh in secret, and cannot make known what they suffer, such unhappy objects are worthy of one's *pains* to find out, and relieve.

SATURDAY MORNING

IT is hardly right to trouble either of you, my honoured correspondents, with an affair, that has vexed me a good deal, and, indeed, *should* affect me more than any other mistress of a family, for reasons which will be obvious to you, when I tell you the case And this (it is so at present with me) I cannot forbear doing.

A pretty genteel young body, my Polly Barlow,

Barlow, as I call her, having been well recommended, and indeed behaved with great prudence till this time, is the occasion.

My dear Mr B and the two ladies, agreed with me to take an airing in the chariot, and to call in upon Mr Martin, who had a present made him for his menagerie, in which he takes great delight, of a rare and uncommon creature, a native of the East Indies. But that as Sir Jacob was on horseback to accompany them, and the ladies were ready to go, I was taken with a sudden disorder and faintness, so that Lady Davers, who is very kind to me, and watches every change of my countenance, would not permit me to go with them, though my disorder was going off, and my dear Mr B was pleased to excuse me, and meeting with Mr Williams as they went to the coach, they took him with them, to fill up the vacant place. So I retired to my closet, and shut myself in.

They had asked Mr H to go with them, for company to Sir Jacob; but he (on purpose, as I believe, by what followed) could not be found, when they set out. So they supposed he was upon some ramble with Mr Colbrand, his great favourite.

I was writing to *you*, being pretty well recovered, when I heard Polly, as I supposed, and as it proved, come into my apartment; and down she sat, and sung a little catch and cried—'Hem!' twice, and presently I heard two voices. But suspecting nothing, I wrote on, till I heard a kind of rustling and struggling, and Polly's voice crying—'Fie—How 'can you do so!—Pray, Sir—'

This alarmed me much, because we have such orderly folks about us; and I looked through the key-hole, and to my surprise and concern, saw Mr H— fooling with the girl—and taking liberties with Polly, that neither became him to offer, nor, more foolish girl! her to suffer. And having reason to think, that this was not their first interview and freedom—and the girl sometimes encouragingly laughing as, at other times, inconsistently, struggling and complaining in an accent that was too tender for the occasion, I forced a faint cough. This frighted them both. Mr H swore, and said—'Who can that be?—Your lady's gone 'with them, isn't she?'

'I believe so! I hope so!' said the silly girl—'yet that was like her voice!' '—Ma'am, are you in your closet, Ma'am?' said she, coming up to the door. Mr H standing like a poor thief, half behind the window curtains, till he knew whether it was I.

I opened the door; away sneaked Mr H and she leaped with surprise, not hoping to find me there, though she asked the question.

'I thought—Indeed—Ma'am——I 'thought you were gone out.'

'It is plain you did, Polly.—Go and 'shut the chamber door, and come to 'me again.'

She did, but trembled, and was so full of confusion, that I pitied the poor creature, and hardly knew how to speak to her, or what to say.—For my compassion got the upper-hand of my resentment; and as she stood quaking and trembling, and looking on the ground, with a countenance I cannot describe, I now-and-then cast my eye upon her, and was as often forced to put my handkerchief to it.

At last I said—'How long have these 'freedoms past, Polly, between you and 'Mr H?'

She said never a word.

'I am loth to be censorious, Polly, 'but 'tis too plain, that Mr H would 'not have followed you into my cham-'ber if he had not met you at other 'places before.'

Still the poor girl said never a word.

'Little did I expect, Polly, that you 'would have shewn so much imprudence. 'You have had instances of the vile arts 'of men against poor maidens. Have 'you any notion, that Mr H intends 'to do honourably by you?'

'Ma'am—Ma'm—I believe—I hope '—I dare say, Mr H would not do 'otherwise.'

'So much the worse, that you believe 'so, if you have not very good reason 'for your belief.—Does he pretend he 'will marry you, Polly?'

She was silent.

'Tell me, Polly, if he does?'

'He says he will do honourably by 'me.'

'But you know there is but one word 'necessary to explain that other precious 'word *honour*, in this case. It is *ma-'trimony*. That word is as soon spok-'en as any other, and if he *means* it, 'he will not be shy to *speak* it.'

She was silent.

'Tell me, Polly, (for I am really 'greatly

'greatly concerned for you) what you 'think *yourself*: do you *hope* he will 'marry you?'

She was silent.

'Do, good Polly, I hope I may call 'you *good* yet!—Answer me.'

'Pray, Madam!' and she wept, and turned from me, to the wainscot—'Pray, 'Madam, excuse me.'

'But, indeed, Polly, I cannot *excuse* 'you. You are under my protection. 'I was once in as dangerous a situation 'as you *can* be in. And I did not es'cape it, child, by the language and con'duct I heard from you.'

'Language and conduct, Me'm!'

'Yes, Polly, language and conduct. 'For you have heard my story, no doubt, 'all the world has. And do you think, 'if I had sat me down in my lady's bed-'chamber, and sung a song, and hem'd 'twice, and Mr. B. had come to me, 'upon that signal, (for such I doubt it 'was) and I had kept my place, and 'suffered myself to be rumpled, and on'ly in a soft voice, and with an encou'raging laugh, cried—"How can you "do so?" that I should have been what 'I am?'

'Me'm, I dare say, my lord (so all the 'servants call him, and his aunt often, 'when she puts Jackey to it) means no 'hurt.'

'No hurt, Polly! What, and make 'you cry, "*Fie!*"—or do you intend to 'trust your honour to his mercy, rather 'than to your own discretion?'

'I hope not, Me'm!'

'I hope not too, Polly!—But you 'know he was free enough with you, to 'make you say, "*Fie!*' And what might 'have been the case, who knows? had 'I not coughed on purpose, unwilling, 'for your sake, Polly, to find matters so 'bad as I feared, and that you would 'have been led beyond what was reput'able.'

'Reputable, Me'm!'

'Yes, Polly, reputable. I am sorry 'you oblige me to speak so plain. But 'your good requires it. Instead of fly'ing from him, you not only laughed 'all the time you cried out, "*Fie!*' and "*How can you do so?*' but had no other 'care than to see if any body heard you, 'and you observe how he slid away, like 'a guilty creature, as soon as I opened 'my door—Do these things look well, 'Polly? Do you think they do?—And 'if you hope to emulate my good for'tune, do you think *this* is the way?'

'I wish, Me'm, I had never seen Mr. 'H. For nobody will look upon me, 'if I lose your favour!'

'It will still, Polly, (and I took her hand, with a kind look) 'be in your own 'power to keep it, and I will not men'tion this matter, if you make me your 'friend, and tell me all that has passed.'

Again she wept, and was silent.

This made me more uneasy. 'Don't 'think, Polly,' said I, 'that I would 'envy any other person's preferment, 'when I have been so much exalted my'self. If Mr. H. has talked to you of 'marriage, tell me.'

'No, Me'm, I can't say he has *yet*.'

'*Yet*, Polly? Then he *never* will. 'For when men *do* talk of it, they don't 'always *mean* it: but whenever they '*mean* it, how can they confirm a doubt'ing maiden, without *mentioning* it? 'but, alas, alas for you, poor Polly!—'The freedoms you have permitted to 'him, no doubt, previous to those I 'heard, and which would have been 'greater, possibly, had I not surprised 'you with my cough, shew too well, that 'he *need* not make any promises to you.'

'Indeed, Me'm—Indeed, said she, sobbing, 'I might be too little upon my 'guard, but I would not have done any 'ill for the world.'

'I hope you would not, Polly, but 'if you suffer these freedoms, you can't 'tell what you'd have permitted—Tell 'me, do you love Mr. H.?'

'He is a very good-humoured gen'tleman, Madam, and is not proud.'

'No, 'tis not his business to be proud, 'when he hopes to humble you—humble 'you indeed! Beneath the lowest person of 'the sex, that is honest.'

'I hope—'

'You *hope!*' interrupted I.—'You '*hope* too much, and I *fear* a *great* '*deal* for you, because you fear *so little* 'for yourself—But tell me, how often 'have you been in private together?'

'In private, Me'm!—I don't know 'what your ladyship calls *private*!'

'Why that is *private*, Polly, when, 'as just now, you neither imagined nor 'intended any body should see you.'

She was silent, and I saw, by this poor girl, how true lovers are to their secret, though, perhaps, their ruin depends upon keeping it. But it behoved *me*, on

more

more accountable than I would any body else, as I hinted before, to examine this matter narrowly, because if Mr H should marry her, it would have been laid upon Mr B's example.—And if Polly should be ruined, it would be a sad thing, and people would have said—' Ay, she could ' take care enough of herself, but none at ' all of her servant *her* waiting-maid had ' a much more remiss mistress than Pa- ' mela found, or the matter would not ' have been thus

' Well, Polly, I see, continued I, ' that you will not speak out to me. You ' may have *several* reasons for it, possi- ' bly, though not *one* good one But ' as soon as Lady Davers comes in, who ' has a great concern in this matter as ' well as Lord Davers, and are answer- ' able to Lord H in a matter of so much ' importance as this, I will leave it to ' her ladyship's consideration, and shall ' no more concern myself to ask you ' questions about it—For then I must ' take her ladyship's directions, and part ' with you, to be sure '

The poor girl, frighted at this, (for every-body fears Lady Davers) wrung her hands, and begged, for God's sake, I would not acquaint Lady Davers with it.

' But how can I help it?—Must I not ' connive at your proceedings, if I do ' not? You are no fool, Polly, in other ' cases Tell me, how is it possible for ' me, in my situation, to avoid it?

' I will tell your ladyship the whole ' truth, indeed I will—if you will not ' tell Lady Davers I am ready to sink ' at the thoughts of Lady Davers's know- ' ing any thing of this.

This looked sadly I pitied her, but yet was angry in my mind, for I saw too plainly, that her conduct could not bear a scrutiny, not even in *her own* opinion, poor creature

I said—' Make me acquainted with ' the whole.'

' Will your ladyship promise—

' I'll promise nothing, Polly —When ' I have heard all you think proper to ' say, I will do what befits me to do, ' but with as much tenderness as I can ' for you—and that's all you ought to ' expect me to promise

' Why then, Madam,—But how can ' I speak it?—I can speak sooner to any- ' body, than to Lady Davers and you, ' Madam—For her ladyship's passion, ' and your ladyship's virtue—How shall ' I —And then she threw herself at my feet, and hid her face with her apron

I was in agonies for her almost, I wept over her, I raised her up, and said —' Tell me all You cannot tell me ' worse than I apprehend, nor, I hope, ' so bad! O Polly, tell me soon—For ' you give me great pain —

And my back, with grief and compassion for the poor girl, was ready to open, as it seemed to me—In my former distresses, I have been overcome by fainting next to death and was deprived of sense for some moments—But else I imagine, I must have felt some such affecting sensations, as the unhappy girl's case gave me

' Then, Madam, I own, said she, ' I have been too faulty

' As how!—As what!—In what ' way!—How faulty?—asked I, as quick as thought ' you are not ruined, ' are you?—Tell me, Polly?'

' No, Madam, but—'

' But what?—Say, but what?'

' I had consented—'

' To what?

' To his proposals, Madam '

' What proposals?

' Why, Madam, I was to live with ' Mr H

' I understand you too well—But is it ' too late to break so wretched a bar- ' gain,—have you already made a sa- ' crifice of your honour?'

' No, Madam, but I have given it ' under my hand

' Under your *hand*!—Ah! Polly, it ' is well if you have not given it under ' your *heart* too But what foolishness ' is this! What consideration has he ' made you?'

' He has given it under his hand, that ' he will always love me, and when his ' lordship's father dies, he will own me.'

' What foolishness is this on both ' sides!—But are you willing to be re- ' leased from this bargain?

' Indeed I am, Madam, and I told ' him so yesterday But he says he will ' sue me, and ruin me, if I don't stand ' to it.

' You are ruined, if you do!—And I ' wish—But tell me, Polly, are you not ' ruined as it is?

' Indeed I am not, Madam '

' I doubt then, you were upon the ' brink of it, had not this providential ' indisposition kept me at home —You ' met, I suppose, to conclude your shock-

' ing

'ing bargain—O poor unhappy girl!—'
'But let me see what he has given under his hand?'

'He has 'em both, Madam, to be drawn up fair, and in a strong hand, that shall be like a record.'

Could I have thought, Miss, that a girl of nineteen could be so ignorant in a point so important, when in every thing else she has shewn no instances like this *stupid folly*?

'Has he given you money?'

'Yes, Madam, he gave me—he gave me—a note. Here it is. He says any body will give me money for it.'

And this was a bank-note of fifty pounds, which she pulled out of her stays.

I instantly thought of those lines of Cowley, which my dear lady several times made me read to her, though these supposed an infinitely more excusable case—*Marriage* for money.

> 'Take heed, take heed, thou lovely maid!
> 'Nor be by glitt'ring ills betray'd!
> 'Thyself for money! O let no man know
> 'The price of beauty fall'n so low!
> 'What dangers ought'st thou not to dread,
> 'When Love, that's *blind*, is by *blind* Fortune led?'

The result was, he was to settle one hundred pounds a year upon her and *hers*, poor, poor girl—and was to *own* her, as he calls it, (but as wife or mistress, she stipulated not) when his father died, and he came into the title and estate.

I *told her, it was impossible for me to* conceal the matter from Lady Davers, if she would not, by her promises to be governed intirely by me, and to abandon all thoughts of Mr. H. give me room to conclude, that the wicked bargain was at an end.

And to keep the poor creature in some spirits, and to enable her to look up, and to be more easy under my direction, I blamed *him* more than I did *her*: though considering what virtue requires of a woman, and custom has made shameless in a man, I think the poor girl inexcusable, and shall not be easy while she is about me. For she is more to blame, because, of the two, she has more wit than the man.

'But what can I do?' thought I. 'If I put her away, 'twill be to throw her directly into his hands. He won't stay here long, and she *may* see her folly. But yet her eyes were open, she knew what she had to trust to—and by their wicked beginning, and her encouraging repulses, I doubt she would have been utterly ruined that very day.

I knew the rage Lady Davers would be in with both. So this was another embarrass. And yet should my good intentions be frustrated, and they should conclude their vile bargain, and it appeared that I knew of it, but would not acquaint her, then should I have been more blamed than any mistress of a family, circumstanced as I am.

Upon the whole, as to the girl, I resolved to comfort her as well as I could, till I had gained her confidence, that my advice might have the more weight with her, and, by degrees, be the more likely to reclaim her: for, poor soul! there would be an end of her reputation, the most precious of all jewels, the moment the matter was known, and that would be a sad thing.

And as to the man, I thought it best to take courage (and you, that know me, will say, I must have a good deal more than usual) to talk to Mr. H. on this subject.

And the poor body consenting I should, and, with great protestations, declaring her sorrow and repentance, begging to get her note of hand again, on which she laid a foolish stress, and desiring me to give him back his note of fifty pounds, I went down to find him.

He shunned me, as a thief would a constable at the head of a hue and cry. As I entered one place or room, he went into another, looking with conscious guilt, but yet confidently humming a tune. At last I fixed him speaking to Rachel, bidding her tell Polly he wanted to send a message by her to her lady. By which I doubted not, he was desirous to know what she had owned, in order to govern himself accordingly.

His back was towards me, and I said—'Mr. H. here I am myself, to take your commands.'

He gave a caper half a yard high—'Madam, I wanted—I wanted to speak to—I would have spoken with—'

'You wanted to send Polly to me, perhaps, Mr. H. to ask if I would take a little walk with you in the garden.'

'Very true, Madam!—Very true, indeed!—You have guessed the matter—I thought it was pity, this fine day, as every-body was taking an airing'—

'Well then, Sir, please to lead the 'way, and I'll attend you

'Yet I fancy, Madam, the wind is a 'little too high for you—Won't you 'catch cold?

'No, never fear, Mr H. I am not 'afraid of a little air

'I will attend you presently, Ma-'dam. You'll be in the great gravel 'walk, or on the terrace—I'll wait upon 'you in an instant

I had the courage to take hold of his arm, as if I had like to have slipt, 'For, thought I, 'thou shalt not see the girl, 'worthy friend, till I have talked to 'thee a little, if thou dost then—Excuse 'me, Mr H.—I hope I have not hurt 'my foot.—I must lean upon you

'Will you be pleased, Madam, to 'have a chair? I fear you have sprain-'ed your foot.—Shall I help you to a 'chair?

'No, no, Sir, I shall walk it off, if I 'hold by you

So he had no excuse to leave me, and we proceeded into the garden But never did any thing look so silly—So like a *foolish fellow*, as his aunt calls him He looked, if possible, half a dozen ways at once, hem'd, cough'd, wriggled about, turned his head behind him every now-and-then, and started half a dozen silly subjects, in hopes to hinder me from speaking

I appeared, I believe, under some concern how to begin with him, for he would have it I was not very well, and begged he might step in one minute to desire Mrs Jervis to attend me

So I resolved to begin with him, lest I should lose the opportunity, seeing my eel so very slippery And placing myself on the seat at the upper end of the gravel walk, I asked him to sit down He declined it, and would wait upon me presently, he said, and seemed going So I began—'It is easy for me, Mr H. to 'penetrate the reason why you are so 'willing to leave me but tis for your '*own* sake, that I desire you to hear 'me, that no mischief may ensue among 'friends and relations, on an occasion to 'which you are no stranger

'Laud, Madam, what can you mean? '—Surely, Madam, you don't think 'amiss of a little innocent liberty, or so!'

'Mr H. replied I, 'I want not any 'evidence of your inhospitable designs 'upon a poor unwary young creature, 'whom your birth and quality have 'found it too easy a task to influence

'*Inhospitable designs*! Madam!—A 'harsh word, by Gad—You very nice 'ladies cannot admit of the least free-'dom in the world!—Why, Madam, I 'have kissed a lady's woman before now, 'in a civil way or so, and never was 'called to an account for it, as a breach 'of hospitality

''Tis not for me, Mr H. to proceed 'to *very nice* particulars with a gentle-'man who can act as you have done, by a 'poor girl, that could not have had the 'assurance to look up to a man of your 'quality, had you not levelled all dis-'tinction between you, in order to level 'the weak creature to the common dirt 'of the highway I must tell you, that 'the poor girl heartily *repents* of her 'folly, and, to shew you, that it signi-'fies nothing to deny it, she begs you 'will give her back the note of her hand 'you have extorted from her foolish-'ness, and I hope you'll be so much of 'a gentleman, as not to keep in your 'power such a testimony of the weak-'ness of any of the sex

'Has she told you that, Madam!—'Why, may be—indeed—I can't but 'say—Truly it may'nt look so well to 'you, Madam but young folks will 'have frolicks—It was nothing but a 'frolick—Let me *be hanged*, if it was!'

'Be pleased then, Sir, to give up her 'note to me to return to her—Reputa-'tion should not be frolicked with, Sir, 'especially that of a poor girl, who has 'nothing else to depend upon'

'I'll give it to her myself, if you 'please, Madam, and laugh at her into 'the bargain Why, tis comical enough, 'if the little pug thought I was in ear-'nest I must have a laugh or two at 'her, Madam, when I give it her up'

'Since 'tis but a frolick, Mr H. you 'won't take it amiss, that when we are 'set down to supper, we call Polly in, 'and demand a sight of her note, and 'that will make every one merry as well 'as you'

'Cot so, Madam, that may'nt be so 'well neither!—For, perhaps, they will 'be apt to think it is in earnest, when, 'as I hope to live, tis but a jest no-'thing in the world else, upon honour!'

I put on then a still more serious air—'As you *hope to live*, say you, Mr H.! '—and *upon your honour*!—How fear 'you

'you not an instant punishment for this 'appeal! And what's the *honour* you 'swear by?—Take that, and answer 'me, Sir: do gentlemen give away bank-'notes for *frolicks*, and for *mere jests*, 'and *nothing in the world* else!—I am 'sorry to be obliged to deal thus with 'you. But I thought I was talking to 'a gentleman who would not forfeit his 'veracity, and that in so solemn an in-'stance as this!'

He looked like a man thunder-struck. His face was distorted, and his head seemed to turn about upon his neck, like a weathercock in a hurricane, to all points of the compass, his hands clenched as in a passion, and yet shame and confusion struggling in every limb and feature.

At last he said—'I am confoundedly 'betrayed. But if I am exposed to my 'uncle and aunt,' (for the wretch thought of nobody but himself) 'I am undone, 'and shall never be able to look them in 'the face. 'Tis true, I had a design 'upon her, and since she has betrayed 'me, I think I may say, that she was as 'willing, almost, as I.'

'Ungenerous, contemptible wretch, thought I!—'But such of our sex as can 'thus give up their virtue, ought to ex-'pect no better: for he that sticks not at '*one* bad action, will not scruple *another* 'to vindicate himself: and so, devil-like, 'become the tempter, and the accuser 'too!'

'But if you will be so good,' said he, with hands uplifted, 'as to take no no-'tice of this to my uncle, and especially 'to my aunt and Mr. B. I swear to 'you, I never will think of her as long 'as I live.'

'And you'll bind this promise, will 'you, Sir? by *your honour*, and as you '*hope to live*!'

'Dear, good Madam, forgive me, I 'beseech you, don't be so severe upon 'me. By all that's—'

'Don't swear, Mr. H. But as an 'earnest that I may believe you, give 'me back the girl's foolish note, that, 'though 'tis of no signification, she may 'not have *that* to witness to her folly.'

He took out his pocket-book. 'There 'it is, Madam!—And I beg you'll for-'give this attempt. I see I ought not 'to have made it. I doubt it was a 'breach of the laws of hospitality, as 'you say. But to make it known, will 'only expose me, and it can do no good, 'and Mr. B. will perhaps resent it, and 'my aunt will never let me hear the last 'of it, nor my uncle neither—And I 'shall be sent to travel again—And,' (added the poor creature) 'I was once 'in a storm, and the crossing the sea again 'would be death to me.'

'What a wretch art thou!' thought I—'What could such a one as thou 'find to say to a poor creature that, if 'put in the scale against considerations 'of virtue, should make the latter kick 'the beam?—Poor, poor Polly Barlow! 'thou art sunk indeed! Too low for 'excuse, and almost beneath pity!'

I told him, if I could observe, that nothing passed between them, that should lay me under a necessity of revealing the matter, I should not be forward to expose him, nor the maiden either: but that he must, in his own judgment, excuse me, if I made every body acquainted with it, if I were to see the correspondence between them likely to be renewed or carried on. 'For,' added I, 'in that 'case, I should owe it to myself, to Mr. 'B. to Lord and Lady Davers, and to 'you, and the unhappy body too, to do 'so.'

He would needs drop down on one knee to promise this, and with a thousand acknowledgments, left me, to find Mr. Colbrand, in order to ride to meet the coach on it's return.

I went in, and gave the foolish note to the silly girl, which she received eagerly, and immediately burnt, and I told her, I would not suffer her to come near me but as little as possible, when I was in company, while Mr. H. staid, but consigned her intirely to the care of Mrs. Jervis, to whom only, I said, I would hint the matter, as tenderly as I could: and for this, I added, I had more reasons than one; first, to give her the benefit of a good gentlewoman's advice, to which I had myself formerly been beholden, and from whom I concealed nothing: next, to keep out of Mr. H's way: and lastly, that I might have an opportunity, from Mrs. Jervis's opinion, to judge of the sincerity of her repentance. 'For, Polly,' said I, 'you 'must imagine, so regular and uniform 'as all our family is, and so good as I 'thought all the people about me were, 'that I could not suspect, that she, the 'duties of whose place made her nearest 'to my person, was the farthest from 'what I wished.'

I have ſet this matter ſo ſtrongly before her, and Mrs Jervis has ſo well ſeconded me, that I hope the beſt, for the grief the poor creature carries in her looks, and expreſſes in her words, cannot be deſcribed, frequently accuſing herſelf with tears, ſaying often to Mrs Jervis, ſhe is not worthy to ſtand in the preſence of a miſtreſs, whoſe example ſhe has made ſo bad an uſe of, and whoſe leſſons ſhe had ſo ill followed

I am ſadly troubled at this matter, however, but I take great comfort in reflecting, that my ſudden indiſpoſition looked like a providential thing, which may ſave one poor ſoul, and be a ſeaſonable warning to her, as long as ſhe lives

Mean time I muſt obſerve, that at ſupper laſt night, Mr H looked abject, and mean, and like a poor thief, as I thought, and (conſcious of his diſappointed folly, though I ſeldom glanced my eye upon him) had leſs to ſay for himſelf than ever

And once my Lady Davers laughing, ſaid—' I think in my heart, my nephew ' looks more fooliſh every time I ſee him, ' than the laſt

He ſtole a look at me, and bluſhed, and my lord ſaid—' Jackey has ſome ' grace !—He bluſhes !—Hold up thy ' head, nephew !—Haſt thou nothing at ' all to ſay for thyſelf ?

Sir Jacob ſaid—' A bluſh becomes a ' young gentleman !—I never ſaw one ' before though, in Mr H.—What's ' the matter, Sir ?

' Only, ſaid Lady Davers, ' his ſkin ' or his conſcience is mended, that's all

' Thank you, Madam,' was all he ſaid, bowing to his aunt, and affecting a careleſs, yet confuſed air, as if he whiſpered a whiſtle

' O wretch !' thought I, ' ſee what it ' is to have a condemning conſcience, ' while every *innocent* perſon looks round, ' eaſy, ſmiling, and erect !'—But yet it was not the ſhame of a bad action, I doubt, but being diſcovered and diſappointed, that gave him this confuſion of face

What a ſad thing it is for a perſon to be guilty of ſuch actions, as ſhall put it into the power of another, even by a look, to mortify him ! And if poor ſouls can be thus abjectly ſtruck at ſuch a diſcovery as this, by a fellow creature, how muſt they appear before an unerring and omniſcient Judge, with a conſcience ſtanding in the place of a thouſand witneſſes ? and calling in vain upon the *mountains to fall upon them*, and the *hills to cover them* !

How ſerious this ſubject makes one !

SATURDAY EVENING

I Am juſt retired from a fatiguing ſervice, for who ſhould come hither to dine with Mr B but that ſad rake Sir Charles Hargrave, and Mr Walgrave, Mr Sedley, and Mr Floyd, three as bad as himſelf, inſeparable companions, whoſe whole delight, and that avowedly, is drinking, and hunting, and lewdneſs, but otherwiſe, gentlemen of wit and large eſtates ? Three of them broke in upon us, at the * Hall, on the happieſt day of my life, to our great regret, and they had been long threatening to make this viſit, in order to ſee me, as they told Mr B

They whipt out two bottles of Champaign inſtantly, for a *whet*, as they called it, and went to view the ſtud, and the kennel, and then took a walk in the garden till dinner was ready, my Lord Davers, Mr H and Sir Jacob, as well as Mr B (for they are all acquainted) accompanying them

Sir Charles, it ſeems, as Lord Davers told me afterwards, ſaid, he longed to ſee Mrs B She was the talk wherever he went, and he had conceived a high opinion of her before hand

Lord Davers ſaid—' I defy you, gen ' tlemen, to think ſo highly of her as ' ſhe deſerves, take mind and perſon to- ' gether

Mr Floyd ſaid, he never ſaw any woman yet, who came up to what he expected, where fame had been laviſh in her praiſe

' But how, brother baronet, ſaid Sir Charles to Sir Jacob, ' came *you* to be ' reconciled to her ?—I heard that you ' would never own her

' Oons, man, ſaid Sir Jacob, ' I was ' taken in—I was, by my ſoul !—They ' contrived to clap her upon me, as Lady ' Jenny C and pretended they'd keep ' t'other out of my ſight, and I was ' plaguily bit, and forced to get off as ' well as I could '

* See Vol. II. p 205.

'That was a bite indeed,' said Mr Walgrave 'and so you fell a praising 'Lady Jenny, I warrant, to the skies

'Ye—s,—by my soul, (drawling out the affirmative monosyllable) 'I was 'used most scurvily faith I was. I bear 'em a grudge for 't still, I can tell 'em 'that,—for I have hardly been able to 'hold up my head like a man ever since '—but am forc'd to sneak about, and 'go and come, and do as they bid me 'By my troth, I never was so manage'able in my life'

'Your Herefordshire neighbours, Sir 'Jacob,' said Mr Sedley, with an oath, 'will rejoice to hear this, for the whole 'county there canno manage you

'I'm quite cow'd now, by my soul, 'as you will see by-and-by nay, for 'that matter, if you can set Mrs B a 'talking, there's ne'er a puppy of you 'all will care to open your lips, except 'to say as she says

'Never fear, old boy, said Sir Charles, 'we'll bear our parts in conversation I 'never saw the woman yet who could 'give me either awe or love for six mi'nutes together.—What think you, Mr 'B? Have you any notion, that your 'lady will have so much power over 'us?'

'I think, Sir Charles, I have one of 'the finest women in England, but I 'neither expect, nor desire, you rakes 'should see her with my eyes

'You know, if I have a mind to love 'her, and make court to her too, Mr 'B I will and I am half in love with 'her already, although I have not seen 'her

They came in when dinner was near ready, and the four gentlemen took each a large bumper of old-hock for another whet

The countess, Lady Davers, and I, came down together The gentlemen knew our two noble ladies, and were known to them in person, as well as by character Mr B in his usual kind and encouraging manner, took my hand, and presented the four gentlemen to me, each by his name Sir Charles said, pretty bluntly, that he hoped he was more welcome to me now, than the last time he was under the same roof with me, for he had been told since, that *that* was our happy day

I said, Mr B's friends were always welcome to me

'Tis well, Madam,' said Mr Sedley, 'we did not know how it was We 'should have quartered ourselves upon 'Mr B for a week together, and kept 'him up day and night

I thought this speech deserved no answer, especially as they were gentlemen who wanted no countenance, and addressed myself to Lord Davers, who is always kindly making court to me 'I 'hope, my good lord, you find your'self quite recovered of your head ach?' (of which he complained at breakfast)

'I thank you, my dear sister, pretty 'well

'I was telling Sir Charles, and the 'other gentlemen, niece, said Sir Jacob, 'how I was cheated here, when I came 'first, with a Lady Jenny

'It was a very lucky cheat for me, 'Sir Jacob, for it gave you a prepos'session in my favour, under so advan'tageous a character, that I could never 'have expected otherwise'

'I wish, said the countess, 'my 'daughter, for whom Sir Jacob took 'you, had Mrs B.'s qualities to boast 'of

'How am I obliged to your lady'ship's goodness, returned I, 'when 'you treat me with even greater indul'gence than you use to so beloved a 'daughter!'

'Nay, now you talk of treating, said Sir Charles, 'when, ladies, will you treat 'our sex with the politeness which you 'shew to one another?'

'When your sex deserve it, Sir Charles,' answered Lady Davers

'Who is to be judge of that? said Mr Walgrave

'Not the gentlemen, I hope,' replied my lady

'Well then, Mrs B' said Sir Charles, 'we bespeak your good opinion of *us*; 'for you have *ours*

'I am obliged to you, gentlemen, 'but I must be more cautious in declar'ing *mine*, lest it should be thought I am 'influenced by your kind, and perhaps 'too hasty, opinions of me

Sir Charles swore they had *seen* enough of me the moment I entered the parlour, and heard enough the moment I opened my lips, to answer for *their* opinions of me

I said, I made no doubt, when *they* had as good a subject to expatiate upon, as I had, in the pleasure before me, of seeing so many agreeable friends of Mr B s, they would maintain the title they claimed of every one s good opinion

'This, said Sir Jacob, 'is binding 'you over, gentlemen, to your good be- 'haviour—You must know, my niece 'never shoots flying, as you do

The gentlemen laughed 'Is it shoot- 'ing flying, Sir Jacob, returned Sir Charles, 'to praise that lady

'Ads-bud, I did not think of that

'O Sir Jacob, said the countess, 'you need not be at a fault,—for a 'good sportsman always hits his mark, 'flying or no and the gentlemen had 'so fair an one, that they could not well 'miss it

'You are fairly helped over the stile, 'Sir Jacob,' said Mr Floyd

'And, indeed, I wanted it, though 'I limped like a puppy before I was 'lame One can t think of every thing 'as one used to do at your time of life, 'gentlemen

This flippant stuff was all that passed, which I *can* recite, for the rest, at table, and after dinner, was too polite by half for me such as, the quantity of wine each man could *carry off*, that was the phrase, dog, horses, hunting, racing, cock-fighting, and all accompanied with swearing, and cursing, and that in good humour, and out of wantonness (the least excusable and most profligate sort of swearing and cursing of all,) loud laughing, with a little touching now and then on the borders of Sir Simon s beloved subject, to try if they could make a lady shew she *understood* their hints by her *blushes**, a certain indication, that those who seek a blush in others, are past it themselves, and by their turning it into ridicule when they find it in their friends, that they would not for the world have it imputed to them, talking three or four at once, and as loud as if they were in the field pursuing their game, at a quarter of a mile s distance from one another

These were the subjects, and this the entertainment, which held the ladies and me for one hour, after a tedious dinner, when we retired, and glad we were to do so The gentlemen liked the wine so well, that we had the felicity to drink tea and coffee by ourselves, only Mr B [illegible] the gentlemen to par- [illegible] filling in for a few minutes to tell us, they would stick by what they had, and taking a dish of coffee with us

I should not omit one observation that Sir Jacob, when they were gone, said, they were *pure company* and Mr H that he never was so delighted in his *born days*—While the two ladies put up their prayers, that they might never have such another entertainment And being encouraged by their declaration, I presumed to join in the same petition

Yet, it seems, these are men of wit! I believe they must be so—because I could neither like nor understand them.—Yet, if their conversation had much wit in it, I should think my ladies would have found it out

However, this they did find out, and agree in, that these gentlemen were of the true modern cast of libertines and fox-hunters, and, indifferently as they liked them, could not be easily outdone by any of the same stamp in England

God defend my dear Miss Darnford, and every worthy single lady, from such a husband, as a gentleman of this character would make!

I wonder really how Mr B who chooses not this sort of conversation, and always (whatever faults he had besides) was a *sober* gentleman, can sit for hours so easy and cheerful in it, and yet he never says much, when they are in their high delight

When all's done, Miss, there are very unpleasant things, which persons in *genteel* life are forced to put up with, as well as those in *lower*, and were the one to be balanced with the other, the difference, as to true happiness, would not perhaps be so great as people in the latter imagine,—if it did not turn in their favour

The gentlemen, permit me to add, went away very merry, to ride ten miles by owl light, for they would not accept of beds here They had two French horns with them, and gave us a blast, or flourish or two, at going off Each had a servant besides but the way they were in would have given me more concern than it did, had they been related to Mr B and less used to it And, indeed, it is a happiness, that such gentlemen take no more care than they generally do, to interest any body intimately in their healths and preservation, for these are all

* See Vol I p [illegible]

single men Nor is the publick, any more than the private, under any necessity to be much concerned about them, for let such persons go when they will, if they continue single, their next heir cannot well be a worse commonwealth's-man, and there is a great chance he may be better

You know I end my Saturdays seriously And this, to what I have already said, makes me add, that I cannot express how much I am, my dear Miss Darnford,

your faithful and affectionate

P B

LETTER XXXVIII

FROM MRS B TO MISS DARNFORD, IN ANSWER TO LETTERS XXXV AND XXXVI

MY DEAR MISS DARNFORD,

I Skip over the little transactions of several days, to let you know how much you rejoice me, in telling me* Sir Simon has been so kind as to comply with my wishes Both your most agreeable letters came to my hand together, and I thank you a hundred times for them, and I thank your dear mamma, and Sir Simon too, for the pleasure they have given me in this obliging permission How happy shall we be together!—But how long will you be permitted to stay, though? All the winter, I hope —And then, when that is over, let us set out together, if God shall spare us, directly for Lincolnshire, and so pass most of the summer likewise in each other's company What a sweet thought is this!—Let me indulge it a little while

Mr B read your letters, and says, you are a charming young lady, and surpass yourself in every letter I told him, that he was more interested in the pleasure I took in this favour of Sir Simon's than he imagined 'As how, my dear?' said he 'A plain case, Sir,' replied I 'for endeavouring to improve myself by 'Miss Darnford's conversation and be'haviour, I shall every day be more 'worthy of your favour He kindly would have it, that nobody, no, not Miss Darnford herself, excelled me

'Tis right, you know, Miss, that Mr B should think so, though I must know nothing at all, if I was not sensible how inferior I am to my dear Miss Darnford: and yet, when I look abroad now and-then, I could be a proud slut, if I would, and not yield the palm to many others.—But don't let every body know how vain I am Yet they may too, if they take in, at the same time, the grounds of my vanity, for they must then allow, that I have no small reason to be proud, in having so happily won the favour of two such judges, as Mr B and Miss Darnford, and have the good fortune, likewise, to rejoice in that of Lady Davers, and the Countess of C

Well, my dear Miss,

SUNDAY

IS past and gone, as happily as the last, the two ladies, and, at *their* earnest request, Sir Jacob, bearing us company, in the evening part My Polly was there morning and evening, with her heart broken almost, poor girl!—I put her in a corner of my closet, because her concern should not be minded Mrs Jervis gives me great hopes of her —and she seems to abhor the thoughts of Mr. H.—But as there proves to be so little of real love in her heart, (though even, if there had, she would have been without excuse) is she not the wickeder by half for that, Miss? To consent, and take *earnest*, as I may say, to live with a man, who did not pretend to marry her!—How inexcusable this!—What a frailty!—Yet so honestly descended, so modest in appearance, and an example so much better—forgive me to say—before her—Dear, dear, how could it be!

Sir Jacob was much pleased with our family order, and said, 'twas no wonder I *kept* so good myself, that was his word, and made others so, and he was of opinion that the four rakes (for he run on how much they admired me) would be converted, if they saw how well I passed my time, and how cheerful and easy every one, as well as myself, was under it He said, when he came home, he thought he must take such a method himself in *his* family, for, he believed, it would make not only better masters and mistresses, but better children, and better servants too. But, poor gentleman! he has, I doubt, a great deal to mend in

* See p 429

himself,

himself, before he can begin such a practice with efficacy in his *family*.

MONDAY

IN the afternoon, Sir Jacob took his leave of us, highly satisfied with us both, and *particularly*—so he said—with me, and promised that my *two cousins*, as he called his daughters, and his sister, an old maiden lady, if they went to town this winter, should visit me, and be improved by me, that was his word Mr B accompanied him some miles on his journey, and the two ladies, and Lord Davers, and I, took an airing in the coach

Mr B was so kind as to tell me, when he came home, with a whisper, that Miss Goodwin presented her duty to me

I have got a multitude of fine things for the dear little creature, and Mr B promises to give me a dairy-house breakfast, when our guests are gone.

I inclose the history of this little charmer *, by Mr B 's consent, since you are to do us the honour, as he (as well as I) pleases himself, to be one of our family —But keep it to yourself, whatever you do. I am guaranty that you will, and have put it in a separate paper, that you may burn it as soon as you have read it. —For I shall want your advice, it may be, on this subject, having a great desire to get this child into my possession, and yet Lady Davers has given me an † hint, that dwells a little with me When I have the pleasure I hope for, I will lay all before you, and be determined and proceed, as far as I have power, by you You, my good father and mother, have seen the story in my former papers

TUESDAY.

YOU must know, I pass over the days thus swiftly, not that I could not fill them up with writing, as ample as I have done the former but intending only to give you a general idea of our way of life and conversation, and having gone through a whole week and more, you will be able from what I have recited, to form a judgment how it is with us, one day with another —As for example, now-and-then neighbourly visits received and paid Needle work between whiles Musick Cards sometimes, though I don t love them—One more benevolent round—Improving conversations with my dear Mr B and my two good ladies—A lesson from him, when alone, either in French or Latin, a new pauper case or two—A visit from the good dean—Mr Williams s departure, in order to put the new-projected alteration in force, which is to deprive me of my chaplain—(By the way, the dean is highly pleased with this affair, and the motives to it, Mr Adams being a favourite of his, and a distant relation of his lady) Mr H s and Polly s mutual endeavour to avoid one another—My lessons to the poor girl, and cautions, as if she were my sister—

These, my dear Miss Darnford, these, my honoured father and mother, are the pleasant employments of our time, so far as we females are concerned for the gentlemen hunt, ride out, and divert themselves in their way, and bring us home the news and occurrences they meet with abroad, and now-and-then a straggling gentleman they pick in their diversions.—And so I shall not enlarge upon these articles, after the tedious specimens I have already given Yet the particulars of one conversation, possibly, I may give you another time, when I have least to do, because three young ladies, relations of Lady Towers and Mrs Arthur, were brought to visit me, for the benefit of my instructions, for that was the kind compliment of those ladies to me

WEDNESDAY, THURSDAY

COULD you ever have thought, my dear, that husbands have a dispensing power over their wives, which kings are not allowed over the laws ? I have this day had a smart debate with Mr B and I fear it will not be the only one up on this subject Can you believe, that if a wife thinks a thing her duty to do, and her husband does not approve of her doing it, he can dispense with her performing it, and no sin shall lie at her door? Mr. B maintains this point I have great doubts about it, particularly one, that if a matter be my duty, and he dispenses with my performance of it,

* See Vol. II p. 277. † See p 332 of this Volume.

whether

whether, even although that were to clear *me* of the sin, it will not fall upon *him self?* And, to be sure, Miss, a good wife would be as much concerned at this, as if it was to remain upon *her* Yet he seems set upon it What can one do!—Did you ever hear of such a notion before, Miss? Of such a prerogative in a husband? Would you care to subscribe to it?

This is one of Mr B s particularities He has several of them, the effects, as I take it, of his former free life Polygamy, as I have mentioned heretofore, is another That is a bad one indeed Yet he is not so determined on this, as he seems to be on the other, in a certain case, that is too *nice* for me, at present to explain to you, and so I might as well have taken no notice of it, as yet —Only the argument was so present to my mind held within this hour, and I write a journal, you know, of what passes

But I will, some time hence, submit it, at least to *your* judgments, my father and mother You are well read in the Scriptures, and have gone through the occasion often, and both Mr B and I build our arguments on Scripture, though we are so different in our opinions He says, the ladies are of his opinion I m afraid they are, and so will not ask them But, perhaps, I mayn't live, and other things may happen, and so I ll say no more of it at present*

FRIDAY

MR H and my Lord and Lady Davers, and the excellent Countess of C——, having left us this day, a good deal to my regret, and, as it seemed, to their own, the former put the following letter into my hands, with an air of respect, and even reverence You will observe in it, that he says, he spells most lamentably, and this obliges me to give it you *literally*

'DEARE GOOD MADAM,

'I Cannott contente myselfe with com-'mon thankes, on leaving youres 'and Mr B 's hospitabel house, because 'of *thatt there* affaire, which I neede 'not mention, and truly am *ashamed* to 'mention, as I *have been* to looke you 'in the face, ever since it happen d I 'don t knowe *how itt came aboute*, butt 'I thought butt att first of *joking* a littel, '*or soe*, and seeing Polley heard me 'with more attentiveness then I expect-'ed, I was encouraged to proceede, 'and *soe*, now I recollecte, itt *came 'aboute*

'But shee is innosent for me and I 'don t knowe how *thatt* came aboute 'neither, for wee were oute one moone 'lighte nighte together, in the gardin, 'walking aboute, and afterwardes tooke 'a *napp* of two houres, as I beliefe, in the 'summer-house in the littel gardin, be-'ing over-powered with sleepe, for I 'woulde make her lay her head uppon 'my breste, till, before we were awar, 'wee felle asleepe together Butt be-'fore thatt, we hadd agreed on whatt 'you discovered

'Thiss is the whole truthe, and all the 'intimasies wee ever hadd, *to speake off*. 'But I beleefe we shoulde have been 'better acquainted, hadd you nott, luck-'ily *for mee!* prevented itt, by being att 'home, when we thought you abroad. 'For I was to come to her when shee 'hemm d *two or three times*, for hav-'ing made a contract, you knowe, Ma-'dam, it was naturall enough to take 'the first occasion to putt itt in force.

'She coulde not keepe her owne se-'critt, and may have tolde you more, 'perhapps, then is true So what I 'write is to *cleare myselfe*, and to tell 'you, how sorry I am, in such a good 'house as youres, and where their is so 'much true godliness, that I shoulde 'ever be *drawne away* to have a 'thoughte to dishonour itt But I will 'take care of being over-familliar for 'the future with *underlings*, for, see 'how a man may be *taken in!*—If shee 'hadd relented itt att first, when I begun 'to kisse her, *or soe* (for, you knowe, 'we younge fellows will take libertis 'sometimes where they don't become 'us, to our owne disparagements chiefly, '*that s true*) I shoulde have hadd an '*awe* uppon me, or iff shee had *told 'you*, or butt *said* shee woulde, I shoulde 'have *flowne*, as soone as had any 'thoughtes further aboute *the matter*. '—But what had one of oure sexe to do, '*you knowe*, Madam, when they finde '*littel* resistence, and that shee woulde '*stande quietly* and *telle no tales* and

* For the sequel of this matter, see Vol. IV. Letter III.

'make

'make so great a struggle, and not keepe on in the same way rather, but to stay away, on, till one brought itt to more than one at first intended?

'Poor Polley! I pity her too. Don't thinke the worse of her, deare Madam, so as to turn her away, because it may be her ruin. I don't desire too see her. I mought have been drawne in to do strange foolish things, and been ruined at the long run; for who knows where this thing mought have ended? My unkle woulde have never forgiven me. My father too (his lordship, you have hearde, Madam, is a very crosse man, and never loved mee much) mought have cutt off the intaile. My aunt would have despised mee, and scorned mee. I should have been her foolishe fellowe in earnest, not in jeste, as now. You woulde have resented itt, and Mr. B. who knowes? mought have called me to account, (for he is bloody passionate, I hear tell at the Hall, and has foughte two or three duells, as I have hearde) for abusing the freedom of his house, and breaking the laws of hospitality, as you told mee, and so, it is not unlikely, I mought have dyed like a dogge in a ditch, and there would have been an ende of a noble family, that have been peeres of the realme time out of minde. What a sadd thing would this have been! A publicke as well as private losse! for you knowe, Madam, whatt my lady countess sais, and nobody says better things, or knowes more of the matter, than her ladyshipp, That every peere of the realme is a jewell in the crowne. A fine saying! God grante, I may keepe itt in minde, when my time comes, and my father shall happen to die!

'Well, but, good Madam, cann you forgive mee? You see how happy I am in my disappointment. But I must take another sheete of paper.—I did nott thinke too write so much,—for I don't love itt: butt on this ocasion, know not how too leave off.—I hope you cann reade my letter. I knowe I write a clumsy hand, and spelle moste lamentably, for I never had a tallent for these thinges. I was readier by halfe to admire the orcherd robbing picture in Lillie's grammer, then any other parte of the book: excuse my nonsense, Madam: butt many a time have I help'd to fill a sachil, and always supposed that picture was putt there on purpose to tell boyes whatt diversions are allowed them, and are propper for them. Severall of my schoole fellows tooke it for granted, as well as I, and wee coulde never reconsile itt to oure reason, why wee shoulde bee punished for practising a lesson taughte us by our grammers.

'But, hey, whether am I running! I never writt so to you before, and never may againe, unlesse you, or Mr. B. commande itt, for youre servise. So pray excuse me, Madam.

'I knowe I neede give no advise to Polley, to take care of first encouragements. Poore girl! shee mought have suffer'd sadly, as welle as I.—For iff my father, and my unkell and aunte, had requir'd mee to turne her off, you knowe itt woulde have been undutifull too have refus'd them, notwithstanding our bargaine. And want of duty to them woulde have been to have added faulte too faulte: as you once observed, I remember, that one faulte never comes alone, but drawes after itt generally, five or six, to hide or vindicate itt, and they every one perhapps as many more.

'I shall never forgett severall of youre wise sayinges. I have been vexed, may I be hang'd if I have not, many a time, that I coulde not make such observations as you make, who am so much older too, and a man besides, and a peere's son, and a peere's nephew! but my talents lie another way, and by that time my father dies, I hope to improve myselfe, in order to cutt such a figgure, as may make me be no disgrace to my name or countrey; for I shall have one benefitt over many yonge lordes, that I shall be more fond of makeing observations then speeches, and so shall improve of course, you knowe.

'Well, butt whatt is all this to the purpose!—I will keepe close to my texte, and thatt is, to thank you, good Madam, for all the favours I have received in your house, to thank you for disappointing mee, and for convinsing mee, in so kinde, yet so shameing a manner, how wrong I was in the matter of that there Polly, and for not exposing my folly to any boddy but myselfe (for I should have been ready to hang myselfe, if you hadd,) and to begg youre pardon for itt, and to assuer you, that I will never offerr the like as long as I breathe

'breathe I am, Madam, with the 'greatest respecte, *youre moste obliged, moste faithfull, and moste obedient humbell servante,*

'J H.

'Pray excuse blotts and blurrs'

Well, Miss Darnford, what shall we say to this fine letter?—You ll allow it to be an original, I hope Yet, may-be not For how does one know, but it may be as well written, and as sensible a letter as this class of people generally write?—But what then shall we be able to say for such poor creatures of our sex as are *taken in*, as Mr H calls it, by such pretty fellows as this who if they may happen to *write* better, hardly *think* better, or design to *act* better, and are not so soon brought to repentance, and promises of amendment?

Mr H dresses well, is not a contemptible figure of a man, laughs, talks, where he can be heard, and his aunt is not present,—and *cuts*, to use his own word, a considerable figure in a country town—But see—Yet I will not say what I might—He is Lord Davers s nephew, and if he makes his *observations*, and *forbears* his *speeches*, (I mean, can be silent, and only laugh when he sees somebody of more sense laugh, and never *approve* or *condemn* but in *leading-strings*) he may possibly pass in a crowd of gentlemen.—But poor, poor Polly Barlow! What *can* I say for Polly Barlow?

I have a time in view, when, possibly, my papers may fall under the inspection of a dear gentleman, to whom, next to God, I am accountable for all my actions and correspondences; so I will either write an account of the matter, and seal it up separately, for Mr B or, at a proper opportunity, will break it to him, and let him know, (under secrecy, if I can engage him to promise it) the steps I took in it, for fear something should arise hereafter, when I cannot answer for myself, to render any thing dark or questionable in it, A method I believe very proper to be taken by every married lady, and I presume the rather to say so, having had a good example for it for I have often thought of a little sealed-up parcel of papers, my lady made me burn in her presence, about a month before she died.—'They are, Pamela,' said she, 'such as I have no reason to be concerned 'about, let who will see them, could 'they know the springs and causes of 'them but, for want of a clue, my son 'might be at a loss what to think of se'veral of those letters, were he to find 'them, in looking over my other papers, 'when I am no more'

Let me add, that nothing could be more endearing than our parting with our noble guests My lady repeated her commands for what she often engaged me to promise, that is to say, to renew the correspondence begun between us, so much (as she was pleased to say) to her satisfaction

I could not help shewing her ladyship, who was always inquiring after my writing employment, most of what passed between you and me, and she admires you much, and wished Mr H had more wit, that was her word: she should in that case, she said, be very glad to set on foot a treaty between you and him

But that, I fancy, can never be tolerable to you, and I only mention it *en passant* —There s a French woman for you!

The countess was full of her kind wishes for my happiness, and my Lady Davers told me, that if I could give her timely notice, she would be present on a *certain* occasion

But, my dear Miss, what could I say?—I know nothing of the matter!—Only, I am a sad coward, and have a thousand anxieties, which I cannot mention to any body

But, if I have such in the honourable estate of matrimony, what must those poor souls have, who have been seduced, and have all manner of reason to apprehend, that the crime shall be followed by a punishment so *natural* to it? A punishment *in kind*, as I may say, which if it only ends in forfeiture of life, following the forfeiture of fame, must be thought merciful and happy beyond expectation for how shall they lay claim to the hope that is given to persons in their circumstances that *they shall be saved in child bearing*, since the condition is, *if they* CONTINUE *in faith and charity, and* HOLINESS *with* SOBRIETY?

Now, my honoured mother, and my dear Miss Darnford, since I am upon this affecting subject, does not this text seem to give a comfortable hope to a good woman, who shall die in this circumstance, that she shall be happy in the Divine mercies? For the Apostle, in the context, says, that *he suffers not a woman to teach, nor to usurp authority over the man,*

man, but to be in ſilence—And what is the reaſon he gives? Why, a reaſon that is a natural conſequence of the curſe on the firſt diſobedience, that ſhe ſhall be in ſubjection to her huſband.—'For, ſays he, *Adam was* NOT *deceived, but the woman, being deceived, was in the tranſgreſſion*. As much as to ſay—Had it not been for the woman, Adam had kept his integrity, and therefore her puniſhment ſhall be, as it is ſaid—"*I will greatly multiply thy ſorrow in thy conception in ſorrow ſhalt thou bring forth children,—and thy huſband ſhall rule over thee*. But nevertheleſs, if thou ſhalt not ſurvive the ſharpneſs of thy ſorrow, thy death ſhall be deemed to be ſuch an alleviation of thy part of the intailed tranſgreſſion, that thou ſhalt *be ſaved*, if thou haſt CONTINUED in faith, and charity, and HOLINESS with SOBRIETY.'

Thus, my honoured parents, and my dear friend, is *my* paraphraſe, and I reap no ſmall comfort from it, when I meditate upon it.

But I ſhall make you as ſerious as myſelf, and, my dear friend, perhaps frighten you from entering into a ſtate, in which our poor ſex ſuffer ſo much, from the bridal morning, let it riſe as gaily as it will upon a thoughtful mind, to that affecting circumſtance, (throughout the whole progreſſion) for which nothing but a tender, a generous, and a worthy huſband can make them any part of amends.—And when one *is* ſo bleſſed, one has ſo many fears added to one's ſorrows, and ſo much apprehenſion, through human frailty, of being ſeparated from ſo beloved a partner, that one had need of the greateſt fortitude to ſupport one's ſelf. But it may be, I am the weakeſt and moſt apprehenſive of my ſex—It may be, I am!—And when one ſees how common the caſe is, and yet how few die in it, how uneaſy many women are, *not* to be in this circumſtance, (my good Lady Davers particularly, at times) and Rachel and Hannah in Holy Writ, and then how a childleſs eſtate might leſſen one in the eſteem of one's huſband, one ought to bring theſe conſiderations in balance, and to baniſh needleſs fears. And ſo I will, if I can.

But a word or two more, as to the parting with our honoured company. I was a little indiſpoſed, and they all would excuſe me, againſt my will, from attending them in the coach ſome miles, which their dear brother did. Both ladies moſt tenderly ſaluted me, twice or thrice a-piece, folding their kind arms about me, and wiſhing my ſafety and health, and charging me to *think* little, and *hope* much, for they ſaw me thoughtful at times, though I endeavoured to hide it from them.

My Lord Davers was pleaſed to ſay, with a goodneſs of temper that is peculiar to him—'My deareſt, dear ſiſter—May God preſerve you, and multiply your comforts! I ſhall pray for you more than ever I did for myſelf, though I have ſo much more need of it;—I *muſt* leave you—But I leave one whom I love and honour next to Lady Davers, and ever ſhall.'

Mr H. looked conſciouſly ſilly.—'I can ſay nothing, Madam,—but (ſaluting me) 'that I ſhall never forget your goodneſs to me.' Adding, in his frothy way, and with as foppiſh an air—'Now can I ſay, I have ſaluted an angel, if ever there was an angel on earth.'

I had, before, in Mrs Jervis's parlour, taken leave of Mrs Worden and Mrs Leſley, my ladies women: they each ſtole, as it were, at the ſame time, a hand of mine, and kiſſed it, begging pardon, as they ſaid, for the freedom. But I anſwered, taking each by her hand, and kiſſing her—'I ſhall always think of you with pleaſure, my good friends, for you have encouraged me conſtantly by your preſence in my private duties, and may God bleſs you, and the worthy families you ſo laudably ſerve, as well for your ſakes, as their own!'

They turned away with tears, and Mrs Worden would have ſaid ſomething to me, but could not.—Only both taking Mrs Jervis by the hand—'Happy, happy Mrs Jervis!' ſaid they, almoſt in a breath.—'And happy, happy I too,' repeated I, 'in my Mrs. Jervis, and in ſuch kind and worthy well-wiſhers as Mrs Worden and Mrs Leſley.—Wear this, Mrs Worden;—wear this, Mrs. Leſley, for my ſake.' and I gave each of them a ring, with a cryſtal and brilliants ſet about it, which Mr B. had bought a week before for this very purpoſe; for he has a great opinion of both the good folks, and often praiſed their prudence, and their quiet and reſpectful behaviour to every body, ſo different from the impertinence, that was

is word, of most ladies women, who are favourites

Mrs Jervis said—'I have enjoyed 'many happy hours in your conversa- 'tion, Mrs Worden and Mrs Lesley 'I shall miss you very much.'

'I must endeavour, said I, taking her hand, 'to make it up to you, my good 'friend, as well as I can And of late 'we have not had so many opportuni- 'ties together as I should have wished, 'had I not been so agreeably engaged as 'you know—So we must each try to 'comfort the other, when we have lost, 'I such noble, and you such worthy 'companions

Mrs Jervis's honest heart, before touched by the parting, shewed itself at her eyes—'Wonder not, my good friends, said I, to the two gentlewomen, wiping with my handkerchief her venerable cheeks, 'that I always endeavour thus 'to dry up all my good Mrs Jervis's 'tears, and then I kissed her, thinking of *you*, my dear mother, and I was forced to withdraw a little abruptly, lest I should be too much moved myself, because I was going up to our departing company, who, had they inquired into the occasion, would perhaps have thought it derogatory (though I should not) to my present station, and too much retrospecting to my former,

I could not, in conversation between Mr B and myself, when I was gratefully expatiating upon the amiable characters of our noble guests, and of their behaviour and kindness to me, help observing, that I had little expected, from some * hints which formerly dropt from Mr B to find my good Lord Davers so polite and so sensible a man

'He is a very good-natured man, replied Mr B 'I believe I might once or 'twice drop some disrespectful words of 'him But it was the effect of passion, 'at the time, and with a view to two or 'three points of his conduct in publick 'life, for which I took the liberty to find 'fault with him, and received very un- 'satisfactory excuses. One of these, I 'remember particularly, was in a con- 'ference between a committee of each 'house of parliament, in which he be- 'haved in a way I could not wish from a 'man so nearly allied to me by marriage, 'for all he could talk of, was the dignity 'of their house, when the reason of the 'thing was strong with the other, and it 'fell to my lot to answer what he said, 'which I did, with some asperity, and 'this occasioned a coolness between us 'for some time

'But no man makes a better figure in 'private life than Lord Davers, espe- 'cially now, that my sister's good sense 'has got the better of her passions, and 'she can behave with tolerable decency 'towards him For, formerly, Pamela, 'it was not so, the violence of her spirit 'making him appear in a light too little 'advantageous either to his quality or 'merit But now his lordship improves 'upon me every time I see him

'You know not, my dear, continued Mr B 'what a disgrace a haughty and 'passionate woman brings upon her hus- 'band, and upon herself too, in the eye 'of her own sex, as well as ours Nay, 'even those ladies, who would be as glad 'of dominion as she, if they might be 'permitted to exercise it, despise others 'who do, and the man *most* who suffers 'it

'And let me tell you, my Pamela, said the dear man, with an air that shewed he was satisfied with his own conduct in this particular, 'that you cannot imagine 'how much a woman owes to her hus- 'band, as well with regard to *her own* 'peace of mind, as to *both* their reputa- 'tions, (however it may go against the 'grain with her sometimes) if he be a 'man, who has discretion to keep her in- 'croaching passions under a genteel and 'reasonable controul!'

How do you like this doctrine, Miss! —I'll warrant, you believe, that I could do no less, than drop Mr B one of my best curtsies, in acknowledgment of my obligation to him, for so considerately preserving to me *my* peace of mind, and *my* reputation, as well as *his own*, in this case

But after all, when one duly weighs the matter, I can't tell but what he says may be right in the main, for I have not been able to contradict him, partial as I am to my sex, when he has pointed out to me instances in the behaviour of certain ladies, who, like children, the more they have been humoured, the more humoursome they have grown, which must have

* See Vol II p. 195.

occasioned as great uneasiness to themselves, as to their husbands Will you excuse me, my dear —This is between ourselves, for I did not own so much to Mr B For one should not give up one s sex, you know, if one can help it, for the men will be as apt o impose, as the women to incroach, I doubt

Well, but here, my honoured father and mother, and my dear Miss Darnford, at last, I end my journal wise letters, as I may call them, our noble guests being gone, and our time and employments rolling on in much the same manner, as in past days, of which I have given an account

If any thing new or uncommon, or more particularly affecting to me than usual, occurs, I shall not fail to trouble you with it, as I have opportunity But I have now my correspondence with Lady Davers to resume, and how shall I do about that —Oh! I can easily tell it is but trespassing a little on your indulgent allowance for me, my ever honoured parents—And you, my dear Miss, will find it a relief, instead of an occasion for regret, to be eased of a great many impertinencies, which I write to you in my heart's confidence, and in the familiarity of friendship.—Besides, I shall have the happiness of changing our paper-correspondence into personal conversation with you, when at London —And what a sweet change for me will that be!—I will end with the joyful thought, and with the assurance that I am, *my dearest father and mother, and best beloved Miss Darnford, your dutiful and affectionate*

P B

LETTER XXXIX

MY DEAR MISS DARNFORD,

I Hear that Mrs Jewkes is in no good state of health I am very sorry for it I pray for her life, that she may be a credit (if it please God) to the penitence she has so lately assumed —For if she die it will look discouraging to some thoughtless minds, who penetrate not far into the methods Providence takes with it's poor creatures, that as soon as she had changed her manner of living, and was in a reformed state, she was taken away though 'tis certain, that a person is fitter to die, when worthiest to live And what a mercy will it be to her, if she should *not* live long, that she saw her errors, and repented before 'twas too late?

Do, my dear *good* Miss Darnford, vouchsafe to the poor soul the honour of a visit she may be low spirited—She may be too much sunk with the recollection of past things.—Comfort, with that sweetness which is so natural to Miss Darnford, her drooping heart, and let her know, that I have a true concern for her, and give it her in charge to take care of herself, and spare nothing that will administer either to her health, or peace of mind

You ll pardon me, my dear, that I put you upon such an office, an office indeed unsuitable from a lady in your station, to a person in her's, but not to your piety and charity, where a duty so eminent as that of visiting the sick, and cheering the doubting mind, is in the question

I know your condescension will give her great comfort, and if she should be hastening to her account, what a pleasure will it give such a lady as you, to have illuminated a benighted mind, when it was tottering on the verge of death!

But I hope she will get the better of her indisposition, and live many years a thankful monument of God s mercies, and to do more good by her example in the latter part of her life, than she may possibly have done evil in the former

I know she will want no spiritual help from good Mr Peters, but then the kind notice of so generally esteemed a young lady, will raise her more than can be imagined, for there is a tenderness, a sympathy, in the good persons of our sex to one another, that (while the best of the other seem but to act as in office, saying to one those things, which though edifying and convincing, one is not certain proceeds not rather from the fortitude of their minds, than the tenderness of their natures) mingles from one woman to another with one s very spirits, thins the animal mass, and runs through one's heart, in the same lisy current, (I can t clothe my thought suitably to express what I would express) giving assurance, as well as pleasure, in the most arduous cases, and brightening our misty prospects till we see the Sun of Righteousness rising on the hills of comfort, and dispelling the heavy fogs of doubt and diffidence

This it is makes me wish and long as I do, for the company of my dear Miss

Miss Darnford O when shall I see you? When shall I?—To speak to my present case, it is *all* I *long for*, and, pardon my freedom of expression, as well as thought, when I let you know in this instance, how *early* I experience the *ardent longings* of one in the way I am in.

But I ought not to set my heart upon any-thing that is not in my own power, and which may be subject to accidents, and the controul of others But let whatever interventions happen, so I have your *will* to come, I must be rejoiced in your kind intention, although your *power* should not prove answerable

And now, my dearest, honoured mother, let me tell you, that I build no small consolation in the hope, that I shall, on a certain occasion, have your presence, and be strengthened by your advice and comfortings For this was a proposal of the best and most considerate of men, who is every day, if he sees but the least thoughtful cloud upon my brow, studying to say or to do something to dispel it But I believe it is the grateful sense I have of his goodness to me, that makes me thus over-anxious for the apprehensions of a separation from such an excellent husband, from hopes so chearing, prospects so delightful, must, at times, affect one, let one's affiance and desires be ever so strong where they ought to be preferably placed.—Then one would live to do a little more good, if one *might!*

I am a sad weak, apprehensive creature, to be sure I am! How much better fitted for the contingencies of life, are the gay, frolick minds, that think not of any thing before it comes upon them, than such thoughtful *futurity pokers* as I am!

But why should I trouble you, my honoured and dear friends, with my idle fears and follies—just as if nobody was ever in my case before?—Yet weak and apprehensive spirits will be gloomily affected sometimes, and how can one help it?—And if I may not hope for the indulgent soothings of the best of parents, and of my Miss Darnford, in whose bosom besides can one disburden one's heart, when oppressed by too great a weight of thought?

You *will* come, and be in the house with me, my dear mother, for some time, when my best friend sends to you — won't you? And you will *spare*, my dear mother, my best of fathers: won't you?—Yes, yes, I am sure you will—And I am sure my Miss Darnford will be with me, if she can, and these are my comforts But how I run on!—For I am so much a novice, that—

But I will say no more, than that I am, my honoured father and mother, your ever-dutiful daughter, and, my dear Miss Darnford, *your affectionate and obliged*

P B.

LETTER XL

FROM MISS DARNFORD TO MRS B.

MY DEAR MRS B

WE are greatly obliged to you for every particular article in your entertaining journal, which you have brought, sooner than we wished, to a conclusion. We cannot express how much we admire you for your judicious charities, so easy to be practised, yet so uncommon in the manner, and for your inimitable conduct in the affair of your frail Polly, and the silly Mr. H

Your account of the visit of the four rakes, of your parting with your noble guests, your verses, and Mr H's letter, (an original indeed!) have all greatly entertained us, as your prerogative hints * have amused us but we defer our opinion of those hints, till we have the case more fully explained

But, my dear friend, are you not in danger of falling into a too thoughtful and gloomy way? By the latter part of your last letter, we are afraid you are, and my mamma, and Mrs Jones, and Mrs Peters, enjoin me to write, to caution you on that head. But there is the less need of it, because your prudence will always suggest to your reasons, as it does in that very letter, that must outbalance our fears *Think* little, and *hope* much, is a good lesson in your case, and to a lady of your temper, and I hope Lady Davers will not in vain have given you that caution After all, I dare say, your thoughtfulness is but symptomatical, and will go off in proper time

Meantime, permit me to choose you a subject, that will certainly divert you. You must know, that I have been a diligent observer of the conduct of people in the married life to each other; and

* See this Volume, p 444.

have often pronounced, that there cannot be any tolerable happineſs in it, unleſs the one or the other makes ſuch ſacrifices of their inclinations and humours as renders it a ſtate very little deſirable to free and generous minds. Of this I ſee an inſtance in our own family; for though my papa and mamma live very happily, it is all owing to one ſide, I need not ſay which. And this, I am ſure, muſt be the caſe between Mr. B. and you: for you muſt, even through fire if required, ſacrifice to Moloch. I know your prudence will oblige you to make the beſt of it; and like a contented good wife, you will ſay, you have your own will in every thing: a good reaſon why, becauſe you make your own will his. This, long ago, we all agreed, any lady muſt do, be her quality ever ſo great, who would be happy with Mr. B.—Yet my ſiſter once hoped (*entre nous*) to be the perſon.—Fine work would there have been between two ſuch ſpirits, you may believe!

But to wave this: let me aſk you, Mrs. B. is your monarch's conduct to you as *reſpectful*, I don't mean fond, when you are alone together, as when in company?—Forgive me, Madam—But you have hinted two or three times, in your letters, that he always is moſt complaiſant to you in company; and you obſerve, that *wiſely* does he act in this, becauſe he thereby does credit with every-body to his own choice. I make no doubt, that the many charming ſcenes which your genius and fine behaviour furniſh out to him, muſt, as often as they happen, inſpire him with joy, and even rapture; and muſt make him love you more for your mind than for your perſon—but theſe rapturous ſcenes laſt very little longer than the preſent moment. What I want to know is, Whether in the *ſteadier* parts of life, when you are both nearer the level of us common folks, he gives up any thing of his own will in compliment to yours? Whether he acts the part of a reſpectful, polite gentleman in his behaviour to you; and breaks not into your retirements, in the dreſs, and with the brutal roughneſs of a fox-hunter?—Making no difference, perhaps, between the field or his ſtud, I will not ſay kennel, and your chamber or cloſet?—Policy, for his own credit ſake, as I mentioned, accounts to me well, for his complaiſance to you in publick. But his regular and uniform behaviour to you in your retirements, when the converſation between you turns upon uſual and common ſubjects, and you have not obliged him to riſe to admiration of you, by ſuch ſcenes as thoſe of your two parſons, Sir Jacob Swynford, and the like, are what would ſatiſfy my curioſity, if you pleaſe to give me an inſtance or two of it.

Now, my deareſt Mrs. B. if you can give me a caſe, partly or nearly thus circumſtanced, you will highly oblige me.

Firſt, Where he has borne with any infirmity of your own; and I know of none where you can give him ſuch an opportunity, except you get into a vapouriſh habit, by giving way to a temper too thoughtful and apprehenſive.

Next, that, in complaiſance to *your* will, he recedes from his *own* in any one inſtance.

Next, whether he breaks not into your retirements unceremoniouſly, and without apology or concern, as I hinted above.

You know, my dear Mrs. B. all I mean, by what I have ſaid; and if you have any pretty converſation in memory, by the recital of which, this my bold curioſity may be anſwered, pray oblige me with it; and we ſhall be able to judge by it, not only of the inborn generoſity which all that know Mr. B. have been willing to attribute to him, but of the likelihood of the continuance of both your felicities, upon terms ſuitable to the characters of a fine lady and fine gentleman, and of conſequence, worthy of the imitation of the moſt delicate of our own ſex.

This is the taſk your Polly Darnford preſumes to ſet her beloved Mrs. B. And why? For your own diverſion, in the *firſt* place: For my edification, in the *next*: And that when I have the pleaſure I hope for, of attending you in London, I may ſee what there is in the conduct of you both, to admire, or remonſtrate againſt, in the *third*. For, where there is ſo little wanting to perfection between you, I ſhall be very free with you both, in my cenſures, if he impoſes, through prerogative, or you permit, through an undue compliance, what I ſhall imagine ought not to be in either caſe. I know you will excuſe me for what I have ſaid, and well you may, ſince I am ſure, I ſhall have nothing to do, when I am with you, but to admire and to imitate *you*, and to wiſh, if ever I marry, I may have juſt ſuch a huſband (though not quite ſo haughty perhaps) as Mr B. But pray, let not the lordly man see this letter, nor your anſwer, nor the copy of it, till you may conclude I have the latter, if then, that you may not be under any undue influences

Your obliging *longings*, my beloved dear lady, for my company, I hope, will be ſoon, very ſoon, anſwered My papa was ſo pleaſed with your ſweet earneſtneſs on this occaſion, that he joined with my mamma, and both, with equal cheerfulneſs, ſaid, you ſhould not be many days in London before me Murray and his miſtreſs go on ſwimmingly, and have not yet had one quarrel The only perſon, he, of either ſex, that ever knew Nancy ſo intimately, and ſo long, without one!

This is all I have to ſay, at preſent, when I have aſſured you, my dear Miſs B how much I am *your obliged and affectionate*

POLLY DARNFORD

I muſt add, however, that I expect from you almoſt as many letters as there are poſt days between this and the time I ſee you, for I will not part with my correſpondent for any body, no, not for Lady Davers

But I muſt inſiſt upon your giving me the converſation with the young ladies related to Lady Towers and Mrs Arthur

I will obſerve every-thing you ſay in relation to Mrs Jewkes, who is much as ſhe was, but not better

LETTER XLI.

MY DEAREST MISS DARNFORD,

I Was afraid I ended my laſt letter in a gloomy way, and I am obliged to you for the kind and friendly notice you take of it It was owing to a train of thinking which ſometimes I get into, of late; I hope, only ſymptomatically, as you ſay, and that the cauſe and effect will ſoon vaniſh together

But what a taſk, my dear friend, I'll warrant, you think you have ſet me! I thought, in the progreſs of my journal, and in my letters, I had given ſo many inſtances of Mr B's polite tenderneſs to me, that no new ones would be required at my hands, and when I ſaid he was always *moſt* complaiſant before company, I little expected; that ſuch an inference would be drawn from my words, as would tend to queſtion the uniformity of his behaviour to me, when there were no witneſſes to it But I am glad you give me an opportunity to clear up all your doubts on this ſubject To begin then,

You firſt deſire an inſtance, where Mr B has borne with ſome infirmity of mine

Next, that in complaiſance to my will, he has receded from his own

And, laſtly, Whether he breaks not into my retirements unceremoniouſly, and without apology or concern, making no difference between the field or the ſtud, and my chamber or cloſet?

I know not, my dear, what the diſtance is, at which the polite ladies, and thoſe of rank think it proper to endeavour to keep their huſbands but I will give you by-and bye the ſubject of one converſation only, which will anſwer all you mean, as I apprehend, and at the ſame time acquaint you with the notions and behaviour of us both, with reſpect to this diſtance, and my retirements, and then leave you to judge as you think fit

As to the firſt, his bearing with my infirmities; he is daily giving inſtances of his goodneſs to me on this head, and I am aſhamed to ſay, that of late I give him ſo much occaſion for them as I do but he ſees my apprehenſiveneſs, at times, though I endeavour to conceal it, and no huſband was ever ſo ſoothing and ſo indulgent as Mr B He gives me the beſt advice, as to my malady, if I may call it one treats me with redoubled tenderneſs, talks to me upon the ſubjects I moſt delight to dwell upon, as of my worthy parents, what they are doing at this time, and at that, of our intended journey to London, of the diverſions of the town, of Miſs Darnford's company; and when he goes abroad, ſends up my good Mrs Jervis to me, becauſe I ſhould not be alone at other times, takes me abroad with him, brings this neighbour and that neighbour to viſit me, and carries me to viſit them talks of our journey to Kent, and into Lincolnſhire, and to my Lady Davers's, to Bath, to Tunbridge, and I can't tell whither, when the apprehended time ſhall be over —In fine, my dear Miſs Darnford, you cannot imagine one half of his tender goodneſs and politeneſs to me! Indeed you cannot!—Then, as to what you call *reſpectful*, he watches every motion of my eye, every turn of my countenance, ſeldom gives his opinion upon ſubjects that he kindly imagines within my capacity,

city, till he has heard mine, and I have the less fear of falling into mean compliances, because his generosity is my guardian, and never fails to exalt me more than I can debase myself, or than it is possible I can deserve Then he hardly ever goes out to any distance, but he brings me some pretty present, that he thinks will be grateful to me when at home he is seldom out of my company, delights to teach me French and Italian, and reads me pieces of manuscript poetry, in several of the modern tongues (for he speaks them all,) explains to me every-thing I understand not, delights to answer all my questions, and to encourage my inquisitiveness and curiosity, tries to give me a notion of pictures and medals, and reads me lectures upon them, for he has a fine collection of both, and every now and then will have it, that he has been improved by my questions and observations.

What say you to these things, my dear? Do they come up to your first question? or do they not? Or is not what I have said, a full answer, were I to say no more, to *all* your inquiries? Can there be any such thing as *undue compliances* to such an husband, on my side, think you? And when I have charm'd to sleep, by my grateful duty, that watchful dragon, *Prerogative*, as Lady Davers, in one of her letters, calls it*; and am resolved not to awake it, if I can help it, by the least disobliging or wilfully perverse act, what have I to apprehend from it?

O my dear, I am thoroughly convinc'd, that half the misunderstandings, among married people, are owing to trifles, to petty distinctions, to mere words, and little captious follies, to over-weenings, or unguarded petulances and who would forego the solid satisfaction of life, for the sake of triumphing in such poor contentions, if one could triumph?

Are such foibles as these to be dignified by the name of *inclinations* and *humours*, which to be given up, would be making such a *sacrifice, as shall render the married life little desirable to free and generous minds?*

But say not, my dear, to *free* and *generous minds*: for every high spirit deserves not these epithets nor think what I say, a partiality in behalf of my own conduct, and an argument for tameness of spirit, and such an one as would lick the dust, for, let me tell you, my dear friend, that, dearly as I love and honour my Mr B if he were to require of me any-thing that I thought it was my duty not to comply with, I should be the unhappiest creature in the world, because I am sure I should withstand his will, and desire him to excuse my non-compliance

But then I would reserve my strength for these *greater* points, and would never dispute with him the *smaller*, although they were not entirely to my liking and this would give both force and merit to the opposition, when I found it necessary but to contest every little point, where nothing but one's stubborn will was in the question, what an inexcusable perverseness would that be! How ready to enter the lists against an husband, would it make one appear to him? And where besides, is the merit of obliging, were we only to yield to what will oblige ourselves?

But you next require of me an instance, where, in complaisance to *my* will, he has receded from *his own?* I don't know what to say to this When Mr B. is all tenderness and indulgence, as I have said, and requires of me nothing, that I can have a material objection to, ought I *not* to oblige him? Can I have a will that is not his? Or would it be excusable if I *had?* All little matters, as I have said, I cheerfully give up great ones have not yet occurr'd between us, and I hope never will One point, indeed, I have some apprehension *may* happen, and that, to be plain with you, is, we have had a debate or two on the subject (which I maintain) of a mother's duty to nurse her own child, and I am sorry to say it, he seems more determined than I wish he were, against it

I hope it will not proceed so far, as to awaken the sleeping dragon I mentioned, *Prerogative* by name; but I doubt I cannot give up this point very contentedly But as to lesser points, had I been a dutchess born, I think I would not have contested them with my husband

Upon the whole of this question then, I have really had no will of my own to contend for, so generous is Mr B and so observant and so grateful have I thought it my duty to be, yet I could give you many respectful instances, too, of his receding, when he has desired to

* See this Vol p 336.

see

see what I have been writing, and I have told him to whom, and begg'd to be excused One such instance I can give since I began this letter. This is it

I put it in my bosom, when he came up: he saw me do so.

'Are you writing, my dear, what I 'must not see?'

'I am writing to Miss Darnford, Sir, 'and she begg'd you might not, at pre'sent'

'This augments my curiosity, Pa'mela, What can two such ladies write, 'that I may not see?'

'If you won't be displeased, Sir, I 'had rather you would not, because she 'desires you may not see her letter, nor 'this my answer, till the latter is in her 'hands.'

'Then I will not,' returned Mr B.

Will this instance, my dear, come up to your demand for one, where he recedes from his own will, in complaisance to mine?

But now, as to what both our notions and our practice are on the article of my retirements, and whether he breaks in upon them unceremoniously, and without apology, let the conversation I promised inform you, which began on the following occasion.

Mr B rode out early one morning, within a few days past, and did not return till the afternoon, an absence I had not been used to of late; and breakfasting and dining without him being also a new thing with me, I had such an impatience to see him, having expected him at dinner, that I was forced to retire to my closet, to try to divert it, by writing; and the gloomy conclusion of my last, was then the subject He returned about four o'clock, and indeed did *not* tarry to change his riding-dress, as your politeness, my dear friend, would perhaps have expected, but came directly up to me, with an impatience to see me, equal to my own, when he was told, upon inquiry, that I was in my closet

I heard his welcome step, as he came up stairs, which generally, after a longer absence than I expect, has such an effect upon my fond heart, that it gives a responsive throb for every step he takes towards me, and beats quicker and faster, as he comes nearer and nearer, till tapping my breast, I say to it sometimes—'Lie still, busy fool as thou art! Canst 'thou not forbear letting thy discerning 'lord see thy nonsensical emotions? I love 'to indulge thee in them, myself, 'tis 'true, but then let nobody else observe 'them, for, generous as thy master is, 'thou mayest not perhaps meet with 'such favourable interpretations as thou 'deservest, when thou art always flut'tering thus, as he approaches, and 'playest off all thy little joyful frolicks 'into the glowing cheek, and brighten it 'eye of thy mistress, which makes her 'look, as if she were conscious of some 'misdemeanour, when, all the time, it 'is nothing in the world but grateful 'joy, and a love so innocent, that the 'purest mind might own it'

This little flutter and chiding of the busy simpleton, made me meet him but at the closet-door, instead of the entrance of my chamber, as sometimes I do.—'So, my dear love, how do you?' folding his kind arms about me, and saluting me with ardour 'Whenever I have 'been but a few hours from you, my 'impatience to see my beloved, will 'not permit me to stand upon the for'mality of a message to know how you 'are engaged, but I break in upon you, 'even in my riding dress, as you 'see.'

'Dear Sir, you are very obliging, 'But I have no notion of *mere* forma'lities of this kind,' (How unpolite this, my dear, in your friend!) 'in a married 'state, since 'tis impossible a virtuous 'wife can be employed about any thing 'that her husband may not know: and 'so need not fear surprizes.

'I am glad to hear you say this, my 'Pamela, for I have always thought the 'extraordinary civilities and distances 'of this kind, which I have observed 'among several persons of rank, altoge'ther unaccountable For, if they are 'exacted by the lady, I should suspect 'she had reserves, which she herself be'lieved I could not approve of If not 'exacted, but practised of choice by the 'gentleman, it carries with it, in my 'opinion, a false air of politeness, little 'less than affrontive to the lady, and dis'honourable to himself, for does it not 'look, as if he supposed, and *allowed*, 'that, probably, she might be so em'ployed that it was necessary to apprise 'her of his visit, lest he should make 'discoveries not to her credit, or his 'own?'

'One would not, Sir,' (for I thought his conclusion too severe) 'make such a 'harsh supposition as this, neither for

'there are little delicacies and moments 'of retirement, no doubt, in which a 'modest lady would be glad to be indulged by the tenderest husband.

'It may be so, in an *early* matrimony, 'before the lady's confidence in the honour and discretion of the man she has 'chosen has disengaged her from her 'bridal reserves.'

'Bridal reserves! dear Sir, permit 'me to give it, as my humble opinion, 'that a wife's behaviour ought to be as 'pure and circumspect, in degree, as 'that of a bride, or even of a maiden 'lady, be her confidence in her husband's honour and discretion ever so 'great. For, indeed, I think a gross 'or a careless demeanour little becomes 'that modesty, which is the peculiar excellency and distinction of our sex.'

'You account very well, my dear, 'by what you now say, for your own 'over-nice behaviour, as I have sometimes thought it. But are we not all 'apt to argue for a practice we make 'our own, because we *do* make it our 'own, rather than from the reason of 'the thing?'

'I hope, Sir, that is not the present 'case with me, for, permit me to say, 'that an over-free or negligent behaviour of a lady in the married state, 'must be a mark of disrespect to her 'consort, and would shew, as if she was 'very little solicitous about what appearance she made in his eye. And 'must not this beget in him a slight opinion of her, and her sex too, as if, supposing the gentleman had been a free 'liver, she would convince him, there 'was no other difference in the sex, but 'as they were within or without the 'pale, licensed by the law, or acting in 'defiance of it?

'I understand the force of your argument, Pamela. But you were going to say something more.

'Only, Sir, permit me to add, that 'when, in my particular case, you enjoin me to appear before you always* 'dressed, even in the early part of the 'day, it would be wrong, if I was less 'regardful of my behaviour and actions, than of my appearance.'

'I believe you are right, my dear, if 'a precise or unnecessary scrupulousness be avoided, and where all is unaffected, easy, and natural, as in my 'Pamela. For I have seen married ladies, both in England and France, 'who have kept a husband at greater 'distance than they have exacted from 'some of his sex, who have been more 'intitled to his resentment, than to his 'wife's intimacies.

'But to wave a subject, in which, as 'I can with pleasure say, neither of us 'have much concern, tell me, my dearest, how you were employed before I 'came up? Here are pen and ink: here 'too, is paper, but it is as spotless as 'your mind. To whom were you directing your favours now? May I not 'know your subject?

Mr. H.'s letter was a part of it, and so I had put it by, at his approach, and not choosing he should see that—'I am 'writing,' replied I, 'to Miss Darnford: but I think you must not ask 'me to see what I have written *this* time. 'I put it aside, that you should not, 'when I heard your welcome step. The 'subject is our parting with our noble 'guests; and a little of my apprehensiveness, on an occasion upon which 'our sex may write to one another; but, 'for some of the reasons we have been 'mentioning, gentlemen should not desire to see.'

'Then I will not, my dearest love.' (So here, my dear, is another instance—I could give you an hundred such—of his receding from his own will, in complaisance to mine.) 'Only,' continued he, 'let me warn you against too much apprehensiveness, for your own sake, as 'well as mine, for such a mind as my 'Pamela's, I cannot permit to be habitually over-clouded. And yet there 'now hangs upon your brow an overthoughtfulness, which you must not 'indulge.'

'Indeed, Sir, I was a little too 'thoughtful, from my subject, before 'you came, but your presence, like the 'sun, has dissipated the mists that hung 'upon my mind. See you not, and I pressed his hand with my lips, 'they are 'all gone already?' smiling upon him, with a delight unfeigned.

'Not quite, my dearest Pamela, and 'therefore, if you have no objection, I 'will change my dress, and attend you 'in the chariot for an hour or two, whither

* See Vol. II. p. 216. 219.

'ther you pleaſe, that no one ſhadow may 'remain viſible in this dear face, tenderly ſaluting me

'Whitherſoever you pleaſe, Sir. A 'little airing with you will be highly 'agreeable to me'

The dear obliger went and changed his dreſs in an inſtant, and he led me to the chariot, with his uſual tender politeneſs, and we had a charming airing of ſeveral miles, returning quite happy, cheerful, and delighted with each other's converſation, without calling in upon any of our good neighbours for what need of that, my dear, when we could be the beſt company in the world to each other?

Do theſe inſtances come up to your queſtions, my dear? or, do they not?—If you think not, I could give you our converſation in the chariot, for I wrote it down, at my firſt leiſure, ſo highly was I delighted with it for the ſubject was my deareſt parents, a ſubject ſtarted by himſelf, becauſe he knew it would oblige me. But being tired with writing, I may reſerve it, till I have the pleaſure of ſeeing you, if you think it worth aſking for And ſo I will haſten to a concluſion of this long letter

You will perceive, my dear, by what I have written, in what ſenſe it may be *juſtly* ſaid, that Mr B is *moſt* complaiſant to me before company, perhaps, politically, as you ſay, to do credit to his own generous choice —but that he is more tender, yea, *reſpectfully* tender, (for that's the word with you) and not leſs polite to me, in our retired hours, you will have no doubt, from what I have related, and could further relate, if it were neceſſary for every day produces inſtances equal to what I have given you.

Then, my dear, let me ſay to you, what I could not ſo freely ſay to any other young lady, that I never could have hoped I ſhould be ſo happy as I am, in other particulars, from a gentleman who has given himſelf the liberties Mr B has done for I never hear from him, in company, or when alone, the leaſt ſhocking expreſſion, or ſuch frothy jeſts, as tend to convey impure ideas to the moſt apprehenſive mind There is, indeed, the leſs wonder in this, and that we can glory in a true conjugal chaſtity, as I have the vanity to think, his love, as well as my own, is the love of the mind, rather than that of perſon, and our tendereſt and moſt affecting moments, are thoſe which lift us up above ſenſe, and all that ſenſe can imagine But this is a ſubject too delicate to be dwelt upon, even to you; and you'll better comprehend all I mean, when your pure mind meets with a gentleman of exalted ſenſe, like Mr B whom, if you *find* him not ſo good as you wiſh, your example will *make* ſo.

Permit me to add, for the ſake of you, my dear parents, as well as for the ſakes of my much-reſpected friends, who have joined in the kind caution you ſo obligingly give me, againſt getting into too thoughtful and gloomy a way, that there is no great fear I ſhould continue long in it, when I have ſo kind and ſo generous a comforter as Mr B For, at his preſence, all my fearful apprehenſions are diſſipated, and vaniſh like a morning dream And depend upon it, that ſo ſure as the day ſucceeds to the night, ſo ſure will my mind, while capable of the leaſt ſenſe of gratitude be illuminated the moment he ſhines out upon me, let it be ever ſo overcaſt in his abſence, through imaginary doubts, and apprehended evils

I have only farther to add, for my comfort, that next Thurſday ſe'ennight, if nothing hinders, we are to ſet out for London And why do you think I ſay *for my comfort?* Only that I ſhall then ſoon have the opportunity, to aſſure you perſonally, as you give me hope, how much I am, my dear Miſs Darnford, *your truly affectionate*

P B

I will ſhew you, when I ſee you, the converſation you require about the young ladies.

LETTER XLII

MY DEAR MISS DARNFORD,

ONE more letter, and I have done for a great while, becauſe I hope your preſence will put an end to the occaſion I ſhall now tell you of my ſecond viſit to the Dairy houſe, where we went to breakfaſt, in the chariot and four, becauſe of the diſtance, which is ten pretty long miles

I tranſcribed for you, from letters written formerly to my dear parents, an *ac-

* See Vol II p 277

count of my former dairy-house visit, and what the people were, and whom I saw there, and although I besought you to keep that affair to yourself, as too much affecting the reputation of my Mr B to be known any farther, and even to destroy that account, when you had perused it, yet, I make no doubt, you remember the story, and so I need not repeat any part of it

When we arrived there, we found at the door, expecting us, (for they heard the chariot-wheels at a distance) my pretty Miss Goodwin, and two other Misses, who had earned their ride, attended by the governess's daughter, a discreet young gentlewoman As soon as I stepped out, the child ran into my arms with great eagerness, and I as tenderly embraced her, and leading her into the parlour, asked her abundance of questions about her work, and her lessons, and among the rest, if she had merited this distinction of the chaise and dairy-house breakfast, or if it was owing to her uncle's favour, and to that of her governess? the young gentlewoman assured me it was to both, and shewed me her needleworks, and penmanship, and the child was highly pleased with my commendations

I took a good deal of notice of the other two Misses, for their school-fellow's sake, and made each of them a present of some little toys, and my Miss, of a number of pretty trinkets, with which she was highly delighted, and I told her, that I would wait upon her governess, when I came from London into the country again, and see in what order she kept her little matters, for, above all things, I loved pretty housewifely Misses, and then, I would bring her more

Mr B observed, with no small satisfaction, the child's behaviour, which is very pretty, and appeared as fond of her, as if he had been *more* than her *uncle*, and yet seemed under some restraint, lest it should be taken, that he *was* more. Such power has secret guilt, poor gentleman! to lessen and restrain a pleasure, that would, in a happier light, have been so laudable to have manifested! But how commendable is this his love to the dear child, compared to that of most wicked libertines, who have no delight, but in destroying innocence, and care not what becomes of the unhappy infants, or of the still more unhappy mothers!

I am going to let you into a charming scene, resulting from this perplexity of the dear gentleman A scene that has afforded me high delight ever since, and always will, when I think of it, but I will lead to it as gradually as it happened

The child was very fond of her uncle, and told him, she loved him dearly, and always would love and honour him, for giving her such a good aunt. 'You 'talked, Madam,' said she, 'when I 'saw you before, that I should come 'and live with you—Will you let me, 'Madam? Indeed I will be very good, 'and do every thing you bid me, and 'mind my book, and my needle, indeed 'I will

'Ask your uncle, my dear,' said I, 'I should like your pretty company of 'all things'

She went to Mr B and said—'Shall 'I, Sir, go and live with my aunt?—'Pray let me, when you come from London again'

'You have a very good governess, 'child,' said he, 'and she can't part 'with you'

'Yes, but she can, Sir, she has a great 'many Misses, and can spare me well 'enough, and if you please to let me ride 'in your coach sometimes, I can go and 'visit my governess, and beg a holiday 'for the Misses, now and-then, when I 'am almost a woman, and then all the 'Misses will love me'

'Don't the Misses love you now, Miss 'Goodwin?' said he 'Yes, they love 'me well enough, for matter of that, 'but they'll love me better, when I can 'beg them a holiday Do, dear Sir, let 'me go home to my new aunt, next time 'you come into the country'

I was much pleased with the dear child's earnestness, and permitted her to have her full argument with her beloved uncle, but was much moved, and he himself was under some concern, when she said—'But you should, in pity, let me live with 'you, Sir, for I have no papa, nor 'mamma neither they are so far off!—'But I will love you both as if you were 'my own papa and mamma, so, dear 'now, my good uncle, promise the poor 'girl that has never a papa nor mamma!'

I withdrew to the door 'It will rain, 'I believe,' said I, and looked up And, indeed, I had almost a shower in my eye, and had I kept my place, could not have refrained shewing how much I was affected.

Mr.

E F Burney del | Heath sculp

Plate IX

Published as the act directs by Harrison & C° [illegible]

Mr B as I said, was a little moved; but for fear the young gentlewoman should take notice of it—'How! my dear,' said he, 'no papa and mamma!—Did 'they not send you a pretty black boy 'to wait upon you, a while ago? Have 'you forgot that?'—'That's true,' replied she 'but what's a black boy to 'living with my new aunt?—That's 'better a great deal than a black boy!'

'Well, your aunt and I will consider 'of it, when we come from London Be 'a good girl, mean time, and do as your 'governess would have you, and then 'you don't know what we may do for 'you'—'Well then, Miss Bett,' said she to her young governess, 'let me be set 'two tasks instead of one, and I will 'learn all I can to deserve to go to my 'aunt'

In this manner the little prattler diverted herself, And as we returned from them, the scene I hinted at, opened as follows

Mr B was pleased to say—'What 'a poor figure does the proudest man 'make, my dear Pamela, under the 'sense of a concealed guilt, in company 'of the innocent who know it, and even 'of those who do not!—Since the casual 'expression of a baby shall overwhelm 'him with shame, and make him unable 'to look up without confusion. I blushed 'for myself, continued he, 'to see how 'you were affected for me, and yet withdrew, to avoid reproaching me so much 'as with a look. Surely, Pamela, I 'must then make a most contemptible 'appearance in your eye! Did you not 'disdain me at that moment?'

'Dearest Sir! how can you speak 'such a word? A word I cannot repeat 'after you! For at that very time, I 'beheld you with the more reverence, 'for seeing your noble heart touched 'with a sense of your error, and it was 'such an earnest to me of the happiest 'change I could ever wish for, and in 'so young a gentleman, that it was one 'half joy for that, and the other half 'concern at the little charmer's accidental plea, to her best and nearest friend, 'for coming home to her new aunt, that 'affected me so sensible as you saw'

'You must not talk to me of the 'child's coming home, after this visit, 'Pamela; for how, at this rate, shall I 'stand the reproaches of my own mind, 'when I see the little prater every day 'before me, and think of what her poor 'mamma has suffered on my account! ''Tis enough, that in *you*, my dear, I 'have an hourly reproach before me, for 'my attempts on your virtue, and I 'have nothing to boast of, but that I 'gave way to the triumphs of your innocence and what then is my boast?'

'What is your boast, dearest Sir? You 'have every thing to boast, that is worthy of being boasted of—Brought up 'to an affluent fortune, uncontrouled in 'your will, your passions uncurbed, you 'have nevertheless permitted the Divine 'grace to operate upon your truly noble 'heart, and have seen your error, at a 'time of life, when others are rushing 'into vices, in the midst of which, perhaps, they are cut off

'You act generously, and with a laudable affection, to a deserving baby, 'which some would have left friendless 'to the wide world, and have made more 'miserable, perhaps, than they had 'made the very miserable mother and 'you have the comfort to think, that, 'through God's goodness, this mother 'is not unhappy, and that there is not 'a lost *soul*, any more than a lost *body*, 'to lay to your charge

'You have inspirited, by your generous example, and enabled, by your 'splendid fortune, another person, whom 'you have made the happiest creature in 'the world, to do good to the poor and 'destitute all around her, besides making every one who approaches you, 'easy and happy, with the bounty of your 'own hands

'You are the best of husbands, the 'best of landlords, the best of masters, 'the best of friends, and, with all these 'excellencies, and a mind, as I hope, 'continually improving, and more and 'more affected with the sense of its past 'mistakes, will you ask, dear Sir, what 'is your boast?'

'O my dearest, dear Mr B and then I pressed his hand with my lips, 'whatever you are to yourself, when you 'give way to reflections so hopeful, you 'are the glory and the boast of your 'grateful Pamela! And permit me to 'add, tears standing in my eyes, and holding his hand between mine, 'that I 'never beheld you in my life, in a more 'amiable light, than when I saw that 'noble consciousness which you speak 'of, manifest itself in your eyes, and

'your

'your countenance—O Sir! this was a 'sight of joy, of true joy! to one who 'loves you for your dear soul's sake, 'as well as for that of your person; and, 'who looks forward to a companionship 'with you, beyond the term of this 'transitory life!'

The dear gentleman looked down sometimes, and sometimes upon me, without offering to interrupt me, and when I had done speaking, I began to fear, by his silence, that I had offended him, remembering just then, one of his former* cautions to me, not to throw a gloom upon his mind by my over-seriousness, and I said, putting my arms round his arm, as I sat, my fearful eye watching his—'I fear, Sir, I have been 'too serious! I have, perhaps, broken 'one of your injunctions! Have cast a 'gloominess over your mind! And if I 'have, dear Sir, forgive me!

He clasped his arms around me 'O 'my beloved Pamela,' said he, 'thou 'dear confirmer of all my better purposes! How shall I acknowledge your 'inexpressible goodness to me? I see 'every day more and more, my dear 'love, what confidence I may repose in 'your generosity and discretion! You 'want no forgiveness, and my silence 'was owing to much better motives than 'to those you were apprehensive of

Judge ye, my honoured parents, what pleasure must overspread my heart, encouraged in a manner so agreeable to all my wishes, and at the hopeful prospect of a thorough reformation, which I had so often prayed for, and which so happily began to open to my delighted mind, on this occasion

Indeed I could not find words to express my joy, and so was obliged to silence in my turn, being only able to raise my swimming eyes to his encouraging ones, and to press his hand between both mine, to my lips, which, by their quivering motion, shewed their readiness to perform their part of speech, could my backwarder *tongue* have given utterance to my meanings.

He saw my grateful transport, and kindly said—'Struggle not, my beloved 'Pamela, for words to express sentiments 'which your eyes and your countenance 'much more significantly express than 'any words *can* do Every day produces 'new instances of your affectionate concern for my *future* as well as *present* 'happiness and I will endeavour to 'confirm to you all the hopes which the 'present occasion has given you of me, 'and which I see by these transporting 'effects, are so desirable to you'

If, my dear Miss Darnford, you are not at present able to account for this speechless rapture, as I may call it, I am confident you will, if it should be your lot to marry such a gentleman as Mr B one who is capable of generous and noble sentiments, and yet has not been so good as you could wish, whenever it shall happen, that the Divine grace, and your unaffected piety, shall touch his heart, and he shall give hopes like those I have the pleasure to rejoice in.—Hopes so charming, that they must, if confirmed, irradiate many a gloomy appearance, which, at times, will cast a shadow over the brightest and happiest prospects

The chariot brought us home sooner than I wished, and Mr. B handed me into the parlour 'Here, Mrs Jervis,' said he, meeting her in the passage, 'receive your angelick lady —I must take 'a little tour without you, Pamela, for 'I have had *too much* of your dear company, and must leave you, to descend 'again into myself, for you have raised 'me to such a height, that it is with 'pain I look down from it.'

He kissed my hand, and went into his chariot again, for it was but half an hour after twelve, and said he would be back by two at dinner He left Mrs Jervis wondering at his words, and at the solemn air with which he uttered them But when I told that good friend the occasion, I had a new joy in the pleasure and gratulations of the dear good woman, on what had passed

Were I, my dear friends, to recount to you every conversation that gives me delight, when we are *alone*, (my Miss Darnford) as well as when we are in company, I should do nothing but write Imagine the rest from what I have (but as *so many specimens of my felicity*) informed you of, and then think, if there can possibly be a happier creature on earth, than I am at present

My next letter will be from London, and to you, my honoured parents, for to you, my dear, I shall not write again, expecting to see you soon But I must

* See Vol II p. 196.

now

now write seldomer, because I am to renew my correspondence with Lady Davers, with whom I cannot be so free, as I have been with Miss Darnford, and so I doubt, my dear father and mother, you cannot have the particulars of that correspondence, for I shall never find time to transcribe.

But every opportunity that offers, you may assure yourselves, shall be laid hold of by your ever-dutiful daughter

And now, my dear Miss Darnford, as I inscribed this letter to you, let me conclude it, with the assurance, that I am, and ever will be, *your most affectionate friend and servant,*

P. B.

END OF THE THIRD VOLUME.

CPSIA information can be obtained
at www.ICGtesting.com
Printed in the USA
LVHW101353280921
698925LV00011B/409